AMNESTY INTERNATIONAL REPORT 1981

This report covers the period
1 May 1980 to 30 April 1981

AMNESTY INTERNATIONAL is a worldwide movement which is independent of any government, political grouping, ideology, economic interest or religious creed. It plays a specific role within the overall spectrum of human rights work. The activities of the organization focus strictly on prisoners:

—It seeks the *release* of men and women detained anywhere for their beliefs, colour, sex, ethnic origin, language or religion, provided they have not used or advocated violence. These are termed *"prisoners of conscience"*.

—It advocates *fair and early trials* for *all political prisoners* and works on behalf of such persons detained without charge or without trial.

—It opposes the *death penalty* and *torture* or other cruel, inhuman or degrading treatment or punishment of *all prisoners* without reservation.

AMNESTY INTERNATIONAL acts on behalf of the United Nations Universal Declaration of Human Rights and other international instruments. Through practical work for prisoners within its mandate, Amnesty International participates in the wider promotion and protection of human rights in the civil, political, economic, social and cultural spheres.

AMNESTY INTERNATIONAL has over 2,500 adoption groups and national sections in 40 countries in Africa, Asia, Europe, the Americas and the Middle East, and individual members, subscribers and supporters in a further 111 countries. Each adoption group works on behalf of at least two prisoners of conscience in countries other than its own. These countries are balanced geographically and politically to ensure impartiality. Information about prisoners and human rights violations emanates from Amnesty International's Research Department in London.

AMNESTY INTERNATIONAL has consultative status with the United Nations (ECOSOC), UNESCO and the Council of Europe, has cooperative relations with the Inter-American Commission on Human Rights of the Organization of American States and is a member of the Coordinating Committee of the Bureau for the Placement and Education of African Refugees of the Organization of African Unity.

AMNESTY INTERNATIONAL is financed by subscriptions and donations of its worldwide membership. To safeguard the independence of the organization, all contributions are strictly controlled by guidelines laid down by AI's International Council and income and expenditure are made public in an annual financial report.

AMNESTY INTERNATIONAL REPORT 1981

Amnesty International Publications
10 Southampton Street ● London WC2E 7HF ● United Kingdom

First published 1981 by Amnesty International Publications
10 Southampton Street, London WC2E 7HF, United Kingdom

ISBN 0 86210 040 2
AI Index: POL 01/01/81
Original Language: English

Printed, designed and typeset in Great Britain by
Redesign, 9 London Lane, London E8
Maps by Andras Bereznay

Regional maps have been included in this report to indicate the location of countries and territories cited in the text and for that purpose only. It is not possible on the small scale used to indicate precise political boundaries. Larger territories whose disputed status is a matter of unresolved concern before relevant bodies of the United Nations have been indicated by striping. Amnesty International takes no position on territorial disputes.

Contents

Introduction

Deliberate cruelty threatens prisoners of conscience everywhere. Who is to help when your arms are held and you know it is useless to struggle; when the cell door closes and you have no say in when it will open again; when the first blow warns that there is worse to come; when the sentence of death tells you that your life will end at the hands of the people who now guard and feed you?

Faced with extensive and entrenched violation of human rights — often sanctioned at the highest levels of government — what can the ordinary citizen do? Twenty years ago this question led to the founding of a new movement: Amnesty International.

In these 20 years, Amnesty International's efforts have shown that committed individuals can work together — regardless of politics — and help individual victims. Since 1961 it has worked to free prisoners of conscience, to get political prisoners fair trials, to halt torture and executions. Often it is impossible to demonstrate how much has been achieved. Seldom can Amnesty International show a direct link between its work and the desired results; it does not claim credit. But prisoners do emerge after years of solitary confinement, having received not one letter out of the hundreds sent by groups, yet insisting that they knew of the worldwide efforts, that they knew their families were supported, and, above all, that they shared that most human of qualities, hope. Many say that it was hope alone that gave them strength to face another indistinguishable, unnumbered day; to withstand the certainty of more torture to come; to stay sane as the date of execution approached; to cope with imagining the suffering of those they love.

Tragedy near to home affects people more easily than distant disaster: a murder in the next street more than a massacre abroad. But Amnesty International insists on the principle of international responsibility for the protection of human rights. Its members work impartially and without discrimination for prisoners held in countries other than their own; they do not take up cases of prisoners in their own country. No members are expected to provide information on their own country and no members have responsibility for action taken or statements issued by the international organization on their own country. Research into human rights violations is the responsibility of an international secretariat working under the authority of an executive committee elected by the membership. Elected representatives of the entire membership determine Amnesty International's policy.

What started as a small group working to secure the release of those imprisoned for the peaceful expression of their opinions has become a worldwide movement and something of an institution. It has refined its terms of reference, logically and within strict limits. If it was necessary to work for the release of those convicted of non-violent political offences and imprisoned, it was just as necessary to work for fair trials for all political prisoners, and for those detained without any trial at all. As evidence was gathered about the repression of dissent, it became clear that torture was not an unthinkable aberration of a less civilized past but a routine technique of many modern governments. Amnesty International decided to campaign against torture and against the death penalty.

As it enters the 1980s, the movement has established a precise role for itself in the overall field of human rights work. It has a threefold mandate: it seeks the immediate and unconditional release of all prisoners of conscience (those imprisoned because of their beliefs, colour, sex, ethnic origin or language who have not used or advocated violence); it advocates fair and prompt trials for all political prisoners and works on behalf of such prisoners detained without charge or trial; it opposes torture and the death penalty in all cases.

Amnesty International does not work against any government; only against repressive policies and practices. It says nothing about the merits of the views of the victims. Its members are of many religions and of none, they are conservative and communist, rich and poor, black and white, from east and west, from colonial powers and from their former colonies. They can join in Amnesty International's work because its mandate is precise and incontrovertible.

Amnesty International does not claim that working against the repression of opinion is more important than working against poverty or disease: just that it is vital. It demands that governments adhere to laws, national and international. It does not interfere in the internal affairs of sovereign states but bases its work on the standards established by the Universal Declaration of Human Rights and the International Covenant on Civil and Political Rights. It tries to persuade international bodies to elaborate new standards and supplies them with information to help them implement existing standards.

When governments use methods, illegal even under their own laws, to kidnap and kill their own citizens — without acknowledgement, let alone trial — Amnesty International insists that they accept responsibility for the "disappeared" and murdered. It has made representations to the United Nations Commission on Human Rights, the United Nations Sub-Commission on Prevention of Discrimination and Protection of Minorities and the United Nations Working Group on Enforced or Involuntary Disappearances. Amnesty International now sees the need to launch a major publicity campaign about "disappearances" and to focus on the problem of extrajudicial killings to increase understanding of these threats to human rights and to fix the offending governments with responsibility for their actions, both before the United Nations and in the eyes of the world.

The pages that follow describe Amnesty International's work and its concerns throughout the world in the 12 months from 1 May 1980 to 30 April 1981. No comparisons are made because there are no ways to quantify the misery caused by the repression catalogued here. Not only does censorship limit the availability of information about human rights abuses, but the techniques of repression and their impact vary widely. Nor is it possible to establish whether repression is increasing; certainly awareness of it is. It is now harder for states to hide repression. That may explain why Amnesty International is often attacked by governments whose abuses it exposes to public scrutiny.

Human rights have been violated not only by governments, but also by groups supporting various causes. The taking of hostages, the use of torture and the execution of political opponents are unacceptable regardless of the motives or identities of the perpetrators. Amnesty International regards any violation of the fundamental human rights within its mandate as a threat to the rights and dignity of all people. It concentrates on trying to halt violations comitted or tolerated by governments, because it is they who are responsible for upholding the standards agreed by the international community.

Amnesty International has been dismayed by a tendency among governments to regard certain abuses as more acceptable when committed by friends than by enemies. Human rights are indivisible and must be understood — in theory and in practice — to be the birthright of all people, transcending the boundaries of nation, race or belief. If the international community is to progress in the defence of human rights, its members must be willing to confront political imprisonment, torture and executions wherever they occur. They must be willing to treat allegations and evidence of such abuses in any country as a matter of the utmost concern, regardless of their own foreign policy objectives. The hypocrisy about human rights must be ended. To do less is to risk undermining respect for human rights everywhere.

Prisoners of conscience today

Prisoners of conscience are held by governments in all the geographical regions of the world, in countries with the most diverse political, social and economic systems. There is just as much diversity among the prisoners themselves, their beliefs and the background to their arrests. During the year Amnesty International worked for the release of prisoners of conscience in more than 60 countries.

Prisoners of conscience are people imprisoned because of their political, religious or other conscientiously held beliefs, their ethnic origin, sex, colour or language, provided that they have not used or advocated violence. Amnesty International's term has been adopted in recent years by human rights activists in a number of countries. It reflects the principle on which Amnesty International was founded, that all people have the right to express their convictions and the obligation to extend that freedom to others. The imprisonment of individuals because of their beliefs or origins is a violation of fundamental human rights, rights that are not "bestowed" on individuals by states, and cannot be retracted for political convenience.

Amnesty International seeks the immediate and unconditional release of all prisoners of conscience. It does not seek to support the beliefs or the activities of those who have been imprisoned, nor does it claim to speak for them. It calls for their right to speak — in freedom and peace — for themselves.

Most of the prisoners of conscience whose cases were taken up during the year were detained for trying to exercise their rights to freedom of expression, association, assembly or movement. But imprisonment on grounds of conscience took other forms too. Some prisoners of conscience were conscientious objectors refusing to do military service. Others were imprisoned simply because members of their families were political or religious activists. Some prisoners of conscience were held for actions undertaken as individuals; others had been part of a group or movement. Some had acted in direct opposition to the government in power or the established system of government; others deliberately worked within their country's political system and could not even be described as being in opposition to the government.

Involvement with political parties in opposition to the government resulted in many people being imprisoned, even though neither their activities nor those of their party were violent. Members of national minorities were jailed in a number of countries for trying to achieve some degree of autonomy. Trade union activity or participation in strikes or demonstrations was a common cause of imprisonment. In certain countries members of religious groups were incarcerated for religious practices prescribed by their faith which contravened the limits set by the state on religious activity.

Simply criticizing or questioning the government was, in many countries around the world, enough to send someone to prison. A large number of prisoners of conscience were held for trying to publicize human rights violations in their own countries: often where secrecy and suppression of information were major obstacles to improving respect for human rights.

Most states holding prisoners of conscience have signed and ratified or otherwise voted for international human rights agreements, declarations and resolutions, under the auspices either of the United Nations or of a regional body, or both. These human rights instruments guarantee the rights to freedom of conscience, freedom of expression, freedom of association and similar fundamental rights. They also regulate the restrictions that may be placed on those rights. For example, the International Covenant on Civil and Political Rights says that the right to freedom of expression may be restricted by law when this is necessary either "for the respect of the rights and reputations of others" or "for the protection of national security or of public order or of public health or morals". Many governments abuse international human rights law by invoking such clauses to justify restrictions on civil and political rights that result in individuals being imprisoned for expressing views inconvenient to the authorities.

Few states admit openly that they have detained people in violation of internationally recognized standards. Government responses to expressions of concern about prisoners of conscience vary widely. Some offer their own interpretations of international standards: claiming for example that freedom of expression does not include the right to advocate communism, or alternatively, to agitate against communism. Other governments assert they do not send people to prison for their beliefs, but only for criminal acts; while their legislation makes the expression of dissenting ideas a criminal offence. Some governments admit to holding particular individuals, but claim they were involved in violence, despite evidencc to the contrary. Many states refer to a threat to national security and apply legislation which defines the threat so broadly that anyone believed to be critical of the government can be locked away. Other governments simply refuse to comment or to supply information about the prisoners. Common to most official responses to concern about prisoners of conscience is an effort to obscure or withhold the facts, usually both from the local populace and from international public opinion.

Imprisonment itself takes different forms. Most individual prisoners of conscience adopted by Amnesty International have been held in places of incarceration such as prisons, camps, investigation centres or army barracks. Many others, however, have been held under conditions which are so physically restrictive as to amount to imprisonment. Examples are house arrest and "banning" or internal exile to some remote locality. In some countries people have been diagnosed as mentally ill and forcibly confined to psychiatric hospitals, because they exercised their human rights and not for authentic medical reasons.

In some parts of the world people are not formally arrested or detained, but are abducted by government personnel, or by groups operating with the connivance of the authorities. If the government refuses to acknowledge that individuals have been detained, or to reveal their fate, it is often difficult to ascertain whether they are alive and in detention, or have been murdered. In such cases Amnesty International continues to work until it knows what has happened to the people who "disappeared", and may adopt the victims as prisoners of conscience where this would help to free them or clarify their fate.

Every day the news media report arrests of people trying to exercise their human rights in non-violent ways. But for every prisoner of conscience whose case becomes news, there are many more who are unknown; and even those who gain wide publicity tend to be forgotten over time. Amnesty International aims to give attention to all the forgotten prisoners, to put their cases into the public record, to ensure that they remain a public concern, and that they are cared for individually as long as they remain in prison. The organization assigns individual cases to Amnesty International adoption groups around the world, after their case histories have been investigated by the Research Department in the International Secretariat. When the facts show the individual is a prisoner of conscience, the adoption group works by publicizing the case, involving various sections of the community, and persistently appealing to the offending government for the prisoner's release. When Amnesty International does not have enough information to be certain of the reasons for imprisonment, or the individual's present circumstances, the case is given to an adoption group for further investigation. Group activity is coordinated with other national and international initiatives.

The work of Amnesty International groups for prisoners of conscience can be frustrating. Governments frequently refuse to reply to or even acknowledge letters. A case can be worked on for years with no new information emerging, or the news may be bad: the prisoner may have been ill-treated, or denied medical care. It is often impossible even to contact the prisoner's family or send the material aid that is usually needed. Yet Amnesty International's experience after 20 years of this work reaffirms the forecasts of its founders: that persistent work for the individual prisoner in face of all obstacles is frequently the only help the prisoner is receiving; that silence on the part of the government is not a reason for giving up on a case; and that Amnesty International's activities often have more positive effects than can be traced from far away.

A fair trial?

Prisoners in many countries around the world are convicted in trials that violate internationally agreed standards, or are held for years, sometimes decades, without any form of trial at all. As well as working to free prisoners of conscience, Amnesty International strives to ensure a fair trial within a reasonable time for all political prisoners. Amnesty International intervenes in cases where people are taken into custody for administrative internment; where they are not brought to trial for an extended period of time; and where there may have been politically motivated miscarriages of justice.

All the major international human rights documents cover the right to a fair trial. "No one shall be subjected to arbitrary arrest, detention or exile" says Article 9 of the Universal Declaration of Human Rights. Article 10 goes on to state: "everyone is entitled in full equality to a fair and public hearing by an independent and impartial tribunal..." Specific minimum guarantees for the conduct of criminal cases are provided in Article 14 of the International Covenant on Civil and Political Rights, and the covenant also states: "anyone arrested or detained on a criminal charge... shall be entitled to trial within a reasonable time or to release". The European and American conventions on human rights have similar provisions.

Amnesty International's work for fair and prompt trials extends beyond prisoners of conscience, whose release is sought regardless of criminal proceedings, to cover all political prisoners. While the term "prisoner of conscience" is strictly defined, the phrase "political prisoner" confers no status whatever and applies to anyone who is imprisoned where there is a political element in the case, for example where the motivation of the authorities or of the prisoner appears to be political. Where political prisoners, such as suspected members of opposition groups that use violence, may not be prisoners of conscience, Amnesty International urges that they be given a fair trial within a reasonable time, or, if charges are not brought, released.

Administrative internment is probably the most widespread problem encountered in this area of work. In many countries, either under the ordinary law or under special temporary measures to deal with states of emergency and the like, the authorities put people in prison without charging them with any criminal offence. In some cases such imprisonment lasts for decades. Where Amnesty International has definite information that detainees are prisoners of conscience it demands their release. Sometimes, however, the authorities have faced violent opposition, and it is difficult to establish whether or not individual prisoners have been involved in armed activities. Here Amnesty International urges the authorities to bring the prisoners to trial, or else to release them. It may also advocate setting up independent review bodies to examine the evidence against each prisoner, so that those against whom there is credible evidence of criminal activity may be tried, and the others freed.

In some countries people are arrested on suspicion of politically motivated criminal activity but there are substantial delays before the trial. Some people are kept under arrest for months or even years before criminal charges are preferred. In other cases, even after being charged, the accused are kept in prison for very long periods before the charges are actually heard in court.

Often when trials do take place, prisoners are convicted under procedures that fall short of internationally agreed standards of fairness. Hearings are conducted behind closed doors, making any assessment of their fairness impossible; or, while the trial is nominally public, the authorities select who should be admitted in such a way as to make the proceedings indistinguishable from those held behind closed doors. Prisoners are denied the right to have lawyers of their own choice to defend them. Cases are heard by special tribunals and military courts whose composition is incompatible with an independent impartial hearing, or whose procedures and rules of evidence fall short of those in ordinary courts. The defence is sometimes not even allowed to call witnesses or present any evidence on behalf of the accused; and there are cases where defence lawyers in political trials are persecuted themselves.

On occasion criminal charges are brought against individuals in order to harrass them for lawful political or religious activity. Amnesty International may try to acquire independent information to judge the credibility of the charges, and will seek to ensure that any such charges are tested in a fair trial. However it does not have the resources to mount sophisticated investigations of every alleged political miscarriage of justice. For example, if someone claiming to be a prisoner of conscience has been convicted of an ordinary crime after a proper trial, Amnesty International will rarely possess enough information to conclude that there has been a miscarriage of justice. Amnesty International sends lawyers and other experts on missions to represent the organization, conduct negotiations on its behalf and collect on-the-spot information about prisoners of conscience, legal procedures and other matters of direct concern. In its work for fair trials Amnesty International sends foreign lawyers to observe the trials of prisoners of conscience and political prisoners, in order to assess the proceedings. The mission report is usually submitted to the government in question, and, where appropriate, published.

Publicity is an important means of pressing governments to bring legal proceedings and practice into line with international standards. In its representations to governments and in its published reports Amnesty International recommends measures to ensure fair and prompt trials, and highlights procedures and legislation that deny citizens a fair hearing. Where people are held without any trial at all, urgent action appeals, special campaigns, news releases, and direct approaches to government are all brought to bear. Some prisoners convicted after trials that failed to conform to standards of fairness are allocated to Amnesty International groups who gather as much information as they can about the case, and urge the government to review it. Where prisoners of conscience, or individuals likely to become prisoners of conscience, need help in securing a lawyer, Amnesty International may assist with funds or legal aid.

Torture and the death penalty

Few international standards are as generally accepted as the banning of torture. There are few, if any, states which do not prohibit torture in their legislation. In reply to United Nations questionnaires governments invariably refer to these legal provisions, claiming that this means that torture does not take place in their country. Yet each year Amnesty International receives countless reports on individuals who have been tortured and ill-treated in prisons and detention centres throughout the world.

The Universal Declaration of Human Rights and the International

Covenant on Civil and Political Rights are unequivocal: "No one shall be subjected to torture or to cruel, inhuman or degrading treatment or punishment." The United Nations Declaration on the Protection of All Persons from Torture and Other Cruel, Inhuman or Degrading Treatment or Punishment goes further: "Exceptional circumstances such as a state of war or a threat of war, internal political instability or any other public emergency may not be invoked as a justification of torture or other cruel, inhuman or degrading treatment or punishment."

Torture and ill-treatment are used extensively to gain information, force confessions, and to punish, intimidate and terrorize. Torture humiliates the victim and dehumanizes the torturer. Among the techniques reported during the year were: hanging people upside down and pouring water into their nostrils; electric shocks; beating the soles of the feet; smashing toes and fingers with a hammer; rape; forcing prisoners to eat live frogs and beetles; pushing people's heads into a bathtub filled with water, blood, vomit, excrement and food; deprivation of sleep; mock executions; and threats against relatives, including children. In some countries certain methods, such as flogging and amputation, were carried out in public.

Amnesty International is unconditionally opposed to torture and the death penalty. The movement is committed to resisting, by all appropriate means, the execution or torture of any prisoner. Amnesty International opposes the death penalty because it is a violation of the right to life and a violation of the right not to be subjected to cruel, inhuman or degrading treatment or punishment. This opposition applies to all executions whether in political or criminal cases.

During the year under review, positive developments towards the abolition of the death penalty included the adoption by Peru of a new constitution abolishing it for peacetime offences, and the defeat of a bill before the Papua New Guinea Parliament to re-introduce the death penalty as a discretionary punishment for wilful murder. By 30 April 1981, 23 countries had completely abolished the death penalty, and 17 had abolished it for ordinary crimes only.

During the year January to December 1980, 1,229 people are known to have been executed in 29 countries and 1,295 people sentenced to death in 41 countries. In addition a number of "executions" of prisoners by opposition groups were reported. These figures include only cases known to Amnesty International: the true figures are certainly higher. Execution methods included shooting, electrocution, hanging, stoning and decapitation. Some executions were carried out in public, although most were not.

Wherever there are fears that a prisoner may be tortured or executed, immediate appeals are sent to the appropriate authorities by Amnesty International. In cases of torture, the authorities are urged to guarantee the prisoner's safety, to allow access to a lawyer or member of the family and to provide for medical care. Where execution is threatened Amnesty International appeals for clemency on humanitarian grounds.

The more than 4,000 doctors in 26 countries in Amnesty International's medical program play an important role in this work: from medical letter-writing campaigns for prisoners in ill-health or suffering medical neglect to studying the after-effects of torture and helping rehabilitate its victims. Amnesty International doctors were sent on missions to a number of countries, and systematically examined former detainees, adding the weight of their evidence to the allegations of torture in several of Amnesty International's published reports during the year.

The rehabilitation of torture victims requires medical and psychiatric treatment, and medical groups encouraged the establishment of independent centres for this work. The United Nations Commission on Human Rights has agreed to recommend that the General Assembly establish a voluntary fund for the victims of torture.

Amnesty International seeks to alert doctors to the ethical abuses of participation in executions, cruel treatment and torture. In March 1981 a declaration was adopted calling on doctors not to participate in executions (Appendix VI). A similar draft declaration adopted by the Central Committee of the Irish Medical Association was transmitted to the World Medical Association for consideration at its 1981 assembly.

As well as intervening in individual cases, Amnesty International presses governments to take structural measures to prevent torture in the future. Experience shows that it is not enough to prohibit it in the constitution or penal code. Other measures are necessary, for example: the abolition of incommunicado detention; providing early access to a judge to decide on the lawfulness of the detention; providing medical examinations; and training police officials in the ethics of their profession as defined, for example, in the United Nations Code of Conduct for Law Enforcement Officials.

Amnesty International — a worldwide campaign

What does it mean to be a member of Amnesty International? It means doing something practical to protect the rights of others. It can mean subscribing to the monthly newsletter, sharing it with friends, and writing letters on behalf of prisoners of conscience or those threatened with torture or execution. It can mean joining a group and working for as long as it takes to help win the release of the prisoners of conscience for whom the group has a special responsibility. It can mean raising money on street corners, going to public meetings, selling publications or helping to run a national office.

This spirit of practical commitment helped get the Amnesty International movement off the ground 20 years ago. The story has often been told of a morning in early 1961 when British lawyer Peter Benenson read in the newspaper of two students in Portugal who had been arrested in a restaurant and sentenced to seven years' imprisonment for raising their glasses in a toast to freedom. Indignant, his first reaction was to go to the Portuguese Embassy in London and protest personally, but he realized that more than an individual gesture was needed. He conceived the idea of a one-year campaign to publicize the plight of people detained throughout the world — under all political systems — for the peaceful expression of their beliefs: prisoners of conscience. The campaign, launched with a newspaper article, "The Forgotten Prisoners", attracted wide interest. Within months, thousands of people had offered their help, and what had started as a brief publicity campaign, became a permanent movement: AMNESTY INTERNATIONAL.

Today there are more than 250,000 members, subscribers and supporters in 151 countries or territories, with national sections in 40. There are 2,560 adoption groups, of from three to sometimes more than 50 members. Each group is allocated responsibility for two or three prisoners of conscience or possible prisoners of conscience. The cases are balanced politically and geographically to reflect impartiality. If a case is still under investigation, because there is not enough evidence to determine whether the prisoner is a prisoner of conscience, the group seeks further information and urges the government to supply details of the charges against the prisoner. With a prisoner of conscience, the group puts its energy into writing letters, circulating petitions, publicizing the case and calling on the authorities for the prisoner's immediate and unconditional release. The group may also raise money to send relief assistance, such as money, medicine or clothing, to the prisoner and the prisoner's family.

A unique aspect of Amnesty International's casework — placing the emphasis on the need for international protection of human rights — is the fact that each group works on behalf of prisoners held in countries other than its own.

Group members also take part in national and international campaigns that attract wide publicity. Some join the special networks set up to respond with a minimum of delay in cases where torture or executions are feared. Some are organized into groups of members of the same profession, for example lawyers or medical doctors. Doctors intervene on behalf of prisoners in need of medical treatment, or threatened with torture; on Amnesty International missions they examine alleged torture victims; and medical groups assist the rehabilitation of torture victims. Organizations like churches and trade unions and individuals like artists, parliamentarians and government officials are approached at national and local level to exercise influence on behalf of prisoners within their own spheres of activity.

Group members, as well as the individual members and affiliates, participate in decision-making meetings at the national level which vary with the differing organizational structures in each country. Delegates from national sections then go forward to an annual International Council, attended by some 200 participants. The council is the supreme governing body of the movement; for example, the Statute of Amnesty International can be changed only by a two-thirds vote of all the delegates. The council determines the international budget and decides on main policy questions.

The council also elects members to the International Executive Committee, a nine-member body responsible for carrying out the decisions of the council and supervising the International Secretariat. The committee approves all missions sent to a country to meet government officials, investigate allegations of human rights abuses and interview former prisoners. All Amnesty International Publications are issued under the committee's authority.

This structure ensures that the vital decisions of the movement are controlled by the membership and its elected representatives. The role of the International Secretariat is to collect information on the human rights questions of concern to Amnesty International, evaluate it and make recommendations for policy and action. The secretariat, with a staff of 150 people of some 30 nationalities, has to compile details about prisoners, answer the numerous queries about them, and keep the members, groups and sections up to date on cases, campaigns and new projects.

The funds to sustain these activities are raised by Amnesty International members themselves. At its council meeting in September 1980 Amnesty International reaffirmed its policy of relying for finances on the efforts of members and donations from the public. Amnesty International does not accept government money for its international budget. It will accept such funds only for its program of humanitarian relief assistance, provided that these are distributed under the sole control of Amnesty International. This financial independence is essential to keep the movement free from interference by governments, funding agencies or pressure groups and to keep it true to its original spirit.

That spirit was reflected during the year in work on behalf of 1,475 new cases of known or possible prisoners of conscience. In the same period the International Secretariat learned of the release of 894 prisoners for whom groups had worked.

A total of 317 urgent action appeals were issued during the year. These were on behalf of thousands of prisoners in more than 60 countries, including many held without charge or trial following mass arrests, prisoners threatened with torture, or facing execution, individuals who had become critically ill in prison, and people abducted by security forces acting with the connivance of the authorities. In every case of a prisoner being sentenced to death, appeals for clemency were sent.

The annual Prisoners of Conscience Week, in October, focused on "Different Faces of Imprisonment". It drew attention to short-term arrests, "disappearances" and "banning": all methods of silencing or restricting opponents.

A major effort was launched in March 1981 to draw attention to human rights violations in the Republic of Korea and through the year Amnesty International members and groups, in addition to their normal activities, cooperated in special actions to help prisoners in the German Democratic Republic, Guatemala, Pakistan, Romania, Singapore, Spain, Turkey and Zaïre.

On 22 October 1980 International Executive Committee Chairperson José Zalaquett presented to United Nations Secretary-General Kurt Waldheim and General Assembly President Rüdiger von Wechmar an appeal calling on the UN and its member states "to take all necessary steps for the immediate and total abolition of the death penalty throughout the world". The appeal was signed by six heads of government and over 150,000 people in more than 100 countries including judges, lawyers, members of parliament, religious and labour leaders, scientists, doctors, artists and writers. Although the UN General Assembly did not pass a resolution on the abolition of the death penalty it did adopt a resolution expressing alarm at the incidence in different parts of the world of summary and arbitrary executions.

The relief program aims to alleviate the suffering of prisoners of conscience and their families and to assist the recovery of victims of torture by providing money and material assistance. It is not a substitute for the principal objectives of securing the release of prisoners of conscience and abolishing the practice of tortuure altogether. When relief payments are distributed by intermediaries or bodies outside Amnesty International, the organization is careful to stipulate the precise, prisoner-related purposes for which the relief is intended, and whenever possible obtains documentation of receipt from the intended beneficiary. The relief program of the International Secretariat is supervised by a sub-committee of the International Executive Committee. The Relief Committee also advises national sections on their relief activities. During the year the International Secretariat distributed £144,306 in relief. Groups and national sections also sent help directly to prisoners and their families. The assistance ranged from facilitating family visits to prisons and medical care for prisoners, through to helping with education and money for families left without a breadwinner.

Despite the range of activities undertaken by Amnesty International members, much of the work was frustrating and difficult. For Amnesty International members the challenge remains twofold: to combat political, religious and racial intolerance internationally, and to overcome the indifference to human rights issues that they confront all too often in their own communities.

International organizations

The promotion and protection of human rights is an international responsibility, which has been recognized by the United Nations (UN) and other international organizations, and is the very foundation of Amnesty International's work. Amnesty International gives great importance to working through and strengthening international mechanisms for the protection of human rights, and has encouraged and supported the establishment and implementation of international standards. It has consistently worked with the UN, whose charter pledges member states to work for "universal respect for, and observance of, human rights and fundamental freedoms for all without distinction as to race, sex, language or religion".

Amnesty International has consultative status (category II) with the Economic and Social Council (ECOSOC) of the UN which allows it to participate in the work of ECOSOC and its specialist sub-bodies on human rights matters within its expertise. The Commission on Human Rights is a functional commission of ECOSOC composed of 43 member states elected by the council. It is the principal body dealing with human rights within the UN. The commission is serviced by the Sub-Commission on Prevention of Discrimination and Protection of Minorities composed of 26 individuals elected by the commission who serve in a personal capacity.

The Committee on Crime Prevention and Control, a body of 25 individuals elected by ECOSOC, is responsible for the preparatory work for the UN Congress on the Prevention of Crime and the Treatment of Offenders, which takes place every five years. These congresses have adopted major international human rights standards, for example the first in 1955 drew up the UN Standard Minimum Rules for the Treatment of Prisoners; the fifth in 1975 the UN declaration against torture (the Declaration on the Protection of All Persons from Torture and Other Cruel, Inhuman or Degrading Treatment or Punishment).

Amnesty International looks to these bodies to fulfil three major tasks: to develop and promote new international standards to protect prisoners about whom Amnesty International is concerned; to establish effective mechanisms to monitor compliance with existing standards; and to enforce these standards when necessary.

By and large the existing international standards cover the human rights questions of concern to Amnesty International: political imprisonment, fair trial, torture. Only on the death penalty are the universal standards less than precise. However the system has been slow to enforce those standards, be it at the national level or through international mechanisms. Amnesty International has consistently pressed all governments to adhere to the international covenants on human rights and the Optional Protocol to the International Covenant on Civil and Political Rights. The Human Rights Committee, established under the International Covenant on Civil and Political Rights, composed of 18 individual experts elected by the states that have ratified the covenant, monitors compliance with the covenant. It studies reports submitted by States Parties, and, under the Optional Protocol to the covenant, considers complaints concerning individuals whose rights under the covenant are reportedly violated. Amnesty

International welcomed the creation of a special mechanism to deal with the particular problem of "disappearances": the Working Group on Enforced or Involuntary Disappearances established by the Commission on Human Rights in 1980.

Over the last few years Amnesty International has frequently provided information about human rights violations to UN bodies. Every year it presents evidence on a number of countries to the UN Secretary-General under the procedure established by ECOSOC whereby the Commission on Human Rights investigates reports referred to it by its sub-commission that "appear to reveal a consistent pattern of gross and reliably attested violations of human rights". With the establishment of the commission's Working Group on Enforced or Involuntary Disappearances, Amnesty International has submitted information on a number of countries where "disappearances" have taken place. It also works under special procedures for dealing with human rights violations in particular countries or regions: it regularly provides information to the commission's Ad Hoc Group of Experts on southern Africa and to the Special Rapporteur on the Situation of Human Rights in Chile. Amnesty International has also testified before such bodies as the Fourth Committee of the General Assembly on human rights violations in East Timor and Namibia and the Special Committee on Apartheid on violations in southern Africa.

Amnesty International seeks to draw the attention of member states to particular types of human rights violations through its written and oral statements. For example during the 1981 session of the commission Amnesty International addressed the problem of extra-judicial executions by governments, referring in some detail to Bolivia, El Salvador and Guatemala. By providing concrete information Amnesty International seeks to encourage enforcement of mechanisms and procedures set up by the UN to respond to violations of human rights. These are in many respects still lacking in power and subject to political pressures. However some significant advances have been made in recent years, and the human rights situations in a number of countries such as Bolivia, El Salvador, Guatemala and Kampuchea are now being examined, in addition to those in southern Africa, Israel (Occupied Territories) and Chile which have been considered by the UN for several years.

In the United Nations Educational, Scientific and Cultural Organization (UNESCO), where Amnesty International has category B status, a special procedure for dealing with human rights violations within UNESCO's mandate was established in 1978. Amnesty International has begun systematically to submit cases to the Committee on Conventions and Recommendations which deals with such complaints. It has also promoted greater activity by UNESCO in the field of human rights education and awareness. Through meetings of non-governmental organizations, by participation in the 1978 UNESCO International Congress on the Teaching of Human Rights, and by intervening and lobbying at the UNESCO General Conference, Amnesty International has pressed for the inclusion of human rights education, which has now been made an important plank of the UNESCO program.

Amnesty International has no formal status with the International Labour Organisation (ILO), but its information on such issues as forced labour, and the imprisonment and "disappearance" of trade unionists has been made available to organizations which do work formally with the ILO.

Amnesty International has also cooperated with regional inter-governmental organizations on its concerns within these regions. Amnesty International has consultative status with the Council of Europe and has testified on a number of occasions over the years before the Committee on Migration, Refugees and Demography of the Council's Parliamentary Assembly. Most recently it did so on the problem of internal and external refugees in El Salvador. It also submitted information on Argentine prisoners who were potential refugees. Amnesty International has given evidence before the Political Affairs Committee of the Assembly, most recently on the state of human rights in Turkey, a member country of the Council of Europe. Amnesty International often gives information about the European Commission of Human Rights to individuals and their lawyers. It also lobbied the Council of Europe on such issues as the abolition of the death penalty and the right of conscientious objectors to military service not to be imprisoned.

The regional organization of the Americas is the Organization of American States (OAS). Amnesty International regularly submits information about human rights violations within its mandate to the Inter-American Commission on Human Rights (IACHR) of the OAS. For the past three years Amnesty International has been invited to attend the OAS General Assembly as a special guest and has made available to the delegations documents outlining its concerns in the region.

At present the Organization of African Unity (OAU) does not have any body specifically constituted to deal with human rights questions, but Amnesty International has been watching with interest moves within the OAU to draft an African Charter of Human and People's Rights. Amnesty International continues to be a member of the Coordinating Committee of the OAU's Bureau for the Placement and Education of African Refugees, and has attended some meetings of the bureau. Africa has a large refugee population; many are former prisoners on whose behalf Amnesty International has worked.

Amnesty International maintains working relations with many international non-governmental organizations, both within the structures at the UN and other international bodies, and bilaterally. The nature of the relations with other organizations depends on how far these organizations work in areas connected with Amnesty International's statutory concerns.

Responsibility for relations with international organizations is vested in the International Executive Committee and the International Secretariat. However Amnesty International national sections play an important role, in particular by lobbying their own governments and parliamentarians in support of Amnesty International's objectives within particular international organizations. This work is increasing and is also of relevance to Amnesty International groups around the world, particularly where they can invoke international standards relevant to the individual cases for which they work.

Contributions to meetings of international organizations

Date	*Meeting*	*Activity*
1980 June	UN Working Group on Enforced or Involuntary Disappearances (Geneva)	Written submissions on "disappearance" cases
June	Political Affairs Committee, European Parliament (Brussels)	Oral statement on implementation of Helsinki Final Act
July	Human Rights Committee (Geneva)	Information for members of the committee on the reports of States Parties under consideration
August	Ad Hoc Working Group of Experts on Southern Africa of the UN Commission on Human Rights (London)	Oral statement on situation of political prisoners in South Africa and Namibia

Date	*Meeting*	*Activity*
August-September	UN Sub-Commission on Prevention of Discrimination and Protection of Minorities (Geneva)	Oral statement on "disappearances". Written submissions on a "consistent pattern of gross violations" in Afghanistan, Argentina, Ethiopia, Indonesia, Paraguay and Uruguay
August-September	Sixth UN Congress on the Prevention of Crime and the Treatment of Offenders (Caracas)	Seminar on death penalty. Oral statements on death penalty, torture and "disappearances". Written statements on death penalty and torture
September-October	UNESCO General Conference (Belgrade)	Oral statements on human rights education
September	UN Working Group on Enforced or Involuntary Disappearances (Geneva)	Written submissions on "disappearances" cases
October	UN General Assembly (New York)	Petition on death penalty presented to UN Secretary-General and to President of the General Assembly
October	UN Special Committee against Apartheid (New York)	Oral statement on political imprisonment in South Africa
October	Human Rights Committee (Geneva)	Information for members of the committee on the reports of States Parties under consideration
October-November	Fourth Committee of UN General Assembly (New York)	Oral statements on concerns in East Timor and Namibia
November	NGO Conference on Security and Cooperation in Europe (Madrid)	Oral statement on implementation of Helsinki Final Act

Date	*Meeting*	*Activity*
November	OAS General Assembly (Washington)	Memorandum on concerns in Latin America
November	Council of Europe Conference on Terrorism (Strasbourg)	Written statement on possible dangers of anti-terrorist measures
December	Council of Europe NGO symposium on police and human rights in Strasbourg	Written statement on need to implement police codes of ethics
December	UN Working Group on Enforced or Involuntary Disappearances (Geneva)	Written submissions on "disappearances" cases
1981 February	Committee on Migration, Refugees and Demography, Parliamentary Assembly, Council of Europe (Paris)	Oral statement on refugees from El Salvador
February	Council of Europe meeting on handling human rights information	Participation in establishing networking structure
February-March	UN Commission on Human Rights (Geneva)	Written statement on "disappearances". Oral statements on "disappearances" and "murder by governments"
March-April	Human Rights Committee (New York)	Information for members of the committee on the reports of States Parties under consideration
April-May	UN Economic and Social Council (New York)	Written statement on draft code of medical ethics
April	Political Affairs Committee, Parliamentary Assembly, Council of Europe (Paris)	Oral statement on torture in Turkey

Africa

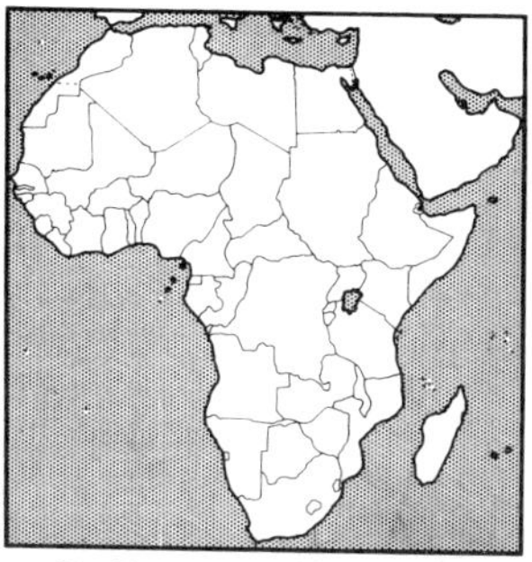

There were promising developments in respect of human rights both at the international level and in a number of African countries during the year 1 May 1980 to 30 April 1981. Further progress was made towards establishing an African regional mechanism for the protection of human rights and new efforts were made to focus international attention on the plight of Africa's refugees, estimated to number five million.

In January 1981 a meeting of Ministers of Justice of the member states of the Organization of African Unity (OAU) adopted a draft Charter of Human and People's Rights and agreed that this should be submitted to the annual summit meeting of OAU Heads of State and Government due to take place at Nairobi, Kenya, in June 1981. If accepted, the charter would come into force when a majority of OAU member-states have ratified it. An African Commission on Human and People's Rights would then be established to promote the charter, protect the rights laid down in it, and investigate serious abuses of the charter with a view to rectifying or remedying them.

As yet relatively few African countries have ratified the International Covenant on Civil and Political Rights and other international instruments for the protection of human rights. Of those that have, the majority did so shortly before the covenant came into force in 1976. No African countries signed or ratified the covenant in the year under review.

In several countries governments took action to improve human rights. In Zimbabwe repressive laws such as the Indemnity and Compensation Act and certain provisions of the Emergency Powers Regulations were repealed, and thc independence amnesty was extended. In Ghana the civilian administration of President Hilla Limann released most of those imprisoned by special courts during the previous administration. In the Central African Republic opposition politicians were freed from detention and their parties were legalized under a new constitution approved by national referendum. In a number of other countries too, the year saw the release of significant numbers of prisoners of conscience. All long-term political detainees were freed in Swaziland and long-term prisoners were released in Angola and Cameroon. All detainees were freed by the government in Seychelles, but some were forced to go into exile.

There were also some releases in Ethiopia, but the number freed was small in proportion to the hundreds of long-term political detainees who remained in prison. The government has still not accounted adequately for 16 prisoners who "disappeared" from prison in July 1979 and may have been murdered by security officials. In Guinea the release during the year of most remaining political prisoners, some of whom had been held for almost 10 years, was accompanied by grave fears about the fate of several hundred others not seen since their arrest several years ago.

There were violations of human rights of concern to Amnesty International in a majority of African countries. The incidence and extent of such violations varied considerably in the 41 countries described in this report. Insufficient information was received about Amnesty International concerns in six countries or territories — Cape Verde, Mauritius, Nigeria, Senegal, Sierra Leone and Upper Volta — to allow their inclusion in this report.

There were continuing extensive violations of human rights in South Africa, where black opposition to *apartheid* resulted in determined student protest and unprecedented industrial unrest nationwide. This was met with mass arrests and detentions, many involving school students, with a series of political trials and with the banning of more black community leaders. In Namibia opponents of continued South African occupation were detained and in a number of cases tortured.

Human rights abuses in Zaïre, the subject of a major Amnesty International report in May 1980, persisted throughout the year. In Mali students and teachers were arrested and ill-treated. In Liberia the overthrow of the Tolbert government in April 1980 resulted in several hundred detentions and other human rights violations. In Uganda former President Idi Amin's brutal rule left a legacy of political turmoil, violence and widespread disregard for human rights. Godfrey Binaisa was deposed as President and detained under house arrest for more than seven months. He was freed after the December election which resulted in Milton Obote's return to power. Many political opponents of the new government were detained in the months following the outbreak of anti-government guerrilla activity in February 1981. The civil war in Chad continued, affected by foreign military intervention and accompanied by severe violations of human rights and the summary killing of prisoners by various parties to the conflict.

With the exception of Cape Verde, the legislation of all African countries retains the death penalty. During the past year death sentences and executions were reported in a number of countries including Angola, Burundi, Ethiopia, Kenya, Liberia, Mozambique, South Africa and Zaïre. A number of convicted prisoners were sentenced to death in Ghana and Zimbabwe, although in Ghana all prisoners who had spent more than one year on death row were granted clemency in September 1980, and in Zimbabwe all sentences of death imposed during the first year of independence were commuted by President Canaan Banana in April 1981.

Amnesty International published a major report on human rights violations in Zaïre in May 1980. During the year submissions relating to human rights violations in Djibouti, Ethiopia, Mali, Namibia, South Africa, Uganda and Zaïre were presented by Amnesty International to the United Nations and other intergovernmental and non-governmental organizations.

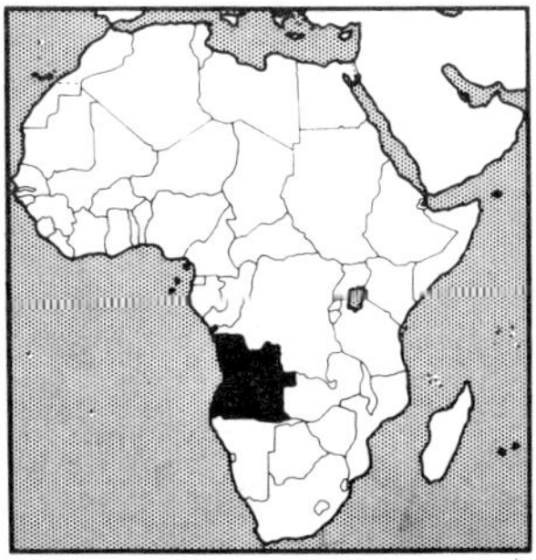

Angola

Amnesty International's main concerns were detention without trial, unfair trial procedures and the death penalty.

Throughout the year there was sporadic fighting in the central and southern parts of the country between government security forces and guerrillas belonging to the *União Nacional para a Independência Total de Angola* (UNITA), National Union for the Total Independence of Angola, led by Dr Jonas Savimbi. The UNITA was responsible for regular sabotage along the Benguela railway and for bomb explosions in the capital, Luanda, and in other cities in central Angola. In addition Kunene and Kuando-Kubango provinces were repeatedly attacked by South African forces.

The conflict between the UNITA and the government of the *Movimento Popular de Libertação de Angola — Partido de Trabalho* (MPLA-PT), People's Movement for the Liberation of Angola — Labour Party, resulted in prisoners being taken by both sides. At the end of 1980 the UNITA was reported to be holding Angolan and Portuguese civilians as well as captured government soldiers. For its part the government had detained several hundred people suspected of UNITA connections. Some had been captured while fighting for the UNITA; for example more than 50 people were held in Luanda's *Casa de Reclusão* (detention centre) without charge or trial. Others were merely suspected of supporting the UNITA and were detained without trial. Both sides executed opponents. In August 1980 the UNITA summarily tried and executed 15 people described as MPLA-PT soldiers after 25 UNITA members had been executed in Luanda.

In addition to those imprisoned for supporting the UNITA a small number of people accused of supporting the *Frente Nacional de Libertação de Angola* (FNLA), Angola National Liberation Front, which had fought the government in 1975 and 1976, were still being held in mid-1980 at Tari detention camp, near Kibala in Kuanza-Sul province.

Despite the armed conflict many long-term detainees were released during the year. They included suspected members of dissident left-wing groups held since late 1977 and early 1978 and detainees of several nationalities who had been detained without charge or trial in Luanda, some for as long as four and a half years.

Members of the *Organização Comunista de Angola* (OCA), Angola Communist Organization, and the *Nucleo José Staline,* Joseph Stalin Group, had been detained without trial since 1977 and early 1978. Members of both these organizations were released in January 1980, and by May 1980 about 15 remained in detention who had all been adopted as prisoners of conscience. In February and March 1980 at least four of the detainees appeared before a special judicial commission composed of members of the People's Revolutionary Tribunal which summarily examined their cases and sentenced them to periods of two and three years' administrative detention. The detainees had no right to defend themselves. At the beginning of May 1980 three of them were transferred from São Paulo prison in Luanda to Tari detention camp. Later in May three women teachers held at São Paulo prison on account of suspected links with the OCA went on hunger-strike for 12 days to protest against their continuing detention. The three were released in June along with a fourth teacher, Dulce Fonseca, who had been detained in 1978 and sentenced to two and a half years' administrative detention in February 1980.

In July 1980 the seven men still in detention at São Paulo prison because of links with the two dissident groups went on hunger-strike. At the same time the three who had been transferred to Tari camp refused to work. During the hunger-strike Amnesty International appealed for the release of all the detainees. The hunger-strike lasted 28 days and by the time it ended all seven hunger-strikers had been transferred to hospital and the authorities had indicated that their cases would be reviewed. The seven detained at São Paulo and the three at Tari camp were all released unconditionally in August 1980. In October 1980 Amnesty International received a reply to its appeals from a senior member of the MPLA-PT Central Committee, but it did not refer to detainees still being held on whose behalf Amnesty International was appealing.

Amnesty International investigated the detention without trial of Sabino dos Santos da Cunha Matos and eight other prisoners from Sao Tome and Principe who had been living in Angola and who were arrested in Luanda in April 1979, apparently suspected of criticizing the Government of Sao Tome and Principe. They were reportedly released in August 1980.

More than 20 detainees held in the *Casa de Reclusão* in Luanda went on hunger-strike in September 1980, protesting against their detention. Four of them were Zaïrians who had been detained since July 1976, a few months after seeking political asylum in Angola. Prisoners from Zaïre, Portugal, Chile and other countries had been detained in 1977 and 1978, apparently because the authorities saw them as a threat to national security. Several Cape Verdeans were released in October 1980. In March 1981 the Zaïrians and a number of other non-Angolan detainees held in Luanda were released to the United Nations High Commissioner for Refugees for resettlement outside Angola. In December 1980 Amnesty International learned that four Portuguese nationals captured before independence in 1975 while fighting for the FNLA, who had since been detained without trial, had been released and deported to Portugal.

Although a number of political detainees were released during the year Amnesty International remained concerned by the prolonged detention without charge or trial of civilians arrested on suspicion of being "counter-revolutionaries". Amnesty International received reports of a number of civilians detained for between six and 12 months after being denounced to the authorities, although no evidence had been presented that they had actually committed offences.

During 1980 and early 1981 some 50 people accused of being members of the UNITA and of causing bomb explosions and civilian deaths were sentenced to death by the People's Revolutionary Tribunal, sitting in Bie, Huambo, Kuito and Luanda. The condemned prisoners were allowed to appeal to a special Appeals Tribunal formed in April 1980 to hear appeals against death sentences and prison terms exceeding 20 years. Only one appeal against the death sentence, in January 1981, was successful; the sentence was commuted to imprisonment. At the same hearing a prisoner who had been given a long prison sentence had it changed on appeal to a death sentence. Sixteen prisoners condemned to death in July 1980 and nine condemned in August 1980 are reported to have been executed; it is not clear how many other condemned prisoners have been executed.

Amnesty International repeatedly appealed to the Angolan authorities not to impose the death penalty and to commute death sentences, both during and after trials in 1980 and early 1981. In April 1980 and again in September 1980 the organization wrote to senior officials explaining its opposition to the death penalty and why it sought to prevent executions from taking place. No reply was received.

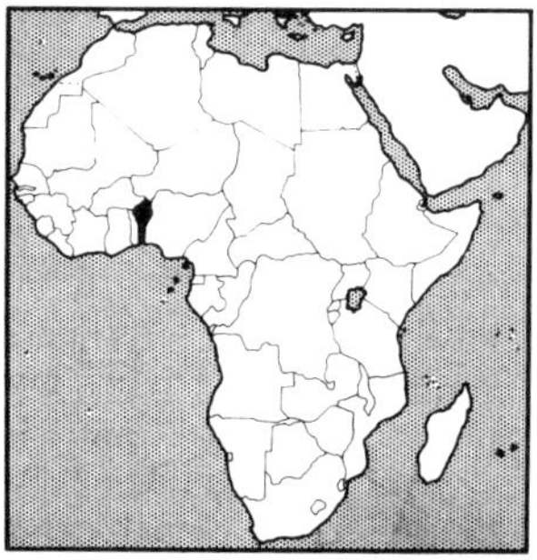

Benin

The main concerns of Amnesty International were: the detention without trial of suspected political opponents; unfair trials of political prisoners; and the cruel, inhuman and degrading treatment of some prisoners.

Throughout the year Amnesty International sought the release of 22 students and teachers held without trial for alleged involvement in protests against government policies in education. With the exception of Paul Iko, held since September 1978, they were arrested between March and November 1979 when meetings and strikes were organized to call for improvements in university education, and to oppose government-controlled student associations. Several reports suggest that in early 1980 up to 50 students and teachers were detained but that by late 1980 some of these had been released after hurried court hearings that passed sentences of three and four months.

Amnesty International continued to appeal for the release of three former Presidents, Hubert Maga, Sourou Migan Apithy and Justin Ahomadegbe, held under house arrest without charge or trial since the military coup led by Colonel Mathieu Kerekou in October 1972. In late April 1981, they were reportedly released from house arrest.

Amnesty International also sought the release of Abbé Alphonse Quenum and former Agriculture Minister Adrien Glele who were among 13 people arrested in 1975 and convicted of participation in attempts to overthrow the government. There were serious shortcomings in their trial, including the absence of defence counsel and denial of the right of appeal. Inquiries were also made about Claude

Midahuen, a former official in the Ministry of Finance, who was arrested in 1975 and sentenced to 10 years' imprisonment. He was not permitted to be present at his trial.

In November and mid-December 1980 two waves of arrests took place throughout the country and as many as 100 people are reported to have been detained. Some of the arrests were of high-ranking government officials suspected of opposing the leadership of President Kerekou. Others included primary school teachers who allegedly opposed government attempts to impose a new trade union structure. Most are believed to have been released by the end of April 1981. In early January 1981 Amnesty International appealed publicly for the release of these and all other detainees held without charge or trial in Benin; the appeals also drew attention to prisoners convicted in unfair trials, and called for improvements in prison conditions. The authorities have not responded.

In March 1981 Amnesty International appealed to the government for the release or trial of Guy Midiouhouan. In early February he had been deported from Gabon to Togo after being arrested for writing articles critical of President Oumar Bongo. Two weeks later he was deported from Togo to Benin where he was detained. In April 1981 Amnesty International was informed of his release.

In September 1980 Amnesty International appealed to the government for the release of all prisoners of conscience in Benin, for an end to detention without trial, pointing out that rights enshrined in the Beninese constitution, *Loi fondamentale*, had been violated. This law guarantees the rights to freedom of conscience, expression and association, to freedom from arbitrary arrest and to defence counsel. No answer has been received.

Amnesty International was concerned by reports of harsh prison conditions and ill-treatment of detainees at the *Commissariat central* (central police station) in Cotonou, the capital. Prisoners were held in overcrowded cells, which are poorly ventilated and unsanitary. One cell, known as *la grille* (the cage), was so overcrowded that many detainees were forced to remain standing. Medical facilities were reported to be inadequate and many detainees to suffer recurrent ill-health. In October 1980 students and teachers held in the Central Prison, Cotonou, were apparently beaten and harassed by prison officers, after asking to be held separately from prisoners convicted of criminal offences. The conditions of detention and medical facilities at the Central Prison in Cotonou and the civilian prison in Porto Novo were also known to be poor.

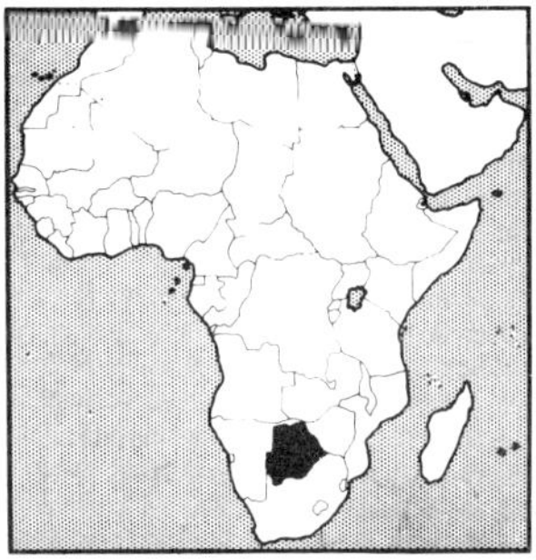

Botswana

Amnesty International was concerned about the forcible repatriation of four South African refugees.

Despite the return home of more than 20,000 Zimbabweans in the first months of 1980, and the resulting reduction in the refugee problem, there were signs of increasing tension between the government and the South African refugee community. After the departure of the Zimbabwean refugees the Botswana Government announced its intention to relocate the great majority of South African refugees in a vacated settlement camp at Dukwe, in a remote area some 130 kilometres northwest of Francistown. The refugees resisted this move, apparently out of fear that the camp was vulnerable to attack by South African security forces and out of misgivings about conditions. Some refugees went into hiding in Gaborone, but they eventually went to Dukwe after the authorities threatened to deport them back to their country of origin. A few refugees are said to have opted for repatriation rather than move to Dukwe.

Tension between the Botswana Government and the South African refugees reached a peak in January 1981 when Daniel Kwelagobe, Minister of Public Service and Information, visited Dukwe and issued a strong warning that refugees absent from the camp without permission would be liable to summary repatriation. He announced that four refugees had already been "de-recognized" by the authorities and deported to South Africa. This was confirmed by the South African authorities, who acknowledged that four refugees had been detained at the border on 15 January 1981.

Amnesty International expressed concern to the Botswana authorities about the summary deportation, and asked for clarification of the number and identities of those deported. Some unconfirmed reports had suggested that more than four refugees had been deported, and that at least one of those subsequently detained had died in security police custody in South Africa. The Botswana authorities named the refugees as Michael Lithoko, Wilson Fanyana Mashaba, Joseph Minare and Strike Mashilane. On 25 February 1981 Louis Le Grange, South Africa's Minister of Police, told the House of Assembly in Cape Town that no refugees deported from Botswana since the beginning of the year were in police custody at that time. He stated also that there were no cases in which charges had been brought against such deportees. However it was not clear from the Minister's statement precisely when the four refugees had been released from detention in South Africa.

Towards the end of March 1981 the Minister of Public Service and Information issued a public assurance that Botswana had not changed its policy of granting asylum to political refugees from South Africa. He insisted that "genuine and well-behaved refugees who co-operated with the government would never be harassed during their stay at Dukwe camp".

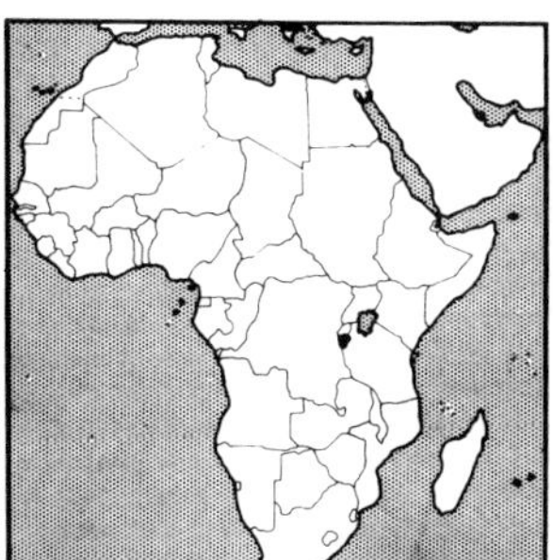

Burundi

Amnesty International's main concerns were detention without trial and the death penalty.

Amnesty International received information about a number of students detained during the year. In late July 1980 Ladislas Nzohabonayo and Mathias Niyonzima, both leading members of the ruling party's youth wing, the *Jeunesse révolutionnaire Rwagasore* (JRR), Revolutionary Rwagasore Youth, were arrested while attending a national conference of the JRR. They were accused of disturbing the proceedings after they had apparently criticized the leaders of the JRR and encouraged them to adopt more radical policies. They were detained without charge or trial until November, when they were released. Their cases were investigated by Amnesty International.

At least two other students were arrested in early August 1980. Both had been studying abroad, one in Romania and the other in Libya. They were obliged to return home after they had protested against the reduction of their overseas study grants together with other students from Burundi. One of those detained was Antoine Nkeshimana, who had been studying in Bucharest. He was sent home with several other students in July 1980 and was arrested on 3 August 1980, apparently because of the protests against grant reductions. Amnesty International investigated his case. He was released uncharged in November 1980.

In July 1980 Amnesty International learned that six people had been executed in Bujumbura. Four had been convicted of violent crimes, and two of membership of the illegal *Nanga Yivuza* religious sect and of ritual cannibalism.

Cameroon

The major concerns of Amnesty International were long-term detention without trial of suspected political opponents and poor prison conditions.

In a year which brought the release of most prisoners of conscience known to Amnesty International, high-ranking members of the government and of the judiciary publicly stated their belief that human rights were respected in Cameroon. At the reopening of the Supreme Court in November 1980, its President drew attention to legal safeguards to protect the rights of the accused. However individuals arrested on suspicion of political offences have not benefited from such safeguards; they have either been tried before military tribunals without defence counsel or have been held without charge or trial.

Amnesty International continued to seek the release of all the detainees held without charge or trial since July 1976, when some 200 students, teachers and white-collar workers were arrested for allegedly distributing anti-government leaflets. In February 1980 Amnesty International publicly appealed for the release of some 50 members of this group held in the *Prison de production*, labour camp, at Yoko and at the so-called Re-education Centre at Tchollire. Both of these institutions contain sections which are effectively administrative internment centres. After a decree remitting sentences for convicted prisoners on Cameroon's National Day on 20 May, most of these untried detainees were freed. Only Gaspard Mouen, Martin Ebelle-Tobo, Emmanuel Bille and André Moune were still reported to be in detention. No adequate explanation has been given by the authorities to justify their continued detention without charge or trial. Amnesty International was also concerned by reports that other political prisoners were being held without charge or trial, including three army officers, arrested in September 1979 after an alleged coup attempt, and an unknown number of Jehovah's Witnesses.

Although no new reports of torture against identified detainees have been received, Amnesty International was concerned by claims that suspects held in custody by the police or the paramilitary police, known as the *Brigade mixte mobile*, have been beaten and ill-treated as a matter of course. Standards of food and hygiene were reported to be very poor at both Yaounde central prison and the administrative internment centre at Tchollire. Both prisons lacked adequate medical facilities, and access at Tchollire to families and friends was severely restricted.

Central African Republic

Amnesty International's main concerns were detention without trial and the death penalty.

In November and December 1980 the government released Ange Patasse, leader of the *Mouvement de libération du peuple centrafricain* (MLPC), Central African People's Liberation Movement, and several other political detainees. This was apparently part of an attempt to form a national coalition between the ruling *Union démocratique centrafricaine* (UDC), Central African Democratic Union, and opposition political parties. Charges of endangering state security which had been brought against Ange Patasse and nine others were dropped after an examining magistrate ruled that they were without foundation. Most of the detainees released at this time, including Ange Patasse and the journalist Joseph Tchendo, had been detained since November 1979.

In early December, the government convened a national seminar in Bangui to discuss the country's future and invited all political groups. The seminar recommended that political parties in addition to the ruling UDC should be legalized, and allowed to compete for power within a democratic framework. This was accepted by the government and led to the legalization of existing opposition parties and to the formation of several new ones in late December and early January. On 1 February 1981 a national referendum approved a new constitution by a large majority.

In August 1980 President David Dacko, who had assumed office after the overthrow of Emperor Bokassa almost one year earlier, dismissed two senior government officials. Vice-President Henri Maidou and Prime Minister Bernard Christian Ayandho were both placed under house arrest for several weeks. Their removal led to the formation of a new government under Prime Minister Jean-Pierre Lebouder, which included members of the MLPC.

The new constitution introduced after the February referendum guarantees freedom of activity for political parties. It provides for a single-chamber national assembly, and an elected president to hold office for six years. The first presidential election under the new constitution took place on 15 March 1981, organized on the French model. President Dacko was confirmed in office at the first round of voting with an official return of 50.23 per cent, and Ange Patasse, who stood as the MLPC's presidential candidate, received 38 per cent of the votes. Even before the official results were announced on 19 March there were violent demonstrations in Bangui, where Ange Patasse had been the most successful candidate. At least four people are believed to have been killed. The results were challenged by the unsuccessful candidates who claimed that the poll had been rigged in the President's favour. On 20 March 1981, in response to the demonstrations in Bangui and other towns such as Bossangoa, President Dacko proclaimed a state of siege, but this was lifted after 10 days. After the election President Dacko formed a new government composed exclusively of UDC members, under the premiership of Simon Bozanga.

In August and September several MLPC supporters who had been held under house arrest or restricted to provincial towns were set free. They had been adopted as prisoners of conscience by Amnesty International, as were the members of the MPLC released in November and December 1980, who included Joseph Beninga and Gabriel Dote-Batakara. Several supporters of the *Front patriotique oubangien* (FPO), Oubangui Patriotic Front, were also freed, including Nditifei Boysembe Marc, who had been detained at Ngaragba prison since 16 August 1980 accused of plotting to overthrow the government, and Cyriaque Bomba and Emmanuel Majot, who had been banished *(assignés à résidence)* to Boda and Bossangoa respectively after their arrest on 9 March 1980. Also set free was Massemba Ngolio, a journalist arrested in August 1980 for having filed a report to an international news agency which was considered to be insulting to President Dacko.

There were several trials of former officials accused of crimes committed during the rule of Emperor Bokassa. In December 1980 Emperor Bokassa's elder sister, Catherine Gbagalama, was convicted of carrying out arbitrary arrests, causing bodily harm and abusing the authority which she had held as Mayor of Pissa, a town 80 kilometres from Bangui. She was sentenced to three years' imprisonment, two of them suspended. She was released immediately as she had already spent 15 months in pre-trial custody. In December 1980, Louis Lakouama, a former Minister of Defence, and Jean-Robert Zana, a former Minister of Interior, were put on trial. They were both acquitted of charges connected with the killing of young people at Ngaragba prison in April 1979. In early 1981 several officials accused of crimes during the Bokassa era were still in prison awaiting trial: they included the former Prime Minister, Elisabeth Domitienne.

Former Emperor Bokassa, in exile in Ivory Coast since his overthrow in September 1979, was tried in his absence in December 1980. He was accused of responsibility for numerous murders, particularly of political prisoners, and also of expropriating and misusing public funds. He was convicted and sentenced to death.

Six people were convicted of having committed murders while Bokassa was in power and sentenced to death. They included former prison guards found guilty of killing children at Ngaragba prison in April 1979. They were initially condemned to death by Bangui's Central Criminal Court in February 1980, but these sentences were annulled by the Supreme Court in August 1980. The six were tried again in September 1980 and were once again sentenced to death. Amnesty International appealed for these sentences to be commuted. The six prisoners also appealed to the President to commute their sentences. However all six were executed by firing-squad at the end of January 1981 and their bodies publicly displayed.

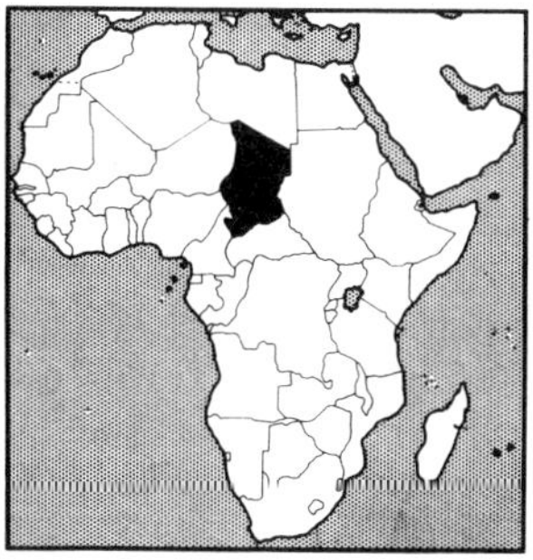

Chad

Amnesty International was concerned by reports of executions of prisoners captured during the civil conflict which continued to dominate events throughout the year. The general dislocation and breakdown of administrative control which accompanied the conflict made it difficult either to obtain detailed information or to intercede effectively for the protection of human rights.

The transitional government of national unity formed after negotiations in Lagos, Nigeria, in August 1979 functioned ineffectively for most of 1980. Renewed fighting broke out in March 1980 between the *Forces armées du nord* (FAN), Armed Forces of the North, led by Defence Minister Hissène Habré, and the *Forces armées populaires* (FAP), People's Armed Forces, supporting Goukouni Oueddei, President of the transitional government. A third group led by Vice-President Wadal Abdoulkader Kamougue took no part in the conflict but consolidated its control over the southwest of the country. In the capital, N'Djamena, fighting continued until December 1980, when Libyan troops intervened in support of Goukouni Oueddei. The FAN were forced to retreat from N'Djamena but further skirmishes between the FAN and FAP and Libyan forces occurred in March 1981 in Biltine province in eastern Chad.

Shortly after the FAN withdrew from N'Djamena, more than 100 corpses and skeletons were discovered in an area which the FAN had occupied near the Chari river. According to observers they were the remains of prisoners summarily executed by the FAN, still bound at the wrist. FAN forces claimed that the corpses were of their own soldiers killed during the fighting.

Further allegations of summary executions were made in February 1981 after Libyan troops occupied the town of Guereda in Biltine province. Unconfirmed reports alleged that 56 suspected FAN supporters were summarily executed at Guereda between 3 and 9 February 1981. In April 1981 press reports in neighbouring Sudan indicated that more summary executions of suspected FAN supporters had taken place at Abeche in Ouaddai province.

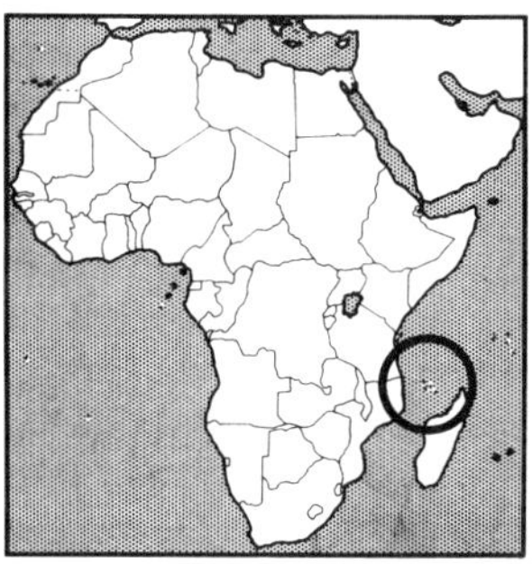

Comoros

Amnesty International's concerns were detention without trial, unfair trials, ill-treatment of prisoners, and harsh prison conditions.

In response to an invitation from the government, Amnesty International was preparing for a mission in May 1981. Amnesty International had repeatedly called on the government to try or release about 30 civilian officials and soldiers arrested when the present government of President Ahmed Abdallah came to power in May 1978, and still detained without charge or trial in April 1981. They included members of the former government of President Ali Soilih such as Salim Himidi, former Minister of the Interior, Ali Toihir "Keke", former Secretary General for Defence, and Abdulwahab Mohamed, teacher and former member of parliament. Toyib Dada and Nassor Khalifa, both former presidential aides detained since 1978, had been freed in May 1980.

Thirteen others who had been detained in 1978 were brought to trial in December 1980 and early 1981, before a special court established to deal with people detained in 1978. Eleven of them, all former members of the security forces, were convicted of killing 11 people in a mosque in Iconi, Grande Comore, on 18 March 1978. They were sentenced to prison terms ranging from six months to life imprisonment. The defendants were not legally represented and had no right of appeal.

A number of students were arrested in February and August 1980 for striking or criticizing the government's educational policies, and some were reportedly ill-treated by the security forces. Most were released within a short time, but some were sentenced to six months' imprisonment. Amnesty International was also investigating the detention of Fatouma Said Abdallah who was charged with murder, since it believed that she may have been arrested for her political views.

In February 1981 over 50 people including prominent officials were arrested for alleged possession of subversive documents and video cassettes. Eleven were still held without charge, in Voidjou military camp at the end of April 1981.

Amnesty International was concerned about harsh prison conditions at Moroni central prison, where the 1978 detainees were held. According to Amnesty International's information prisoners were denied visits from relatives, lawyers or religious representatives, correspondence, writing materials, and books except for the Quran. They were denied beds and sleeping mats, and slept on the earthen floor. Until January 1981 the cells were overcrowded, with windows blocked up. Prisoners were allowed out into the open air very rarely, and were forbidden to change their clothes or wash for long periods. Medical treatment was often refused. When the prison jurisdiction was transferred in January 1981 from the security force to the army, overcrowding was reduced, the windows were unblocked, and some outdoor exercise was permitted. Some prisoners were admitted to hospital, although contact with relatives was still denied.

In Voidjou military camp, 40 kilometres from Moroni, prisoners were held incommunicado in darkened cells, without beds or sleeping mats, and denied medical attention. Prisoners there were reportedly frequently beaten. Some of the 1978 detainees have also from time to time been taken there from Moroni central prison and beaten.

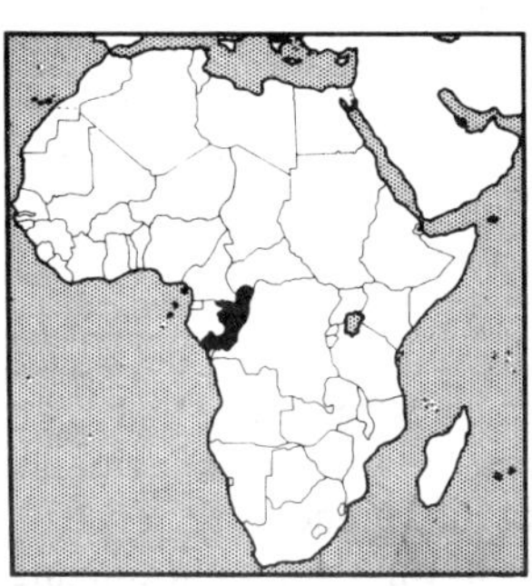

Congo

Amnesty International's main concern was detention without trial.

Former head of state Joachim Yhombi-Opango, who was replaced as President in February 1979 by Colonel Denis Sassou-Nguesso, has been held in detention since March 1979. He was initially accused of high treason but has not been brought to trial. First held at Makola military camp, he has been detained at Pointe-Noire since late 1979. Three associates of former President Yhombi-Opango — Pierre Aboya, Pierre Anga and Jean-Claude Itoua — have also been detained without trial since 1979. All four cases were being investigated by

Amnesty International. Two other detainees arrested at the same time — Bonaventure Engubu and Gaston Issambo — were released in August 1980.

Amnesty International received information about a number of short-term detentions. In September 1980 Bernard Mackiza, editor, and Albert Mianzoukouta, a journalist, both employed by the newspaper *La Semaine africaine,* were arrested in Brazzaville and detained for two weeks. Albert Mianzoukouta had written an article criticizing the construction of a new railway bridge to link the administrative centre of Brazzaville with the residential quarter where most senior government officials live. They were reportedly denied food during the first few days in detention.

A number of refugees from Zaïre were also detained during 1980. Most were students who fled from Zaïre after a strike and demonstrations by students in Kinshasa during March and April 1980. Some, such as former student leader Pascal Nzogu, were released and allowed to leave the country within a few weeks, but others are believed to have been detained for about six months. By early 1981 all the Zaïrian detainees known to Amnesty International had been released and permitted to travel to other countries of asylum under the auspices of the United Nations High Commissioner for Refugees.

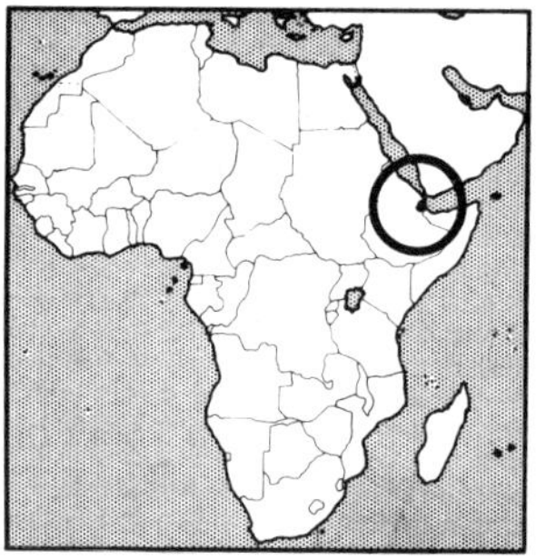

Djibouti

Amnesty International's concerns in Djibouti centred on the cases of 41 people arrested in 1979. They were detained on charges of being involved in two separate attacks on army camps at Randa and at Khor Angar. Most are believed to have been tortured immediately after their arrest. Nineteen of the detainees were discharged and freed in early 1981, and others who had earlier been provisionally released were also discharged at the same time. The remaining 22 detainees went on trial before the state security tribunal in March 1981.

The two trials relating to the Randa and Khor Angar incidents resulted in the acquittal and release of 15 of the defendants. Seven — mostly soldiers — were sentenced to terms of imprisonment ranging from three to seven years on the lesser charge of criminal association. No charge relating to actual participation in the attacks was sustained. There is no right of appeal against the tribunal's verdict or sentence. The counsel of the defendants' choice, a member of the Paris Bar, was not permitted to plead, but the defendants were represented by lawyers of the Djibouti Bar.

Amnesty International's concern over the treatment of the detainees arrested after the Randa and Khor Angar incidents had been brought to the attention of President Hassan Gouled's government during an Amnesty International mission to Djibouti in March 1980. Particular disquiet had been expressed about the alleged torture of the detainees, many of whom appeared to have been arrested because of their previous membership of a banned opposition party, *Mouvement populaire de libération,* the Popular Liberation Movement.

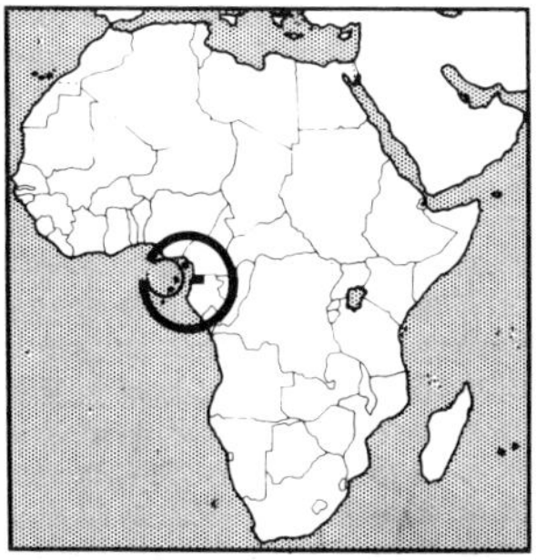

Equatorial Guinea

For most of the year the increased respect for human rights which followed the overthrow and execution of President Masie Nguema in late 1979 was maintained by the government of President Obiang Nguema Mbasogo. However in April 1981 the President announced that a plot against the government had been discovered and ordered the arrest of more than 100 people. Most were reportedly members of the Fang ethnic group from Ebebiyin and Mikomeseng districts. They included naval officers such as Captain Luis Oyono, and former senior officials such as Antonio Mba Ndong, who was reportedly dismissed as Technical Secretary General of the Ministry for Foreign Affairs in early 1981, and Angel Masie Ntutumu, who had been Minister of the Interior until 1976. The detainees were held incommunicado, and by the end of April 1981 the charges against them were still not known.

In March 1980 the United Nations Commission on Human Rights received the report of the special rapporteur appointed in March 1979 to make a thorough study of human rights in Equatorial Guinea, and recommended, in view of the changes that had taken place in the country, the appointment of an expert to assist the new government to restore human rights and fundamental freedoms. The expert, in consultation with the government, visited the country in late 1980 and reported to the commission in February 1981. He paid particular attention to legislation and advised the revision of existing laws, the drafting of new laws, including a constitution, and noted the need to train lawyers. He recommended that the United Nations assist by providing experts in these areas. In March 1981 the commission decided to keep the human rights situation in Equatorial Guinea under review, and to take steps to implement the expert's recommendations.

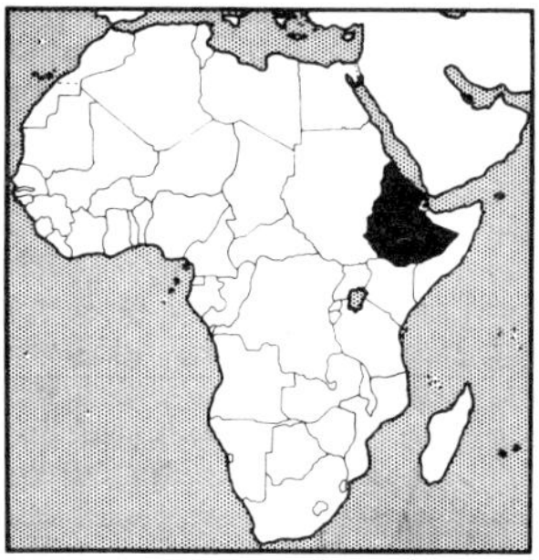

Ethiopia

Amnesty International's concerns were detention without trial, torture, "disappearances", political killings, harsh prison conditions, and the use of the death penalty.

Armed conflict continued in Eritrea, Tigrai, the Ogaden, and the Oromo-populated southern provinces, where opposition movements fought for self-determination. The Eritrean conflict entered its 20th year and in late 1980 the conflict in the Ogaden caused relations with Somalia to deteriorate further. Civilians in these areas suffered from the fighting, with many fleeing from the upheavals and related political persecution. The number of refugees from Ethiopia rose to over two million, while a further million or more people were displaced within the country as a result of the fighting and famine. In June 1980 the ruling Provisional Military Administrative Council (PMAC) promulgated an amnesty for refugees in Djibouti, though few are believed to have returned. A small number of refugees returned from Sudan, but were detained on arrival for a lengthy screening process by security officials.

In May 1980 Amnesty International submitted to the United Nations Commission on Human Rights its fourth communication on human rights violations in Ethiopia. The report stated: "the pattern of large-scale and often prolonged political imprisonment under harsh conditions, torture, and summary executions, has persisted through most of the country". It added that a number of "disappearances" took place in July 1979. It noted that the PMAC had taken measures to end the previously widespread pattern of arbitrary arrests and executions by local administrative organizations, both *kebelles* (urban-dwellers' associations) and peasant associations.

The number of new political arrests appeared to have decreased, except in the areas of armed conflict, and a small number of long-term political prisoners were released. There were some improvements in prison conditions in certain prisons. Nevertheless there were still believed to be several thousand people detained without charge or trial on political grounds; torture was still reported to be widely used; "disappearances" which took place in 1979 had never been explained by the authorities; many prisoners were allegedly executed outside the framework of the law; and prison conditions generally remained harsh.

Six years after the revolution which overthrew the imperial government in 1974, about 200 former government officials were still in indefinite detention without charge or trial. Some of their wives and children were also held. It appears that no review mechanism exists for examining the allegations against these prisoners individually and impartially, or for recommending the release of certain categories such as elderly women and men, women and their children detained together, or chronically ill detainees, or for offering release through a "rehabilitation" process. Amnesty International regards most of the 1974 detainees as prisoners of conscience, detained for their political views or position, and has frequently called for their release.

Among the long-term detainees — many believed to be prisoners of conscience — were people arrested in the first few years of the revolution. Although supporters of the revolution they were arrested for opposing the PMAC. Some were apparently victims of arbitrary arrests of members of nationalities or ethnic groups where guerrilla movements existed. Others were members of certain Protestant and Pentecostal churches — such as the Ethiopian Evangelical Mekane Yesus Church — which had become targets of government-instigated campaigns of persecution for allegedly harbouring counter-revolutionaries.

Political prisoners in Addis Ababa were held in the PMAC headquarters in the former Menelik palace; the fourth army division headquarters; Akaki prison (where women detainees have been held since 1975); the Central Revolutionary Investigation Department (known as the "third police station"), and the military police barracks. Some were also said to be held in various unidentified "safe houses" in the capital. Few political prisoners were held in *kebelle* prisons for more than a short time, since people arrested by *kebelle* officials were transferred to one of the 25 "higher *kebelles*" in the city and from there to the Central Revolutionary Investigation Department. Amnesty International learned that during the year, sometimes as many as 100 people a week were transferred to the Central Revolutionary Investigation Department for interrogation after arrest on political grounds. Political prisoners were also held in provincial prisons and military barracks throughout the country, with particularly large numbers of political prisoners in Eritrea and Hararghe.

Torture was widespread. A common method was beating on the back and feet in a variety of contorted positions, and there was also sexual torture, such as a bottle of water or ice being tied to the testicles. Suspected political opponents were beaten to intimidate and "punish" them.

Most political prisoners were held in indefinite detention without charge or trial. The trial of six senior officials in 1980 was exceptional, since no other trials of this nature have taken place before or since. Four were sentenced to death in July 1980 for "anti-socialist and counter-revolutionary activities" and espionage, and two others imprisoned for life and 20 years. Most of the trial, held before the Supreme Military Tribunal, was *in camera*, and details were not published. There was no right of appeal. Amnesty International appealed for the commutation of the death sentences but the executions are believed to have been carried out without delay.

The cases of the 16 people who "disappeared" in July 1979 remained unexplained by the authorities. Fifteen of them were long-term untried political detainees: 10 former high officials under Emperor Haile Selassie's government, and five leaders of the Marxist-Leninist *Me'isone,* All-Ethiopia Socialist Movement, which was banned in 1977. The Reverend Gudina Tumsa, General Secretary of the Ethiopian Evangelical Mekane Yesus Church, "disappeared" after being abducted by unidentified gunmen presumed to be government security agents.

Amnesty International had submitted their cases to the United Nations Working Group on Enforced or Involuntary Disappearances. The working group reported on 26 January 1981 that the Ethiopian representative described the facts in the submission as "false rumours", but did not provide any details on any of the cases under investigation. The government has given no official explanation for the "disappearances", and no trace of the "disappeared" has been found. Different government sources have disseminated conflicting information: that the Reverend Gudina Tumsa was in prison and could be visited by a foreign diplomatic representative, although no such visit has been permitted; or that he had been taken away for his own safety by the opposition Oromo Liberation Front (OLF), which is unsubstantiated, and denied by the OLF.

Prison conditions for detainees held in the Menelik palace, fourth army division headquarters, and Akaki prison, improved slightly. Prisoners received food and clothing from their relatives outside prison, and could pass short messages to them, although only one or two short visits were allowed in the year. They had access to a prison medical doctor who could recommend hospital admission for serious complaints or provide treatment in prison. Some exercise and recreational activity were occasionally permitted. More reading and study material was allowed. However no international humanitarian organization has been permitted to inspect the conditions of political prisoners since shortly after the revolution.

Conditions were still particularly harsh for the 180 former high-ranking government officials held since 1974 in the Menelik palace cellars. Sanitation was very poor, and most prisoners suffered from the effects of long-term confinement underground in damp unhygienic conditions. Prisoners held in the military police barracks were also treated harshly, being held incommunicado in solitary confinement in small concrete cells without windows or furniture.

Amnesty International was concerned about the threatened repatriation of Ethiopian refugees, particularly from Bulgaria, Czechoslovakia, Hungary and the Soviet Union. A number of Ethiopians studying in those countries feared political persecution if forced to return to Ethiopia, and tried to go to other countries where they could seek asylum. It appears that most were eventually allowed to go to other countries to seek asylum.

Amnesty International pressed the authorities for clarification of the fate of the "disappeared"; campaigned on behalf of the hundreds of Oromo women and men detained in February 1980 and allegedly tortured; called for the release of all prisoners of conscience, an end to torture and executions, and improvements in prison conditions.

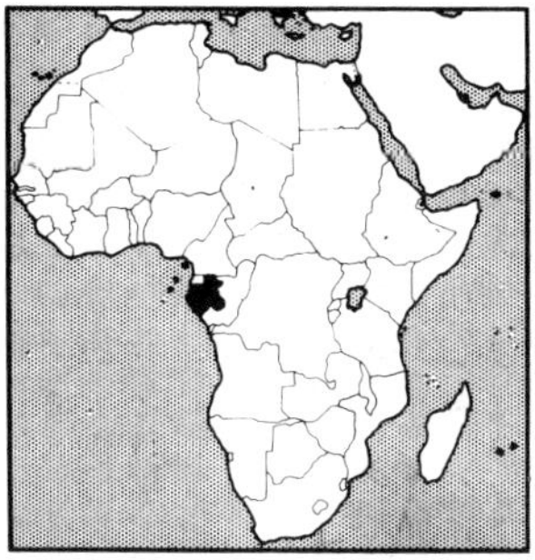

Gabon

Amnesty International's major concern was detention without trial.

Dominique Diata and Augustin Irigo, two soldiers held without charge or trial for more than two years and adopted as prisoners of conscience by Amnesty International, were released in June 1980. They had been arrested in March 1978 apparently suspected of left-wing sympathies.

In January 1981 Amnesty International learned of the arrest of Guy Ossito Midiouhouan, a teacher of Beninese nationality. He was apparently detained for several weeks because he had written an unpublished article containing comments held to be insulting to President Omar Bongo, and is believed to have been ill-treated. On 6 February 1981 Amnesty International asked the authorities for the reasons for his arrest and on 16 February 1981 they replied that he had been expelled to Togo, where, according to independent reports, he was again arrested. His wife and child who had been placed under house arrest after his detention were also expelled from Gabon. He was later deported from Togo to Benin.

In February 1981 it was reported that the government intended to increase the penalty for criticizing or insulting the head of state or other senior government officials. Those convicted may in future be liable to up to 10 years' imprisonment.

Reports received by Amnesty International suggested that significant numbers of detainees were being held without charge or trial at Libreville central prison. The identities of most were not known to Amnesty International, but they appeared to include both political and criminal suspects, many of them victims of arbitrary arrest. Unable to obtain release by legal means, as a result some are believed to have been imprisoned under harsh conditions for several years.

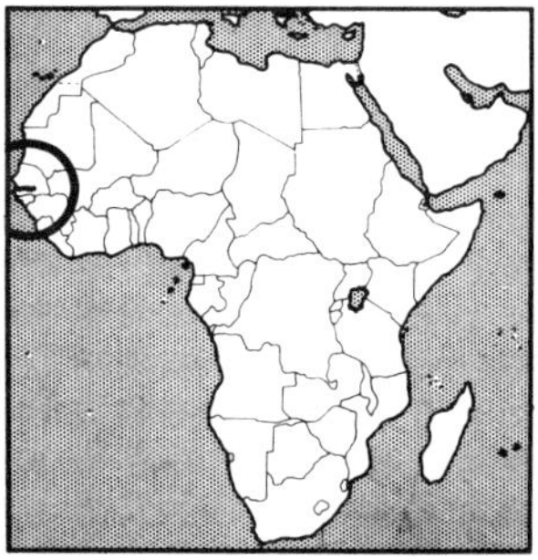

Gambia

On 31 October 1980 six members of a political group called the Movement for Justice in Africa (MOJA) were arrested in the capital, Banjul, and charged with "managing an unlawful society" and "possessing firearms and ammunition". Less than 48 hours earlier, MOJA and another organization called the Gambia Socialist Revolutionary Party (GSRP) had been declared "unlawful societies" under the terms of the 1971 Societies Act, which empowers the President to outlaw any society deemed to be "prejudicial to or incompatible with the interests of the defence of the Republic, public safety, public order, public morality or public health . . .". MOJA and GSRP were banned shortly after the killing of Eku Jacob Mohoney, Deputy Commander of the Field Forces, the Gambia's army, and official announcements that Libyan agents had been involved in an attempt to overthrow the government. At President Dawda Jawara's request, Senegalese troops intervened to protect strategic points in Banjul. Diplomatic relations with Libya were severed.

Trial proceedings against the six accused, all of whom were released on bail in December 1980, began in the Magistrates' Court in late November 1980. On 4 April 1981 the court ruled that four of the accused — Bekai Jobe, Pamodu Jobe, Mamadou M'Boge and Solomon Tamba — had no case to answer and should be released. Proceedings continued against the two remaining defendants — Fakkeba Juwara and Koro Tijan Sallah — and had not finished by the end of April 1981.

Amnesty International expressed concern that the charges against the six accused might relate to their activities as members of MOJA before it was banned, activities which were then lawful. In addition some of the accused were specifically charged with "possession of arms and ammunition", although authoritative sources suggested that a police search at the home of Koro Tijan Sallah had uncovered nothing more dangerous than a bow and arrows and several shotgun cartridges. In response the government insisted that the trial was a criminal one without political connotations. However the authorities allowed an Amnesty International observer to attend the trial in late December 1980 and early January 1981.

In December 1980 Mustapha Danso, a private in the Field Forces, was convicted of murdering the Deputy Commander of the Field Forces, Eku Jacob Mohoney, and sentenced to death. He was granted the right to appeal, but no appeal proceeding had been lodged by the end of April 1981.

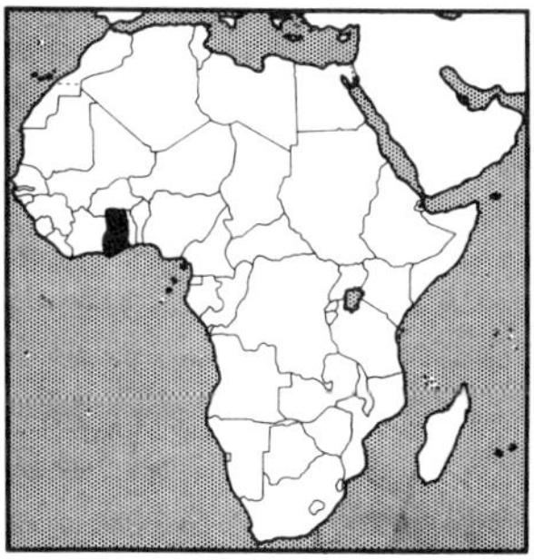

Ghana

The main concerns of Amnesty International originated before the present civilian administration took office and related to difficulties between the present government and supporters of former head of state, Flight-Lieutenant Jerry Rawlings.

Most prisoners sentenced to prison by special courts during the term of office of the Armed Forces Revolutionary Council (AFRC), between June and September 1979, were freed during the year after applying to the courts for reconsideration of their convictions. However at the end of April 1981 at least 27 prisoners were still being held. Their sentences of between five and 95 years' imprisonment were imposed after hurried trials without defence counsel. In July 1980 all had submitted *habeas corpus* applications to the Accra High Court, which referred the cases to the Supreme Court in late September. In February 1981 the Supreme Court considered the cases but had not, by the end of April 1981, made public its decision as to whether the applications would be received.

In June 1980 Amnesty International publicly appealed to the authorities to review all sentences passed by the AFRC Special Courts, in view of their unfair proceedings. In a public statement in late September 1980 President Hilla Limann announced an amnesty for all political exiles and refugees, except those sentenced *in in absentia* by the AFRC. He is reported to have said later that "the time is not ripe" for a decision on the fate of prisoners convicted by the AFRC Special Courts.

In mid-October 1980 the government announced that a number of agricultural development schemes established by Flight-Lieutenant Jerry Rawlings were being turned into camps "for training active subversives . . . with the aim of overthrowing the government of Ghana by unlawful means". During October and November about 10 people were arrested and questioned. Amnesty International was only able to obtain the name of one of them, Wilhelm Harrison Buller, a British national, who was allegedly "chief instructor" in the camps. After nearly two months in detention without charge or trial, all were released, and Buller was deported. In late November 1980 Amnesty International had asked for the reasons for Buller's detention.

One of those detained in late November 1980, Kojo Tsikata, a former army captain and close associate of Flight-Lieutenant Jerry Rawlings, was alleged to have been severely assaulted during interrogation by military intelligence officers. Kojo Tsikata had previously brought an action against senior members of military intelligence to stop the harassment he claimed he had suffered for several months.

The presidential amnesty of September 1980 commuted to life imprisonment the death sentences of all prisoners who had spent one year or more on death row. Amnesty International does not know how many they were.

Guinea

Amnesty International's concerns were political imprisonment, detention without trial of suspected political opponents of President Sekou Toure's government, ill-treatment of detainees and poor prison conditions.

Fears about the fate of the thousands reported arrested in the massive waves of arrests in 1971 and 1976 were increased following the release in late 1980 of virtually all the long-term political prisoners still held at Boiro camp. Sixteen long-term prisoners were released in October 1980. They included Nabaniou Cherif, Baba Kourouma and El-Hadj Mamadou Fofana (see *Amnesty International Report 1980*), and Sory Conde, Saliou Coumbassa, Sekou Fofana and Yoro Diarra, all of whom had formerly held high political office. Of approximately 500 long-term political prisoners known to Amnesty International and who are not believed to have been released, no more that 10 were reported alive in detention. There were strong reasons to fear that the remainder, which included many former senior officials and military officers arrested in 1971 and 1976, were either killed in prison or died from ill-treatment or harsh conditions. The government has failed to provide their relatives or international humanitarian organizations with any information about their fate.

Despite an amnesty for all political exiles declared in 1975, a number who returned to Guinea were arrested shortly afterwards and held without charge or trial. In late 1979 Mahmoud Bah and Moucktar Diallo returned to Guinea and were arrested for allegedly planning to dynamite several public buildings. At least six individuals arrested in Boke at the same time are reported to have died in Boiro camp after being deprived of food and water. Amnesty International investigated the case of another former exile, Mamady Magassouba, who was detained from mid-1980 until his release in April 1981 after apparently being denounced for anti-government activities.

On 14 May 1980 a grenade exploded in the audience at the *Palais du peuple* (People's Palace) in the capital, Conakry, killing one person and injuring some 50 others. Although President Sekou Toure and government officials escaped unhurt there were fears that the attack might lead to arrests on the scale of those in 1971 and 1976. Shortly after the explosion *le Conseil national de la Révolution* (CNR), National Council for the Revolution, Guinea's legislative body, called for a purge to "unmask and once more crush the enemy internally and externally", and some 100 individuals are believed to have been detained. Although some were released shortly afterwards, including army photographer Lieutenant Himy Sylla whose case was investigated by Amnesty International, as many as 40 remained in detention. In late February 1981 a series of bombs exploded at Conakry airport, but no fatalities were reported.

In early 1981 a large number of people were detained, ostensibly in order to apprehend those responsible for the 1980 and 1981 explosions. As many as 100 people were reportedly taken into custody. They included members of the presidential guard on duty at the time of the February 1981 airport bombing, as well as trainee pilots and airport staff. The authorities also encouraged the neighbouring states of Senegal and Ivory Coast, with large Guinean exile communities, to extradite Guinean citizens. In April 1981, the Ivorian authorities are believed to have helped in the forcible repatriation of three Guineans to Conakry, where on arrival they were badly beaten by Guinean soldiers and prison officers. Two have since been returned to Ivory Coast, but Barry Moucktar remained in detention in Boiro camp. He had lived in Ivory Coast for 16 years. Amnesty International was concerned that the recent arrests may have been an attempt to stifle opposition to the authorities, given the absence of guarantees against detention without trial.

Amnesty International has continued investigating the cases of students detained in April 1979 at Kankan and in March 1980 at Kindia, following protests against poor educational facilities. Up to 100 students may have been arrested on each occasion. Some of the detainees are believed to have been forcibly conscripted into the army after several months in detention, while others are thought still to be detained. Amnesty International was also investigating reports of the arrest of students in Kankan in January 1981 after the appearance of wall slogans hostile to the authorities.

By late 1980 conditions of imprisonment in Boiro camp had improved, although the standard of sanitation and nutrition remained poor. Reports have suggested that the number of prisoners in Boiro camp may have reached the levels of the early 1970s, and there were fears that conditions would again have deteriorated. Amnesty International was concerned by reports that prisoners were frequently beaten with rifle butts and sticks in Boiro camp. The government has yet to allow an inspection of its prisons by an international humanitarian organization.

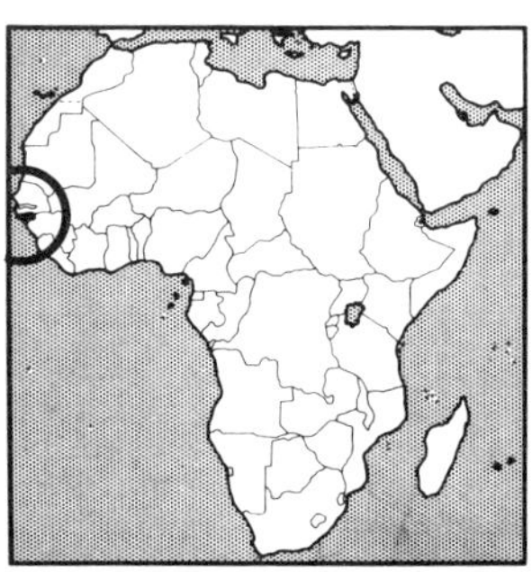

Guinea-Bissau

Amnesty International's concerns were the detention without trial of suspected political opponents and the death penalty.

On 14 November 1980 a coup led by Prime Minister Major Joao Bernardo Vieira overthrew the government of President Luis Cabral. The only reported fatalities were officials Antonio Buscardini and Otto Schatt who were killed by troops loyal to the Prime Minister when allegedly resisting arrest. Both the government and the *Assembleia Nacional Popular* (ANP), National Popular Assembly, were dissolved, and the new *Conselho da Revoluçâo,* Council of the Revolution, assumed executive and legislative powers.

One of the first results of the coup was the revelation of serious and repeated violations of human rights before the coup. The new administration promptly ordered the release of at least 100 prisoners who had been secretly and arbitrarily detained by the police and National Security officials. Many had apparently been arrested on suspicion of political opposition to the previous administration. Also released was Rafael Barbosa, former President of the *Partido Africano da Independência da Guiné e Cabo Verde* (PAIGC), African Party for the Independence of Guinea and Cape Verde, the country's sole political party. Although detained since 1975 he was among 22 people brought to trial in August 1980 charged with involvement in an abortive coup attempt in November 1978. Following the State Prosecutor's demand in early August 1980 for the death penalty for Rafael Barbosa and two other defendants, Amnesty International appealed to President Cabral to exercise clemency if the death penalty should be imposed. However on 18 August 1980 the trial was indefinitely postponed. One of those for whom the death sentence had been requested, Malam Sanha, was reported to have committed suicide in prison in October 1980.

At a large public meeting on 21 November 1980 in the capital, Bissau, Major Vieira announced the discovery of mass graves in various parts of the country containing some 500 corpses. According to government sources as many as 400 were shot by a small secret commando unit and another 100 were asphyxiated at Farim prison. Records found after the coup revealed that large numbers of *comandos africanos*, African soldiers who had fought with the Portuguese colonial forces, had been executed in the first six months after independence in July 1974, as had many people allegedly linked to the abortive armed coup attempt in November 1978. A partial list of those executed was published in late November 1980 and foreign journalists and diplomats visited a mass grave.

Immediately after the coup the former President of the Republic, Luis Cabral, and seven high-ranking officials were arrested. The new authorities announced that some of them would be tried for involvement in the secret executions. One of the detainees, former Army Chief of Security Andre Gomes, is reported to have committed suicide in prison in late December 1980. In a statement to the press in January 1981 President Vieira announced that all political prisoners, including those arrested after the coup, would be freed in due course.

In late February 1981 some 200 students were arrested in Bissau after demonstrations against proposed educational reforms and the arrest of four other students. All had been released by early March 1981. In late March 1981, Rafael Barbosa was arrested once more along with several other people for alleged anti-government activities. In late April 1981 Amnesty International appealed to the authorities to try the detainees without delay or to release them.

Ivory Coast

Amnesty International's concerns were detention without trial, the forcible conscription of suspected trade union activists, and the gross ill-treatment of detainees, some of whom died.

In November and early December 1980 some of the personnel at the headquarters of the *Office des postes et télécommunications,* the post office; the *Radio-Télévision ivoirienne* (RTI), the national broadcasting agency; and the *Agence ivoirienne de presse* (AIP), the national press agency, went on strike for salary increases and improvements in training programs. On 12 December a number of journalists and technicians at the RTI and AIP suspected of being trade union activists were arrested, and forcibly conscripted into the army. Sports journalist Eugène Kacou was among at least 18 transported to the military camp at Daloa. Conscription in the Ivory Coast is not universal and has in the past been selectively applied against critics of government policies.

Also arrested between 4 and 18 December were eight white-collar workers suspected of holding an unofficial union meeting and possessing Marxist literature. All were held in overcrowded conditions at the *Commissariat central* (the central police station) in the capital, Abidjan. In its appeals to the authorities in January and April 1981 Amnesty International called for the rapid release or trial of all these individuals. No answer has been received.

In March 1981, 46 people died in custody. Most were Ghanaians, who were among several hundred arrested during an operation against urban crime. All 46 detainees apparently died of asphyxiation after being crowded into a small and badly ventilated cell at the *Gendarmerie* (police station) at Agban, a suburb of the capital. President Houphouët-Boigny is reported to have condemned these deaths and to have ordered an official inquiry. Amnesty International was concerned that many migrant workers from neighbouring West African states were apparently singled out for arbitrary arrest, and that without relatives to bring them food, their conditions of detention have been particularly harsh. Reports suggested that detainees held in Abidjan, and particularly at the *maison d'arrêt* (remand centre), received insufficient food and medical attention and that many were in poor health.

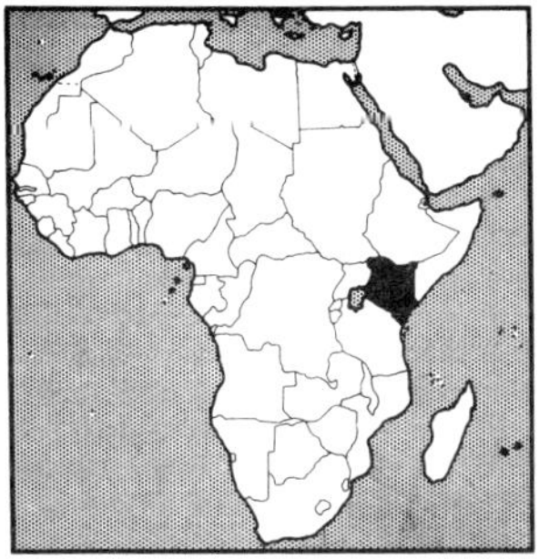

Kenya

Amnesty International's main concern was the use of the death penalty. On 27 August 1980 Amnesty International appealed to President Daniel arap Moi to exercise presidential clemency on behalf of all those under sentence of death, and deplored reports that six people had been executed at Kamiti prison in Nairobi on 4 August. It was not known whether further executions were carried out.

Although no details were issued by the government Amnesty International believes that in August 1980 over 100 people were in Kamiti prison under sentence of death, mainly for robbery with violence. Those charged with this offence are tried by a resident magistrate, are not eligible for state legal aid, and are subject to a mandatory death sentence on conviction. Most are not legally represented and few of those sentenced succeed in completing the legal formalities to appeal against sentence.

Amnesty International was also concerned at incidents in Garissa, capital of the north eastern province, in November 1980. The majority of people in this area are of Somali ethnic origin, and it has been a restricted area since the secessionist conflicts of the 1960s, when a Somali movement fought unsuccessfully for the area to become part of Somalia.

On 2 November 1980 a government district officer was murdered near Garissa, and seven others — mostly government officials — were killed in another attack in Garissa on 9 November. After the second incident the security forces engaged in reprisals against ethnic Somalis in Garissa. They reportedly burned down a section of the town, committed numerous assaults, and killed an unknown number of people. Virtually the whole ethnic Somali population of Garissa was rounded up and detained in the open for several hours; some were held under these conditions for two days without food or water. Many ethnic Somalis living in other parts of Kenya were also arrested for short periods and interrogated. By April 1981 no one had been charged in connection with the murders in Garissa.

Lesotho

During the year there were several detentions under the Internal Security (General) Amendment Act of 1974. This empowers the police to detain people incommunicado and without charge or trial for a period of 60 days, after which successive detention orders may be issued. In June 1980 at least four academic staff members of the National University were detained under this provision for several weeks. They were later released uncharged after protests by students and other university staff. One of them, Thabeng Ramarumol, a law lecturer, was later reported to have left the country and to have sought asylum in Botswana. There were further detentions in early August, when Godfrey Kolisang, a well-known lawyer and General Secretary of one faction of the Basutoland Congress Party (BCP) and other BCP supporters were arrested. Godfrey Kolisang had previously been adopted as a prisoner of conscience by Amnesty International when he was detained under the same act in November 1975.

Amnesty International called upon the government to grant these detainees access to their families and to legal representation, and asked the authorities to publish the names of all detainees together with details of their places of imprisonment. Concerted appeals were made on behalf of one of the detainees, 66-year-old Tsolo Kalake, a former political prisoner in South Africa who was reported to be seriously ill. Amnesty International also urged the government to ensure that the detainees were charged or released without delay. In response the government said that Godfrey Kolisang and the other detainees had been arrested for alleged subversive activities and would be prosecuted, unless the Director of Public Prosecutions decided otherwise. All the detainees, including Godfrey Kolisang, were later released uncharged, although the Prime Minister's private secretary claimed that some had confessed under interrogation to subversive activities in support of the armed guerrillas of the Lesotho Liberation Army (LLA). On 20 October 1980 in response to further inquiries from Amnesty International, the government reported that no detainees were then being held under the Internal Security (General) Amendment Act.

The first major political trial since 1975 began in early March 1981 when 11 alleged supporters of the LLA appeared in court at Maseru charged with high treason. The accused were all said to have been arrested in May 1980 after an attack on a police station in

Mafeteng district, which resulted in two deaths. The trial was still in progress at the end of April 1981.

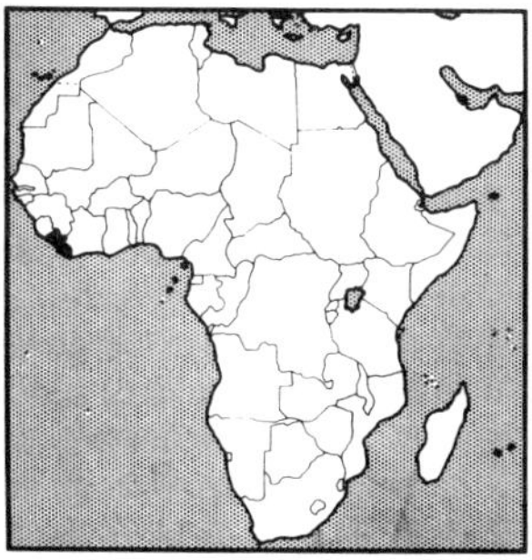

Liberia

The concerns of Amnesty International were political imprisonment, detention without charge or trial, unfair trials, poor prison conditions, the ill-treatment of detainees, and the death penalty.

Immediately after the armed coup which brought Master-Sergeant Samuel Doe to power on 12 April 1980, many former officials, senior officers and managing directors of publicly-owned corporations were arrested. The newly-formed People's Redemption Council (PRC), the supreme legislative and executive body composed of soldiers from the lower ranks, issued a decree defining the crime of high treason, effective retroactively and punishable by the death penalty or imprisonment of 10 years to life. *Habeas corpus* was suspended and all political activity was banned. The PRC established a Special Military Tribunal consisting entirely of soldiers, which, within a week of the coup, began hearings against 14 former senior officials charged with "high treason, rampant corruption, misuse of public office and the abuse of civil and human rights". The defendants were allowed neither defence counsel nor to present evidence. After hurried proceedings the military tribunal submitted its verdict on 13 of the accused to the PRC, which ordered their execution. On 22 April 1980 they were publicly executed by firing squad.

These executions provoked protests from many foreign heads of state, international organizations and religious bodies. Shortly afterwards the new government stated that no more former officials would be executed and that only 101 individuals on a public list would be tried for activities before the coup. However by then about 500 people had reportedly been arrested and detained in prisons and detention centres in the capital, Monrovia, although about 200 were freed within a month. Many were associates or relatives of former prominent officials and had been arbitrarily detained on the orders of a member of the PRC or of the government. Many others were harassed by soldiers from the lower ranks. Head of State Doe made several attempts to control the soldiers and curb the violence against civilians, and to end the administrative confusion: at least nine soldiers were imprisoned during 1980 for assault or harassment of civilians.

A PRC decree made public in mid-May 1980 restricted the power of arrest to the Ministry of Justice and county authorities but it was not consistently followed. The Commanding General of the armed forces ordered the arrest of armed forces chaplain Major Edwin Lloyd, who had reportedly criticized the execution of former government officials in a sermon. Officials claimed he was arrested for helping a photographer to take unauthorized pictures. He was taken to Bella Yallah prison. A.B. Tolbert, son of the late President, William Tolbert, and former member of the House of Representatives, was arrested in mid-June 1980 when troops forcibly entered the French Embassy where he had sought refuge. An unknown number of civilians were held for allegedly assisting him while he was hiding. In October 1980 Stephen Neal was arrested in Harper for having allegedly criticized the execution of his brother in April. In February 1981 three dock-workers' leaders were arrested following strikes, which had been banned by the PRC in June 1980.

These arrests appear to have been carried out solely on executive orders, without reference to legislation existing before the coup or independent judicial authority. Despite official claims most detainees have not been charged or given reasons for their arrest. Powers of extrajudicial arrest were increased by Head of State Doe in September 1980 when he publicly authorized members of the security forces to arrest anyone found to be "sabotaging the interests of the PRC". His call for all "anti-revolutionary elements . . . to immediately be executed" was later retracted. In February 1981 Head of State Doe was reported to have warned that anyone attempting to "disorganize the nation" would be arrested and shot by firing-squad if found guilty. The legal status of these crimes remains unclear, and it is not known whether any detainees have been accused of committing them.

In late April 1980 the Special Military Tribunal resumed its hearings against civilians accused retroactively of "high treason, rampant corruption and misuse of public office". Throughout May, 22 former ministers and senior officials were given hurried trials, without the right to defence counsel or to appeal. The military tribunal is believed to have submitted its verdicts for ratification to the PRC, but these were never made public and the accused remained in detention without knowing their sentences. In July 1980 the trial of nine soldiers arrested in May and accused of plotting a counter-coup, including Brigadier General Rudolph Kolako and Colonels Bedell, Solo and Benson, opened before the Special Military Tribunal. The defendants were allowed defence counsel and the right to present evidence and call witnesses. They denied the charges. On 11 December 1980, the day before the verdict was due, the Chairman of the Special Military Tribunal, General Frank Senkpeni, was arrested. He was accused of withholding information provided by the prisoners and of delaying the court's judgment. Shortly afterwards two other members of the tribunal, Colonels Taylor and Coleman, were also arrested, apparently on similar grounds. Although all three were replaced, the tribunal has not sat again and the verdicts against the nine soldiers have not been made public.

Appeals for the prompt trial of all political prisoners before civilian courts or their release have been regularly addressed to the PRC. The diplomatic representatives of France and the United States publicly appealed for a general amnesty on several occasions and the European Economic Community reinforced its call for releases by suspending aid to Liberia for several months. Similar appeals were made by several African heads of state. In June and September 1980 Amnesty International appealed to Head of State Doe to release between 200 and 400 detainees held without charge or trial; to ensure that trials of political prisoners took place before independent courts with adequate defence counsel; to improve prison conditions in Monrovia; to end the ill-treatment of detainees; and to return prisoners transported to the remote prison of Bella Yallah to Monrovia. From October 1980 onwards Amnesty International repeatedly submitted this appeal to the Head of State and to members of the PRC and of the government. After a request from Foreign Minister Gabriel B. Matthews in December 1980 Amnesty International made a number of recommendations to improve respect for human rights including the publication of a list of all political detainees and the release of those against whom proceedings were not intended. The authorities have yet to respond to these proposals or to agree to an Amnesty International mission to their country.

Many public appeals have been made within Liberia: civilian members of the government, including the Ministers of Foreign Affairs, Economic Affairs and Planning, and Justice, called on the PRC to release or try all political prisoners before civilian courts; as did representatives of the Roman Catholic Church and other prominent personalities.

In July 1980, 19 detainees were freed, and the late President's wife, Victoria Tolbert, and her three daughters were released from house arrest. Three further groups of political prisoners were released in November and December 1980 and April 1981, when 23, 22 and 19 detainees were freed. In all some 120 prisoners were reported to have been released by the end of April 1981, the majority detainees, but also at least 15 former senior officials tried in May 1980. Although it is difficult to establish the number of prisoners left, records suggest that between 80 and 200 people were still imprisoned at the end of April 1981.

In the first three months after the coup Amnesty International received several reports that detainees in Monrovia were frequently being beaten with whips and automobile fan belts. Although recent reports indicated that this had been stopped Amnesty International remained concerned by reports of very poor prison conditions in the Post Stockade at the Barclay Training Centre and in the South Beach prison, both in Monrovia. Conditions were believed to be most insanitary and the food insufficient and of poor quality. Medical care was inadequate and at least two prisoners are believed to have died as a result. Visits by friends and relatives of prisoners have been banned for long periods. In September 1980 the commanding officer of the Post Stockade, Captain Reeves T. Buoah, banned all visits to prisoners and is reported to have warned that attempts to circumvent this ruling would be severely punished.

Amnesty International was also concerned by penalties to counter the smuggling and use of illegal drugs which involved cruel and degrading treatment, and were reportedly to be imposed extrajudicially. Minister of Defence Major Samuel B. Pearson announced in September 1980 that individuals found in possession of illegal drugs would be forced to consume immediately whatever quantities were found upon them. In March 1981 the Liberian press announced a government decision that before prosecution 25 lashes would be inflicted on anyone importing drugs into Liberia through Robertsfield airport.

Statements by government officials suggested that the death penalty would apply to those convicted of "illegally attempting to influence the conduct of armed and police forces and security personnel for personal benefit and against the interest of the State" or of "disorganizing the nation". Seven people were executed by hanging in early March 1981. Government sources claimed that all had been convicted of murder and sentenced to death before the coup.

Madagascar

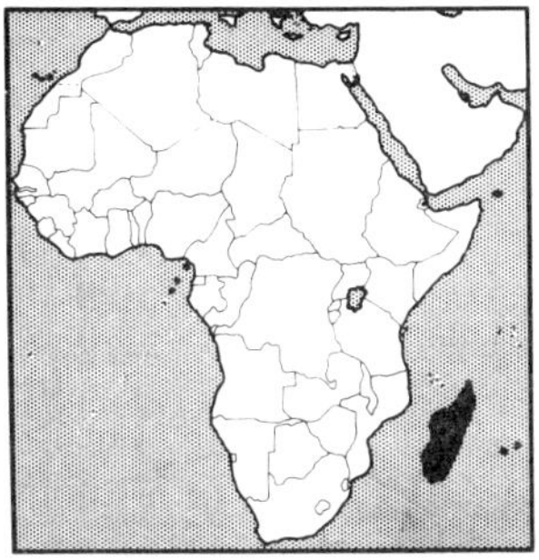

Amnesty International's main concerns were the imprisonment of prisoners of conscience, prolonged pre-trial detention, torture and harsh prison conditions.

The cases of three long-term detainees were being investigated by Amnesty International: Richard Andriamaholison and Marson Rakotonirina, both senior police officers; and Jean-Astier Rakoto-Abel, an army officer. They were arrested in October 1977 and eventually charged with endangering or plotting against state security. They were still being held in pre-trial detention at the end of April 1981, although the 20-month maximum period of such detention permitted by Malagasy law had been exceeded. The authorities have failed either to acknowledge or respond to Amnesty International's repeated requests for the reasons for their continued detention without trial. There was particular concern about Richard Andriamaholison, who was reportedly seriously ill in Manjakandriana prison in April 1981. Amnesty International medical groups appealed to the authorities to allow him full access to qualified medical treatment, if necessary in hospital.

On 30 November 1980 Monja Jaona, the 70-year-old President of the *Mouvement national pour l'indépendance de Madagascar* (MONIMA), the National Independence Movement of Madagascar, was placed under house arrest (*assignation à résidence fixe*) in a remote army camp near Ihosy, 600 kilometres from the capital, Antananarivo. This followed demonstrations in Toliary by MONIMA supporters. Amnesty International appealed for his release if he was not to be charged, and for access to his relatives, doctor and lawyer, but no response was received. Amnesty International later issued an urgent appeal calling for his unconditional release as a prisoner of conscience. He was released in March 1981, after agreeing to reintegrate MONIMA into the ruling National Front for the Defence of the Malagasy Socialist Revolution.

More people were arrested after demonstrations in Antananarivo on 3 February 1981 by students protesting about academic issues and demanding the release of Monja Jaona. At least six people were killed in the ensuing rioting. Four members of the Union of Teachers and Researchers in Higher Education, who had been involved in a strike committee coordinating university protests since the previous November, were detained. They included Professor Randriamampandry, Dean of the Faculty of Medicine and President of the Malagasy

Human Rights Committee (which had been active on behalf of political prisoners in 1971 and 1972); Dovo Rabetsitonta, a lecturer and senior MONIMA party official; Régis Rakotonirina, a research technician and MONIMA official; and Herimanana Razafimahefa, a student leader. The strike committee was accused of instigating the rioting, and charges of endangering state security and criminal association were brought against the four detainees and other strike committee members sought by the police. Professor Randriamampandry was arrested without legal formalities and detained incommunicado beyond the 12-day maximum permitted period of detention without charge. Régis Rakotonirina "disappeared" after abduction by unidentified government agents. About a month later however he was taken to hospital and then prison, having been severely ill-treated. Amnesty International issued an urgent appeal on behalf of the four detained strike committee members on 25 February 1981, and later adopted them as prisoners of conscience.

Amnesty International made further inquiries about the delays in bringing certain prisoners charged with serious security offences to trial. Valev Dimitrov, a refugee from Bulgaria, and Milan Knezić, a refugee from Yugoslavia, had been detained since 1978. In another case, Walter Markl, an Austrian architect, and Roland Lachman and Constantin Centziedes, citizens of the Federal Republic of Germany, had been arrested in September 1979. Their trials took place in December 1980, and the security charges were all dismissed. The two refugees were sentenced to one and three years' imprisonment for illegal entry, while the other three were acquitted.

Valev Dimitrov alleged after his release that he had been tortured in the security police headquarters, *Direction générale d'investigation et de documentation* (DGID), during the first five months of his detention, by means of systematic beatings on the body and feet, electric shocks, simulated execution, and frequent denials of food. He alleged that Milan Knezić had also been tortured in this way, and that both had attempted to commit suicide. Towards the end of his detention he was held in several different prisons where there was severe overcrowding, poor hygiene and diet, inadequate medical attention, and frequent ill-treatment of prisoners. Dave Marais, a South African, was allegedly also ill-treated in the security police headquarters and was still being held there incommunicado in poor health in early 1981. He and another South African, John Wight, were arrested in 1978 and sentenced later that year by a military tribunal to five years' imprisonment for illegal entry.

Malawi

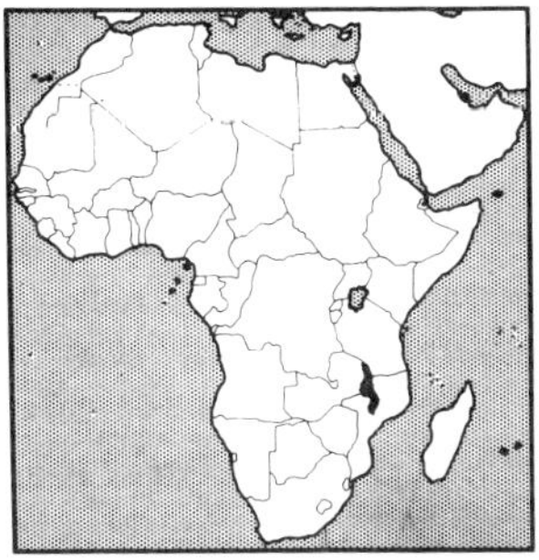

Amnesty International's concerns were the use of detention without trial and the trial of two senior politicians accused of sedition.

The sedition trial began in November 1980 and ended in March 1981 with the conviction and imprisonment of the two defendants. It was the first major political trial to take place since 1977. One of the defendants, Gwanda Chakuamba, was a former cabinet minister and confidant of Life President Hastings Kamuzu Banda. For many years he had been one of the most senior and powerful political figures in the country. Until his dismissal from office in February 1980 he held two ministerial portfolios, with responsibility for both the southern region and for Youth and Culture. He was also Commander of the Young Pioneers, youth wing of the ruling Malawi Congress Party (MCP), and Chairman of the key MCP Disciplinary Committee.

Gwanda Chakuamba was detained without charge until late November 1980 when he was brought to trial before the southern region Traditional Court at Blantyre. He appeared together with a political associate, Sofiliano Faindi Phiri, a nominated member of parliament for Chikwawa South. Both defendants were charged with "uttering seditious words" with the intent of "raising discontent or dissatisfaction among the subjects" of President Banda. Three other charges were brought against Gwanda Chakuamba alone. He was alleged to have contravened public security regulations by having in his possession photographs of several exiled former government ministers and by the illegal possession of firearms, two pen pistols. One of these was said to have been loaded with one bullet. He was also accused of possessing prohibited publications, notably copies of the London-based *New African* magazine, and *To The Point*, a South African publication.

The main charge, that of "uttering seditious words", related to a political meeting held on 18 November 1979 at Chikwawa, in the southern region. At the meeting Faindi Phiri was alleged to have committed sedition by claiming that all developments in the Lower Shire area had been brought about through the personal efforts of Gwanda Chakuamba, and to have said that the country as a whole would have been better developed if there were more people of Gwanda Chakuamba's calibre. The essence of the sedition charge against Gwanda Chakuamba was that he did not dissociate himself from Faindi Phiri's remarks and emphasize to those attending the meeting that all developments in the area were in fact due to "the wise and dynamic leadership of President Banda".

The trial of Gwanda Chakuamba and Faindi Phiri was conducted before a panel of five chiefs, headed by Chief Nazombe. Legal representation is not permitted in the Traditional Court. After several adjournments the trial ended on 20 March 1981. Gwanda Chakuamba was convicted on all four counts and sentenced to 22 years in prison. Faindi Phiri was also convicted and received a five-year prison term for sedition.

Amnesty International's request for permission to observe the trial was not accepted by the government.

One aspect of the trial proceedings which gave cause for particular concern was a reference by the prosecutor to the continuing imprisonment of an unspecified number of people arrested for possessing photographs of exiled former government ministers. Cross-examining Gwanda Chakuamba on 18 February 1981, the state prosecutor claimed that many people had been arrested for this reason in the past by the Young Pioneers and that some of them were still in custody. Neither the number nor the identities of those to whom he referred were known to Amnesty International.

No official information has been made available about the number of detainees and political prisoners and it was not possible for Amnesty International to estimate their number. The identities of only a few were known. They were believed to include several detainees held since the early 1970s and about 15 political associates of Gwanda Chakuamba arrested in late 1979 or early 1980. Aleke Banda, a former Secretary General of the MCP and cabinet minister, and more recently managing director of the government-controlled Press Holdings company and other quasi-governmental institutions was also believed to be detained. He was dismissed from all his posts and from the MCP in January 1980 for alleged "gross breaches of party discipline". However David Basa Kaunda, another former cabinet minister who had been similarly dismissed in February 1980, was formally reinstated in the MCP in January 1981. The rumours of his detention referred to in *Amnesty International Report 1980,* appear to have been without foundation.

The opposition group which appeared to cause the government greatest anxiety was the Socialist League of Malawi (LESOMA), headed by Dr Attati Mpakati. In early April 1981 President Banda was reported to have told a rally in Lilongwe that Dr Mpakati would be "shot on sight" if he should enter Malawi.

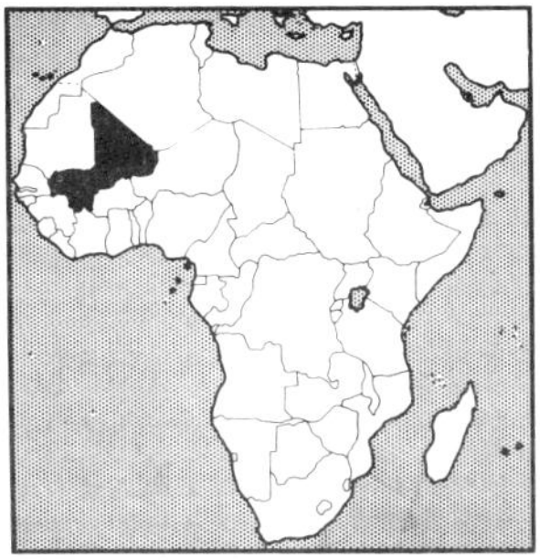

Mali

Amnesty International's main concerns were political imprisonment, detention and banishment without charge or trial, torture, poor prison conditions and the death penalty.

The conflict between the government and students, which culminated in March 1980 in numerous detentions, the death in custody of a student leader, and clashes between troops and demonstrators, and led to large numbers of students being suspended indefinitely from their studies and the closure of numerous schools and colleges, was followed in the second half of 1980 by an open confrontation between the government and the teaching profession. In mid-July 1980 about 20 teachers were arrested in Bamako, the capital, after the breakdown of negotiations over teachers' demands for better pay. Some of those arrested are believed to have been beaten and tortured with electric shocks. Most were alleged to have been active members of the *Commission des comités syndicaux des enseignants*, Commission of Teachers' Trade Union Committees, an autonomous trade union body formed in late 1979 to represent teachers working in and around Bamako. This body replaced local sections of the official *Syndicat national de l'éducation et de la culture,* National Union of Education and Culture, which had been disbanded some months earlier after internal disputes. During early 1980 the commission had been negotiating with the government for better pay, but negotiations broke down and teachers refused to supervise examinations held in July 1980.

In early September 1980, 13 of the detainees were tried in Bamako, the remainder having been freed after several days' detention. They were convicted of "opposition to the legitimate authority", defined as "offending public order or impeding the execution of administrative or judicial functions". Eleven of the teachers were sentenced to three months' imprisonment, and a 12th was given a suspended sentence. Modibo Diakite, the commission's Secretary General, was sentenced to four months' imprisonment. The teachers were transported to the remote desert town of Menaka where they remained until the end of their sentences. They were all adopted as prisoners of conscience by Amnesty International.

All the teachers were stopped by the authorities at Segou on their return to Bamako and forcibly returned to Gao, where an appeal against their conviction lodged the previous September was heard *in camera*. The appeal court confirmed the sentences imposed in

September and already completed but the teachers were dismissed from the Ministry of Education, put "at the disposal of the Ministry of the Interior", and banished in early December to remote administrative outposts. Amnesty International continued to intervene on their behalf, appealing for the lifting of all restrictions. Three of the teachers were reportedly allowed to return to Bamako at the end of 1980.

Between 13 and 26 November 1980, 21 teachers were arrested in Bamako at meetings of the commission. All were held for several weeks without charge in one of Bamako's police stations, and some were reportedly beaten and tortured with electric shocks. In early December 20 were transported to remote outposts in the Gao region, where some were reportedly held in military camps. Despite government claims that the teachers were "working freely", it was clear that they were sent against their will. In April 1981 they were charged with the "establishment of a secret association", an offence which carries a penalty of up to three years' imprisonment. All the teachers detained and subsequently banished have been adopted as prisoners of conscience by Amnesty International. Ibrahima Samba Traore, a teacher recently returned from France, who has been held in Bamako without trial since September 1980 has also been adopted as a prisoner of conscience. He is believed to have been tortured at the *Brigade d'investigation criminelle,* Criminal Investigation Bureau, having been found in possession of documents published by foreign-based movements critical of the government.

Between January and March 1981 a student found in possession of documents published by a banned student organization and 12 more teachers belonging to the commission were arrested and held without trial in police stations in Bamako. The teachers were charged in April 1981 under the penal provision relating to secret association and were adopted as prisoners of conscience by Amnesty International.

During the year Amnesty International received confirmation of the release of all the students arrested in March 1980. On 2 July 1980, 37 students and teachers were reportedly injured when police violently attacked a peaceful gathering to commemorate the death in detention of student leader Abdul Karim Camara in March 1980. Several days later at least one school pupil died and several were seriously injured in Sevare near Mopti when police charged at marchers protesting against the arrest of another pupil.

Amnesty International continued to work on behalf of Dr Mamadou Gologo and Idrissa Diakite, who were convicted on charges of "insulting the Head of State" and sentenced to four years' imprisonment in October 1979 after the distribution of leaflets criticizing the government. After appeals from several organizations including

Amnesty International, Dr Gologo was allowed to leave Nioro du Sahel prison and return to Bamako for treatment for an eye ailment.

Conditions of detention in the police stations of the first, third and fifth *arrondissements* (districts) of Bamako were reported to be harsh. Many political detainees were held with criminal suspects in dark, overcrowded and poorly-ventilated cells. Standards of sanitation and hygiene are very low. Torture has been reported at several of these police stations, as well as at the *Gendarmerie* camp and the Djikoroni military base. Prisoners at the *Prison centrale* (Central Prison), Bamako, suffer overcrowding and poor food, and prison officers reportedly beat them. Conditions at the Taoudenit "Special Re-education Centre" were still harsh. Its extreme Saharan temperatures and the severity of the regime made imprisonment here a brutal form of punishment. Many prisoners were reported to be forced to march barefoot some 20 to 40 kilometres a day. The one meal provided daily was of low nutritional value, and some prisoners were reported to suffer severe and prolonged stomach complaints.

In early February 1981 Amnesty International made a public appeal to the delegates attending an extraordinary congress of the country's sole political party, the *Union démocratique du peuple malien* (UDPM), the Democratic Union of the Malian People, calling for the release of all prisoners of conscience in the country, an end to torture, and an improvement in prison conditions. No reply was received. In mid-March 1981 Amnesty International representatives met the Minister of Foreign Affairs, Blondin Alioune Beye, and repeated these concerns.

In late June 1979 the Special State Security Court sitting in Timbuctoo (Tombouctou) imposed death sentences on Kissima Doukara, formerly Lieutenant-Colonel and Minister of Interior, Defence and Security, and Nouhoun Diawara, former army captain. Both were convicted of "embezzlement, corruption and extortion". In mid-March 1981 the same court, sitting in Bamako, imposed three more death sentences, one *in absentia,* against three gendarmes allegedly involved in a plot to assassinate President Traore on New Year's Eve 1980. None of these death sentences had been carried out by 30 April 1981. On 21 August 1980 Mamadou Keita and Karuba Coulibaly, both sentenced to death in 1980 for murder, armed robbery and other offences, were executed by firing-squad.

Mauritania

The main concerns of Amnesty International were detention without charge or trial and house arrest, unfair trials, torture, judicial amputations and floggings, and the death penalty.

In early March 1980 demonstrations in the capital, Nouakchott, and several major towns called for greater equality for the *Haratine*, a black Arabic-speaking minority composed of freed slaves of the politically dominant Maure (Arab-Berber) community. Demonstrators also called for the release of four *Haratine* who had earlier been arrested after protests against the sale in Atar of a young woman by her slave-master. As many as 50 suspected members of a clandestine *Haratine* movement known as *El Hor* were arrested after these demonstrations and some are believed to have been badly beaten in detention. Most were released shortly afterwards, but 17 were tried in early May 1980 before the newly-formed Special Military Court on state security charges. All received three-month suspended prison sentences and fines. A further 18 *Haratine* were arrested in March 1980 in Atar, apparently accused of trespass after trying to prevent the sale of the young slave. They were freed in late 1980 after being held without trial for several months. Also freed in late 1980 was Ahmedou Ould Abdallah, director of the nationalized SNIM mining company, whose case was investigated by Amnesty International after he was arrested in April 1980 and accused of involvement in the *Haratine* movement. In early July 1980 the ruling *Comité militaire de salut national* (CMSN), the Military Committe for National Salvation, announced that it had abolished slavery, and that a national commission had been formed to evaluate the compensation due to former slave-owners.

Throughout the year the authorities detained without trial suspected opponents of their policies. In April 1980 school inspectors Bal Fadel and M'Bodj Samba Bedou, former teacher Sy Omar Satigui, entrepreneur Ba Youssouf and government official Kane Saïdou were detained for alleged opposition to government policies. All are believed to have been tortured after their arrest, and to have been held incommunicado until their release in November 1980. Also arrested in April 1980 were former Ministers Sidi Cheikh Ould Abdellahi, Mohammed Ould Sidi Babah, Abdoulaye Baro and Abdallah Ould Ismael, apparently suspected of sympathy with opposition movements. All were placed under house arrest. Their cases were taken up by Amnesty International.

In mid-December 1980 around 120 pupils at the *Lycée franco-arabe* (secondary school) in Nouakchott were briefly held in detention after protests against some members of the teaching staff. Police are reported to have severely beaten demonstrators. Four former senior officials — Taleb Mohammed Ould M'Rabott, Dah Ould Abdel Jelil, Mourio Ould Hassen and Malokif Ould El Hassen — were arrested in the same month after demonstrations in Nouakchott calling for a return to civilian rule. Amnesty International was investigating their cases. In late December 1980 Ahmed Baba Miske, Mauritania's former Ambassador to the United Nations, and at least four others were arrested after the authorities claimed to have uncovered a "pro-Libyan" plot to overthrow the government. Ahmed Baba Miske and Mohammed El-Wafi were placed under house arrest in Akjoujt, while the others are believed to have been imprisoned. Charges against them were dismissed by a civil court in late February 1981 and all were released. Amnesty International was concerned about the continued house arrest of four former officials arrested in June and October 1979 including former Ministers Abdallah Ould Bah, Ahmed Ould Daddah and Hamdi Ould Mouknass. The last was seriously ill, and was allowed out of the country temporarily in October 1980 for medical treatment after a number of interventions on his behalf.

On 16 March 1981 an armed attempt to overthrow the ruling CMSN was staged in Nouakchott led by former senior officers of the Mauritanian army who had joined the clandestine *Alliance pour une Mauritanie démocratique* (AMD), an opposition movement associated with former President Moktar Ould Daddah, whose leading members were exiled in Morocco and France. About 10 soldiers and civilians were killed in the attack, which was repulsed by forces loyal to the CMSN. In the days after the attack Mauritania broke off diplomatic relations with Morocco; head of state Lieutenant-Colonel Mohammed Ould Haidalla claimed it had been directly involved in training and transporting the insurgents. At least nine rebels were arrested, and the authorities are reported to have detained about 50 sympathizers in Nouakchott. After a trial before the Special Military Tribunal Lieutenant-Colonel Ahmed Salem Ould Sidi, former Vice-President of the CMSN, Lieutenant-Colonel Mohammed Ba Ould Abdel Kader, former Minister of Education and member of the CMSN, and Lieutenants Moustapha Niang and Mohammed Doudou Seck, were convicted of "high treason, murder and conspiracy with the enemy", and sentenced to death. Five others received sentences of life imprisonment with hard labour. Despite appeals for clemency from Amnesty International and other organizations, the four men sentenced to death were executed in late March 1981. About 20 alleged supporters of the AMD who had been arrested were reportedly freed in late March. Amnesty International continued its investigations into the identities of those in detention and the charges against them.

Amnesty International was concerned about reports of trials held in the absence of the accused, *in camera*, and without defence representation. In mid-November 1980 former President Moktar Ould Daddah was sentenced in his absence to imprisonment for life with hard labour by the Special Military Court on charges of "high treason, violation of the constitution and of the nation's economic interests." The court also sentenced Lieutenant-Colonel Mohammed Ba Ould Abdel Kader to death in his absence on charges of "desertion, treason, plotting against the internal and external security of the State". In February 1981 the Special Military Court sentenced Lieutenant Moustapha Niang to death in his absence on similar charges, and handed down long terms of imprisonment to six other absent defendants. Both Lieutenant-Colonel Kader and Lieutenant Niang were executed in late March 1981 after participating in the failed attack on Nouakchott. In mid-March 1981 the Special Military Court convened to deliver three death sentences *in absentia* to individuals allegedly involved in the March attack.

Amnesty International is also concerned about the cruel penalties which have been imposed by the *Shari'a* or Islamic law court. This court was formally established in July 1980 to ensure what Minister Colonel Dia Amadou termed "good, swift and effective justice" to combat rising crime. It promptly imposed two death sentences and one sentence of amputation of the right hand. On 19 September 1980, near Nouakchott, in front of several thousand people, the first prisoner was executed by firing-squad. Three others were then led into a tent to have their right hand cut off by a medical auxiliary from Nouakchott hospital. After each amputation, performed without general anaesthetic, the medical auxiliary left the tent and held up the amputated hand for the crowd to see. All three hands were finally held up to public view on a rope. In its appeals to the government and to the medical association in Mauritania Amnesty International called for an end to these penalties and to the participation of medical personnel in contravention of the Hippocratic Oath and the World Medical Association's Declaration of Tokyo. It was later learned that the *Association des médecins, pharmaciens et odontologistes de Mauritanie*, the Mauritanian Association of Doctors, Pharmacists and Dentists, had protested vigorously to the authorities about involving a member of the medical profession in the amputations.

In early October 1980 nine men were publicly given from 10 to 30 lashes of the whip after being convicted of theft by the *Shari'a* court. After being convicted of murder by the same court Mouhamed Ould

Alioune was publicly executed in early December 1980. In a statement commemorating International Human Rights Day on 10 December 1980 the Minister of Foreign Affairs is reported to have stated that the application of *Shari'a* law in Mauritania was motivated by the government's "constant preoccupation . . . to safeguard human rights".

Mozambique

Amnesty International's concerns were detention without trial, the conduct of trials before the Revolutionary Military Tribunal and the death penalty.

During the year there were reports of fighting between government forces and guerrilla fighters belonging to the *Movimento Resistencia de Mozambique* (MRM), Mozambique Resistance Movement, which allegedly receives South African backing. In July 1980 more than 270 MRM personnel were reported killed and 300 captured when government forces destroyed a major MRM base near the Zimbabwe border. However further clashes occurred and in December 1980 refugees fleeing into Zimbabwe alleged that the MRM had launched a campaign of terror and carried out atrocities against civilians in the Espungabera area. The government also faced armed opposition from *Africa Livre,* the Free Africa Movement.

There was also increasing tension with South Africa, particularly after South African soldiers raided a suburb of Maputo, the capital, at the end of January 1981 and destroyed houses occupied by members of the African National Congress (ANC). Following the raid, in which a number of South African refugees were killed, eight members of the armed forces were paraded at a rally and accused of treason and corruption in connection with the attack. Six United States citizens allegedly engaged in espionage were expelled and a number of other foreign nationals and Mozambique citizens were detained. Most were reportedly released by mid-April 1981.

Long-term detention without trial remained one of Amnesty International's primary concerns.

It was not possible to estimate accurately the number of long-term detainees, and difficult to discover their identities. In May 1980 a US journalist estimated that as many as ten thousand people might be detained in "re-education camps", one of which he had visited, and that up to three thousand of these might be held for political reasons.

A number of releases were reported. In May 1980 it was announced that the resettlement in Niassa province of 600 former prisoners granted amnesty in October 1979 would be completed by 1 June 1980. At the end of 1980 a further 600 prisoners held since an abortive revolt in December 1975 were also pardoned, though 15 others also detained at that time may yet face trial before the Revolutionary Military Tribunal.

In June 1980 three prison guards accused of ill-treating prisoners were prosecuted. All were convicted and sentenced to short terms of imprisonment and fines. They included the chief prison officer at Machava Central Prison in Maputo.

At least seven people convicted of politically-motivated offences were sentenced to death and executed. In October 1980 three people were sentenced to death by the Revolutionary Military Tribunal in Maputo after being convicted of espionage and military sabotage. They were executed within a few days. Amnesty International protested against these executions and appealed to President Samora Machel to exercise clemency in any future cases. Amnesty International made a new appeal for clemency in February 1981 when four alleged members of *Africa Livre* were sentenced to death, but they too were executed.

All seven death sentences were imposed by the Revolutionary Military Tribunal, a military court established in March 1979 to hear cases involving treason or other security offences. The tribunal, over which military officers preside, meets *in camera.* Defendants are not permitted legal counsel.

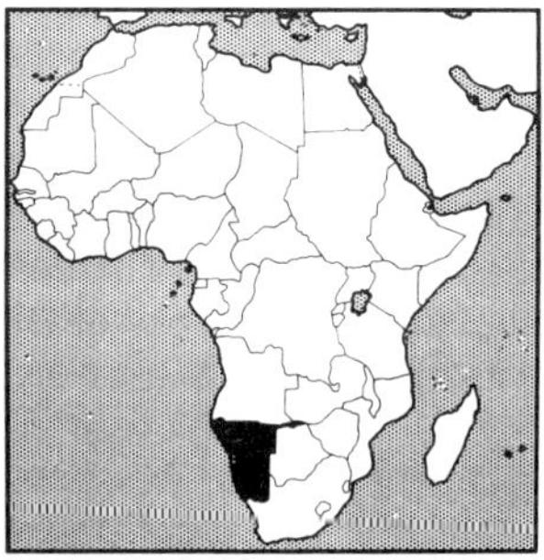

Namibia

The main concerns of Amnesty International were detention without trial and administrative restriction, torture, prison conditions, and the death penalty.

International efforts to obtain a political settlement leading to the independence of Namibia and the withdrawal of South Africa's administration and military forces continued but were unsuccessful. The gradual process of transferring power from the South African Government to an internal administration dominated by Dirk Mudge's Democratic Turnhalle Alliance (DTA) continued throughout the year. In July 1980 a 12-member Council of Ministers was formed from among the 50 members of the National Assembly. Headed by

Dirk Mudge as Chairman, and composed of representatives from each of the 11 officially-designated population groups, the council was given certain executive powers and control over more than 20 government departments previously administered directly by the South African authorities. However South Africa's Administrator-General retained power of veto over the council's actions; and direct control over key aspects of policy such as defence and security, foreign relations and negotiations concerning Namibia's independence remained with the South African Government.

In October 1980 the South African State President extended military service to all black men aged between 16 and 25 years. Many are believed to have left the country to avoid conscription.

This exodus prompted the leaders of five main churches to address a petition to the South African President at the end of October 1980, in protest against the extension of military service to blacks.

Throughout the year there were further extensive violations of human rights. Many people were detained without trial and others were restricted under administrative orders. There were allegations of torture and two important political trials took place, one of which resulted in the imposition of the death penalty. There were renewed attacks into Angola by South African military forces at war with the South West Africa People's Organization (SWAPO) guerrillas, and this reportedly resulted in the deaths of many civilians. In early 1981 a foreign mercenary who deserted from the South African Defence Force (SADF) alleged that the military unit to which he had been attached had carried out atrocities in Angola.

Earlier, in June 1980, disturbing reports had appeared in a Lutheran church publication and a Windhoek newspaper. These alleged that a secret assassination squad had been established by the South African authorities under the code-name *Koevoet*, and that a death list of 50 names had been drawn up. Those included on the list, some of whose names were published, were said to be targets because of their supposed sympathy for SWAPO, recognized by the United Nations as the sole legitimate representative of the people of Namibia. They were said to include Bishop Kleopas Dumeni, a leading Lutheran pastor based in Ovamboland. These allegations were denied by Dr Viljoen, then Administrator-General. However in November 1980 the Lutheran church printing press at Oniipa in Ovamboland was destroyed by a bomb explosion widely attributed to South African security agents. The printing press had previously been destroyed in a similar way in May 1973, but had been rebuilt in 1975.

Several long-term political detainees who had been adopted as prisoners of conscience by Amnesty International were released during the year. They had mostly been held since May 1979 under

Proclamation AG26 of 1978, which empowers the Administrator-General to order the indefinite incommunicado detention of any person whom he considers likely to promote "political violence and intimidation". The Administrator-General is not obliged to state why an individual is detained and detainees are denied any effective means of challenging their detention orders. Those freed included Axel Johannes, Administrative Secretary of the legal, internal wing of SWAPO, who was released in late July 1980. He had been held without trial for some 15 months, and had been imprisoned without trial for most of the period since 1974. Like a number of other former detainees, he was immediately restricted under a "release warrant" issued by the Administrator-General. As a result he was subjected to partial house arrest, ordered to report regularly and frequently to the police, prohibited from receiving visitors at his home and restricted to a particular district. Those subject to release warrants are also prohibited from working as teachers or in the public service. Some detainees were restricted at the time of their release to districts far from their homes and families. These release warrants, similar in form to banning orders imposed on dissidents in South Africa, are of unlimited duration.

In addition to the powers of preventive detention under AG26, the South African authorities possess wide powers of detention without trial under the Administrator-General's Proclamation AG9 of 1977. This provision, which is applicable throughout most of northern Namibia in those areas designated "security" districts, appeared to be most extensively used to hold people for interrogation. Detainees were held incommunicado and at any place designated by the authorities whether or not it fell within a security district. They may be held indefinitely, and have no recourse to the courts or other legal means to effect their release. No details were provided by the South African authorities of the numbers and identities of those detained, and official secrecy surrounded the location of detention camps and interrogation centres. Relatives and lawyers of detainees have no right to information about their detention, let alone the reasons for their arrest or the conditions under which they are held. AG9 thus provides a potential for the "disappearance" of individual detainees.

One known group of almost 120 detainees held under AG9 were about to enter their fourth year of continuous incommunicado detention at the end of April 1981. They have been held since they were abducted by South African military forces in May 1978 from a camp for Namibians at Kassinga in southern Angola. Some 200 people are believed to have been seized at that time, but about 60 were released within a few weeks. The International Committee of the Red Cross has been permitted to visit those who are still held near

Mariental, southeast of Windhoek at least three times since mid-1980. However, the identities of those detained have not been disclosed and it is believed that no visits by relatives have been permitted. Several were reported to have escaped in December 1980, but all but one appear to have been recaptured.

It is not clear what was the legal basis for their arrest in the period between their abduction in May 1978 and the introduction of legislation, one year later, amending AG9 to authorize indefinite detention. Before May 1979 the maximum period of incommunicado detention without charge under AG9 was 96 hours. It has not been possible to verify allegations that the detainees were tortured in the months after their abduction, or whether this group of detainees, together with those 60 or so who were released shortly after the attack on Kassinga, were the only people captured during South African raids into Angola.

The use of indefinite incommunicado detention for interrogation has long been associated with the use of torture. In September 1980 Amnesty International received information from authoritative sources naming several detainees who had been tortured and ill-treated while detained under AG9 in mid-1980. One detainee was reported to have been taken blindfolded to a secret detention centre and then interrogated under torture. Similar allegations of torture were made by Rauna Nambinga, a former nurse and member of SWAPO, after leaving the country in late 1980. She claimed that she had been tortured with electric shocks while detained at Oshakati in July 1980. She was held under AG9 from mid-July until November.

Earlier in the year the South African authorities had arrested four members of the Namibia National Front (NNF) political party who alleged that another NNF member, Albertus Kanguootui, had been ill-treated by security police while in detention. They made this claim after visiting Kanguootui at the Katutura State Hospital in Windhoek. He was alleged to have told them that he had been "brutally assaulted" and required hospital treatment as a result. Kanguootui was not called as a witness by the state and, as he was still in detention at that time, could not be called by the defence, but a medical report submitted to the court suggested that his allegations were false. The four NNF officials were convicted and fined. Kanguootui was eventually freed uncharged in January 1981 after more than five months in detention.

Two major political trials ended in October 1980. One resulted in the conviction of Ida Jimmy for statements she had made at a SWAPO rally in Luderitz in mid-July, and a seven-year prison sentence. The other trial, which ended on 13 October 1980, involved two farmworkers from the Grootfontein area charged under the South

African Terrorism Act which is applied in Namibia. Markus Kateka and Hendrik Kariseb were jointly charged with helping SWAPO guerrillas responsible for an attack on the farm of their employer. No one was injured or killed as a result of the attack, but upon conviction Kariseb received a 10-year prison term and Markus Kateka was sentenced to death. The trial judge denied Kateka leave to appeal, but this was later granted by the Chief Justice of South Africa. His appeal was due to be heard by the South African Appeal Court at Bloemfontein in May 1981.

Amnesty International continued throughout the year to work for the release of individual prisoners of conscience. In addition, concerted international appeals were made on behalf of two groups of detainees arrested in mid-1980 and held incommunicado without charge or trial, and on behalf of Markus Kateka, sentenced to death in October 1980. Amnesty International also reported formally on human rights violations in Namibia to the United Nations Commission on Human Rights in August 1980, and to the Fourth Committee of the United Nations General Assembly in November 1980.

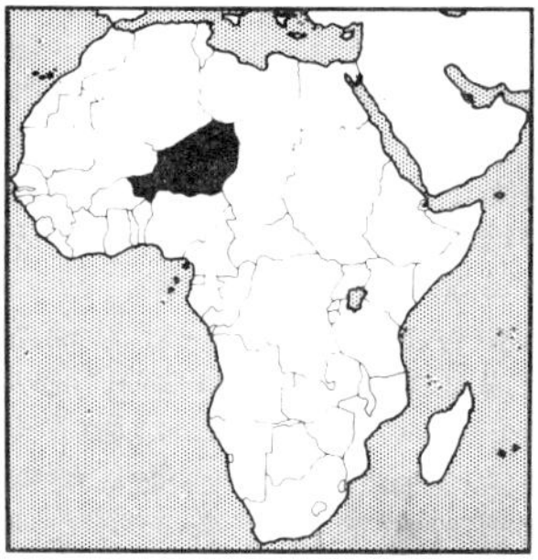

Niger

Amnesty International's concerns were detention without trial and prison conditions.

On 15 April 1980 former President Hamani Diori and former leader of the *Sawaba* (Freedom) Party Djibo Bakary were released from detention. Hamani Diori had been detained since his overthrow in April 1974 by the present head of state, Colonel Seyni Kountche. Djibo Bakary had been detained without trial since 1975 for alleged involvement in an attempted coup. Hamani Diori and his son Mounkaila were effectively placed under house arrest in Niamey. However some 17 people, relatives of Hamani Diori and former officials in his government, remained in detention without charge or trial. They included Hamani Diori's brother, Djiba Balle, and two former government ministers, Aboubacar Moussa and Ibrahima Issa.

Most of the detainees were held in the remote desert prison at Agadez in the Saharan region, where conditions of detention were reported to be harsh. The remainder were held at Tillabery in southern Niger. They were apparently allowed to receive visits or letters from their families only rarely, and visits were very brief and closely supervised by prison guards. Medical facilities were also said to be inadequate. At least two of the detainees were believed to be seriously ill. Ibro Djibo was moved to Niamey in late April 1980 where he had an operation for cancer of the bladder. The authorities freed him when they learned that the illness might prove terminal.

Three other detainees have been held for more than five years for alleged involvement in plots against the government. Cyrille Gabriel and Mai Tourare Gadjo were arrested in 1975; Sanoussi Jackou was reportedly tried *in camera* by a military tribunal after his arrest in 1976 but no judgment has been made public.

Shortly before the 21st anniversary of independence on 15 April 1981 Amnesty International appealed to the authorities to bring to trial or release all these detainees. No answer was received.

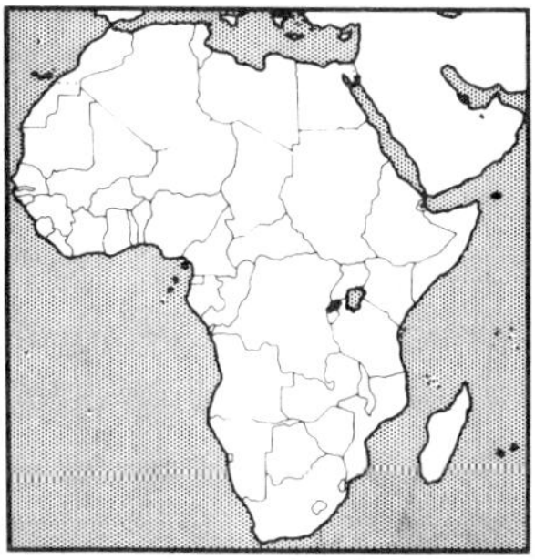

Rwanda

Amnesty International's main concern was the detention without trial of alleged opponents of the government, more than 30 of whom were still held at the end of April 1981.

About 40 people were arrested in April and May 1980 after the distribution of a number of leaflets in the capital, Kigali, during March 1980. Although the leaflets criticized the head of state, President Juvenal Habyarimana, they did not advocate his overthrow but accused him of misusing his office to accumulate a large personal fortune and of favouritism towards his own Bashiro clan in preference to the rival Bagoyi clan. The Bashiro and Bagoyi clans originate in the northwest and belong to the majority Hutu ethnic group.

The leaflets, which first appeared in Kigali in early March 1980, were initially concerned about the dispute between Emile Birara, Governor General of the National Bank of Rwanda, and three military officers. The officers had apparently accused Emile Birara of corruption, leading him to publicize a letter he had written to President Habyarimana refuting the criticisms and in turn accusing the officers of corruption and nepotism. This led to more leaflets, some of them anonymous and apparently written by members of the Bagoyi clan, complaining about the extent to which their clan had been deprived of power in recent years as a result of President Habyarimana's policies.

On 17 April 1980 Major Théoneste Lizinde, a prominent member of the Bagoyi clan, was arrested in Kigali. At the time he was Director General of Foreign Policy at the presidency, and had formerly been head of the Security Police until December 1979. Within a few weeks of his arrest about 40 other people were detained, many of them members of the Bagoyi clan. They included a number of soldiers and former senior officials such as Alphonse-Marie Kagenza, a former Ambassador to Uganda, and Donat Murego, a former Director General of the presidency. Spiridion Shyirambere, Secretary General the national university, was also detained as were the wives of Alphonse-Marie Kagenza and others. Several of the detainees are believed to have been released later, but some 30 were still being held at the end of April 1981.

In mid-May 1980 the government claimed that the detainees were suspected of conspiring against the government. At the same time President Habyarimana stated that they would be charged and tried before a civilian court without delay. The President repeated this assurance in December 1980 but no trial had taken place by the end of April 1981.

It is believed that all the detainees were held incommunicado at Ruhengeri prison in a special unit for political detainees, which Major Lizinde himself had designed when he was head of the Security Police. According to reports a number have been physically ill-treated but the circumstances of their detention make it impossible to verify this.

Amnesty International is investigating several of the detainees' cases. In August 1980 an appeal was made to President Habyarimana for information on the charges against those detained and the likelihood of their being brought to trial. No response has been received.

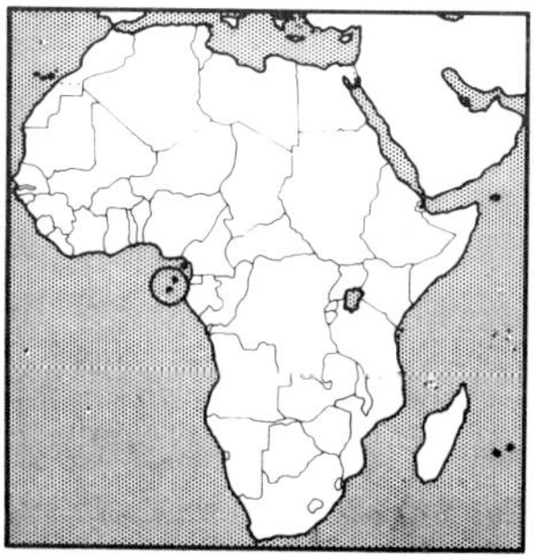

Sao Tome and Principe

Amnesty International's main concern was the continued detention without trial of former Prime Minister Miguel Trovoada, who has been adopted as a prisoner of conscience. He was arrested in October 1979 after taking refuge in the local office of the United Nations Development Program (UNDP) and was accused of plotting against the government of President Pinto da Costa. However no formal charges have yet been brought against him and the authorities have not replied to inquiries or appeals for his release.

Amnesty International is investigating the cases of Alcino de Lima and Albertino Neto, who are serving prison sentences of 22 and 21 years respectively. They were convicted of conspiring against the government with three others in March 1979. Orlando da Graça, who had been adopted by Amnesty International as a prisoner of conscience, and Maria Bragança Neto, whose case was being investigated by Amnesty International, were released in July 1980 under an amnesty granted by President da Costa on the fifth anniversary of independence. The third defendant, Fernando Alvim, was released during 1980 after completing his two-year prison sentence.

Two Portuguese nationals, Antonio Ferreira and Antonio Martins, were arrested in November 1980 and accused of plotting to overthrow of the government. Two Portuguese diplomats were expelled at the same time.

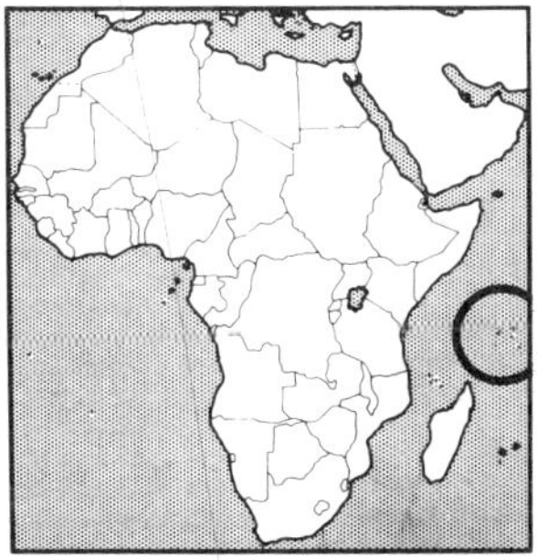

Seychelles

In July 1980 the government released the remaining 13 prisoners detained without charge or trial since the previous November, on condition that they went immediately into exile. Some were allegedly threatened with future reprisals if they expressed opposition to the government from abroad. The detainees, held under the Preservation of Public Security (Detention) Regulations, included Gerard Hoarau, principal immigration officer; Bernard Verlaque, journalist and publisher of the recently banned *Weekend Life;* and Max Racombo, secretary to the government's Planning Authority.

These detainees and 65 others released earlier had been publicly accused by the government of conspiracy to overthrow it by creating internal disturbances designed to facilitate a mercenary invasion. There was no invasion and no detainee was charged with any offence.

Amnesty International had sent a mission in January 1980 to express concern over their detention without trial and their prison conditions and had taken up their cases for investigation.

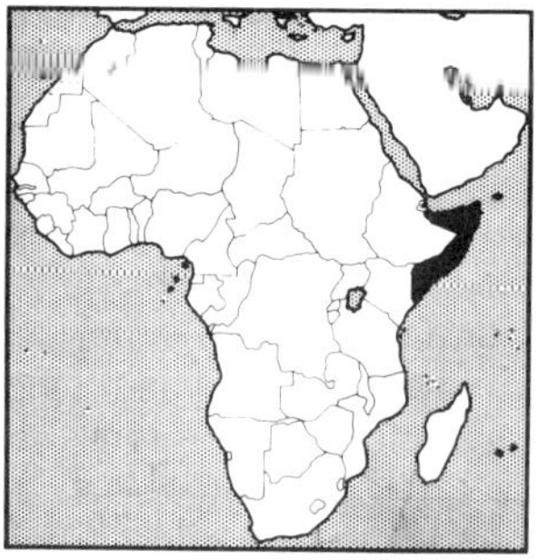

Somalia

Amnesty International's concerns were detention without trial, unfair trials, allegations of torture, harsh prison conditions, and the use of the death penalty.

Somalia continued to receive large numbers of refugees fleeing from the armed conflict in the Ogaden region and other parts of Ethiopia. The number of refugees — about 1.3 million — was equivalent to one third of Somalia's population. There were also a number of armed confrontations between Somali forces and Ethiopia-based Somali exile opponents — the Somali Salvation Front (SOSAF).

President Siyad Barre decreed a state of emergency on 21 October 1980 and reconstituted the military Supreme Revolutionary Council, which had ruled the country from the overthrow of the civilian government in 1969 until it was replaced by the Somali Revolutionary Socialist Party (SRSP) in 1976. The President said that the state of emergency was needed because "a few opportunists were threatening stability at a time when Somalia was menaced by Ethiopia".

New regional and district revolutionary committees consisting of security officials and SRSP party officers were created throughout the country and empowered to detain or sentence people to three months' imprisonment for "counter-revolutionary offences", including suspicion of "engaging in such actions as have brought about the need for a declaration of the state of emergency". These powers were not subject to judicial constraints.

Sixty-eight prisoners had been adopted as prisoners of conscience by Amnesty International or were being investigated in April 1981. Most were held in indefinite detention without charge or trial under the National Security Law of 1970. No independent detention review mechanism exists, and the government publishes no details of those it detains. Some had been tried and convicted by security courts whose proceedings do not accord with international standards of fair trial. The prisoners included Mohamed Abshir Musse, a police brigadier general, detained under house arrest after the 1969 coup, released in 1975, arrested two months later and since then detained; Abdullahi Farah Ali "Holif", also a police brigadier general, detained in 1975 after holding ambassadorial posts under the military government; Mohamed Haji Ibrahim Egal, former Prime Minister, detained under house arrest after the 1969 coup, released in 1975 and appointed Ambassador to India, detained since 1976; and Yusuf Osman Samantar "Barde Ad", Secretary General of the Somali Democratic

Union until 1969, arrested several times since then for short periods, and detained since 1976.

Amnesty International was investigating the cases of other prisoners arrested over the last few years. They included businessmen, civil servants, former politicians, and several members of the armed forces detained after the April 1978 coup attempt, but not charged in the subsequent treason trial in which 17 defendants were condemned and executed. Some of the prisoners were allegedly arrested because they belonged to the Majarten tribe, which is a target of persecution.

Many arrests followed a series of bomb blasts in Mogadishu in January 1981, in which two people were injured. It was alleged that some of those arrested were tortured but Amnesty International was unable to verify this. Those detained without charge or trial included prominent public figures such as members of parliament Mohamed Yusuf Weirah (former Finance Minister), Mohamed Ali Warsame (former Education Minister, and SRSP central committee member), and Colonel Abdullahi Warsame (former Auditor General); former Labour Minister Abdulaziz Nur Hersi; Abukar Hassan Yare, a university law lecturer; Mohamed Farah Hassan, a trade union leader; Warsame Ali Farah, Mayor of Mogadishu; and a director general in the Ministry of Justice and Religious Affairs, Ahmed Abdi Hashi.

Only a few prisoners whose cases had been taken up by Amnesty International were released including Jama Khalef Farah and Colonel Mohamud Mohamed Gouled, and a businessman who returned to Somalia in 1979 under an amnesty for exiles, but was detained on arrival.

In November 1980 Amnesty International issued an urgent action appeal on behalf of seven detainees known to be seriously ill. They included Yusuf Omer Azhari (former Ambassador to the United States of America), Yusuf Ali Barre (teacher and poet), Yusuf Osman Samantar "Barde Ad", and Saida Botan Elmi, who had allegedly been assaulted several times in detention. Amnesty International called for full medical treatment and asked for their release to be urgently considered on medical grounds. It said their medical complaints could be caused by harsh prison conditions, poor diet, lack of exercise, and absence of prompt qualified medical attention. The Minister of Justice and Religious Affairs replied that all prisoners were given full medical attention, with regular visits by prison doctors, but made no comment on individual cases or prison conditions generally. None of the prisoners were released.

Most prisoners of conscience and political detainees were held in Labatan Jirow prison near Baidowa or Lanta Bur prison near Afgoi. In these remote maximum security prisons diet was poor and medical attention inadequate. Visits and correspondence with relatives, lawyers or religious representatives were not allowed. Reading material, association with other prisoners, exercise and access to the open air were permitted to some detainees but not others. The most prominent political detainees such as Mohamed Abshir Musse and Mohamed Haji Ibrahim Egal, were reportedly held in permanent solitary confinement, in small, permanently lit, underground cells. Conditions in Mogadishu central prison were less rigid, but detainees complained of overcrowding and poor hygiene.

The death sentence was imposed and carried out a number of times during the year for offences including mutiny, embezzlement and homicide. Four students sentenced to death by a security court in June 1979 for demonstrating against the government in Garowe had their sentences commuted and were released in late 1980. Amnesty International had appealed to President Siyad Barre for commutation of the sentences.

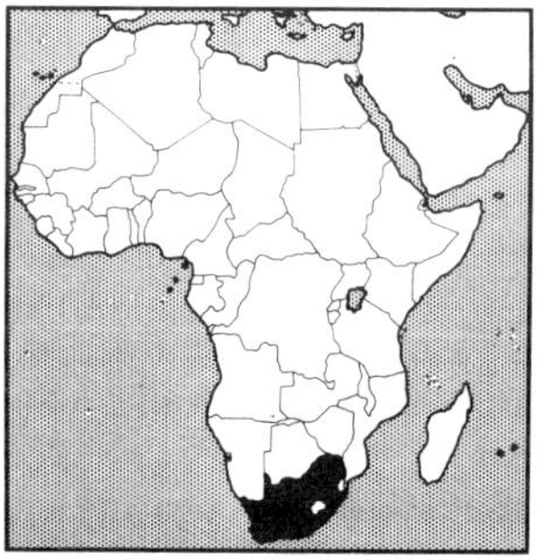

South Africa

The main concerns of Amnesty International were detention without trial and the imprisonment of prisoners of conscience, bannings, torture and the death penalty.

There were changes in the constitution during the year. The exclusively white Senate was abolished by legislation enacted during the 1980 parliamentary session and replaced by a new body, the President's Council, which includes representation from the "Coloured", Indian and Chinese communities as well as the white population group. Representatives of the majority African population were, however, specifically excluded from participation in the President's Council which, unlike the former Senate, has advisory and not legislative powers.

This constitutional change coincided with a long and bitter boycott of schools by "Coloured" and black students protesting at inequalities in education. The boycott began and received wide support in the Western Cape area, where the majority of the "Coloured" population lives.

Black opposition to government policies was not confined to education. Black trade unionism grew rapidly, and there was an almost unprecedented number of strikes and industrial disputes. Violent opposition to the government also grew, particularly by members of the banned African National Congress (ANC).

The government's response to black protest, non-violent as well as violent, was marked by large-scale violations of human rights. The schools boycott, the rash of strikes and industrial disputes and the upsurge of ANC activity were met by waves of arrests and detentions, political trials and bannings. The press also came under renewed pressure. *Post,* the main newspaper for blacks since the banning of *The World* in October 1977, was effectively suppressed by the government in late 1980. Five black journalists, all leading members of the Media Workers' Association of South Africa (MWASA), were restricted under banning orders and thus prevented from working as journalists. Among them were MWASA President Zwelakhe Sisulu, the son of a jailed ANC leader, Walter Sisulu, serving life imprisonment on Robben Island, and Albertina Sisulu, a veteran opponent of *apartheid* who has been held under repeated banning orders for over 16 years. The banned journalists were all adopted as prisoners of conscience by Amnesty International.

The ruling National Party government of Prime Minister P. W. Botha also took strong action against its opponents abroad. In January 1981 South African military forces entered Mozambique attacking and destroying houses occupied by ANC members in the Matola area of Maputo. At least 15 people, mainly refugees from South Africa, were killed in the raid and several others were captured and taken back to South Africa. In February 1981 Dhaya Pillay, a South African refugee employed as a schoolteacher in Swaziland, was abducted and secretly repatriated by agents apparently acting on behalf of South Africa. He was subsequently handed back by the South African authorities after several of his abductors were arrested by police in Swaziland, but no information was given by the government in Pretoria to indicate why, or at what place, he had been detained incommunicado for some three weeks. Amnesty International's inquiries about Dhaya Pillay's abduction and detention received no response from the South African Government.

The authorities continued throughout the year to use detention without trial extensively against critics and opponents. In mid-1980 several hundred people were arrested in the Western Cape and other areas where the schools boycott had spread. As well as school students, many of them children under 16 years of age, the arrested included teachers, community leaders and others who supported the boycott or in other ways backed the students' stand. More than 130 detainees were placed in preventive detention under Section 10 of the Internal Security Act. They were generally allowed regular visits from close relatives and most were released by mid-August 1980. They were not charged. Many of the detainees were adopted as prisoners of conscience by Amnesty International. Those who remained in detention beyond August 1980, some of whom went on hunger-strike to protest against their continued imprisonment without trial, were also adopted by Amnesty International.

Most of those detained in connection with the schools boycott were held under other detention provisions, such as Section 6 of the Terrorism Act, which stipulate that detainees be held incommunicado and permit the security police to withhold all information about those detained. After interrogation a number of detainees were charged and brought to trial. Others were not charged but were kept in detention for long periods because they were considered potential state witnesses. For example at least 10 school students aged between 13 and 17 years, who were the subject of a concerted Amnesty International appeal shortly after their arrest in August 1980, were still believed to be detained more than seven months later.

Trade unionists in a number of industrial disputes were also detained without trial. Joseph Mavi, President of the Black Municipal Workers' Union (BMWU), was detained incommunicado in late July 1980 during a strike by some 10,000 black employees of the Johannesburg municipality, many of them BMWU members. He and two other BMWU officials were later charged with sabotage. This charge was withdrawn and replaced by a lesser charge, of which they were acquitted in March 1981. The strike was broken when large numbers of black workers were forcibly removed from Johannesburg to their respective "homelands". In the Eastern Cape at least 15 leading members of unregistered black trade unions were detained for several weeks at the end of 1980. They were held in the Ciskei "homeland" under legislation authorizing incommunicado detention without trial. Several went on hunger-strike. More Eastern Cape trade unionists were detained in April 1981.

Bonisile Norushe, an official of the African Food and Canning Workers Union was arrested in June 1980 and detained incommunicado until February 1981 when he was required to testify as a state witness in a political trial. He refused to do so and was then jailed for one year by the trial judge for contempt of court. He was adopted as a prisoner of conscience by Amnesty International. Mandla Gxanyana, the defendant against whom he was required to testify, was convicted, fined and sentenced to six months' imprisonment.

Many other suspected opponents of the government were detained during the year. They included leaders of political organizations such as the Azanian People's Organisation (AZAPO), Natal Indian Congress (NIC) and the Labour Party. Leading members of the black Congress of South African Students (COSAS) and the white National Union of South African Students (NUSAS) were also detained, as were several journalists, church and community workers. Among the latter were Alfred Metele and Mzwandile Msoki, employed by the South African Council of Churches to assist political prisoners and their families. Alfred Metele was twice detained in the Ciskei; Mzwandile Msoki was detained without trial for more than nine months.

Amnesty International campaigned against detention without trial and intervened with the authorities on behalf of many of those detained, urging that they should be released if not charged.

There were many political trials during the year. At a number defendants and witnesses made allegations of torture. Almost without exception, it was impossible to verify these reports since the alleged victims were held in incommunicado detention by security police. However one claim was resolved when the Minister of Police agreed an out-of-court settlement for damages with Cynthia Montwedi, a former political detainee who claimed that she had been tortured by security police in Johannesburg in April 1978.

One of the most significant political trials, and one in which torture allegations were made, was of nine alleged members of the ANC charged with treason and offences under the Terrorism Act. The trial came after several violent acts earlier in the year, including an attack on a police station in January 1980 and the seizure of a bank in Pretoria the same month, which resulted in the deaths of three ANC guerrillas and several civilian hostages. In November 1980 all nine defendants were convicted of treason: three were sentenced to death and the others received prison sentences ranging from 10 to 20 years. This was the only political trial to result in the imposition of the death penalty.

In a number of other major political trials defendants charged under the Terrorism Act or the law against sabotage received severe prison sentences upon conviction for non-violent offences. Some were adopted as prisoners of conscience. The Terrorism Act and the law governing sabotage carry a five-year mandatory minimum sentence. Several young people under the age of 18 were among those convicted at such trials and sentenced to terms of imprisonment on Robben Island.

In February 1981 the Minister of Justice announced that certain categories of convicted prisoners would be granted additional remission of sentence at the end of May 1981 to mark the 20th anniversary of the Republic. However prisoners convicted of political offences were specifically excluded from this amnesty. It is government policy to deny political prisoners any remission of sentence, although most convicted criminals receive up to one-third remission. Earlier, in mid-1980, a major campaign in South Africa for the release of ANC leader

Nelson Mandela, imprisoned on Robben Island since he was jailed for life in 1964, proved unsuccessful. Paul David, a lawyer and one of the campaign organizers, was detained without trial and the Prime Minister stated publicly that Nelson Mandela would not be released.

Several new banning orders were imposed during the year. The Minister of Justice banned Curtis Nkondo and Fanyana Mazibuko, respectively Chairman and Secretary of the Soweto Teachers' Action Committee, in mid-1980. Helen Joseph, a well-known opponent of *apartheid,* was banned for the fourth time in June 1981. Aged 75, she had first been placed under a restriction order in 1957 and in 1962 had been the first banned person to be placed under partial house arrest. She had previously been under a banning order until 1971. Saravanan Chetty, who had also been banned before, was served with a new order in February 1981. Among other restrictions, he was subjected to partial house arrest with only two specified relatives allowed to visit his home. His banning order was imposed after he apparently called for the NIC to boycott official anniversary celebrations. Most banned people were adopted as prisoners of conscience by Amnesty International.

Two conscientious objectors were also adopted by Amnesty International. Peter Moll and Richard Steele were both sentenced to one-year terms of imprisonment in detention barracks following their refusal to undertake military service in the Defence Force. They were prosecuted as military defaulters because, as Baptists, they did not belong to one of the "peace" churches recognized by the government when granting conscientious objector status. During their imprisonment both men refused treatment different from that accorded to recognized conscientious objectors, and as a result they were punished and placed in solitary confinement. After some time the authorities conceded their recognition as conscientious objectors. Peter Moll was released in December 1980; Richard Steele was freed in February 1981.

The death penalty remained a major concern. It was extensively used and may be applied for a wide range of offences. According to official statistics, a total of 130 executions were carried out at Pretoria prison in 1980. Forty-three of those hanged were officially classified as "Coloured" and 85 were black. One white and one Indian were also executed. None of those hanged had been convicted of political offences, they had mostly been convicted of murder. James Mange, an alleged ANC member who had been sentenced to death for treason in November 1979, had his sentence commuted to 20 years' imprisonment by the Appeal Court in September 1980. Ncimbithi Johnson Lubisi, Petrus Tsepo Mashigo and Naphtali Manana, the three alleged ANC members convicted and sentenced to death in

November 1980, also on treason charges, were awaiting the outcome of their appeal in April 1981.

Amnesty International appealed to the government to grant clemency to these prisoners. Similar appeals had earlier been made on behalf of James Mange. Appeals for commutation of sentence were also made on behalf of people sentenced to death for non-political offences. For several months in mid-1980 Amnesty International campaigned against the death penalty and tried to influence the authorities towards abolition, but by April 1981 no reduction in the use of the death penalty had become apparent. In February 1981 Helen Suzman, an opposition member of the House of Assembly, called for a committee of inquiry into the death penalty when the Minister of Justice announced that 130 executions had taken place in 1980, but this was not accepted by the government.

Amnesty International made formal submissions concerning human rights in South Africa to the United Nations Commission on Human Rights and the United Nations Special Committee Against Apartheid.

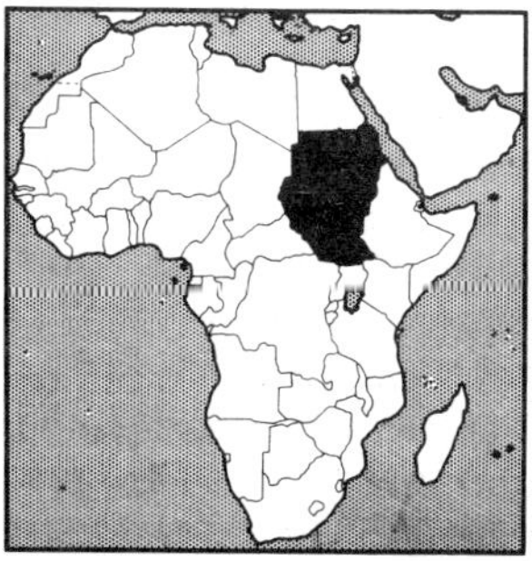

Sudan

Amnesty International's concerns were detention without trial, unfair trials, and poor prison conditions. Sudan retains the use of the death penalty.

One hundred and forty people detained indefinitely without charge or trial under the State Security Law were adopted by Amnesty International as prisoners of conscience. Of these, 66 were released during the year, mostly in August 1980. A further 70 known detainees were being adopted in April 1981, when the total number of political detainees was believed to be at least 300.

Since 1979 the government of President Jaafar Numeiri has detained without trial a substantial number of members or alleged supporters of opposition political parties banned since the Sudanese Socialist Union was decreed the sole political party in 1971. Detained members of the Arab Ba'athist Socialist Party include Omer Mohager Mohamedeen, a lawyer, and Mohamed Ali Jadeen, Deputy Secretary in the Ministry of Finance. An urgent appeal was launched in October 1980 for another detainee, Youssif Himat Hassan, a bank manager who was suffering from a perforated ulcer.

About 60 members of the Democratic Unionist Party were detained in May 1980 for allegedly planning a coup. The majority had been released uncharged by the end of 1980, although Seif Abdel-Magid, a doctor, was still detained in April 1981 and held in solitary confinement at the National Security headquarters.

The largest single group of detainees consisted of members or alleged supporters of the Sudan Communist Party. They included party central committee member Youssif Hussein, lawyer Kemal al-Gizooli, trade unionist Mokhtar Abdullah, and Edward Lino Wor, senior official in the Southern Region Development Corporation. Most were arrested after demonstrations and strikes in mid-1979, but some, like the party central committee member el-Tigani el-Tayeeb, were arrested in late 1980.

In May 1980 Mohamed Murad, a Khartoum University lecturer, and four others were tried before a security court on charges of membership of an illegal organization — the Sudan Communist Party. They were found guilty and given the minimum sentence of six months' imprisonment. They were due for release since the sentence began at the time of arrest, but were immediately rearrested. Seven Ba'athists were tried on similar charges, five of whom were convicted and sentenced to imprisonment for six to 18 months. They too were detained again on expiry of their sentences.

Prisoners released during the year included: Samuel Aru, former Vice-President of the southern region's High Executive Council; poet Mahgoub Sharif; two members of the Sudan Communist Party central committee — Saudi Daraj and Suleman Hamid; Osman Abdel-Nabi a doctor; and Maker Benjamin, a civil servant.

The majority of the detainees were held in Kober prison, Khartoum. They were permitted short supervised family visits, reading material and recreational activities. The main complaint was about inadequate medical treatment and serious delays in obtaining hospital admission.

Kober prison detainees went on hunger-strike on 28 February 1981 against worsening conditions under a new prison commandant. Writing material had been forbidden, their diet had deteriorated, access to independent medical specialists was denied, and other previously recognized rights were arbitrarily withdrawn. After three days the strike ended when the authorities agreed to remedy their complaints.

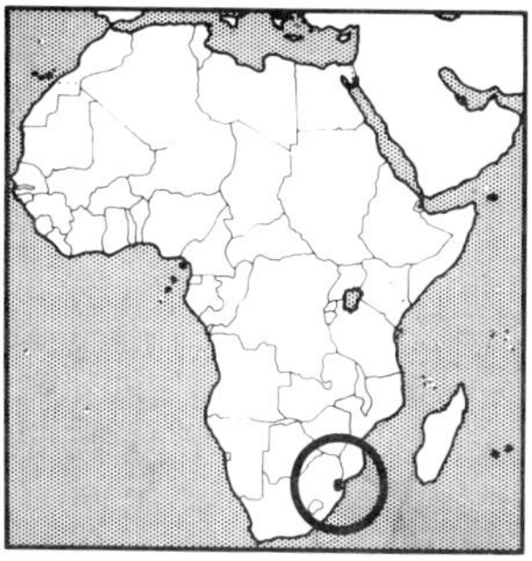

Swaziland

All 14 long-term political detainees still held at the beginning of May 1980 were released unconditionally later that month by order of Prime Minister Prince Mabandla Fred Dlamini. On the day of their release, 28 May 1980, the detainees were taken to the Cabinet office where they were addressed by the Prime Minister and other government ministers, who reportedly admitted that their long imprisonment had been unjustified but encouraged them not to harbour grievances. Seven of the detainees had been adopted as prisoners of conscience by Amnesty International.

Those freed on 28 May included Ambrose Simelane, formerly a leading supporter of Dr Ambrose Zwane's Ngwane National Liberatory Congress (NNLC), which was declared illegal in April 1973 when King Sobhuza II summarily suspended the independence constitution and dissolved parliament. Simelane had been detained continuously under a series of 60-day detention orders since February 1978. Other former office-holders in the NNLC, including Sam Myeni and Kislon Shongwe, had similarly been detained without trial for two years. They had been arrested in mid-May 1978. Musa Shongwe, a well-respected attorney detained in August 1978 shortly after defending three South African refugees charged with arms offences, was also freed unconditionally on 28 May 1980.

The first indication that the detainees might be released had been given about two weeks earlier by Prime Minister Dlamini when commenting upon a report which appeared in the London-based *New African* magazine. This had described the use of detention without trial in Swaziland and had suggested that an international campaign would be launched to obtain the detainees' release. While questioning the motives behind such a campaign, the Prime Minister indicated that he was reviewing the whole issue of political detainees in Swaziland.

Amnesty International welcomed the release of the detainees in early June and urged Prime Minister Dlamini to avoid further use of administrative detention orders.

The situation of refugees from Mozambique and South Africa also gave cause for concern. In early June 1980 it was reported that more than 60 Mozambican refugees had been handed back by the Swazi authorities. The identities of those returned were not known to Amnesty International and were not disclosed by the government, but it was feared that some may have had valid grounds to expect imprisonment for reasons of conscience on their return. More Mozambicans seeking asylum in Swaziland are believed to have been repatriated later in the year, and in February 1981 it was reported that there were only 20 Mozambicans left in the country recognized as refugees by the United Nations High Commissioner for Refugees.

Shortly before the first large-scale repatriation of Mozambican refugees in June 1980 Prime Minister Dlamini had visited Maputo for talks with the Mozambique Government. As a result, suspicions were aroused that a reciprocal agreement might have been reached between the two governments under which refugees would be returned. These suspicions gained credence in late August 1980 when four Swazi refugees were summarily repatriated from Mozambique. Three of them were subsequently charged with leaving Swaziland illegally, and one received a jail sentence. However one other, who is not believed to have been charged, was permitted by the authorities to return to Mozambique.

The vulnerability of the 4,000 South African refugees who live in Swaziland was vividly illustrated twice during the year. In June 1980 at least two members of the banned African National Congress (ANC) were killed when houses occupied by the organization were destroyed in a bomb explosion allegedly caused by South African security agents.

In February 1981 Dhaya Pillay, an alleged member of the ANC who had been a refugee in Swaziland since November 1977, was forcibly abducted by several men apparently acting on behalf of the South African security police. Four of those held responsible were arrested in Swaziland and charged in connection with the kidnapping. Three of them were said to be members of a Mozambique opposition group and the other a black South African, but their identities were not revealed by the Swaziland authorities. They were brought to court in early March 1981 but the proceedings were held *in camera.* They were then released on bail, and may have been able to leave the country.

Dhaya Pillay, who had been employed as a schoolteacher at the time of his abduction, was returned to Swaziland by the South African authorities on 11 March 1981. He later told a press conference in Mbabane that he had been taken blindfolded to a place of detention in South Africa and interrogated. After four days the white official in charge of his interrogation told him: "We made a mistake". After a further two weeks in detention, he was blindfolded again and driven in a car back to Mbabane.

After reports of Dhaya Pillay's abduction Amnesty International appealed to South African Prime Minister P. W. Botha to clarify whether or not he was detained in South Africa and to investigate fully his removal from Swaziland. There was no response to this appeal but an official statement issued by South Africa claimed that Dhaya Pillay had been "detained at the border for alleged contravention of South Africa's immigration laws and then allowed to go".

Tanzania

Amnesty International's main concerns were detention without trial and the retention of the death penalty.

The one remaining person adopted by Amnesty International as a prisoner of conscience, Nasreen Mohamed Hussein from Zanzibar whose movements had been restricted since becoming a "forced bride" in 1971, was finally, in July 1980, able to leave the country to be reunited with her relatives in exile.

Amnesty International was concerned about detention without trial on the mainland under the Preventive Detention Act of 1962. This empowers the authorities to detain any person without charge or trial for an indefinite period. It has been used against political opponents and people suspected of serious criminal offences. Amnesty International believes that more than 100 detainees were held under this act.

A similar detention act in Zanzibar was invoked in June 1980, amid widespread short-term arrests of suspected political opponents, to detain 16 people publicly accused of plotting to overthrow the ruling Zanzibar Revolutionary Council (ZRC). ZRC Chairman Aboud Jumbe announced the following month that the detainees would be charged and tried when investigations were completed. Ten of the 16 detainees were released uncharged on 26 April 1981. Attorney General Damian Lubuva announced that they had been "pardoned". The six remaining detainees were still held without charge or trial. There was no response from the authorities to Amnesty International's requests for information about these detainees and their treatment, or its call for them to be charged and tried or released.

Over 6,000 prisoners were freed by presidential amnesty in 1980, the great majority of whom were convicted ordinary criminals. They included Eliyah Chipaka and John Chipaka, who had been convicted of treason and sentenced to life imprisonment in 1971. A number of untried detainees were also released during the year. Released detainees were often subject to administrative restrictions prohibiting them from employment in public service or travelling abroad.

The government's investigations into allegations of torture and killing of prisoners in Mwanza and Shinyanga in 1976 finally led to the prosecution of those responsible. In two separate trials, 12 senior security and police officers including two Regional Police Commanders were sentenced to prison terms ranging from five to eight years for causing the death by torture of prisoners arrested in Mwanza and Shinyanga in January 1976. They had led a special security operation on the instructions of a high-level security committee chaired by the then Prime Minister, Rashidi Kawawa, inquiring into a wave of unsolved murders in the two regions. According to evidence produced in court, over 800 men and women were arrested and systematically tortured; at least four victims died as a result. A doctor who administered methedrine, a "truth drug", to the prisoners at the request of security officers was later disciplined by the Tanzania Medical Council, and left the medical service.

Togo

Amnesty International's main concerns were detention without trial and prison conditions. The imprisonment of five alleged opponents of the government after a trial which fell short of internationally recognized standards continued to give cause for concern.

Detention without trial or "administrative detention" was used against individuals suspected of political opposition who were often held for periods of several years. In October 1980 Amnesty International appealed to head of state General Gnassingbe Eyadema to provide information about the judicial status of the detention of five people arrested between late 1973 and August 1980 and held without trial. Among these were Agbeshie Pascal Sassou, an official of the Ministry of Foreign Affairs, who was arrested in 1979. Although official sources reported his release on 1 May 1980 Amnesty International received several reports that he was confined to Tokoin hospital against his will throughout 1980. In late March 1981 the Togolese authorities provided Amnesty International with information on all five detainees. Three detainees including Agbeshie Pascal Sassou were said to have been freed between November 1980 and

February 1981, one was being held on corruption charges and one was unknown to the authorities. In early February 1981 Amnesty International appealed to the government to give the reasons for the arrest of Guy Midiouhouan, who had been deported from Gabon to Togo in January 1981. The authorities replied that they had deported him to Benin in late February, claiming that he was not a Togolese national.

Amnesty International was still investigating the cases of Kodjovi Emmanuel de Souza, Kouao Stéphan Sanvee, Kwassi Jean Savi de Tove, Kouassivi Alphonse de Souza and Abalo de Souza, who were convicted by Togo's State Security Court of conspiracy to overthrow the government in August 1979. Death sentences against the first two were commuted to life imprisonment, and the others received prison sentences of between five and 10 years. The trial failed to establish adequately the guilt of the accused and the sentences passed appeared unwarranted and severe. There had been procedural irregularities, particularly with regard to the right to defence counsel at all stages of the judicial process (see *Amnesty International Report 1980*).

Conditions of detention at the *gendarmerie* headquarters in the capital, Lome, were reported to be harsh. Detainees were said to be held in dark overcrowded cells, with little ventilation, poor sanitation and no exercise. Visits were believed to be very restricted.

In late April 1980 an Amnesty International mission visited Togo at the request of the authorities. The delegates were received by President Eyadema, Director of the Presidential Office O. F. Natchaba, the Minister of Justice, and the President of the Supreme Court, and were told that they had free access to any other officials or individuals they might wish to meet. Among the subjects raised by the delegates was the frequency of "administrative detention" and the apparent absence of judicial redress. The authorities were asked to ensure an early hearing before an independent and impartial tribunal for all detainees with defence counsel of their own choosing. Although acknowledging that detainees were held without trial on presidential or ministerial order, often for several years, government officials stressed that the use of such measures was exceptional and designed to counter threats to national security. Interviews with officials confirmed reports that detainees held on executive order could obtain no redress through the courts. The Amnesty International delegates were allowed to visit the "Petite Porte" detention centre at the *gendarmerie* headquarters in Lome. After an appeal to President Eyadema five prisoners held without trial for suspected political opposition were reportedly freed by presidential order on 1 May 1980. Two of these are believed to have been held for possessing literature critical of the government.

In February 1981 a Swiss citizen, Rudolf Eigenmann, was sentenced to death after being convicted of murder. His sentence was later commuted to life imprisonment by the President.

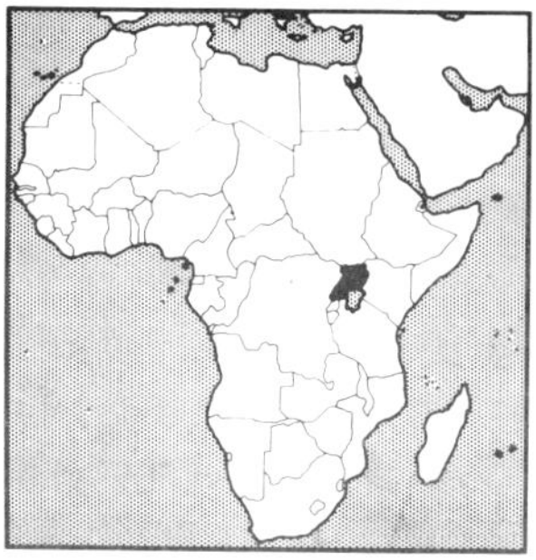

Uganda

Amnesty International's concerns were detention without trial, "disappearances" and extrajudicial killings, torture, harsh conditions of imprisonment, and the death penalty.

On 13 May 1980 President Godfrey Binaisa was deposed and detained by the Military Commission of the ruling coalition Uganda National Liberation Front. The Military Commission headed by former Interior Minister Paulo Muwanga held power until the parliamentary elections of December 1980.

Amnesty International appealed to the Military Commission on 19 May to try or release Godfrey Binaisa and expressed fears for his safety. Paulo Muwanga informed Amnesty International that Godfrey Binaisa was "still living in State House" and had not been mistreated. He was later detained in a private house under the guard of Tanzanian security officers, but no charges were preferred. Amnesty International later adopted him as a prisoner of conscience. He was freed in December 1980.

Amnesty International had also urged the Military Commission to investigate the illegal detention by the army of several people arrested in early May, including journalist Roland Kakooza, editor of *The Economy,* whose release President Binaisa had failed to obtain. Roland Kakooza and others were severely tortured at Makindye military police barracks and Malire army barracks. Others detained by the army on political grounds in the succeeding weeks included Sam Njuba, Chairman of the Uganda Law Society. Roland Kakooza and Sam Njuba were released in July 1980.

Uganda continued to suffer from the chronic insecurity and violent crime prevailing since the overthrow of Idi Amin in April 1979. Allegations that many murders during 1980 were politically motivated were mostly impossible to verify. Two major crises underlined the problems of such insecurity: the famine in Karamoja, caused as much by banditry as by drought, and the upheavals in the West Nile district. In early October 1980 anti-government forces invaded West Nile and killed about 300 soldiers in Koboko. Army reinforcements not only attacked the remaining invaders but also arbitrarily killed, raped and looted the civilian population, apparently in revenge for the killings between 1971 and 1979 of thousands of members of the Acholi and Lango ethnic groups by Idi Amin's security forces, of whom many came from West Nile. Within a short period about a quarter of a million people — virtually the whole population of the district — fled across the border to Zaïre and Sudan. Amnesty International called on the government to initiate an independent inquiry into the West Nile incidents. By late 1980 as the situation became more stable many of these refugees were beginning to return home.

A total of 5,800 prisoners were captured in 1979 by Tanzanian and Ugandan forces during the fighting to overthrow the Amin government, or arrested immediately afterwards. They have been detained since then under the control of Tanzanian security officers in Uganda, and their fate remained unclear. Under Godfrey Binaisa's government a few hundred were released, including civilians seized by the Tanzanian forces during the overthrow of Idi Amin, transported to prison in Tanzania, and later repatriated to custody in Uganda. The government announced that steps would be taken to establish special courts for these detainees, who were mostly members of the army and repressive branches of the Amin government: the State Research Bureau, Public Safety Unit, Military Police, and Anti-Corruption Unit. (The head of the Public Safety Unit, Kassim Obura, was sentenced to death for murder by the High Court, but the case proceeded to appeal.) In mid-1980 conditions for these detainees so deteriorated that a number died of starvation, and others were being routinely ill-treated. Amnesty International urged that they should be tried or released. It called for them to be treated humanely and in accordance with the law.

The December 1980 elections were held in an atmosphere described in the Commonwealth Observer Group's report as "turbulent and troubled . . . the signs of economic and social collapse were everywhere, as were the psychological traumas caused by exposure to brutality on a massive scale". Four political parties contested the elections. Dr Milton Obote — President of Uganda from 1962 to 1971 — was returned to power as leader of the Uganda People's Congress, which had obtained the majority of parliamentary seats. The Democratic Party and Uganda Patriotic Movement formed the parliamentary opposition, although they disputed the validity of many poll results.

President Obote stated at his inauguration: "We shall work for human compassion, rights and dignity. We shall work for reconciliation. We shall insist on no revenge." He pledged that he would lead "a government of law". One of his first acts was to release former

President Binaisa from detention. He later ordered the release of 300 of the detainees arrested in 1979 and stated that the cases of the rest would be reviewed.

In early February two opposition guerrilla forces — the Uganda Freedom Movement and the People's Revolutionary Army — attacked army, police and prison establishments in different parts of the country. In subsequent anti-guerrilla army operations, large numbers of political opponents as well as suspected guerrillas were arrested. Some prisoners were later revealed to be detained under the Public Order and Security Act (1967), which permits indefinite detention without charge or trial. Some were arrested by or in the presence of Tanzanian security officers, to ensure they were not ill-treated by the Ugandan army. Others were arrested by the Ugandan army, without legal authority, and in many cases ill-treated, tortured, made to "disappear" or murdered.

The detainees arrested in February included four Democratic Party (DP) members of parliament, one of whom, Professor Yoweri Kyesimira, was still held at the end of April 1981. Prominent officials of the Uganda Patriotic Movement (UPM), including defeated parliamentary candidates, were also detained, such as Rhoda Kalema (released after two months), Jaberi Bidandi-Sali, Bakulu-Mpagi Wamala, and the Reverend Christopher Okoth.

Amnesty International urged President Obote to guarantee all those arrested the full protection of their basic human rights, and asked for information on the grounds for their detention, their legal status and whereabouts. When no reply was received, fears for the safety of those arrested prompted an urgent appeal. A second urgent appeal expressed extreme concern over reports that Bakulu-Mpagi Wamala had been bayoneted or shot during his arrest by soldiers and tortured in the army interrogation centre at the Nile Mansions Hotel. The detainees' cases were then investigated by Amnesty International as possible prisoners of conscience. Further arrests of DP and UPM supporters, including two more members of parliament and a lawyer, took place in April 1981. Some were reportedly ill-treated. The DP leader alleged that several hundred people had been arrested. By the end of the month Amnesty International was investigating the cases of 25 known detainees. Amnesty International submitted the cases of the detained members of parliament to the Inter-Parliamentary Union.

Amnesty International issued another urgent appeal on behalf of four Makerere University students arrested on campus on 22 February 1981. Demonstrations had been held against the government ban on the student union for protesting against the arrest of a woman student who was later released. In the ensuing violence by the army and pro-government civilian groups against suspected student opponents, several student leaders fled the country. There were fears for the safety of the four arrested students — Paschal Bahikayo, Joseph Essanyu, Silvio Ewaku, and Charles Mukembo — who were adopted by Amnesty International as prisoners of conscience. By the end of April 1981 there was no news of their fate.

Amnesty International called on President Obote on 2 April to establish an independent inquiry into the deaths of about 60 people found murdered in Kampala and believed to have been killed by the security forces.

By April 1981 the security situation in Uganda had deteriorated with armed opposition groups based in several parts of the country claiming responsibility for sabotage and assassinations of government leaders, while anti-guerrilla operations by the Ugandan army made life increasingly dangerous for civilians in areas of alleged guerrilla activity. During April at least 150 people were killed in Kampala, most of them reportedly civilian victims of arbitrary killings by the security forces.

It was announced on 28 April that 10,000 Tanzanian security forces, who had remained in Uganda at the government's request after the defeat of Idi Amin's forces, would be withdrawn by the end of June 1981.

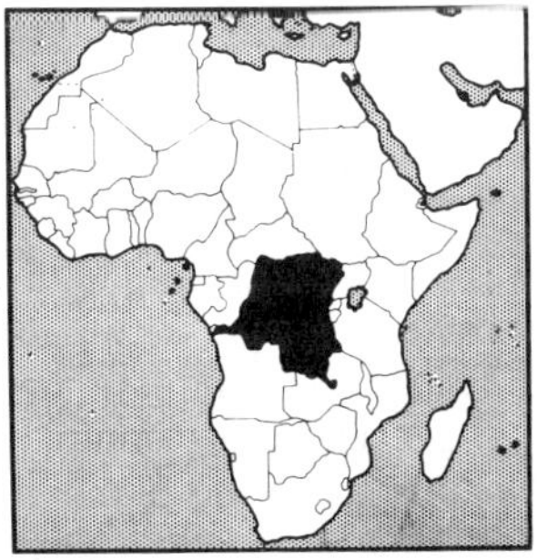

Zaïre

Amnesty International's main concerns were detention without trial, administrative banishment *(relègation),* torture and death in detention, and the death penalty. Amnesty International was also concerned about reports of harsh prison conditions and about unfair trials for alleged government opponents.

In May 1980 Amnesty International published a 22-page report documenting these concerns in detail. Amnesty International members throughout the world participated in a campaign to improve respect for human rights. They sought the release of all prisoners of conscience and a full review of the cases of all political detainees held without trial, an immediate end to torture and extrajudicial executions and the commutation of all death sentences.

Three months before the publication of the report Amnesty International had submitted a memorandum to the government of

President Mobutu Sese Seko. This summarized Amnesty International's concerns in Zaïre and recommended a number of measures to prevent violations of human rights. In May 1980 three government departments replied formally: the *Centre national de documentation* (CND), National Documentation Centre, the security police responsible for arresting political prisoners; the *Parquet général de la République*, the Procurator General's Office; and the *Auditorat général*, the Office of Military Justice responsible for prosecutions both of soldiers and of civilians suspected of complicity with soldiers.

These responses expressed the view that Amnesty International had exaggerated the extent of violations such as torture and harsh prison conditions. As a result they did not feel it necessary to comment on Amnesty International's recommendations on these issues. On the question of detention without trial the Prosecutor General's Office agreed that greater safeguards were needed and recommended that a special commission should regularly review such cases. However there are no signs that this recommendation has been put into effect.

Replying in detail on several individual cases the departments said that a number of prisoners had been released and claimed that others cited by Amnesty International were not prisoners of conscience. In the case of Kasongo Lukika, a military officer convicted with more than 70 others in March 1978 and sentenced to 10 years' imprisonment, the Office for Military Justice said that he was an ordinary criminal because he had been convicted of disobeying orders. He was convicted for belonging to the Mahikari religious sect and was adopted by Amnesty International as a prisoner of conscience. He was eventually released under a special presidential order in February 1981.

Following the publication of Amnesty International's report in May 1980 the Zaïre Government tried to create the impression that the report was exaggerated and inaccurate. The State Commissioner for Foreign Affairs, Nguza Karl-i-Bond, suggested that Amnesty International had a political motive in publishing the report and had not acted purely out of concern for human rights. However a year later, after resigning from his government post in April 1981, Nguza Karl-i-Bond retracted his remarks and admitted that he had been tortured himself while in prison in late 1977. President Mobutu Sese Seko claimed both in September 1980 and again in December that there had been no political prisoners in Zaïre for at least two years.

After receiving new reports of torture during the first half of 1980 Amnesty International published in September 1980 a short document entitled *The Ill-treatment and Torture of Political Prisoners at Detention Centres in Kinshasa.* This contained detailed information on torture at detention centres in Kinshasa: particularly at the headquarters of the security police, which changed its name in April 1980 to the *Centre national de recherches et d'investigations* (CNRI), National Research and Investigation Centre; at a prison known as the *Deuxième Cité de l'OUA,* Second OUA City; and at another centre known as "B2". In response the authorities referred to the fact that the International Committee of the Red Cross (ICRC), had been granted access to each of these places of imprisonment. They claimed that the ICRC had published a report describing conditions as satisfactory but no such report has in fact been published.

In November 1980 a senior official visited London on the initiative of the government for discussions with Amnesty International about human rights in Zaïre. After this visit a new memorandum outlining Amnesty International's concerns was submitted to President Mobutu's government, and Amnesty International was invited to send representatives to Kinshasa to discuss these issues.

Many students were arrested between February and April 1980 after demonstrations in Kinshasa and Lubumbashi. In May the government stated that only 24 had been arrested and that they had all been released during the visit to Zaïre of Pope John Paul II at the beginning of May 1980. However Amnesty International believes that over 100 students had been arrested and that some were still in detention in June 1980; one of the five students who had been introduced to the Pope after his release at the beginning of May was reported to have been rearrested and assaulted.

In Lubumbashi 16 students were detained on 22 April 1980; immediately after their arrest eight were summarily tried by an army officer and by members of the youth wing of the ruling party, the *Jeunesse du mouvement populaire de la révolution* (JMPR), People's Movement for the Revolution Youth. The students were not allowed to defend themselves and were sentenced to be expelled from the university, imprisoned and eventually banished to their home villages for at least one year.

Amnesty International learned of the arrest of teachers in Kinshasa and the provinces after illegal strikes for higher wages in early 1980 and early 1981. Some teachers were also accused by the CNRI of counter-revolutionary activities and of opposition to the government. Another strike for higher wages by school teachers which began in November 1980 led to arrests in Kinshasa and in Kivu and Shaba regions. In March 1981 some 50 teachers were detained in Shaba region. Most were soon released but some were kept in custody for several weeks. In January 1981 the Secretary of the National Teachers' Federation, part of the National Trade Union, was taken into custody for several days suspected of complicity in the teachers' strike.

After their arrest in Bas-Zaïre region at the end of March 1980 a group of more than 20 people were transferred from Matadi to the CNRI headquarters in Kinshasa in May 1980. They were apparently suspected of links with an illegal political party, the *Mouvement national d'union et de réconciliation du Zaïre* (MNUR), Zaïre National Movement of Union and Reconciliation. Most of those arrested came from the Mayumbe area of Bas-Zaïre region as did former President Kasa-Vubu, who was overthrown by President Mobutu in 1965. After six months in custody, during which some of the detainees are reported to have been seriously ill-treated, all but four were released without being charged. The four remaining in prison, Kambu Mavungu, Ngoyo Fuakatinu, Mpongo Malanda and Nlandu Pholo, were charged with conspiring to overthrow Zaïre's constitution. Membership of any party other than the ruling *Mouvement populaire de la révolution* (MPR), People's Movement for the Revolution, is prohibited under Zaïre's one-party constitution. Three of the four prisoners, all of whom were adopted by Amnesty International as prisoners of conscience, were convicted by the State Security Court in November 1980. Kambu Mavungu and Nlandu Pholo were sentenced to three years' imprisonment; Mpongo Malanda was sentenced to 10 months' imprisonment and was released in January 1981. Ngoyo Fuakatinu was reportedly acquitted.

Suspected members of the illegal *Mouvement national congolais/ Lumumba* (MNC/L), Congolese National Movement/Lumumba, were also held in custody without charge or trial during the year. MNC/L members arrested in Kinshasa and Kisangani between September 1979 and May 1980 were reportedly released from prison in September and October 1980 and banished to their towns or villages of origin. In November 1980 Kapepa Inongu was arrested on suspicion of belonging to the MNC/L; and in January 1981 several Zaïrians who usually lived in Brazzaville were arrested by the CNRI in Kinshasa on suspicion of links with the MNC/L or with exiled opposition leaders such as the former State Commissioner for Higher Education, Mungul Diaka. Amnesty International sent repeated inquiries about them but received no replies.

Throughout 1980 large numbers of people were reported to have been arrested and held without charge or trial by the security forces in southeastern Kivu region. Thirty were reportedly still in detention in early 1981. Observers said the total number detained was much higher. The arrests continued in 1981 when Msembe Heri, a student, was detained in Uvira by the CNRI at the end of January. He was reportedly tortured. On 17 March 1981 six young men were arrested in Uvira. The bodies of two of them, Sadiki and Shindano, were later found at the edge of Lake Tanganyika shot through the head.

Amnesty International tried without success to obtain information from the authorities about the reasons for the detentions in Kivu region. The detainees included a number of people who were formerly refugees in Burundi: for example Jean Anzuruni left Zaïre in the late 1960s after playing a major role in the Kivu rebellion against the central government, and returned to Zaïre in 1978 under an amnesty for refugees granted by President Mobutu in June 1978. The detainees also included many farmers, as well as teachers, agricultural extension officers and a 16-year-old fisherman, Zabulone Fujo, whose father has been an active opponent of President Mobutu's government.

In January 1981, 13 People's Commissioners were arrested and accused of signing an open letter to President Mobutu which contrasted many policy statements he had made since he took power in 1965 with what he had actually done.

The 13 were stripped of their parliamentary immunity and their cases were examined by the newly created Disciplinary Commission of the MPR Central Committee, which also examined the case of Kibassa Maliba, a member of the Political Bureau accused of complicity. The Disciplinary Commission found all 14 guilty of serious offences against the discipline of the party and ordered that they should be deprived of their civil and political rights for periods of from one year (in one case) to five years (in 11 cases). Although the legal charges against the People's Commissioners were later dropped the loss of civil and political rights resulted in all 14 people being banished. Some were later held under house arrest in the towns to which they had been banished.

Amnesty International learned of the release of a number of prisoners of conscience during the year. These were military prisoners convicted in March 1978 of complicity in a plot to overthrow President Mobutu and sentenced to three or five years' imprisonment. Some were released after serving their sentences while others, such as Kasongo Lukika, were released under special presidential orders. By April 1981 seven officers serving sentences of between five and 20 years were still imprisoned at Angenga Military Prison in Equateur region and at N'Dolo Military Prison in Kinshasa.

As well as the extrajudicial killings of two young men arrested in Uvira on 17 March 1981, Amnesty International received reports of others killed after their arrest in Kivu region between July and November 1980. In September 1980 for example, Faustin Kinuku and Vincent Waziwazi, both from Luvungi village between Bukavu and Uvira, were reported to have been arrested and killed.

On 26 March 1981 a social sciences professor from the Kinshasa campus of Zaïre's national university, Dikonda wa Lumanyisha, was arrested by the CNRI, beaten and tortured. He was apparently suspected of having been interviewed incognito on a Belgian television program. He was also scheduled to address a human rights seminar at the end of April. Following reports that Professor Dikonda was vomiting blood and had lost consciousness Amnesty International appealed to President Mobutu to intervene and to ensure that Professor Dikonda was given medical attention.

Amnesty International remained concerned by harsh conditions at many prisons and detention centres, despite the closure of the detention camp with the worst mortality rates — Ekafera Camp in Equateur region — in April 1980. Elsewhere in the country conditions were reported to be most severe at centres administered by the army and the security police. Some civilian prisons were also reported to maintain severe regimes, for example Goma in Kivu region, although it appeared that efforts were being made to improve conditions at some other prisons.

After the publication of its report in May 1980 Amnesty International appealed to the authorities to commute all death sentences. In October 1980 President Mobutu commuted the death sentences of all civilians awaiting execution in a special measure to mark his 50th birthday. This measure is believed to have benefited some 130 death-row prisoners. However, it did not apparently help prisoners who had been condemned to death but who were still appealing against their sentences. In March 1981, 17 people originally convicted in January 1980 of armed robbery and murder were executed. Final appeals by some of them were rejected in February 1981 and the executions took place after the 17 had allegedly tried to escape from the prison at Luzumu.

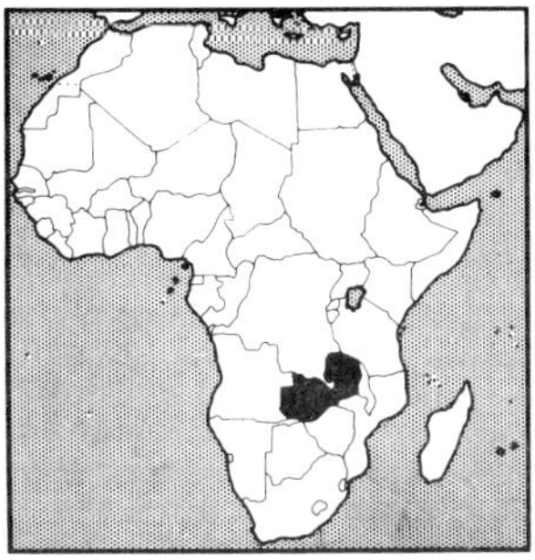

Zambia

The main concern of Amnesty International was the detention without trial of real or suspected opponents of the government. Most were held under administrative detention orders signed by the President in accordance with the Preservation of Public Security Regulations, which allow unlimited detention outside the jurisdiction of the courts.

As economic conditions failed to improve following the independence of neighbouring Zimbabwe there was a series of confrontations between the government and the trade unions and growing criticism from the business community. At one point 17 leading trade unionists were expelled from the United National Independence Party (UNIP), the ruling political party, membership of which is a requirement for public office.

On 15 October 1980 security forces clashed with a group of about 50 armed men, said mostly to be of Zaïrian origin, at Chilanga, a few miles south of the capital, Lusaka. Several of the gang were killed and within a few days at least 45 were captured. A series of arrests then took place. François Cros, a French journalist known for his contacts among refugees from Zaïre's Shaba province, was detained on 17 October.

On 23 October, the day before independence day, a dusk-to-dawn curfew was imposed in most urban areas and a number of prominent Zambians detained. They included Elias Chipimo and Valentine Musakanya, and a well-respected lawyer and commissioner of the High Court, Edward Shamwana. Elias Chipimo, a leading banker and former diplomat had earlier obliquely criticized the government and had been publicly denounced by President Kaunda. Valentine Musakanya, former governor of the Bank of Zambia, has also been denounced as one of "a gang of dissidents". Brigadier Christopher Kabwe, who had been promoted to commander of the air force on 9 October only to be suspended for alleged corruption two days later, was also detained in connection with the activities of the group at Chilanga. On 27 October President Kaunda publicly alleged that the armed gang had been acting on behalf of dissident Zambians, who had received South African backing and whose intention was to overthrow the government. He gave details of the alleged plot and said that the ring-leaders had been arrested, adding that they would soon be charged and brought to trial and that Chief Justice Annel Silungwe had been recalled from abroad to preside. The armed group were said to have been found on a farm owned by Pierce Annfield, a white South African lawyer resident in Zambia who had left the country a few days before. The South African Government denied any involvement in the alleged conspiracy.

Several of those detained in October 1980 were released within a matter of weeks. Elias Chipimo was freed unconditionally on 5 November, and Patrick Chisanga, director of the state-owned Industrial Mining Corporation, on 13 November. François Cros, made the subject of a presidential detention order on 31 October, was also released on 13 November. Three days earlier, his application for a writ of *habeas corpus* had been rejected by the Lusaka High Court. He was later allowed to leave the country.

With one exception, none of those detained in connection with the alleged conspiracy had been charged and brought to trial by the end of April 1981, although on several occasions government officials publicly reaffirmed that the case would go to trial. For example after an appeal by Amnesty International in January that the detainees should be brought to trial or released, a spokesperson for the Minister of Home Affairs was reported on 9 February to have said that investigations were almost complete and that some 50 people would soon be tried. Earlier, in November 1980, a UNIP Central Committee recommendation that a special military tribunal be established to try the alleged conspirators had been rejected at a full meeting of the National Council of UNIP.

The only detainee to have been charged was Valentine Musakanya. On 26 November the Ndola High Court granted his application for a writ of *habeas corpus* and ordered his release finding that the grounds for his detention were "vague, roving and exploratory". However he was immediately rearrested under a new detention order. On 1 December he was charged with treason and taken before the Lusaka Magistrates Court, only for the charge to be withdrawn without explanation before he was asked to enter a plea. He was then returned to detention. His subsequent attempts to obtain release on a writ of *habeas corpus* were unsuccessful.

Edward Shamwana, another detainee, also applied for a writ of *habeas corpus* in November 1980, arguing that his detention was "unlawful and unconstitutional", that he had not been informed of the grounds for detention within the prescribed 14 days, and that he had been subjected to periods of continuous interrogation by security police trying to find reasons to keep him in detention. His application was rejected at the end of November, and a subsequent appeal against the judge's decision was also dismissed. He made a new but similarly unsuccessful attempt in January 1981, claiming that the authorities' failure to prefer charges and bring him to trial should result in immediate release.

After the failure of attempts to obtain their release through the courts in March 1981 Edward Shamwana and Valentine Musakanya jointly drew up a formal petition addressed to the Speaker and members of the National Assembly. They argued that the President's use of the Preservation of Public Security Regulations to authorize detentions was unconstitutional. Because of a technicality the Speaker could not accept the petition when it was first submitted by Mohamed Mansoor, the lawyer acting for Edward Shamwana. Before it could be resubmitted President Kaunda declared it a prohibited publication by notice in the government gazette of 23 March. Mohamed Mansoor was arrested and charged with possession of a banned document, but he was acquitted on 21 April. The state appealed against the verdict, and almost immediately issued a deportation order against Mansoor who is a Sri Lankan.

Action was also taken against Edward Shamwana and Valentine Musakanya after their preparation of the petition. They were moved from Lusaka central prison to remote places of imprisonment at Chipata and Lundazi, in the eastern part of the country, where they were effectively placed in solitary confinement.

In April 1981 Amnesty International reiterated its concern over the continuing detention of Valentine Musakanya, Edward Shamwana and the other detainees held since October 1980, and appealed to the government to bring them to trial or release them without further delay. An earlier appeal, made in January 1981, had resulted in criticism of Amnesty International in the Zambian press, and a claim by the Minister of Legal Affairs, Gibson Chigaga, that appeals sent in Amnesty International's name were "fake".

A number of long-term political detainees were released during the course of the year. They included John Chisata, a former Minister of State for Labour and Social Services, who had been detained without trial under the Preservation of Public Security regulations since late 1978. In March 1981 an appeal brought by John Chisata and another detainee, Faustino Lombe, against an earlier decision of the Ndola High Court to reject their applications for *habeas corpus* was upheld by the Supreme Court, which also awarded costs to the detainees. Both men were then released. Jackson Mutale, arrested at the same time as John Chisata, had his detention order revoked by President Kaunda in April 1981. However at the end of April 1981 several people were still in detention suspected of supporting the banned United Progressive Party (UPP), which had been declared illegal in 1972.

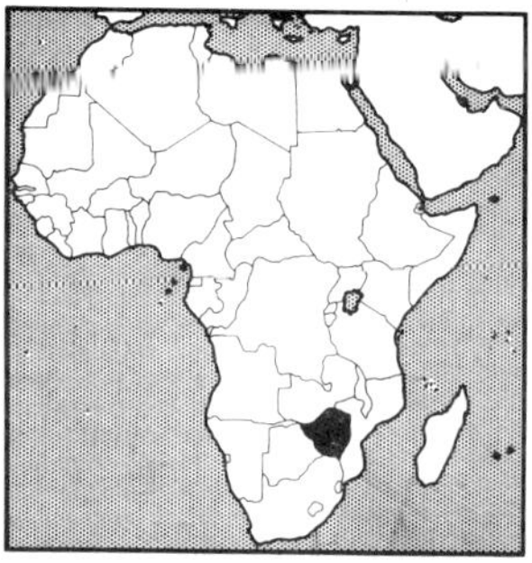

Zimbabwe

Amnesty International's major concerns were the death penalty and the retention of emergency legislation providing for detention without trial.

By the first anniversary of Zimbabwe's independence on 18 April 1981, an estimated one million refugees and displaced persons had been resettled and life in the rural areas most affected by the war appeared to have largely returned to normal. Progress was also made in promoting political reconciliation, not only between the white minority community and the black majority population, but also between the ruling Zimbabwe African National Union (ZANU-PF) and other black political parties.

A crucial problem was the integration of the former ZANU-PF and Patriotic Front (PF) guerrilla forces with what remained of the former Rhodesian security forces, and the reduction of the numbers under arms. Here too, the government of Prime Minister Robert Mugabe achieved progress, though the process was hampered by fighting between former PF and ZANU-PF guerrillas, particularly at Entumbane township, Bulawayo, in November 1980 and February 1981. Partly as a result of the uncertain security situation, the nationwide state of emergency which had been in effect almost continuously since UDI and most recently renewed by Lord Soames in January 1980 was again renewed for a further six months by the new government in July 1980. However a number of provisions affecting fundamental human rights were withdrawn. These included regulations providing for the Special Courts and Special Courts Martial that had been used by previous governments for the trial and sentence of nationalist guerrillas and those suspected of supporting them, and powers to impose collective fines or to enforce compulsory labour.

The state of emergency was again renewed for a further six months in January 1981. Richard Hove, who had replaced Joshua Nkomo as Minister of Home Affairs, told the House of Assembly that this was necessary because of the continuing "unacceptable level of violence", and should not be seen as an intention on the government's part to "infringe human rights".

Although a number of the emergency powers provisions were withdrawn in mid-1980, regulations providing for detention without trial remained intact. The police kept the power to detain any person without charge for 30 days. On 2 September 1980 Senator Simbi

Mubako, Minister of Justice and Constitutional Affairs, told the House of Assembly that there were 117 people detained under such orders. The government retained the power of indefinite detention under the Emergency Powers Regulations, the provision which was used by former governments to detain Robert Mugabe, Joshua Nkomo and many other nationalist leaders and supporters for years. Senator Mubako stated in early September that a total of 69 such detainees were then held on administrative detention orders of indefinite duration. The majority are believed to have been ZANU-PF and PF guerrillas accused of indiscipline. This detention provision is believed also to have been used against at least two members of Joshua Nkomo's PF party who were arrested in late November 1980 at a time of serious tension between the coalition government's ZANU-PF majority and its minority partner, the PF. Several executive members of the PF were detained without charge but, with two exceptions, all were released by 17 December. The two in custody, who are believed to have been the subject of indefinite detention orders, were former Amnesty International adopted prisoners of conscience, Sidney Malunga, an elected member of the House of Assembly, and Mark Nziramasanga, the PF publicity officer. Both were eventually freed unconditionally on 19 January 1981.

In November 1980 the government repealed the Indemnity and Compensation Act, which had been introduced in 1975 by Ian Smith's government. This Act effectively provided indemnity against prosecution to members of the Rhodesian security forces for all acts committed "in good faith" during the course of the guerrilla war. The decision to repeal the Act in November followed the appearance in court of Edgar Tekere, a cabinet minister and the Secretary-General of ZANU-PF, on a charge of murder. Together with seven other ZANU-PF members as bodyguards, he was alleged to have killed a white farmer on 4 August 1980 while carrying out a military-style attack on some soldiers whom he believed had fired upon him the night before. The eight accused admitted the killing, but claimed that they were members of government who had been acting "in good faith" to suppress terrorism, and so were covered by the terms of the Indemnity and Compensation Act. This trial was a major embarrassment to the government and led to Edgar Tekere's removal from the cabinet. It ended on 8 December 1980. The eight defendants were acquitted by a majority verdict on the grounds that they were immune from prosecution due to the Indemnity and Compensation Act.

In early September 1980 the government announced that President Canaan Banana had extended the amnesty granted at the time of independence in April 1980, which had resulted in the release of some ten thousand prisoners. The amnesty had originally covered the period up to 1 March 1980; the amendment announced in September 1980 extended this by six weeks to 18 April 1980. As a result prisoners convicted of stock theft were released, as well as those convicted of or awaiting trial for political offences allegedly committed between 1 March 1980 and 18 April 1980.

A further act of clemency was announced in April 1981, on the first anniversary of independence, when all death sentences imposed during the first year of independence were commuted by President Banana. Although no official figures were given, at least 17 prisoners are believed to have benefited. They included five believed to have been under sentence of death and awaiting execution at the time of independence in April 1980. Announcing the President's decision, the Minister of Justice stated that "This special exercise of the prerogative of mercy does not represent a change in the law in regard to capital punishment or as establishing any precedent".

Amnesty International welcomed this use of presidential clemency as it had been concerned about the government's retention of the death penalty, and about its failure to reject a policy introduced in 1976 by Prime Minister Ian Smith's government under which executions were carried out in secret.

The Americas

Important institutional and constitutional changes took place in several countries of the region during the year covered by this report.

On 17 July 1980 the interim government of President Lidia Gueiler of Bolivia was overthrown in a military coup which involved gross human rights abuses, including political killings, torture, and mass detentions without trial. Political and trade union activity was suppressed and the new government has pursued a policy of enforced exile of members of the opposition, human rights activists and trade unionists. The military coup in Bolivia highlighted some of the human rights violations which most governments resulting from military coups during the last decade in Latin America have perpetrated.

A new constitution came into force in Chile in March 1981, replacing the 1925 constitution and incorporating numerous decrees and laws restricting human rights which the military *junta* has passed since 1973. On 28 July 1980 the first civilian President elected in Peru after 12 years of military government was inaugurated, and a new constitution came into force that abolished the death penalty and ended the jurisdiction of military courts over civilians. In Argentina a new President, General Roberto Viola, was appointed in March 1981. In Uruguay voters rejected a draft constitution proposed by the armed forces in November 1980. In the United States of America President Ronald Reagan took office in January 1981.

Imprisonment of people for the non-violent exercise of their human rights, torture, "disappearances", extrajudicial killings, arbitrary arrests and prolonged detention without trial were reported in many countries of the Americas. In El Salvador thousands of people detained without warrant have "disappeared" or been murdered by the security forces. In Guatemala secret detention and extrajudicial killings by both uniformed and plain clothed members of the security forces were widespread. Amnesty International considers that a government's failure to account for "disappeared" people does not lessen the need for international concern about such people. Governments which have failed to account for people arrested by security forces or others operating with the government's complicity, who later "disappeared", include Argentina, Brazil, Chile, El Salvador, Guatemala, Haiti, Mexico, Paraguay and Uruguay, although there were substantial differences in the extent and circumstances of "disappearances" in these countries. The country entries of this report detail "disappearances" that took place during the year. In many instances relatives of the "disappeared" or members of human rights groups working on their behalf have been harassed, arrested or have even "disappeared" themselves. "Disappearances" in Latin America received worldwide attention with the publication of the report of the Inter-American Commission on Human Rights on Argentina, the reports of the United Nations Commission on Human Rights on Chile and the report of the United Nations Working Group on Enforced or Involuntary Disappearances.

On several occasions the security forces of two or more countries cooperated in killings, "disappearances" and torture. Amnesty International received information that the security forces of Argentina, Bolivia, Peru, El Salvador and Honduras had engaged in such cooperation.

Many Latin American refugees have fled their countries because of human rights abuses, but have not found asylum or protection abroad. In May 1980 hundreds of people, mainly women and children, were reportedly shot and killed by Salvadorian troops as they tried to cross the Sumpul River from El Salvador into Honduras. This was a joint military operation of the Governments of El Salvador and Honduras. Several people died in October 1980 when Haitian police fired on Haitians trying to board a boat in Cap-Haïtien and flee the country. Amnesty International was concerned that Salvadorians, Guatemalans and Haitians were forcibly returned from countries such as the United States of America, the Bahamas, Jamaica and the Dominican Republic to their own countries, where they faced grave risks.

Emergency legislation continued to be used to repress people for the non-violent exercise of their human rights. In some countries the emergency legislation was applied by declaring a state of siege and repeatedly extending it, sometimes for years. Similar results were obtained in countries where parts of the emergency legislation were gradually incorporated into the constitution, penal code or laws of state security. Examples can be found in the legislation of Argentina, Brazil, Chile, Colombia, Cuba, Nicaragua, Paraguay and Uruguay.

Amnesty International continued to be concerned about the imposition of the death penalty and executions. In the United States of America there were 794 people under sentence of death as of 20 April 1981. During the year two executions took place in the English-speaking Caribbean, one in Jamaica and one in the Bahamas; death sentences were passed in Barbados, the British Virgin Islands, Dominica, Guyana, St. Kitts, Trinidad and Cuba.

In May 1980 Amnesty International submitted a statement to the Jamaican Committee on Capital Punishment and Penal Reform, welcoming the government's decision to establish the committee and hoping that its work would pave the way for total abolition of the death penalty in Jamaica. In June 1980 Amnesty International welcomed the passing of the Criminal Law Amendment Act in Bermuda which moved towards abolishing the death penalty, although it retained this punishment for premeditated murder.

Amnesty International pursued a number of individual cases before the Inter-American Commission on Human Rights (IACHR) of the Organization of American States (OAS), from Argentina, Bolivia, Chile, El Salvador, Guatemala and Haiti. Amnesty International attended the annual General Assembly of the OAS held in Washington, D.C. in November 1980 as a special guest. A memorandum to the member states of the OAS conveyed Amnesty International's concerns in those countries on which the IACHR had prepared special reports — Argentina and Haiti — and on which the IACHR's Annual Report had concentrated — Chile, El Salvador, Paraguay and Uruguay. The memorandum also drew attention to human rights abuses in Bolivia after the July 1980 coup. In the memorandum Amnesty International called on member states to ratify and adhere to the American Convention on Human Rights and to accept the compulsory jurisdiction of the Inter-American Court of Human Rights. It called on the assembly to ensure that the judicial remedy of *habeas corpus* was available throughout the region as a protection against torture, death and "disappearance". The memorandum commented on the draft convention defining torture as an international crime which was presented to the assembly, and noted developments regarding the death penalty in the region. The assembly expressed strong support for the work of the IACHR, and asked the IACHR to prepare a report on the human rights situation in Bolivia in the shortest time possible. The assembly adopted a resolution in favour of members ratifying the American Convention on Human Rights and using "the consultative conciliatory and jurisdictional mechanisms" of the convention. It referred the draft convention on torture to member states for comment so that the Permanent Council could submit a final draft to the next General Assembly.

Amnesty International submitted information to other intergovernmental and non-governmental organizations, including the United Nations Commission on Human Rights, the United Nations Educational, Scientific and Cultural Organization (UNESCO), the United Nations High Commissioner for Refugees (UNHCR), and the Council of Europe.

Argentina

Amnesty International's concerns focused on "disappeared" prisoners; the arbitrary arrest and detention without trial of prisoners of conscience; the subjection of political prisoners to torture and to cruel, inhuman and degrading treatment; and the failure of the authorities to conform to internationally recognized standards for a fair trial.

A total of 6,800 people have been registered as "disappeared" by the national human rights organization, the Permanent Assembly of Human Rights. Neither the outgoing administration of President Jorge Rafael Videla nor that of the newly-appointed head of state, General Roberto Viola (who took office on 29 March 1981), has made any move to account for them. High-ranking military authorities have repeatedly said that they will not tolerate any inquiry into these cases, which they claim were caused by the internal disorders. Amnesty International has been investigating the cases of 91 "disappeared" prisoners. Despite evidence to show that these people "disappeared" after being taken into custody by police or military personnel, the authorities have provided no information about their place of detention. Amnesty International also submitted a number of cases to the United Nations Working Group on Enforced or Involuntary Disappearance. In its first report, which was published in January 1981, the working group indicated that it had information on between 7,000 and 9,000 "disappearances" in Argentina. An analysis by the working group of 500 "disappearances" showed that it was highly improbable that the abductions were not carried out by official agents. The working group specifically asked for information on 65 cases where it had a detailed description of the circumstances of the "disappearance" and the people involved had been clearly identified. The government failed to provide any details on these cases but gave assurances that "in cases where . . . the cause of the disappearance is abduction of the person concerned . . . the steps required for all criminal proceedings are taken". Yet of the thousands of *habeas corpus* writs filed by desperate families over the past six years not one has led to the discovery of the victim. Amnesty International is not aware of a single case in which an alleged abductor has been brought to justice by the authorities.

In November 1980 the General Assembly of the Organization of American States considered the report of the Inter-American Commission on Human Rights (IACHR) on the state of human rights in Argentina. The Assembly urged governments to preserve and safeguard the full exercise of human rights, and cited specifically "disappearances". It recommended that central records be established to account for all people detained so that their relatives and friends might promptly learn of any arrest. It also called for arrests to be made only by competent and duly identified authorities, and for detainees to be kept only on premises recognized for that purpose.

Even appeals to the authorities to publish their own list of the "disappeared" have met with a firm refusal. On 25 March 1981 General Albano Harguindeguy, in his last press conference as Minister of the Interior, stated that although the authorities could publish an official list of "disappearances" they had no intention of doing so. However in April 1981 an important precedent was set when the remains of Roberto Daniel Rigone, who was abducted in 1977, were returned to his family. As well as trying to establish what has happened to the people who "disappeared" during the past six years Amnesty International monitored recent abductions which followed the pattern usual in "disappearance" cases. The number of new cases reported has significantly decreased by comparison with previous years: during 1980 about 30 "disappearances" were reported. Since May 1980 Amnesty International has made urgent appeals on behalf of 18 individuals seized in operations usually associated with "disappearances". Three of the victims were subsequently released, another was acknowledged to be in official custody, and the body of a fifth person was found although the cause of death could not be established.

On 24 August 1980 Gervasio Martín Guadix failed to return home. The following day a group of men in civilian clothes, believed to be members of the security forces, raided his home in Villa Lugano, Buenos Aires. A writ of *habeas corpus* was issued on his behalf but received no response from the authorities. It is believed that he was being held in the *Campo de Mayo* (military barracks) in Buenos Aires province. On 18 September Amnesty International issued an urgent appeal on his behalf. In December 1980 the Argentine authorities stated that he had committed suicide on 2 December 1980 near Paso de los Libres, a town in Corrientes province, near the Argentine-Brazil border. It was alleged that he had been a member of a subversive organization. The statement did not clarify the circumstances of his suicide nor has his body been returned to his family.

There is evidence that Argentine military and security forces are carrying out illicit operations outside Argentina. On 30 June 1980 Amnesty International denounced the abduction of four Argentine nationals in the Peruvian capital, Lima. Julia Inés Santos de Acabal, Julio César Ramírez, Noemí Esther Gianetti de Molfino and one other were kidnapped on 12 and 13 June by a group of Argentine security agents who were allegedly helped by members of the Peruvian army intelligence corps. It appears that Federico Frías, a prisoner from Buenos Aires, was brought from Argentina to identify the others. He tried to escape but was wounded in the attempt and has since "disappeared". On 20 June the Peruvian Ministry of the Interior announced that three Argentines, who were not named, had been expelled to Bolivia because their documents were not in order. Amnesty International received unconfirmed reports that one of the kidnap victims, Julia Inés Santos de Acabal, died under torture in Peru. On 21 July the body of Noemí Gianetti de Molfino was discovered in a Madrid flat after an anonymous phone call to the Spanish police. The cause of her death could not be established, nor has there been any satisfactory explanation of how or why she went to Spain without notifying members of her family living in France.

Amnesty International intervened with the authorities to establish the whereabouts of two factory workers who had been abducted from their homes on 11 and 13 March 1981 in Haedo, Buenos Aires province. Armed men in plain clothes abducted Jorge Magrino, and Héctor Orlando Piñón. Although the men were taken away in front of witnesses, local police refused to note formal complaints by relatives. Both men were released after a few days; Amnesty International has received reliable reports that Jorge Magrino had been tortured with electric shocks.

Amnesty International protested against the abduction of 30-year-old Ángel Romano on 27 March 1981 from his home in Quilmes, Buenos Aires province, by armed men in plain clothes. His wife was told that he was being taken to the local police station, but writs of *habeas corpus* presented on his behalf were rejected. For eight days his family had no news of his whereabouts. On 4 April the chief of police of Buenos Aires province stated that Ángel Romano had been officially detained. However he was released on the order of a judge. It was reported that he had been tortured during incommunicado detention.

On 25 March 1981 the government said that they were holding 980 political prisoners: 186 were women, 99 detained before the military coup of March 1976; 803 were men, 475 detained by the previous government; 233 prisoners had been tried and sentenced, 135 charged; 616 were detained without charge in administrative detention *a la disposición del Poder Ejecutivo Nacional* (PEN), at the disposal of the executive power. There is doubt whether these figures were entirely accurate.

Amnesty International has adopted 185 prisoners of conscience and was investigating the cases of a further 115 political prisoners. During the year Amnesty International learned of the release of 30 prisoners of conscience; a number of others were allowed to leave prison but placed under surveillance and restrictions. The official information revealed that the majority of political prisoners had never been charged but remained in prison by presidential decree under Article 23 of the constitution which provides for a state of siege. Most adopted prisoners of conscience fell into this category. The state of siege, in force since November 1974, has been used to justify arbitrary detention without trial of non-violent opponents of the government. In September 1979 the Argentine authorities assured the Inter-American Commission on Human Rights of the Organization of American States (IACHR) that the problem would be gradually resolved, but there has been no evidence of any moves to reduce substantially the number of people detained. In December 1980 the Minister of the Interior announced that 40 prisoners held under PEN would be released. Moreover the right of option — the constitutional right of people detained under PEN to go into exile — was virtually suspended. Only four people were granted the option to leave the country in the month of December 1980. Amnesty International provided information on a number of cases to the Parliamentary Assembly of the Council of Europe which on 25 November 1980 adopted a resolution expressing "grave concern" on behalf of 80 prisoners with visas for European countries whose application for the right of option had been rejected.

On 23 September 1980 a group of Argentine lawyers lodged a collective writ of *habeas corpus* on behalf of 329 prisoners, challenging the right of the government to keep them in detention without trial. On 23 February 1981 the *Federación Argentina de Colegios de Abogados* (FACA), Argentine Federation of Bar Associations, published a statement in *La Nación* drawing the government's attention to the limitations on the power of the executive: "an arrest or transfer by virtue of the state of siege may not be converted by its duration or the nature of its application into a real punishment or sentence". On 13 April 1981 the FACA again called for the state of seige to be lifted and deplored the fact that citizens were being indefinitely deprived of their freedom and denied their constitutional right to a fair trial.

Amnesty International continued to receive reports that political prisoners had been subjected to cruel, inhuman and degrading treatment. In December 1980 prisoners transferred in handcuffs from Unidad 6, Rawson, to Unidad 9, La Plata were severely beaten by military personnel. The physical and mental health of 21 political prisoners is reported to have deteriorated seriously over the past year. Half the prisoners concerned were reported to have serious psychiatric problems. During 1980 Amnesty International made frequent appeals after reports that political prisoners had not received adequate medical treatment and that the prison regime was causing psychological disturbances, particularly among long-term detainees. Gabriel Francisco de Benedetti killed himself in Rawson Prison on 20 June 1980 after serving seven years of a 23-year sentence. Eduardo José Schiavone hanged himself in Caseros Prison in Buenos Aires on 10 July 1980; he had been given a four-year sentence but had been in prison for seven years. Raúl Luis Cominoto who had been in administrative detention for four years hanged himself in La Plata Prison on 19 August 1980 after a month in a special punishment cell. These deaths brought the number of suicides of political prisoners reported since October 1979 to five. Conditions of imprisonment for political prisoners were much harsher than those for ordinary criminal prisoners, and prison conditions failed to comply with Article XXV of the American Declaration of the Rights and Duties of Man and Article 18 of the Argentine Constitution.

In October 1980 Amnesty International campaigned for the release of Eduardo Foti, an adopted prisoner of conscience, arrested in 1975 and held without charge or trial by presidential decree under PEN. During a raid on his home he had been shot in the head and part of his skull was later replaced by a plastic plate. One side of his body was paralysed, he had epileptic attacks and was said to be unable to move or to dress himself unaided. He has been repeatedly punished and denied medical treatment.

Amnesty International has become increasingly concerned about the operations of the *consejos de guerra especiales y estables,* special standing military tribunals, which the military *junta* established in 1976 by Decree 21.264. They not only flout Article 18 of the Argentine Constitution but also fail to conform to internationally recognized standards.

Amnesty International was investigating a number of cases of prisoners sentenced by the military courts. They were mostly convicted on the basis of confessions given to military personnel during interrogation, and there were strong reasons to believe that these statements were extracted by coercion and under torture.

Nicolás Antonio Zárate a 54-year-old Argentine trade union official, was detained in Mendoza on 11 April 1976 and sentenced by a military tribunal on 6 July 1976 to 21 years' imprisonment. The charges, which related to possession of a revolver and subversive documents, were based on evidence allegedly found in his house and which apparently was never fully investigated. His lawyer, appointed by the court, was an army dentist whose defence was limited to endorsing the sentence passed by the tribunal. His trial lasted two days and was held *in camera* in the Police Headquarters in Mendoza, where he had been illegally detained for 60 days during which he was reportedly tortured continuously. His wife, Ana Beatriz Corcino, was abducted in Buenos Aires between November and December 1977 and has "disappeared".

In October 1980 the Nobel Peace Prize was awarded to Adolfo Pérez Esquivel, a former prisoner of conscience who founded *Servicio Paz y Justicia,* the Peace and Justice Service, a non-violent civil liberties organization. He has been closely associated with work for "disappeared" prisoners. Despite his international recognition, individuals and organizations inside Argentina trying to investigate and monitor human rights abuses have been harassed, intimidated and arrested. On a number of occasions demonstrators supporting the Mothers of the *Plaza de Mayo* — a group of relatives of missing people who have been peacefully petitioning for information for the past four years — were detained for short periods. On 10 December 1980, International Human Rights Day, a group of 15 people were arrested and charged with disturbing the peace. They were released after a few days. On 12 March 1981 after another demonstration about 20 people were detained and held for questioning for some hours before being released.

On 28 February 1981 Amnesty International publicly condemned the arrest of six leading human rights activists. On 27 February plain-clothes police raided the Buenos Aires office of the human rights organization, *Centro de Estudios Legales y Sociales* (CELS), Centre for Legal and Social Studies. They arrested two members of CELS: the physicist, José Federico Westerkamp and Carmen Aguiar de Lapacó. During the night of 27/28 February four other prominent members of CELS were arrested: the lawyers Emilio Fermín Mignone, Augusto Conte MacDonell, Boris Pasik and Marcelo Parrilli. Police also confiscated important material documenting human rights violations. The judge in charge of the case, Doctor Martín Anzoátegui, claimed that he had ordered the arrests and seizure of the documents because he had received information that CELS possessed plans of military installations, in violation of Law 224 of the penal code. All were held incommunicado for five days and were released pending further investigation after a week. On 6 March 1981 Amnesty International sent a formal complaint to the Director General of the United Nations Educational, Scientific and Cultural Organization (UNESCO) asserting that these arrests curtailed the rights to freedom of expression and association. Another judge ordered the return of most of the documents. At the end of April 1981 Amnesty International was informed that the public prosecutor, Dr Mugaburu, had called for the case against the members of CELS to be closed and asked a military judge to examine whether military personnel had committed offences. He referred specifically to the case of Elena Holmberg, an Argentine diplomat murdered in December 1978.

Amnesty International made a formal submission to the United Nations Commission on Human Rights under the confidential procedures set up to examine allegations of a "consistent pattern of gross violations". Complaints were presented to the IACHR on behalf of Guillermo Díaz Lestrem, María Antonieta and Rory Céspedes Chung, who met violent deaths after being taken into custody.

On 29 March 1981 Amnesty International wrote to the new President, General Roberto Viola, outlining its concerns and making four recommendations which included the publication of information about "disappeared" prisoners and the release of prisoners detained without charge. No reply was received.

Bolivia

Until 17 July 1980, when the interim civilian government of Lidia Gueiler was overthrown, positive measures to protect human rights were implemented. The military coup led by General Luis García Meza, who was immediately installed as President, prevented the transfer of power to the *Unión Democrática Popular* (UDP), Popular Democratic Union, the coalition party which had won the general election on 29 June 1980. Amnesty International's concerns after the coup were arbitrary arrest, detention without trial, torture, "disappearances" and extrajudicial killings.

By September 1980 between 1,500 and 2,000 people had been detained, all without warrant or charge. *Habeas corpus* was to all intents and purposes suspended. There was evidence of widespread torture and ill-treatment of prisoners, and families were refused information. No political prisoners were brought to trial and many were summarily expelled under threat of death. Many Bolivians were killed by the army or paramilitary groups.

Amnesty International issued urgent appeals after the first wave of arrests and killings. On the morning of 17 July 1980 an emergency meeting held in the building of the *Central Obrera Boliviana* (COB), the Bolivian Workers' Confederation, in La Paz was attacked. About 30 people were seized when the building was stormed by a paramilitary group. Marcelo Quiroga Santa Cruz, the leader of the *Partido Socialista 1* (PS-1), Socialist Party 1, a parliamentarian and lawyer, was singled out and shot, reportedly because he had called for an investigation of human rights violations under former President Bánzer. Among those taken into custody were Juan Lechín Oquendo, the Secretary General of the COB; Simón Reyes, a leader of the *Federación Sindical de Trabajadores Mineros de Bolivia* (FSTMB), Trade Union Federation of Bolivian Mineworkers; Líber Forti, a member of the executive of the COB; and Iván Zegada of the *Asambléa Permanente de los Derechos Humanos,* Permanent Assembly for Human Rights. They were all taken to the *Estado Mayor* (the main military barracks) in Miraflores, La Paz, in ambulances commandeered by Colonel Luis Arce Gómez before the coup.

A similar raid on the *Palacio Quemado* (the presidential palace) led to the arrest of ministers of the interim government, as well as about 25 journalists who were taken to the *Estado Mayor* where they were held in the stables, allegedly forced to lie down in dung and kicked, insulted and threatened.

On 5 August 1980 Amnesty International wrote to General García Meza to appeal for the release of all those detained as a result of the coup. It expressed alarm that the Minister of the Interior, Colonel Luis Arce Gómez, had been unable to provide the press with the names or number of people in custody. It deplored the use of ambulances in armed attacks and for taking away prisoners. It asked for information on the health and whereabouts of 55 prisoners. On 14 August 1980 the government replied that Amnesty International's information was based on falsehoods from the press. The Minister of the Interior would publish a list of the names of all political prisoners and details such as their place of detention and the charges against them. However this information has not been made available.

Sweeping arrests were reported in towns and industrial centres throughout Bolivia. In the mining areas of Huanuni, Catavi and Siglo Veinte, where strikes against the coup had been organized, troops attacked with tanks and heavy weapons to put down any resistance to the military take-over. The armed forces also took over or destroyed the miner's radio stations. On 21 August 1980 Amnesty International publicized reports that in early August troops had killed a group of miners and peasants in the mining district of Caracoles, in the department of Oruro, that women had been threatened and ill-treated by troops, and the bodies of the dead removed before they could be identified. A large number of people were reported missing.

Foreign nationals in Bolivia, particularly missionaries and journalists, were also violently treated. Amnesty International made urgent appeals on behalf of three citizens of the United States of America detained in August. Two Maryknoll priests, the Reverend William Coy and the Reverend John Moynihan, were detained by the army in Riberalto, Pando, and accused of being "pro-communist". They were released after a few days. A journalist, Mary Helen Spooner, was arrested on 6 August 1980 in La Paz after she had written an article about members of the military government being involved in cocaine smuggling. In a statement made after her release and printed in the *Financial Times* of London on 15 August 1980 she said that for six days she had been kept in a closet that was four feet square, and had been threatened with death by the Minister of the Interior.

On 8 September 1980, in a pastoral letter entitled "Dignity and Liberty", the Bolivian Bishops Conference expressed its concern about human rights violations including torture of priests and nuns.

Six weeks after the coup the military allowed some 250 Bolivians who had sought refuge in embassies in La Paz to leave the country. At the same time the government granted access to the prisons to the International Committee of the Red Cross (ICRC) and representatives of the Roman Catholic church.

An Amnesty International delegation visited La Paz from 16 to 25 November 1980 to investigate human rights violations. In talks with government officials the delegates raised Amnesty International's concern about the torture and ill-treatment of political prisoners. The authorities assured them that all remaining political prisoners would be freed by the end of November 1980. During the mission many witnesses reported that arrests were continuing, usually during the curfew. Relatives were generally not told where the prisoner was being taken. Some prisoners belonging to left-wing political parties were taken to private houses and tortured. In February 1981 Amnesty International submitted a memorandum to the Government recommending the release of all prisoners of conscience, the investigation of "disappearances" and an immediate end to torture. Although the government's promise to release all political prisoners by the end of November 1980 was not kept, a substantial number of these prisoners were sent into exile during November and December. Others were placed under house arrest.

On 22 January 1981 Amnesty International expressed its concern to General García Meza about the killing of eight members of the *Movimiento de la Izquierda Revolucionaria* (MIR), Movement of the Revolutionary Left, a political party which won six seats in the 1979 election. On 15 January 1981 a group of civilians and soldiers, acting on the instructions of the Minister of the Interior, surrounded a house in La Paz where the MIR were holding a meeting. Although the people inside were unarmed they were killed; according to some reports they were tortured first. Amnesty International called on the government to investigate these events fully and asked for details of Gloria Ardaya and Gregorio Andrade, who had been taken into custody. Among the dead were Artemio Camargo, the union leader in the COB of the FSTBM. He worked in the Siglo Veinte mine and had been in hiding since the coup. Gloria Ardaya and Gregorio Andrade, a leader of the *Federación de Colonizadores*, Peasants' Federation, were held in incommunicado detention for several weeks and tortured. They went into exile. Amnesty International submitted information on these cases to the Inter-American Commission on Human Rights of the Organization of American States (IACHR).

Since the coup torture has been widely used. One of the main centres for torture was the *Servicio Especial de Seguridad* (SES), a special security department created by Colonel Arce Gómez and under the control of the Ministry of the Interior. The most common methods reported by former prisoners were: beatings, burning with cigarettes, water and electric shock torture.

On 2 February 1981 Amnesty International issued an urgent appeal on behalf of a group of four mineworkers arrested on 12 January 1981 in Siglo Veinte and Catavi. On 16 January 1981 more people were briefly detained and beaten. The four miners originally detained — Octavio Carvajal Dalence, Pablo Rocha Mercado, Asencio Cruz and Germán Gutiérrez Ricaldi — were accused of being "subversive delinquents" by the Commander of the Second Division of the Army in Oruro and expelled to Peru. The forcing of dissidents into exile has left hundreds of families destitute.

On 9 March 1981 Amnesty International issued an urgent appeal on behalf of: Julieta Montaño, leader of the *Unión de Mujeres de Bolivia* (UMBO), the Union of Bolivian Women; and Casiano Amurrio, leader of the *Campesinos Independientes,* a peasant organization. Julieta Montaño was placed under house arrest, and Casiano Amurrio was sent into exile after several weeks detention in *Departamento de Orden Político* (DOP), Department of Political Order, La Paz.

Since the coup most political and trade union leaders have been exiled. By 5 March 1981, according to figures provided by the Intergovernmental Committee for European Migration, 840 people had left Bolivia for political reasons. In February 1981 Amnesty International called upon the authorities to allow all those exiled to return.

Brazil

Amnesty International was concerned by the use of the *Lei de Segurança Nacional* (LSN), law of national security, to curb trade union activity and stifle dissent. Although there have been persistent violations of the rights to freedom of expression and association, Brazil showed some improvement in the protection of human rights. President Figueiredo's policy of *abertura,* a program of gradual liberalization, has come under increasing attack from terrorist acts allegedly committed by right-wing extremists.

Amnesty International has no adopted prisoners of conscience in Brazil. It has been concerned about legal proceedings brought under the LSN against a number of journalists, trade union leaders and parliamentarians. In 1979 after a general amnesty which released most of Brazil's political prisoners, the LSN was reformed. Although the penalties for crimes of subversion were reduced, the scope of the security legislation was not limited, and the LSN has been used to restrict legitimate civil and political rights. In February 1981 three journalists working on the left-wing newspaper, *Hora do Povo*, were sentenced by a military court to 18 months' imprisonment for publishing allegations that government officials had misappropriated public funds. The journalists were freed pending the result of an appeal. João Cunha, a member of the Brazilian Congress, was charged with offending the honour of the President after making a speech in April 1980 accusing him of showing "democratic cynicism" towards a strike by metalworkers in São Paulo. João Cunha's case was to go before the Superior Military Tribunal.

On 25 February 1981 a military tribunal sentenced Luis Inacio da Silva, the President of São Bernardo and Diadema Metalworkers Union, to three and a half years' imprisonment for his part in a strike in April 1980 which stopped car production in São Paulo. As a result of the conviction Luis Inacio da Silva, who was also the leader of the newly formed *Partido dos Trabalhadores* (PT), workers party, has been permanently barred by an electoral court from holding any union or political office. Trade union leaders Djalmo de Souza Bom, Enilson Simões de Moura and Rubens Teodoro de Arruda, were also sentenced to three and a half years' imprisonment. Seven others were given sentences of two or two and a half years' imprisonment. On 4 March 1981 Amnesty International expressed its concern about the conduct of the trial to the Minister of Justice, Ibrahim Abi Ackel. Although the foreign minister had given assurances that the trial would be open to foreign observers, the judge excluded them. The defence lawyers petitioned unsuccessfully for the trial to be adjourned, and although neither they nor their clients were in court the judge proceeded to try the accused in their absence.

In March 1981 a judge in the military court in Amazonas summoned Luis Inacio da Silva, other members of the PT and two leaders of *Confederação Nacional dos Trabalhadores na Agricultura* (CONTAG), rural workers' union, to face charges under the LSN of "having incited class struggle by violent means". In July 1980 Luis Inacio da Silva had participated in a meeting in Brasileia, Acre, to protest about the killing of Wilson de Souza Pinheiro, a leader of the rural workers' union. A few days later, a group of peasants killed a local landowner's foreman who was suspected of having killed the trade union leader.

On 4 August 1980 Amnesty International called on the Minister of the Interior, Mario Andreazza, to instigate an inquiry into the murder by gunmen of two leaders of CONTAG Wilson de Souza Pinheiro and Raimundo Lima. On 10 November 1980 Agenor Martins de Carvalho, a legal adviser to CONTAG and the Secretary General of the *Partido do Movimento Democrático Brasileiro,* Brazilian Democratic Movement Party, in Rondônia, was shot dead.

Amnesty International has become increasingly concerned about violence in the interior directed against smallholders and peasants by landowners trying to expel them from their lands. It has received reports of torture and killings. Those responsible were said to be gunmen hired by the landowners, and their illegal actions to have been tolerated by the local police.

Under the Indian Statute, the demarcation of tribal lands should have been finalized by 1979. But only a few reserves have been defined and the lack of clear boundaries has led to many conflicts between Indians and settlers. On 21 August 1980 21 people, including small children were killed by Kayopó Indians in the state of Para, who feared that settlers were moving in to clear their forest lands. In August 1980 a police captain and a soldier in Maranhão were accused of killing members of the Guajajaras tribe by Colonel Nobre de Veiga, the head of FUNAI (the Brazilian Indian Foundation). On 11 September 1980, Norberto de Paula, an Indian leader from Mangueirinha known as "Paraguai", was killed in a mysterious car accident. Amnesty International has asked the authorities to investigate.

In September 1980 after a series of violent attacks by extreme right-wing groups on politicians and lawyers Amnesty International urged the Minister of Justice to investigate. On 4 July 1980, Dalmo Dallari, a prominent lawyer and member of the Justice and Peace Commission, was kidnapped briefly in São Paulo. He was stabbed and badly beaten before being released. On 10 July a bomb destroyed the car of a Federal Deputy, Marcelo Cerqueira, in Rio de Janeiro. On 27 August 1980 a bomb exploded in the offices of the Brazilian Bar Association in Rio de Janeiro killing a 65-year-old secretary. There is evidence that some attacks were the work of individuals attached to the DOI-CODI (the special anti-guerrilla unit). New evidence has come to light about the illicit activities of those involved in past repression. In October 1980 the São Paulo Regional Medical Council ruled that Harry Shibata, the head of the São Paulo Medical Legal Institute, should be struck off the medical register. Shibata had falsified the death certificate of the journalist, Vladimir Herzog, who died after being tortured in the DOI-CODI headquarters in São Paulo in 1975. (See *Amnesty International Report 1976.*) Inês Etienne Romeu, a former political prisoner and torture victim identified a house in Petropolis used by DOI-CODI agents in Rio de Janeiro as a torture centre. She alleged that nine political prisoners detained in that centre had later "disappeared". She named a doctor who had participated in torture by advising her captors about her state of health. Her allegations, reported in the Brazilian press in February 1981, led to a statement from the ministers responsible for the armed forces deploring the "campaign of revenge" by the press.

In December 1980 Amnesty International supported efforts by the Brazilian Bar Association to investigate the case of two students who "disappeared" in 1973. In July 1980 the bodies of Maria Augusta Thomas and her husband, Marcio Beck Machado, were discovered on a small farm in the state of Goiás. Following the discovery a local judge ordered an investigation, but before a full examination could be made the bodies were removed by men claiming to be police agents.

The government has continued to shelter political refugees from neighbouring countries who are awaiting resettlement. However on 30 July 1980 Amnesty International expressed its concern that the new law on foreigners would enable the summary deportation of *de facto* refugees in Brazil without proper papers, and would not allow them to appeal against the decision or seek resettlement in another country.

Security agents from neighbouring countries were still apparently operating in Brazil. On 1 August 1980 Amnesty International issued an urgent appeal on behalf of Father Jorge Oscar Adur, an Argentine national, who "disappeared" in southern Brazil. There were fears that he might have been forcibly returned to Argentina.

Chile

Amnesty International concerns in Chile were arbitrary detentions, including prisoners of conscience, administrative banishment (*relegación*), torture and political killings.

On 11 March 1981 a new constitution came into force. It replaced the 1925 Constitution which had been largely eroded since the 1973 coup by numerous decrees and four constitutional acts adopted by the military *junta* under General Augusto Pinochet. The new constitution was drawn up by a special commission appointed by the military *junta* with no independent lawyers participating. It was adopted by a referendum which took place on 11 September 1980 under the state of emergency, without electoral registers, with all political parties banned, and supervised by returning officers appointed by the government. Dozens of people were arrested for short periods when trying to hold meetings or speak out against the referendum.

The new constitution consists of 115 articles and 29 interim provisions and will not fully come into force until 1997. It incorporates many of the provisions contained in previous decrees and constitutional acts and severely restricts freedom of association, thought and expression. Many of the articles of the new constitution contradict the International Covenant on Civil and Political Rights to which Chile is a party. For example Article 8 stipulates that all organizations that advocate violence, totalitarian concepts or the class struggle are unconstitutional. Article 23 states that trade union leadership is incompatible with membership of a political party.

President Pinochet has been appointed for a renewable term of eight years. During the transition period to 1997, in addition to the authority granted by the constitution (under the states of exception, Articles 40 and 41), he will exercise extraordinary powers. According to interim provision No. 24 "if . . . acts of violence aimed at disturbing public order occur or if there is danger of internal peace being disturbed, the President of the Republic will thus declare it and will have, for six months renewable, the following powers:

(a) to arrest and detain people for up to five days, in their own homes or in places that are not prisons. If terrorist acts with serious consequences occur, this period can be extended for a further fifteen days;

(b) to limit the right of assembly and freedom of information, the latter being only in as far as the founding, publishing and circulation of new publications is concerned;

(c) to prohibit the entry into national territory, or to expel from it, those who propagate the doctrines mentioned in Article 8 of the constitution, those who are suspected or have a reputation of being followers of those doctrines, and those who carry out acts contrary to the interests of Chile or which constitute a danger for internal peace; and

(d) to order individuals to forcibly remain in an urban locality within the national territory for a period of up to three months. . . . The measures adopted by virtue of this provision are not subject to any kind of appeal, except reconsideration by the authority that ordered them."

Interim provision No. 24(a) extends the scope of Decree 3451 issued on 16 July 1980, a few days after the killing of Lieutenant Colonel Roger Vergara, Director of the Army Intelligence School. Decree 3451 lengthened from five to 20 days the period that suspects could be held without charge by the security forces when investigating offences against the security of the state in which people were killed, injured or kidnapped. The security forces, supported by the Minister of the Interior and the Supreme Court, have applied Decree 3451 to many political activists who had not been involved in such offences. José Benado Medvinsky was detained on 16 July 1980, together with Claire Frances Wilson, and held in incommunicado detention at a secret location and tortured for 15 days. After being tortured with electric shocks for several days and at one point being rushed to see a doctor, he was taken away by car. On arriving at an unknown destination:

"they made me get out and put shackles on my feet, they gave me a pick and a spade, I was still blindfolded, and they made me walk a little and took off the blindfold. They all stood behind me with lanterns. It was night time; they made me go down a slight slope . . . they offered to let me say something before they killed me; I replied that I had nothing to say. Then with the pick and spade they made me dig a hole . . .. Every so often they made me stop and offered to let me speak to save my life; I kept saying that I had nothing to add. When I had finished, they made me lay down on my side in the ditch. I heard someone loading a gun and felt it being pointed at my forehead. Someone else said to him: 'Pull the gun back, otherwise you'll blow his brains out'. Before putting me in the hole, they had removed the shackles from my ankles, and told me that they were going to tie them with wire so that it would be known that the DINA [secret police, later replaced by CNI] had killed me. After a while they took me out of the hole . . . and I was taken back to the same place."

He was brought before a court on 31 July 1980. José Benado was not charged with any of the offences set out in Decree 3451. Many other people were illegally detained for 20 days by the *Central Nacional de Informaciones* (CNI), Chilean secret police, such as Carlos Montes Cisternas, arrested at the end of December 1980 (see below). Where Decree 3451 refers to people being killed, injured or kidnapped, interim provision 24(a) of the constitution refers simply to "terrorist acts with serious consequences".

In March 1981 the President declared a state of emergency under Article 41 of the constitution, and proclaimed that Chile was in the state described in interim provision No. 24. The combined effect of these measures amounted to a virtual state of siege.

Under the powers the President gave himself, Gerardo Espinoza Carrillo, an ex-member of the late President Allende's Popular Unity Government, was arrested and expelled from the country for "criticizing the government" and "propagating totalitarian doctrines" in a speech at the grave of former Popular Unity Minister José Tohá González.

About 150 people, mostly students, have been sent into internal exile by the Minister of the Interior on the orders of the President in accordance with Decree 3168 of February 1980, which has been incorporated into the new constitution. There is no right of trial or appeal. Conditions were reported to be harsh: many of the places were remote and inhospitable; the exiles were restricted in their movement; they had to support themselves and it was virtually impossible for them to find work, especially if they were in tiny villages. At least two people have been banished for two three-month periods within a year.

On 21 February 1981 the *junta* passed Decree 3627, under which regional military commanders are to set up war tribunals to deal with "crimes of any kind that, as their main or subsidiary action, had resulted in the death" of government officials or members of the armed forces or police. The decree lays down that the penalties are to be those applicable in time of war. On 10 March 1981 the decree was amended (by Decree 3655) to cover crimes resulting in injury to (as well as the death of) officials, when it could be assumed that they were injured or killed because of the office they held. Chilean human rights groups have said that this will further restrict the right to a fair trial. The Code of Military Justice states that sentences passed by war tribunals can be reviewed only by a military commander — there is no right of appeal to a civilian court. This would be particularly serious with death sentences since military legislation calls for execution to be carried out within three days of sentence. Military courts have functioned in Chile since the 1973 coup and have been widely criticized by independent lawyers and human rights groups for their arbitrary treatment of opposition members on trial. By contrast members of the security forces found guilty of serious crimes have often been granted amnesties by military courts, under the Amnesty Law of April 1978.

Amnesty International received numerous allegations of torture by the security forces. A consistent pattern emerged from the detailed reports: agents of the CNI, the army or the navy seized people in their homes or on the street; they took them, blindfolded, on the floors of vans or cars to torture centres in military barracks or secret locations. There, they were interrogated and tortured for days at a time: commonly with the *parrilla,* a metal grid to which the victim is tied while electric shocks are administered. Severe beatings, threats and humiliation were also reported.

At the end of May 1980, 33 people were arrested in the towns of Antofagasta, Calama and Taltal by members of the regional security forces, presumed to be from the CNI. They did not identify themselves or produce warrants, nor did they carry out legally established formalities such as informing the detainees' families of the arrests. The 33 were accused of being leaders and members of political parties banned under Decree 77 of 1973. They were taken to secret places of detention, of which two were in Antofagasta: one near a beach; the other formerly the property of a religious order, the Sisters of Divine Providence. The detainees were tortured. They were kept hanging upside down by their feet for hours at a time; they were stripped naked and taken outdoors where icy jets of water from a high-pressure hose were turned on them (it was winter in Chile); they were punched and kicked, and given electric shocks in the most sensitive parts of their bodies. Two detainees, Julio Carrillo Cortes and Nolberto Rivera Videla, were treated with particular cruelty: Nolberto Rivera was forced to swallow human excrement and urine; after eight days their limbs were so swollen and bruised that they could barely move about without help from their companions.

Eduardo Andrés Arancibia Muñoz was arrested on 6 September 1980 and kept incommunicado in a secret place by the CNI until 26 September. In a letter to the Supreme Court, he described the treatment he suffered:

> "I was stripped and moved onto a kind of iron bedstead, to which they tied me . . ., they then proceeded to place electrodes on my arms, legs, nipples, stomach and around the anal zone. I felt unimaginable pain causing me uncontrollable convulsions. Such torture went on for eight days."

Eliana Victoria Bravo, detained for several days in September 1980, declared in a writ of *habeas corpus:* "They put me in a bath and held my head under water so that I almost drowned." The high probability of torture being inflicted on political detainees during the first few days after their arrest led Amnesty International to issue 27 urgent appeals on behalf of more than 180 people.

In February 1981 Amnesty International submitted information on torture and other human rights violations to the United Nations Special Rapporteur on Chile. In its statement to the Tenth General Assembly of the Organization of American States held in Washington in November 1980 Amnesty International expressed concern about the repeated abuses of human rights in Chile.

All political parties have been banned in Chile. Those which supported the government of the late President Salvador Allende were banned by Decree 77 in 1973. During the interim period established by the new constitution all political parties and political activities are forbidden until new government regulations come into force, but in any event no Marxist or allegedly Marxist parties will be tolerated. Many people have been convicted of violating Decree 77. Amnesty International was working on behalf of 48 arrested on that charge in Santiago, Antofagasta, Talca and Linares. Some have been adopted as prisoners of conscience, and others were under investigation. On 31 December 1980 economist Carlos Montes Cisternas was arrested; he was held incommunicado for 20 days and reportedly tortured. He was charged with participating in a clandestine political meeting and being a leader of the banned *Movimiento de Acción Popular Unitario* (MAPU), United Movement of Popular Action. Amnesty International has adopted him as a prisoner of conscience.

Under Chilean law (Decrees 1877, 3168, 3451 and Constitutional Acts 3 and 4) detentions can only be carried out after an arrest warrant has been issued by a competent authority. However the CNI have detained people without warrants. Arrest or remand orders were only given after detentions began, sometimes with explicit instructions that the initial 20-day period after which detainees have to be presented before a judge or released was to begin several days after the actual detention, thus "legally" extending the period during which the prisoner was in the hands of the security forces. This is reported to have happened in the cases of Pedro Drago Domancic Kruger and Patricio Pérez Rosales, who were arrested in October 1980.

Amnesty International continued to work on behalf of the many political prisoners who "disappeared" in Chile between 1973 and 1977. In a few cases bodies have been found (see *Amnesty International Report 1980)* and each time the investigating judges have identified members of the armed forces as responsible. However, the military courts have ruled that those found guilty are covered by the Amnesty Law of April 1978. In January 1981 more bodies were found in Alto Molle east of the northern city of Iquique. Preliminary information gathered by the Association of Relatives of Disappeared Prisoners indicated that the remains of several people had been found, and that there were bullet holes in the skulls. The families of 62 "disappeared" prisoners in the region have asked the Court of Appeal to nominate a special investigating judge to examine the case.

More people have died as a result of torture at the hands of the security forces or in so-called "armed confrontations" with them. On 2 August José Eduardo Jara Aravena, a student of journalism, died after he had been kidnapped and tortured by the so-called *Comando Vengadores de Mártires* (COVEMA), Commando for the Vengeance of Martyrs. It was later disclosed officially that the group was made up of members of the *Servicio de Investigaciones,* detectives, who were, according to the authorities, acting on their own initiative. A COVEMA statement dated 6 August announced that they had acted "because of the inability of the security forces and the police" to deal with the violent activities of opposition groups, such as the killing of Lieutenant-Colonel Roger Vergara Campos in July 1980. On 31 July COVEMA kidnapped and ill-treated two journalists, Guillermo Hormazábal from Radio Chilena and Mario Romero. They were released after 10 hours. Although the Chilean authorities themselves revealed the involvement of individual members of the security forces in the kidnapping, torture and death of Jara Aravena, so far nobody has been charged or remanded in custody.

Disturbing facts surrounded the deaths of Oscar Salazar Jahnsen (28 April 1980), Santiago Rubilar Salazar (2 August 1980), Juan Olivares Pérez and Rubén Eduardo Orta Jopia (8 November 1980), Alejandro Rodrigo Sepúlveda Malbrán (24 December 1980) and José Leandro Arratia Pérez (18 January 1981). Alejandro Sepúlveda was the brother of one of the leaders of the *Coordinadora Nacional Sindical,* a trade union confederation that has been declared illegal by the government. In all these cases, relatives' testimonies and eyewitness reports have led the families and human rights groups in Chile to demand investigations. According to the police, Santiago Rubilar Salazar was shot dead in an armed confrontation with the security forces on 28 July 1980 after taking part in a bank robbery. His family maintained that he was arrested on 26 July, together with his wife and brother, by a group of armed civilians. In other cases preventive writs of *habeas corpus* had been filed by the victims shortly before their deaths, because of heavy surveillance by security forces around their homes.

Political prisoners in the Santiago Penitentiary and their families continued to be harassed and several prisoners went on hunger-strike in protest. At the end of January 1981, 55 prisoners held in Calle 5 of the penitentiary were transferred to other prisons in Santiago and the provinces. Most of the prisoners were being tried in Santiago courts and were awaiting sentence or the results of appeals. The transfers made it difficult for relatives to visit and also seriously hampered the work of defence lawyers. In addition, the political prisoners were no longer segregated from the ordinary criminal prisoners. Although Amnesty International does not ask for special treatment for political prisoners, it was concerned that the Chilean Government had violated an undertaking to separate political from ordinary criminal prisoners made to the United Nations Ad-Hoc Working Group which visited Chile in 1978. The undertaking was confirmed in letter No. 1954 of 21 August 1978 from the Minister of Justice to the Minister of Foreign Affairs. The letter said, "In accordance with the undertaking which I gave to the United Nations *Ad Hoc* Working Group on Human Rights on 24 July last, I immediately issued instructions for the physical segregation, in all gaols and prisons throughout the country, of persons indicted or convicted by military courts and/or for offences against the Control of Firearms Act . . .".

Three prisoners, José Benado Medvinsky, Ulises Gómez Navarro and Nelson Aramburu Soto, were later transferred without warning once again. José Benado and Ulises Gómez were said to be in poor health as a result of hunger-strikes in protest at harassment and poor prison conditions. Nelson Aramburu Soto, adopted as a prisoner of conscience, has been in prison since 1974 and should have qualified for release under the 1978 Amnesty Law. After each transfer his whereabouts were unknown for several days and there were fears for his physical safety. He has still not received his final sentence and Amnesty International was dismayed to learn that his trial dossier had reportedly been "lost", which would further delay and complicate the task of his defence lawyer.

The Chilean Government has been criticized for its human rights record by the United Nations General Assembly, the Inter-American Human Rights Commission of the Organization of American States, the International Commission of Jurists, the Inter-Parliamentary Union and other organizations.

Colombia

In August 1980 Amnesty International presented the Government of Colombia with a 258-page report. Based largely on the findings of a mission to Colombia in January 1980 it documented abuses by government forces including arbitrary arrests, torture, and the unexplained killings of peasant and Indian leaders in rural areas. The report, published on 22 September, expanded a memorandum delivered to the government in April 1980. The report emphasized that the state of siege in force almost continuously for 30 years and recent special security laws had facilitated human rights abuses by security forces; in particular by providing for the trial of civilians by military courts on a wide range of charges and with limited rights to defence.

The report cited more than 600 individual cases, a large number in detail, including many extracts from testimonies of prisoners detained in 1979 and early 1980. It detailed interrogation procedures that included torture: hanging by the arms, the use of drugs, electric shock, rape and near-drowning. It also described Colombian army establishments where torture was alleged to have been practised. A doctor took part in the mission and carried out physical and psychological examinations of 27 of the people whose testimonies alleging torture were included in the report. In most cases he found that the evidence was compatible with the allegations of torture and in some cases that "there was clear evidence that the alleged torture had in fact taken place". The report paid particular attention to abuses of power in the extensive rural areas under military control, the so-called "militarized zones". Security measures intended to combat active guerrilla opposition groups affected the peasant population as a whole through "continual searches, detention and use of torture . . ." which created an atmosphere of "permanent threat and terror". The mission delegates visited 11 prisons in seven cities, two military installations used as detention centres, and two hospitals, with the full cooperation of the authorities.

The government responded at length to the April 1980 memorandum based on the mission, describing it as "libellous" and abusive of Colombia's sovereignty. This commentary was included as an appendix to the report published in September 1980, *Informe de una*

Misión de Amnistía Internacional a la República de Colombia. The response to the September 1980 report was limited to a short telegram in which President Julio César Turbay Ayala deplored the "bias" of Amnesty International.

Several testimonies in the mission report alleging torture in army installations and political killings by military personnel have received independent confirmation from a group of officers and non-commissioned officers formerly attached to the *Batallón de Inteligencia y Contra-Inteligencia "Charry Solano"* (BINCI), the Colombian army's chief military intelligence group. The five officers wrote to Amnesty International and other international organizations on 20 July 1980, claiming they had been wrongfully accused of "common crimes" and jailed by military authorities. They alleged the authorities themselves were responsible for ordering serious criminal acts of political repression. The five alleged that they had been ordered by the intelligence batallion headquarters to torture political detainees. They named batallion personnel who had been detailed to serve as a "terrorist group called the Triple A" which murdered several members of the political opposition, and bombed three Bogotá periodicals *(Alternativa, El Bogotano,* and *Voz Proletaria).* The statement did not reach Amnesty International until January 1981 when it was published in several newspapers in Colombia and Mexico. The situation of the officers remained unknown.

The officers' statement described the torture and killing by military intelligence of guerrilla leader José Martínez Quiróz and other prisoners in 1978 and early 1979. In November 1978 the press had reported leaflets announcing the formation of a "death squad" called the *Alianza Anticomunista Americana* (AAA), American Anti-communist Alliance, which claimed responsibility for killing José Martínez Quiróz.

The officers described their involvement in the interrogation of guerrilla suspects in January 1979 in the *Escuela de Caballeria,* Army Cavalry School, in Usaquen, and in a nearby secret detention centre, known as the *Cuevas de Sacromonte,* Caves of Sacromonte. They described the detention and torture of five prisoners for whom Amnesty International had appealed in January 1979, including Dr Olga López de Roldán and a "tall and dark Uruguayan", later identified as photographer Sergio Betarte Benítez, detained in Bogotá on 3 January. Amnesty International later received detailed testimonies from each of the prisoners who claimed independently that they had been taken from detention in the *Escuela de Caballería* to a secret underground installation they could identify only by the name used by their captors, the "Caves of Sacromonte". While none of the prisoners could describe the entrance to the caves or their exact location as they were blindfolded, the testimony of the five officers identifies the Caves of Sacromonte as part of the Army School of Communications at Facatativá (near Bogotá) used for the interrogation of "very special cases":

> "There is a promontory which can be seen at about 300 metres from the entrance or guardpost of the military installations. It is a sort of anti-aircraft shelter . . . artificial caves with a very long corridor, about 150 metres long. At the sides there are three large rooms".

Each of the prisoners described being beaten while hung by their arms. Dr Olga López said ". . . they put my arms behind, they padded my wrists, and with some ropes lifted me up". Sergio Betarte Benítez also said his wrists were padded "with a blanket in order to leave no marks", before being suspended by a rope hanging over a beam. The officers' statement described the torture in the Caves of Sacromonte in almost identical terms, reporting that prisoners were blindfolded, stripped naked, bound, and beaten systematically while suspended from a roof beam with their hands behind the backs. Dr Olga López was released in January 1981, after two years' detention; Sergio Betarte remained imprisoned without trial.

The *Procuraduría General de la Nación,* the National Office of the Attorney General, which has special constitutional authority to investigate reports of human rights abuses in Colombia, was asked in February 1981 by a group of Colombian parliamentarians to investigate the allegations.

Since the April and August 1980 exchanges with the government there have been several significant developments. The April 1980 memorandum had recommended lifting the state of siege, and noted that Colombia was obliged, under the terms of the International Covenant on Civil and Political Rights and the American Convention on Human Rights, to report to the United Nations and the Organization of American States any extraordinary measures restricting human rights, their reason, what rights are suspended, and for how long. In July 1980 the government notified the Secretary-General of the United Nations that by Decree 2131 of 1976, it had been declared "that public order had been disturbed and that all of the national territory was in a state of siege", and that the measure would be lifted "when the necessary conditions prevail".

Government representatives have also described a law of amnesty as a step towards the eventual lifting of the state of siege. Signed into law by President Turbay on 23 March 1981, it granted a four-month amnesty to insurgents who laid down their arms, providing they were not implicated in kidnapping, extortion, arson and other "acts of ferocity and barbarity". After this period the government was to take into account the guerrillas' response to the amnesty in determining whether to accept petitions from prisoners held on charges of or convicted of rebellion, sedition or rioting *(rebelión, sedición o asonada).*

In March 1981 the Supreme Court challenged the legality of the Security Statute decreed under special state of siege powers by President Turbay on 6 September 1978, which provides heavy penalties for a wide range of acts concerning public order, and conflicts with a new penal code that came into force in January 1981. A court decision was pending on whether the entire Security Statute would be annulled, and whether people convicted under the law would benefit from the more favourable terms of the penal code. Should the law be annulled by the court's decision Article 121 of the Constitution allows the executive to decree a similar emergency law immediately which would override the penal code during the state of siege.

Amnesty International continued to receive reports of abuses in the militarized zones, including apparently arbitrary detentions, torture and the killing of captives by local army patrols. Amnesty International made inquiries into a number of cases including that of *campesinos* (peasant farmers) Luis Orlando Rodríguez and his son Federico Rodríguez Contreras. On 29 October 1980 they were apprehended as they were clearing underbrush on their land at Los Regaderos, Tame, in the *intendencia* (county) of Arauca. An army anti-guerrilla patrol, led by officers whose names are in the possession of Amnesty International, tortured the men on the spot, robbed them and forced them and three other captives as yet unidentified to dig their own graves. They were then shot. Regional and national authorities have reportedly obstructed or ignored requests by local community organizations to investigate the deaths, and have refused permission to exhume the bodies.

Most of the *campesinos* reportedly detained in the militarized zones were charged with having "aided guerrillas" by giving them food or shelter. Most were reportedly apprehended in their homes or while working on their own small farms. Abuses reported in Arauca county are generally attributed to army units under the regional command of the VII *Brigada de Institutos Militares,* Brigade of Military Institutes, in Villavicencio, Meta department, south of Arauca.

The cases of six *campesinos* from the Tame, Arauca region, detained in November 1980 were being investigated. They were held in Villavicencio awaiting court martial on charges of aiding the guerrillas; the 12-year-old son of Celino Jaimes Rozo, one of the six, was detained with them for 20 days. Detailed testimonies from three of the men said that they were held bound to posts in the open air at a rural army campsite for the first few days. After four days' detention at the military air base at Saravena a military intelligence officer arrived (whom they named). He beat and kicked them during interrogation while they were held handcuffed, standing, for 48 hours without food and water. One of the six admitted having once given food to guerrillas passing through his farm, but denied being a collaborator.

Similar cases have been reported from Yacopí, Cundinamarca, another militarized zone. It is reported that a system of military passes has been instituted for local residents, and *campesinos* have to report to the Yacopí military base every three, eight or 15 days. One unexplained killing by an army patrol in the Yacopí area was that of *campesino* José Angel Bustos who was shot dead in his house in the village of Bilbao, and whose body was taken away by helicopter. His body was later recovered by members of the community from the army post at Terán, Cundinamarca.

The procedure by which a zone is "militarized" was illustrated in Caquetá county in southeastern Colombia, an area in which the guerrilla groups FARC and M-19 had reportedly been responsible for four kidnappings and 17 murders in 1980. In January 1981 the *Comandante General* (commander general) of the army, Fernando Landazábal Reyes began "Operation Command Number 12" in Florencia, Caquetá, to coordinate the operations of 5,000 troops being sent to the area. The troops included batallions of *Cazadores* (Hunters) and the elite *Batallón Colombia*, special counter-insurgency forces of the army. Eight military districts were established *(cantones militares),* and special travel restrictions, military passes, and regular reporting to military posts were imposed on the population. Several inquiries have been made by Amnesty International into abuses reported in Caquetá in 1981, including the detention in April 1981 of Ignacio Mora, a leader of the Paujil, Caquetá, city council, and his subsequent death at the Paujil military post.

Recently reported abuses by army forces were not limited to militarized zones. Gerardo Antonio Bermudez was detained on 9 March 1981 in a rural area near Barrancabermeja, Santander department. He was handcuffed, told his captors were from the "death squad", and taken on foot into the hills. There he was hung by his arms from a tree and beaten; and the following day he was taken to a cell in the army complex at Barrancabermeja of the *Nueva Granada* batallion. His testimony described in detail torture there by army interrogators including: beatings; immersion in water; being hung by the arms; burns on the back with cigarrettes; forced standing for five days and nights; and electric shocks, including shocks to the tongue. Uniformed army troops detained Marco Fidel Pasos Martínez and

Luis Eduardo Picaso Estrada on 10 January 1981 in Valledupar, Cesar department. The two young men were found dead two days later; their bodies bore marks of torture, and they had been shot by submachine-gun.

Although serious reports of torture have been received in the past year, they differ to some extent from those of 1979 and 1980 when most involved torture carried out in the major military establishments such as the *Brigada de Institutos Militares* in the capital. Many recent reports have been of *campesinos* apprehended in isolated rural areas, who were tortured on the spot in temporary army bivouacs. The methods required no special equipment or technical sophistication: captives were bound to trees or handcuffed to posts, exposed to the sun by day, and insects by night; forced to remain standing for days on end; hung by the arms while beaten by rifle butts; heads were submerged in dirty water. Captives were frequently threatened with the torture or murder of their families.

There has been some evidence of recent initiatives taken against torture by civil police forces. In its response to the Amnesty International memorandum in April 1980, the government had reported the dismissal and imprisonment of one police official involved in torture. Trade unionist Adolfo Leon Pomo was said to have been "tortured by an agent of the F-2 of the police, who seated him on an anthill resulting in insect bites on his genitals". In a similar case, the Attorney General ordered a disciplinary hearing against two agents of the *Departamento Administrativo de Seguridad* (DAS), the civilian political police, for the arbitrary detention and torture of three suspected thieves in Medellín, Antioquia department in July 1979. The prisoners were reported to have been burned with cigarettes, stripped and beaten, and given electric shocks on the genitals and the back; a medical doctor gave evidence confirming that torture took place. In December 1980 the Attorney General ordered the agents to be dismissed, although no criminal or civil charges were brought. Amnesty International received no information on measures to discipline or prosecute military personnel implicated in torture or other grave abuses against prisoners.

During the year Amnesty International worked on behalf of 33 Colombian prisoners adopted as prisoners of conscience or being investigated. Twenty-one of them were released after trial by court martial, after being held in pre-trial detention for up to two years. Eight prisoners whose cases were being investigated were members of the trade union at the Anchicayá Hydro-Electric Power Station and were detained between May and June 1979 on charges of rebellion; six of them have been released.

In March 1981, 74 members of the guerrilla group M-19 were

taken into military custody in the Ecuador-Colombia frontier region: 27 were reported captured by Colombian troops while inside Ecuador, while 47 others surrendered to Ecuadorian authorities in the town of San Lorenzo. Despite requests for political asylum, the Ecuadorian army summarily returned the 47 to Colombia. Ecuador's Foreign Minister, Dr Alfonso Barrera, publicly expressed to Amnesty International his commitment to remain in personal contact with Colombian authorities to ensure the personal safety of the prisoners.

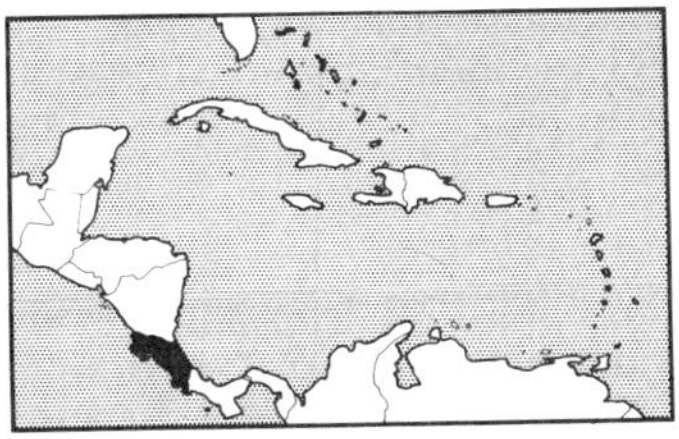

Costa Rica

Amnesty International has been concerned about reports that in the latter half of the year local human rights organizations have been raided and their staff briefly detained, and and that a number of Salvadorian and other refugees have been arrested, apparently without warrant, and expelled from the country. Following a group of such arrests in March 1981 Amnesty International urged Minister of the Interior Arnulfo Carmonoa Benavides not to return a number of Central American refugees to their countries of origin, where in Amnesty International's judgment, their lives would be in danger. Appeals for *habeas corpus* for six exiled Guatemalans who were among the detained were denied, and they were eventually expelled to a third country, on 4 April 1981.

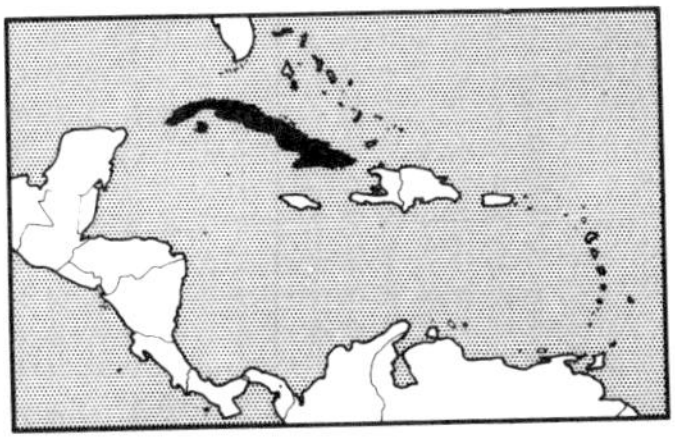

Cuba

The major concerns of Amnesty International were the detention of prisoners of conscience, the death penalty, prison conditions, summary trials, re-sentencing, and allegations of ill-treatment of political prisoners.

About 250 long-term political prisoners were held, most of them in the Combinado del Este maximum security prison in Havana, Boniato prison in Santiago de Cuba and "Kilo 7" prison in Camagüey. The prisoners have refused to obey prison regulations in protest against their treatment as ordinary criminals, and were known as the *plantados*. Many of the 250 political prisoners have spent 15 or more years in prison. Although Amnesty International has not received any evidence that they are prisoners of conscience, it has regularly appealed for their cases to be reviewed and was concerned at reports that many were old and sick, such as Dr José Enrique Velazco Santa Cruz who has spent over 20 years in prison and was said to be suffering from diabetes and cancer of the prostate gland. The *plantados* have gone on several hunger-strikes against alleged ill-treatment and harassment by prison guards. In November 1980 about 100 political prisoners in Boniato prison went on hunger-strike because monthly family visits were suspended. It is alleged that as a result prison guards attacked some of the prisoners; Jorge Vals, Oscar Rodríguez, Onofre Pérez and Ernesto Palomeque were reportedly injured. Amnesty International asked the government for a full investigation and requested that medical treatment be provided to the injured. The protest ended in mid-December, but according to the families of the political prisoners in January 1981 five prisoners were still on hunger-strike. They were: Eloy Gutiérrez Menoyo, Julio Ruiz Pitaluga, Ernesto Díaz Rodríguez, Sergio Montes de Oca and Onofre Pérez. On 23 January Amnesty International asked the government to intervene to protect the health of the five whose lives were thought to be in danger.

Although Amnesty International does not demand special status for political prisoners, it was deeply concerned by allegations that the prison authorities have several times withdrawn food and medical treatment from the political prisoners because they refused to accept new prison regulations. The suspension of family visits was reported to be frequent and arbitrary. Relatives of prisoners in Boniato prison (especially those who were transferred from Havana in July 1979) have sometimes travelled almost 1,000 kilometres from Havana to Santiago de Cuba only to find that the monthly visit had been cancelled without explanation or warning.

Amnesty International believed that only an independent observer with a mandate to visit prisoners and to investigate the allegations of ill-treatment and harassment of the *plantados* could assess their conditions within the context of the general prison regime in Cuba. On 4 December 1980 Amnesty International renewed its appeal to the Cuban authorities to allow such a visit. No answer was received.

The re-sentencing of political prisoners due for release continued to be a major concern. There were at least four prisoners in this category: Fermín Álvarez Santos, Manuel Espinoza Álvarez, Servando Infante Jiménez and José Oscar Rodríguez Terrero, known as "Napoleoncito". The sentences are reported to have been passed without the prisoners having the opportunity to defend themselves.

Amnesty International continued to work on behalf of adopted prisoners of conscience Armando Valladares Pérez and Angel Cuadra Landrove. Both were featured in the *Amnesty International Newsletter* as "prisoners of the month" during the year. An appeal by Angel Cuadra against the remainder of his sentence was rejected by the Supreme Court; the new penal code had reduced the sentence for crimes of the type he allegedly committed. Article 60 of the constitution, on which Angel Cuadra based his appeal, states that penal laws have retroactive effect if favourable to the accused. Amnesty International lawyers' groups continue to campaign for his release. Armando Valladares Pérez has been in the hospital of the Combinado del Este prison since April 1980, after being transferred from an orthopaedic hospital. He has allegedly been kept for several months without medical treatment or exercise in the open air, and without visitors. In a letter smuggled out of the prison, he reported that on 7 February 1981 he was knocked unconscious by a prison guard. It was also alleged that his skin was burnt by a lamp which was held against the back of his neck. Amnesty International has written to the medical authorities at the prison about allegations that Angel Valladares had been denied medical treatment since April 1980.

More than 100,000 Cubans left Cuba during 1980 after some 10,000 had occupied the Peruvian Embassy asking for political asylum (see *Amnesty International Report 1980).* Later in the year the Ecuadorian Embassy and Vatican Legation were occupied by Cubans trying to leave the country, some of whom were armed. In both cases, the Cuban police stormed the premises. It was not clear whether they were authorized by the states involved, and Amnesty International has received reports that after the storming of the Vatican Legation the arrested Cubans, including minors, were summarily tried and some were given 30 year sentences.

Amnesty International received no news of executions during the year, but was concerned about information that death sentences have been passed by the courts and that an unknown number of prisoners in Boniato and Combinado del Este prisons have been sentenced to death for criminal offences. Names received by Amnesty International included: Rodolfo Manuel Alonso Roche, 28 years old; Abilio González Llanes, 26 years old; and Orlando Zuárez (or Suárez) Torres, 20 years old; all reportedly in Combinado del Este; and Reinaldo Masso Garrido (alias "El Caimán") and José Antonio Durruty Faure (alias "Polito"), reportedly in Boniato prison.

Amnesty International was investigating the cases of Adolfo Rivero Caro; Elizardo Sánchez Santa Cruz; Edmigio López Castillo; Ricardo Bofill Pagés, a sociologist and journalist; and Luis Fernández.

They were held on criminal charges such as illegal possession of foreign currency or crimes against the national heritage but their relatives alleged that the real reason was their past political activities and the fact that they have applied for visas to leave the country. It is also alleged that Dr Bofill Pagés and Edmigio López Castillo have been given psychiatric treatment against their will.

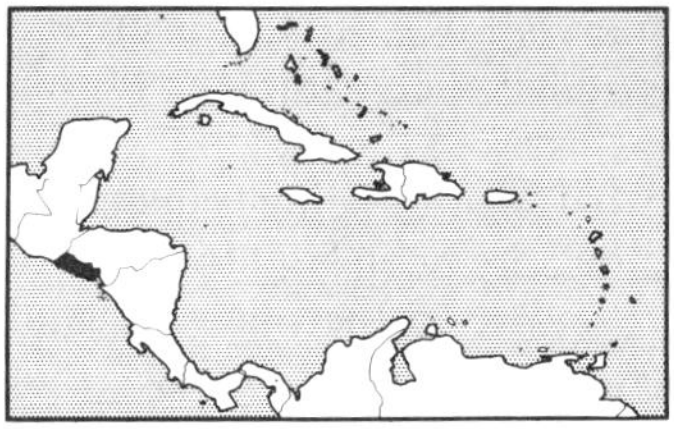

El Salvador

Amnesty International has been concerned about reports that people from all sectors of Salvadorian society have been detained without warrant, have "disappeared" or have been murdered. Although conflict between guerrilla groups and the authorities has escalated and human rights violations by non-government forces have been reported, Amnesty International believes that the majority of the reported violations were inflicted by all branches of the security forces on people not involved in guerrilla activities.

The year has also been characterized by continuing instability in government. Following the overthrow of President General Carlos Humberto Romero in October 1979 by a civilian-military *junta,* the new government announced an amnesty for political prisoners, the restoration of human rights and the implementation of agrarian reform. However in the ensuing months the civilian members of the first *junta* withdrew from the government in protest as the agrarian reform stalled and the repression continued; most went into exile. They had particularly objected to the failure of the authorities either to disband the rural paramilitary group ORDEN (now operating under another name) as recommended in the 1978 Inter-American Commission on Human Rights *Report on the Situation of Human Rights in El Salvador,* or to initiate proceedings against officers implicated in human rights violations. Christian Democrat José Napoléon Duarte joined the government in December 1980 as its civilian President. Colonel Adolfo Majano led the coup which overthrew General Romero in 1979 and had continued to press for land and social reforms. An attempt on his life in November 1980 failed and in December 1980 he was made to leave the *junta.* When he then accused the government of condoning right-wing "death squads" a warrant was issued for his arrest and he was detained in February 1981. Released on 20 March 1981 he reportedly left the country.

Those now in control have implemented what appears to be a systematic and brutal policy of intimidation and repression. When challenged about arbitrary detention, "disappearances" and extra-judicial killings, President Duarte repeatedly responded that his government was under attack from extremist groups of the right and the left who were responsible for many of the abuses. Asked about killings of peasants in strategically important areas where guerrillas were believed to be operating, the government held that many were killed in confrontations with the security forces. In those areas the government appeared to be implementing a counter-insurgency policy that presumed that all civilians were supporters or potential supporters of the armed opposition.

Additional emergency legislation, which contravenes regional and international standards for the protection of human rights, has been passed to legitimize such practices. Decree Law 507, which came into force on 1 January 1981, defines unlawful groups broadly, and under Article 11 statements in the news media that a person belongs to such a group will be sufficient proof. Article 7 permits a secret six-month period of investigation at the pre-trial stage, starting when the detainee is transferred to the custody of the examining judge, and appears to allow at least six months' incommunicado detention. It could be construed as an attempt to legitimize "disappearances".

Many of the "disappeared" and killed were young people; apparently assumed to be sympathetic to the opposition simply on grounds of age. Amnesty International has a photographic record of two arrests on 3 October 1980. Two young men were pictured being arrested by the National Guard who were then shown binding and tying the young suspects before turning them over to men in plain clothes. Five days later their corpses were found showing clear marks of torture.

On 1 November 1980 Gloria del Rosario Rivera, aged 15; Alfonso Román Hernández, aged 22; and 60 others, aged between 14 and 22, were detained in the Colonia Amatepec and Ciudad Credisa in Soyapango, to the east of the capital, by members of the army and security services on a house-to-house search. All were taken away in an armoured lorry. Two days later 15 of their bodies were found in Ilopango. On the same day the bodies of the others were found on the road to Mil Cumbres. All showed signs of torture.

In January 1981, as the guerrillas began their unsuccessful "final offensive", indiscriminate repression against the young intensified. On 10 January troops took 22 teenagers from Mejicanos; all were found tortured and dead. The faces of five of the young women had been obliterated.

On 9 April 1981 Amnesty International publicly urged the

authorities to investigate the massacre which allegedly occurred during the week of 7 April. More than 20 people, including many youths, were killed in the Soyapango suburb of the capital, San Salvador. Unusually, Salvadorian officials, the United States Embassy in El Salvador and the State Department had reportedly acknowledged that an official security unit, the Treasury Police, was involved.

Amnesty International also recorded many abuses directed against children too young to have had any involvement with opposition groups. On 9 July 1980, 31 members of a peasant family by the name of Mojica Santos were reportedly killed by ORDEN members with the complicity of the National Army and the National Police. Those murdered included 15 children under the age of 10. One was only two weeks old.

The children of "displaced persons" fleeing areas of fighting to seek shelter in church-run reception centres in San Salvador and elsewhere have suffered abuses, as have the children of refugees who have sought asylum abroad. Persistent rumours have been received of Salvadorian troops entering Honduras unmolested to pursue refugees, and a number of incidents have been reported in which Salvadorian refugees have been detained with the aid of Honduran troops, taken back across the border into El Salvador, and "disappeared".

A combined military action was reported in May 1980, when hundreds of people, mainly women and children, were killed by Salvadorian troops as they tried to cross the Sumpul River into Honduras, while Honduran troops blocked their way. Both governments initially denied the incident, but a denunciation of the killings by local priests was supported by the Honduran Bishops Council and confirmed by Salvadorian and Honduran human rights groups and eye-witnesses. Later the Salvadorian authorities did state that there had been a confrontation between government forces and guerrillas in the area.

Peasants who survived the massacre later described to visiting foreign delegations of inquiry how Salvadorian soldiers and ORDEN members gathered children and babies together, threw them into the air and slashed them to death with machetes. Some infants were reportedly decapitated and their bodies slit into pieces and thrown to the dogs; other children were reported to have drowned after Salvadorian soldiers threw them into the water.

Similar incidents, involving Salvadorian and Honduran armed forces as well as members of ORDEN, reportedly occurred in March and April of 1981. Amnesty International presented information it had received regarding human rights abuses directed at Salvadorian refugees to international and regional organizations.

Internal refugees or displaced persons fleeing areas where the government's agrarian reform program had been violently imposed and confiscated lands handed over to ORDEN supporters have been removed from church-run relief centres and summarily executed. A government "pacification" program of massive bombings intended to force civilians out of areas controlled by opposition forces had also driven many peasants from their homes.

Clergy, both Salvadorian and foreign, who have denounced such atrocities have themselves been repressed and Amnesty International has repeatedly called for inquiries into the murder and "disappearance" of priests and lay workers including Father Marcial Serrano, parish priest of Olocuilta, kidnapped by the National Guard on 28 November 1980 and still missing.

The assassination of Archbishop Romero, an outspoken defender of human rights, provoked an international outcry. In March 1980 shortly after he had written to President Carter asking the United States of America not to provide military assistance to El Salvador which could be used to perpetrate human rights violations, he was killed while saying mass. Since then there have been reports that the authorities have refused to act upon information about the identities of those behind the Archbishop's assassination.

Slow progress has been made in investigating the murders of four American women whose partially-clothed bullet-ridden bodies were found near Santiago Nonualco, a small town southeast of the capital, on 4 December 1980. All bore marks of strangulation and other physical abuse. A mission of inquiry led by former US Undersecretary of State William Rogers found that there was circumstantial evidence to implicate local security forces. It also found indications that highly placed Salvadorian officials had obstructed efforts to investigate the disappearance and deaths of the four women. The magistrate of the department where the bodies were initially held asked for official protection so that he could give information to the US Ambassador and was reportedly murdered two days later.

After the mission the US suspended assistance to El Salvador until the government clarified the circumstances of the deaths. When the USA resumed its military aid program in January 1981, no charges had been brought nor any criminal proceedings initiated in connection with this incident.

Amnesty International wrote to the US administration of President Jimmy Carter to express its concern at the alleged involvement in human rights violations of official security agencies which could be presumed to be likely beneficiaries of US military aid. In May 1980 the US State Department replied that its assistance was intended to enhance the professionalism of the armed forces.

Following further correspondence with the Carter administration on the subject, Amnesty International welcomed public statements by the new administration of President Reagan when it assumed power in January 1981 that it would continue to be US policy to endeavour to protect human rights in El Salvador; but noted that Amnesty International shared the concern expressed in December 1980 by the United Nations which called upon governments "to refrain from the supply of arms and other military assistance in the current circumstances". After indications that the new administration intended to increase military assistance to El Salvador significantly, Amnesty International announced its intention to urge the new Secretary of State, General Alexander Haig, to review the effects of US assistance programs upon the human rights situation in El Salvador, and to make public the findings of that review.

Academics have been subjected to many abuses. On 10 February 1981 troops burst into a regular meeting of the *Consejo Superior Universitario,* the Supreme University Council, of the National University of El Salvador. Twenty people were detained including the Deans of six faculties and the interim Rector of the National University, Lic. Miguel Parada. Parada's predecessor, Felix Ulloa Martínez, President of the Geneva-based World University Service, died in October 1980 after a machine-gun attack in San Salvador. Ulloa's name had previously appeared on several anonymous death lists. Fourteen of the University Council members detained on 10 February were released shortly afterwards, but there were fears for the safety of the others. However, a journalist eventually located and interviewed them in Santa Tecla prison in the capital.

They described their arrests as the final step in a government campaign to destroy the university, and stated that hundreds of students and professors had been assassinated and the university assaulted by troops on several occassions. The last assault occurred on 26 June 1980 when the institution was completely occupied by troops supported by tanks and helicopters. Students, professors, university administrators and staff, as well as members of left-wing organizations and 15 foreign journalists were taken into custody. At least 22 were reported killed.

Following the publication of their names in the international press, the University Council members were released on 1 April 1981, but approximately 117 other political prisoners remained in Santa Tecla. Many testified that they had been physically and psychologically tortured while in custody. Electric shocks, beatings and the use of hallucinogenic drugs were alleged in attempts to extort confessions of guerrilla involvement. A young teacher, Rafael Carias Flores, displayed large areas of burnt flesh on his arms, legs, body and face, where he said interrogators had thrown sulphuric acid. He also claimed to have been indecently assaulted, and to have had acid poured on his testicles. His two-year-old son was arrested at the same time and has not been located. Four prisoners were reportedly removed from Santa Tecla in September 1980 in reprisal for a hunger-strike calling for a general amnesty and an end to human rights violations and remained missing.

Others held in Santa Tecla included members of the *Sindicato de Trabajadores Empresa Comisión Ejecutiva Hidroeléctrica,* the Hydroelectric Workers Union, which represents workers in the privately-owned electricity-supply industry. They had been jailed after a strike in August 1980. The strike was in protest at a government ruling that the union was unconstitutional under Decree 296 prohibiting trade unions from discussing politics. The discussions in question had dealt with the killings in front of their families of 10 trade unionists who had held meetings to protest against dangerous working conditions.

Also found in Santa Tecla prison was journalist Francisco Ramírez Avelar, who when arrested on 15 January 1981 had been writing for the newspaper *El Independiente*, The Independent, later forced to close. The whereabouts of eight other staff members detained at the same time remained unknown. Ramírez stated that he had not yet appeared before a court, though he had been brought blindfolded and handcuffed before a military judge for questioning, and guns had been jabbed into his chest. He was charged with having served as a link between the news media and the opposition, but he said he had been imprisoned because he had written about the authorities' involvement in political killings. The persecution of *El Independiente* had included several violent attacks on the newspaper's offices, three unsuccessful attempts on the life of its editor, Jorge Pinto, and two failed attempts to arrest him. The only other newspaper that had refused to practice self-censorship, *La Crónica del Pueblo,* the People's Chronicle, closed down in the summer of 1980 after its managing editor and a photographer were abducted. Their bodies were found the next day hacked to death.

Foreign journalists have also suffered. In December 1980 American journalist John Sullivan disappeared from his hotel and has not been heard from since. Nina Bundgaard, writing for the Danish monthly magazine *Politisk Revy* survived detention by the Treasury Police. Arrested on 25 November 1980, blindfolded and interrogated at both Air Force and National Guard Headquarters, the 22-year-old reporter was threatened with death on several occasions and was eventually expelled on 30 November 1980 after intervention by the Danish authorities. Her Salvadorian husband had been killed two days earlier; another friend was kidnapped at his funeral and her dead body later found with torture marks. Mauricio Gamero, a young Salvadorian arrested at the same time as Nina Bundgaard, remained missing. One month later Venezuelan film director Nelson Arrieti was abducted from his hotel by 18 heavily armed members of the security forces in plain clothes. After his release on 18 January 1981 Nelson Arrieti stated that he had been beaten and drugged at the military barracks where he was interrogated.

Salvadorian human rights groups which have tried to inform the international public about human rights abuses have also been decimated by murder and enforced exile. In early October 1980 María Magdalena Enríquez, press secretary of the Human Rights Commission of El Salvador, was abducted and found dead in a shallow grave about 35 kilometres from the capital. Another of its representatives, Ramón Valladares Pérez, was killed on 26 October 1980. The offices of the commission have been bombed frequently since then, and its information and administration secretary, Victor Medrano, was abducted in January 1981 and held by the National Police until 11 February. Attacks have also been mounted against the *Socorro Jurídico,* another body which monitors human rights abuses and which also offers legal assistance to the poor. In mid-December the offices were forced to close temporarily, having been raided 17 times in one week by the National Police, and many of its personnel have been forced into hiding or exile. In early April, a number of *Socorro Jurídico* workers were named on a list issued by the press office of the army as "traitors to their country". Amnesty International issued a press release which expressed regret that the army had published such a list which suggested that official sanction was being given to people wishing to eliminate those who denounced violations of human rights by the security forces. Amnesty International called upon the authorities to protect those named on the list.

Teachers were another profession to suffer repression. From January to October 1980 at least 90 were murdered by uniformed and plainclothes members of the security forces, and at least 19 primary and secondary schools were raided by the security forces. A further 22 teachers were killed in the period 1 January to 1 May 1981, while others have been detained and "disappeared". Many have gone into exile; 85 per cent of the schools in the west of the country have reportedly been closed.

The attacks on teachers appeared to be an attempt to destroy the teachers' union, *Asociación Nacional de Educadores de El Salvador* (ANDES), the National Association of Salvadorian Educators. This union was a member of one of the largest opposition bodies, the *Bloque Popular Revolucionario* (BPR), the Popular Revolutionary Block, which united unions of peasants, teachers, students and shanty town dwellers and was in turn a member of the coalition of opposition parties, the *Frente Democrático Revolucionario* (FDR), the Democratic Revolutionary Front, formed in April 1980.

In November 1980 six FDR leaders, including Secretary General and former Minister of Agriculture under the first post-Romero government, Enrique Alvarez, were kidnapped as they were about to hold a news conference. An estimated 200 men in army and National Police uniform surrounded the area while men in plain clothes arrested the six along with approximately 25 others. The bullet-ridden bodies of the six were later found at a lake near the international airport, showing signs of torture, dismemberment and strangulation.

In December 1980 Amnesty International sent messages to the United Nations, pointing to the overwhelming evidence that Salvadorian troops had been responsible for the killings, and urging member states to condemn these actions which "outraged the minimum standards of government conduct".

A previous submission by Amnesty International to the United Nations Working Group on Enforced or Involuntary Disappearances, included the case of teacher Leonel Meléndez, an ANDES leader. Shot and wounded in May 1980, Meléndez was abducted from the operating theatre of the Rosales Hospital in San Salvador when the hospital was surrounded by vehicles belonging to the National Guard and agents of the National Police.

Throughout the year Amnesty International received similar reports of individuals, in some instances incontestably non-combatants, being removed from hospital and killed, apparently merely because they had sought medical attention after being wounded in the civil conflict. Medical personnel have also been abducted and murdered, apparently for giving treatment to the wounded, including non-combatants. First aid workers have also reportedly been abducted as they tried to transport medical supplies.

In June 1980 and March 1981 Amnesty International launched a campaign to mobilize doctors throughout the world to urge the Salvadorian authorities to protect the health services and bring those who violated its neutrality to justice.

In April 1981 the British charitable agency Oxfam reported that 17 Salvadorians who worked on Oxfam-supported projects in El Salvador had been killed by the army or government-controlled paramilitary forces in the last year. More than 300 people less directly involved in the projects had been killed.

Such atrocities prompted Amnesty International to submit information about the detained and "disappeared" in El Salvador to regional and international organizations. Amnesty International made an oral statement to the UN Commission on Human Rights in

March 1981 in which it estimated that 12,000 people had been killed during 1980 and noted that evidence it had collated from hundreds of individual cases of human rights abuses clearly indicated the responsibility of the regular security forces for the majority. The commission later decided to appoint a special representative to investigate the reported violations. Submissions were also presented to UNESCO and the Inter-American Commission on Human Rights of the Organization of American States. A statement on El Salvador was presented to the Tenth Regular Session of the General Assembly of the Organization of American States, held in November 1980, in which Amnesty International expressed hope that given the continuing gravity of the human rights situation there, the Inter-American Commission on Human Rights would carry out an *in situ* investigation and seek effective means of checking abuses. In March 1981 Amnesty International advised the US section of Amnesty International who testified before the Sub-Committee on Inter-American Affairs to the United States House of Representatives on human rights violations in El Salvador, and urged the sub-committee to uphold human rights considerations as fundamental guidelines in the development of US policy towards El Salvador. In other testimony to the United States House of Representatives a former military doctor in the Salvadorian Army stated that it was the high command of the armed forces, and the directors of the security forces who wielded the power in El Salvador; that the *Escuadrones de la Muerte*, "death squads", were made up of members of the security forces; and that acts of terrorism ascribed to those squads such as political assassinations, kidnappings and indiscriminate murder were in fact planned by high-ranking military officers and carried out by members of the security forces.

During the year, Amnesty International launched 58 appeals on behalf of 472 people believed to have been detained or "disappeared".

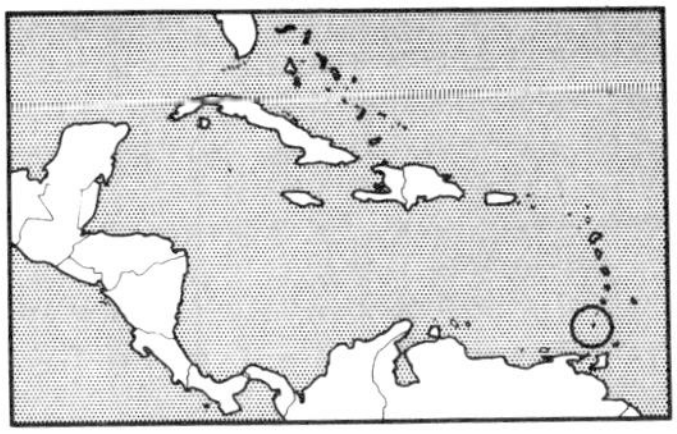

Grenada

The main concern of Amnesty International during the year was the continued detention of over 100 people without charge or trial. Other issues which were raised with the authorities were the alleged ill-treatment of detainees and new legislation providing for the death penalty.

Throughout the year Amnesty International appealed to Prime Minister Maurice Bishop for the release of all detainees not charged with specific offences. Among those held since the coup which brought Maurice Bishop and the New Jewel Movement to power in March 1979 were members of the former government and its supporters. Many people who supported the coup were later accused of plotting to overthrow the present government and detained. Approximately 110 people were held without charge or trial at the beginning of 1981.

An Amnesty International mission visited Grenada in January 1981 to discuss all Amnesty International's concerns with the Prime Minister and in particular to urge that the detainees should be brought to trial, or released. Allegations that some detainees had been ill-treated were also raised.

After this visit Amnesty International wrote to Prime Minister Bishop pointing out that Article 7, paragraph 4 of the American Convention on Human Rights, to which Grenada is a State Party, states: "Anyone who is detained shall be informed of the reasons for his detention and shall be promptly notified of the charge or charges against him". Paragraph 5 of the same article states: "Any person detained shall be brought promptly before a judge or other officer authorized by law to exercise judicial power and shall be entitled to trial within a reasonable time . . .".

Grenada has a mandatory death penalty for murder. The Terrorism (Prevention) Law, 1980, also provides a discretionary death sentence for causing death by explosives or by acts of terrorism. Amnesty International asked the Prime Minister whether the new legislation constituted an extension of the death penalty, and appealed to him for the total abolition of the death penalty in Grenada.

In April 1981 Amnesty International was investigating the cases of 81 detainees.

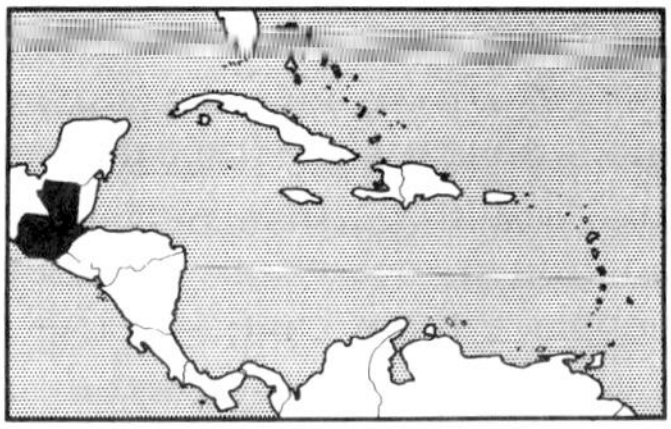

Guatemala

The dominant human rights concern of Amnesty International was that people who opposed or were imagined to oppose the government were systematically seized and frequently tortured and murdered by both uniformed and plain clothed members of the security forces. Arrests without warrant were rarely acknowledged by the authorities, and those detained frequently "disappeared" or were found dead showing clear signs of torture. Often bodies were found far from the place of detention with their features disfigured. To Amnesty International's knowledge the authorities have never conducted a satisfactory investigation into the circumstances under which many thousands of Guatemalans have been killed or "disappeared" in recent years. The authorities have also been unresponsive to repeated requests from Amnesty International and other international humanitarian organizations for such investigations and have consistently failed to address the substance of the complaints submitted to them.

The government attributed such killings to independent groups of the left and right outside its control, or stated that victims died in armed confrontations with the authorities. On 18 February 1981 Amnesty International published a report which concluded that no pro-government groups existed independent of government control, and that government agencies were directly responsible for the killings and kidnappings which the authorities ascribed to extremist "death squads". The report was based on evidence collected since the early 1970s, and included a number of very recent testimonies. One was that of Elias Barahona y Barahona, a former Ministry of the Interior press representative who resigned and fled into exile on 3 September 1980. He stated that the so-called death squads were part of a "program of pacification" carried out by units of the army and police, which used lists of people to be eliminated prepared in a department of the army in the National Palace and approved at meetings held in the palace attended by the Ministers of Defence and the Interior and the Chief of the General Staff of the Army. He said his job at the Ministry of the Interior was to ensure that the press described this government-directed violence as "fighting between clandestine groups of the extreme right and left".

Amnesty International's report included the testimony of a man kidnapped and tortured by the army, who described being beaten and kicked, pulled up by his testicles and smothered with the inner tube of a truck tyre impregnated with quicklime. Before his escape from a military base in Huehuetenango he had witnessed three prisoners being garrotted. A former conscript soldier of Kekchi Indian origin described his training, during which he and other new recruits were told that it was their constitutional duty as soldiers to kill subversives. He related how squads which had killed while in plain clothes were sometimes then ordered to investigate these same murders, this time in uniform.

The report included examples of recent kidnappings and killings, and noted that some 3,000 people had been found murdered after being seized in the first 10 months of 1980 alone. The report was released with a list of 615 people who had "disappeared" after being detained by security forces since President Romeo Lucas García took office in July 1978.

Even before they received the report the Guatemalan Government rejected the conclusions of the report, and accused Amnesty International of interfering in its sovereign affairs and impugning the honour of the President. However when questioned by the press about Amnesty International's findings, the former Vice-President of Guatemala, Dr Villagrán Kramer, stated that he had learned about the system while in government and did not doubt that most killings were decided upon in the presidential palace. Dr Villagrán had threatened to resign if the violence was not controlled, and went into exile in the United States of America on 1 September 1980.

Leaders and potential leaders of popular movements, as well as thousands of peasants and workers, believed to have had no political involvement have been eliminated in government-controlled killings. In many cases the authorities who direct police and army units to kill individuals or cause them to "disappear", are believed to be working from lists of subversives first drawn up after a coup in 1954. These lists are now believed to be held in the central files of the army intelligence division. For instance, some observers attributed the submachine-gun attack in September 1980 on Professor Lucila Rodas de Villagrán, 60, head of a girls' school, to her active membership in her youth of the *Partido Acción Revolucionaria*, Revolutionary Action Party, which ceased to exist more than 25 years ago.

On 28 May 1980 former Christian Democratic Congressman, Julio Hamilton Noriega, was murdered in El Quiché. The *Ejército Secreto Anticomunista* (ESA), the Secret Anti-Communist Army, one of the so-called "death squads", claimed responsibility for this killing. The ESA's name frequently appears on the periodic "death lists", which Amnesty International believes were prepared by the authorities. The killing was apparently a reprisal for the Christian Democrats' statement denouncing violence and the killing of two of its members, and the kidnapping of another on 22 May 1980. After Julio

Hamilton Noriega's death, the Christian Democrats announced that they would close their offices throughout Guatemala, but the killings continued.

Three Christian Democratic mayors were shot in June 1980 and one abducted in November. In February 1981 one person was killed and three wounded in front of the Christian Democratic offices in Guatemala City during an apparent attempt on the life of the party's leader, Vinicio Cerezo Arevalo. Two Christian Democrats arrested after the attempt on Cerezo's life were located in custody and turned over to the jurisdiction of the courts after foreign diplomats had intervened on their behalf. The Christian Democrats appeared to have lost yet another member of their national committee when Joaquín Aguirre Villatoro was kidnapped on 7 April 1981.

Members of the opposition party *Frente Unido de la Revolución* (FUR), the United Front of the Revolution, whose leader Manuel Colom Argueta was killed in 1979 in one of Guatemala's many thousands of unsolved political murders, have also been attacked. Rogelio Barillos, a FUR leader, was killed on 8 May 1980; and Marco Tulio Collado Pardo, a mayor in the department of Escuintla, and Vice-President of the FUR executive committee, was attacked on 8 July with a machine-gun and his bodyguard was killed.

Trade unionists have also been attacked. A list of missing workers, peasants and trade unionists compiled by Amnesty International indicated that between 1 May 1980 and March 1981, 77 workers and trade unionists taken into custody were missing and 47 had been killed.

On 27 May 1980 Marlon Mendizábal García, a trade union leader at the *Embotelladora Guatemalteca S.A.* (EGSA), Guatemalan Bottlers, became the fourth worker to be killed by "death squads" and the third Secretary General of the trade union to die in 17 months. On 20 June 1980 Edgar René Aldana, executive committee member at EGSA, was abducted and his bullet-ridden body was found later that day. When trade unionists met on 21 June 1980 at the headquarters of the *Central Nacional de Trabajadores* (CNT), the Guatemalan Workers' Congress, to discuss René's funeral, police sealed off the road and 25 plain clothes policemen broke into the offices and arrested 27 people. The police originally denied that the trade unionists had been detained, but then Vice-President Villagrán Kramer disclosed that he had asked the President of the Guatemalan Supreme Court to initiate *habeas corpus* proceedings on their behalf. In response to renewed appeals in August 1980, Labour Minister Carlos Alarcón Monsanto wrote that the detained trade unionists had been released. However there has been no further word of the missing people and it is feared they may have been buried in secret graveyards.

In January and February 1981 alone, five such secret burial grounds were found and 45 corpses recovered. In November 1980 Amnesty International received a detailed account of one such secret graveyard near San Juan Comalapa. In March 1980, 38 corpses had been discovered in a deep gorge near that village. Among them was the body of Liliana Negreros, detained during a funeral procession held in memory of 21 Indian peasants who burned to death when police attacked demonstrators in the Spanish Embassy in January 1980. Amnesty International's informant has visited the site and confirmed that at least 30 more bodies had been found in the gorge since the March exhumation. He stated that many corpses still lay in the common grave, and believed the leaders of the local earthquake construction committee, seized and murdered from March to October 1980 by local army units, to be amongst them. They had apparently been killed in line with a general government policy to eliminate any organization which could become a focus for opposition activity.

The policy of intimidating and eliminating leaders or potential leaders of community development projects which might support anti-government activity or provide alternative finance for peasants and thus pose a threat to land owners' labour supplies, has also been directed against foreigners working with legally recognized aid agencies. On 10 October 1980 Veit Nicolaus Stoscheck, a citizen of the USA working as an agricultural assistant in Chimaltenango, was abducted by five gunmen believed to be plain clothes members of the security forces. His body was later found in Antigua, with multiple head injuries and marks of torture.

Lay workers, priests and foreign missionaries have also been defamed in government and anonymous propaganda. The attacks were apparently in retaliation for shielding local Indians from ill-treatment and helping them organize to protect their rights. The Justice and Peace Committee, a human rights monitoring organization founded in 1978, has been vilified and threatened with violence in anonymous press advertisements and leaflets attributed to a non-existent Guatemalan Section of Amnesty International. The Jesuits have been similarly threatened and many foreign priests have been forced to leave the country after receiving death threats. The government withdrew the visas of some religious workers while they were abroad.

Others have been murdered. Father Walter Voordeckers, a Belgian missionary, was killed on 12 May 1980 shortly after he had publicly prayed for the release of his close friend and colleague, Father Conrado de la Cruz, a Filipino member of a Belgian order who had "disappeared" with his assistant Herlindo Cifuentes on 1 May 1980, after being detained with 44 others participating in May Day demonstrations in the capital. The bodies of some of those arrested at the same time as Father de la Cruz and Herlindo Cifuentes have since been found, but the priest and his assistant are still missing.

On 4 June 1980 Father José María Gran Cirera of the Spanish Order of the Sacred Heart was killed with his sacristan Domingo Bats, between Juil and Chajul. The Ministry of Defence alleged that they died in an armed confrontation, but this was denied by the Justice and Peace Committee. Two other priests from the same order were killed in subsequent months. One had been tortured.

Guatemalan priests and lay workers have also suffered repression, often in connection with efforts to help *campesinos* (peasants) claim compensation after their lands had been confiscated by local landowners. Some have been abducted and have since "disappeared", including 11 who "disappeared" from Santiago Atitlán between October 1980 and January 1981.

Increases in killings and "disappearances" in rural areas could often be linked to government suspicions of guerrilla activity in the area, or to the discovery of minerals or other natural resources making Indian lands more desirable. The authorities frequently claimed that the victims have "disappeared" or have been murdered as the result of guerilla actions, or, as was alleged in the case of Father Gran Cirera, that they have died in armed confrontation with official security units.

A number of guerrilla groups have been operating since the mid-1960s, and Amnesty International was aware of reports of escalating conflict, particularly in the countryside, between government and guerrilla forces, with lives lost on both sides. However Amnesty International did not accept government assertions that all or most killings in the rural provinces were the result of armed conflict or the work of agents operating independently of government control. Non-violent community leaders and politically inactive peasants have often been killed by the army in areas where guerrillas were believed to be operating.

On 13 June 1980 approximately 100 men and boys were taken from three villages in the department of Escuintla in a military operation involving the army and the *Guardia de Hacienda* (Treasury Police). Their families initially suspected that they had been forcibly recruited for military service, a frequent occurrence in rural areas with large Indian populations. However there has been no further word of the missing men, and a delegation of relatives which travelled to the capital to ask the President of the Congress to intervene were refused an audience. In July 100 *campesinos* who had taken part in strikes for an increase in the minimum wage "disappeared" from around the Tiquisate area.

The Guatemalan Church in Exile (the bishop, priests and nuns who had been working in El Quiché but were forced to leave in July 1980 after death threats and the killing of some of their colleagues) denounced in early February 1981 the killing by the army of an estimated 168 people in the villages of Papa Chala, Patzaj and Panincac in the municipality of Comalapa, department of Chimaltenango, an area where guerrillas were believed to be operating. A new-born baby was reportedly kicked to death by soldiers.

Some peasants appear to have been killed in reprisals for losses suffered by the army in clashes with the guerrillas. In January 1981 troops who had been ambushed near Santiago, Sololá, retaliated by arresting 14 peasants who were picking cotton nearby. The detainees were flown out of the area in army helicopters. Three days later their bodies were found along the shores of Lake Atitlán, bearing signs of severe torture. All had been garrotted.

In a similar case on 9 April, 24 peasants including a five-year-old child were reportedly hacked to death with machetes by 60 members of the security forces who occupied the village of Chuabajito, in Chimaltenango. There were fears for the lives of two peasants who were left for dead, but survived, and have been removed to the departmental capital for treatment. Amnesty International knows of six witnesses to abuses by the security forces who were removed from hospital and killed in September 1980 alone.

Student Victor Manuel Valverth Morales survived an attempt to remove him from a medical centre where he was being treated after being assaulted by police. He was seized at gunpoint on 19 June 1980 inside the School of Engineering of the National University of San Carlos (USAC) in Guatemala City by two men in plain clothes, who did not identify themselves as law enforcement officers or produce a warrant but shot him several times when he tried to escape. When his attackers tried to remove him from the university medical centre they were overpowered by other students who came to his assistance. Uniformed army troops then attacked the students, who killed one of the two original assailants in reprisal. The students found a card on him which identified him as a military intelligence agent from the "General Aguilar Santa María" army base in Jutiapa province. The second man carried an identity card issued by the *Servicio Especial* (Special Service) of the *Guardia de Hacienda*. The wounded student was eventually able to take advantage of political asylum offered by the Costa Rican Ambassador, but many others have been less fortunate.

The National University of San Carlos has allegedly been the target of a program of government repression intended to destroy it. Officials have often denounced the USAC as a "centre of subversion", and during the year many students have been killed in demonstrations or as a result of indiscriminate police fire. A further 71 have reportedly been killed in detention over the same period. One such incident followed an attack on the Vice-Minister of the Interior, Juan de Dios Reyes Leal, on 19 August 1980. The following day the bodies of nine youths were found on the spot where the official had been wounded, with a note describing them as members of a left-wing guerrilla group. All had apparently been tortured and strangled to death; their bodies were mutilated with machetes. Two were identified as agronomy students detained the previous week. All of the dead had reportedly been in custody and had been executed by the security forces in reprisal.

During the year at least 53 teachers were shot dead while from March to September 1980 at least 27 staff of the University of San Carlos were killed. Amongst those who died at San Carlos were 12 members of the law faculty, while the Guatemalan newspaper *El Grafico* estimated in January 1981 that 35 other lawyers had been murdered by "death squads" in the previous year. In February *El Grafico* reported yet another killing at the university: Oscar Arturo Palencia, Director of Publications. An estimated 50 USAC staff members have gone into exile, following Rector Saul Osorio, who left the country in April 1980.

Many journalists, threatened because of their reporting of the violence, have also fled into exile. The external commission of the *Sindicato de Trabajadores en los Medios de Comunicación Social* (SIMCOS), the Guatemalan journalists' and radio and television commentators' trade union, has listed 12 forced into exile for political reasons from May to December 1980. Many left after their newspaper offices or broadcasting stations had been bombed or shot at by machine-guns. Over the same period the SIMCOS document records the deaths of 13 journalists and the "disappearance" of four others, including Gaspar Culán Yataz, director of the radio station *La Voz de Atitlán* (The Voice of Atitlán), who was twice wounded in the head on 25 October 1980 as he was being apprehended by soldiers in civilian dress. He has not been seen since.

Alaide Foppa, 65-year-old journalist, art critic and professor at Mexico City's National Autonomous University (UNAM) went to Guatemala to visit her family. A resident of Mexico for some years and a member of the Mexican Section of Amnesty International, she was kidnapped and "disappeared" on 19 December along with her chauffeur. Despite inquiries from the Mexican Government and widespread international appeals, her whereabouts are still unknown.

Amnesty International has launched 44 action appeals on behalf of approximately 252 people who have "disappeared" or been kidnapped or arrested over the year. Forty-one "disappearance" cases have been assigned for investigation by Amnesty International groups. Three campaigns by members of Amnesty International medical groups have been initiated on behalf of medical personnel detained or "disappeared" in Guatemala, and on behalf of people who survived attacks and were taken into medical care, but whose lives were still believed to be in danger.

In addition, Amnesty International launched a special campaign on trade unions and companies in Guatemala in March 1981. This campaign was motivated by its concern that employers in Guatemala and international businesses with interests there had avoided responsibility for preventing the kidnapping or killing of their employees. Certain evidence also indicated that some employees of international companies appeared to condone these killings and abductions. The campaign was aimed at making international trade union confederations and international companies aware of human rights abuses in Guatemala, and at securing statements from them expressing concern. It was also hoped to encourage the companies to take steps to protect their employees from human rights violations and to investigate cases where their workers were killed or have "disappeared".

One such agreement was reached on 20 December 1980 between trade union representatives and the new managers of the EGSA, the Coca Cola bottling plant in Guatemala City, after the factory was transferred to a group of Central American investors on 5 September 1980, after an international outcry at the human rights abuses which had been suffered by its employees.

On 12 January 1981 Amnesty International submitted to the United Nations Working Group on Enforced or Involuntary Disappearances a list of 615 people who had "disappeared" in Guatemala after being arrested by the security forces between July 1978 and 31 October 1980. Other smaller groups of cases or individual cases were submitted to this body for consideration with requests for urgent intervention. Amnesty International also made available its report on Guatemala to members of the UN Commission on Human Rights during February 1981. In an oral intervention to the commission Amnesty International drew attention to the problem of politically-motivated government murders there. The commission decided to ask the UN Secretary-General to collect information on the human rights situation in the country and pursue contacts with the authorities.

On 23 September 1980 Amnesty International provided the Inter-American Commission on Human Rights of the Organization of American States with 10 cases which it considered representative and suggested that the commission might visit several government installations which Amnesty International believed to be instrumental in the government's policy of secret detentions, "disappearances" and assassinations. These included the telecommunications centre in the presidential annex, believed to be coordinating secret and extra-judicial security operations. Several alleged interrogation centres, a notorious secret cemetery, and a number of public hospitals where victims of killings were customarily taken for obligatory autopsies were also suggested. Amnesty International urged the commission to pursue its investigation of cases previously raised by Amnesty International which have still not been adequately investigated by the Guatemalan authorities.

Guyana

In June 1980 an Amnesty International observer attended the trial of Dr Walter Rodney, Dr Rupert Roopnarine and Dr Omawale, leading members of the opposition Working People's Alliance. The three academics faced charges of arson after the destruction by fire of a government ministry and offices of the ruling People's National Congress party in July 1979. The trial was adjourned on 6 June 1980. On 13 June Dr Rodney was killed in a bomb explosion. On 18 June Amnesty International urged Prime Minister Forbes Burnham to allow an independent inquiry into his death, in view of the considerable international concern which it had created. No response was received and no independent investigation has taken place.

In December 1980 Amnesty International's observer returned for the resumption of the trial of Drs Roopnarine and Omawale, but after two days it was again adjourned. The trial re-opened in February 1981, but was later adjourned until April.

Allegations that defendants in a treason trial had been ill-treated during interrogation in June 1980 were upheld in April 1981 by the magistrate hearing the case, who ruled that statements made by four defendants were inadmissible because they were not freely given to the police.

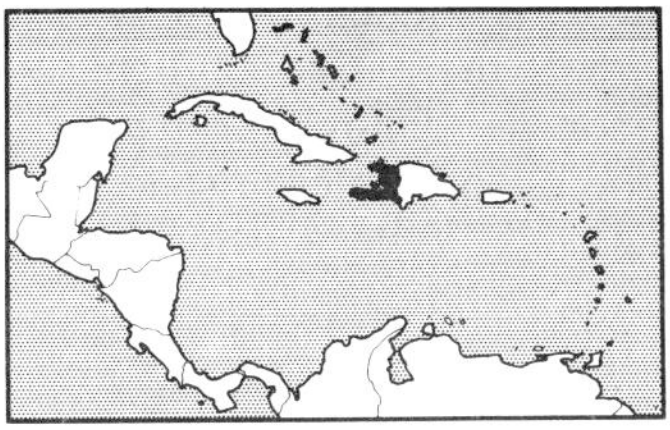

Haiti

Amnesty International was concerned about arbitrary arrests, prolonged detention without trial, allegations of ill-treatment in police custody, torture and poor prison conditions.

Sylvio Claude, who founded the *Parti démocrate chrétien haïtien* (PDCH), Haitian Christian Democrat Party, in 1979, was arrested twice in 1979, released in April 1980, and again arrested in October 1980. Many supporters of his party were arrested in the following few weeks, including his daughter Marie-France Claude, Vice-President of the PDCH, on 27 October, and his son Clervio Claude on 24 November. They were considered prisoners of conscience by Amnesty International.

Between October and December 1980 a wave of arrests took place, the largest and most significant since the amnesty granted to political prisoners by President-for-Life Jean-Claude Duvalier in September 1977. Amnesty International estimated that several hundred politically-motivated detentions took place. Many of those arrested were later expelled from the country, including Pierre Clitandre and Jean-Robert Hérard, editor and deputy editor respectively of *Petit Samedi Soir,* the most important opposition weekly magazine; Grégoire Eugène, founder of the *Parti démocrate chrétien d'Haïti du 27 juin,* Haitian Christian Democrat Party of 27 June, and editor of *Fraternité;* Richard Brisson and Michèle Montas from the independent radio station *Radio Haïti-Inter;* Marc García from *Radio Métropole;* and Yves Richard, a trade unionist and Secretary-General of the *Centrale autonome des travailleurs haïtiens,* Autonomous Congress of Haitian Workers. Yves Richard later gave the following account of his arrrest:

> "I was arrested without warrant at 10 o'clock in the morning during a meeting I was holding at the office of the well-respected Salesian fathers with 35 exploited workers from the textile company DESDAN. Without warning, a group of *tontons-macoutes* [Haitian paramilitary forces] burst in, and, without more ado, started beating up the workers. Fellow trade unionist Siméon Jean-Baptiste was killed by a bullet from the guns of the *tontons-macoutes* of Jean-Claude Duvalier. I was taken with the other workers to Casernes Dessalines (an army barracks) where we were interrogated under torture and accused for the first time of being arsonists and communist agitators. From that moment, I was kept completely separate from the other workers

and transferred to the underground cells hidden below the *Palais national* [National Palace], where there is no daylight. Thanks to the electric torch of the prison guard, however, I was able to distinguish skeletons, probably those of former prisoners, lying here and there on the ground. It was like living a nightmare inside a mass grave under the *Palais national*."

Amnesty International was investigating the cases of about 80 prisoners in detention, most of whom were arrested during 1980. Almost all independent journalists, broadcasters, human rights activists, lawyers defending political detainees and opposition leaders in the country were arrested or expelled during 1980, putting an effective end to the already limited rights to freedom of assembly, association, expression and information. On 30 November 1980 Colonel Jean Valmé, the Chief of Police, explained that the arrests were necessary because "national and international communist agitators connected with the media have for several months been undertaking subversive activities both in the capital and in certain provincial towns with a view to creating a suitable climate for carrying out terrorist and criminal activities". However, with the exception of four people accused of arson whose confessions were allegedly obtained under torture, and Marie-France and Sylvio Claude, the detainees have not been charged or brought before a judge. The so-called "anti-communist" law of 28 April 1969 punishes "communist activities" with the death penalty.

Amnesty International received many allegations of ill-treatment and torture. Lafontant Joseph was arrested on 28 November 1980; a lawyer and the General Secretary of the *Ligue haïtienne des droits humains,* Haitian Human Rights League, he had defended four Amnesty International adopted prisoners of conscience (Ulrich Désiré, Emmanuel Noël, Gustave Colas and Robert-Jacques Telusma) during their trial in August 1980 when they were sentenced to 9 years' imprisonment. He was leaving the Law Courts in Port-au-Prince where he was attempting to represent 60 workers from the national brewery who were under threat of arrest when he was forcibly detained by five men in civilian clothes. He was reported to have been severely ill-treated before being released in December 1980. A demonstration outside the Law Courts by 48 members of the *Centrale autonome des travailleurs haïtiens* in support of the workers from the national brewery was broken up by the *tontons-macoutes* and all 48 workers were arrested. They were taken to Casernes Dessalines where they were reportedly tortured. It is believed they were still in detention at the end of the year.

Evans Paul, a radio journalist, was arrested on 16 October at Port-au-Prince airport after returning on a flight from New York, held incommunicado for 10 days and tortured. He was released without being given any explanation of his arrest. He later described how he was tortured. After being stripped,

> "I was hit in the face. I was slapped (fingers were poked in my eyes and my ears were beaten with the lower part of the palm near the wrist). It's a demoralizing sort of punishment which makes you lose your calm. Almost without a break, several people with sticks took over and gave me a severe beating. A man known as 'Baron' or 'nég marron' came into the room and said, 'But he's too comfortable here. Wait a minute.' Then he took a nylon thread and tied my wrists behind my legs (the scars are still visible). He pushed a long stick between my legs and arms. I was like a ball. I felt as if my body was going to break everywhere. At that point I was beaten with sticks. At one point I felt as though I was going to die. They gave me something to drink. Then they started again even worse. The skin on my buttocks had been torn away. The blood was running down. They weren't put off. On the contrary, you could say that the sight of my blood excited them even more. When I was on the point of dying, they untied me and dragged me to a dark cell. You couldn't see anything. My buttocks felt as if they'd become as big as pumpkins. Next day I had a terrible fever."

Among the people reported to be in detention were several workers and trade unionists who were arrested in July and August 1980 either during industrial disputes or for trying to set up independent trade unions. They included: Antoine Baptiste, Gabriel Marcel, Maurice Lafontant, Massillon Jean, Louis Brutus, Wilner St.-Fort, St.-Armand Mondésir, Ricot Lemoine, Georges Mondésir and Jean-Robert Désir. Two people, René Ermonce (or Hermance) and Ansélus Noël, were held after the Government of the Dominican Republic deported them. They had been refused entry by both the French and Spanish authorities. Amnesty International has expressed its concern to the French authorities about deportations of Haitians back to Haiti where they may face persecution.

Ex-prisoners have described the overcrowded and generally poor conditions found in Haitian prisons. It has been reported that children have been imprisoned for poking their tongues out at the police. Although Amnesty International has not confirmed this, it was consistent with the powers enjoyed by the paramilitary forces known as *tonton-macoutes,* officially named *Volontaires de la sécurité nationale,* National Security Volunteers. They have reportedly arrested people arbitrarily, ill-treated them and then released them for money. One refugee now living in France told Amnesty International that she had been detained by a *tonton-macoute* because she had refused to have sexual relations with him.

A delegation from the Inter-American Commission of Human Rights which visited Haiti in August 1978 published its report during 1980. The findings were consistent with Amnesty International reports on Haiti.

Some of the conclusions were as follows:

> "3. There are reliable indicators that many individuals were victims of torture inflicted in certain cases by the neighbourhood chiefs, both during interrogations after arrests and during imprisonment.
>
> 4. It has been proven that numerous persons are detained without having benefitted from any form of legal procedure, and without having access to an attorney. There is no clear-cut separation of powers in Haiti. Legal guarantees are seriously restricted by virtue of the 'state of seige' which is in effect on an almost permanent basis, and by virtue of the Security Court instituted by the law of August 25, 1977, establishing procedures with limited guarantees as to the right of a legal defence. The Judiciary does not appear to have the independence necessary to exercise its functions.
>
> 5. It may be said that freedom of inquiry, opinion, speech and dissemination of thought does not exist. There are taboo questions which cannot be discussed, such as all matters concerning the President's family, the dictatorship, the extra-budgetary revenues of the *Régie du Tabac,* [state-controlled tobacco industry] etc. There is recourse to procedures such as warnings and admonitions of increasing severity to journalists, issued by the Ministry of the Interior; there is also prior censorship, closing of newspapers, threats, assaults and incarcerations . . .
>
> 7. Freedom of association is extremely restricted. Article 236 (bis) of the 1948 Penal Code, which requires government authorization to form a group of more than twenty people, prevents the creation of any literary, political or other type of association. Trade union freedom does not exist as such. There are neither federations nor confederations or trade unions; the right to strike is limited. The government has made it difficult to form political parties and associations in general."

Amnesty International made a statement to the General Assembly of the Organization of American States held in Washington in November 1980 on human rights violations in Haiti.

Amnesty International has been deeply concerned about Haitian refugees who have fled from their country, often taking great risks, because of the repressive climate. Amnesty International has written to the governments of the United States of America, Jamaica and the Bahamas about the dangers of ill-treatment and imprisonment facing Haitians if they are sent back. In October 1980 the Haitian police fired on Haitians who were trying to board a boat in Cap-Haïtien. Several people were reported drowned or injured in the panic which followed. Amnesty International asked the President-for-Life for a thorough inquiry.

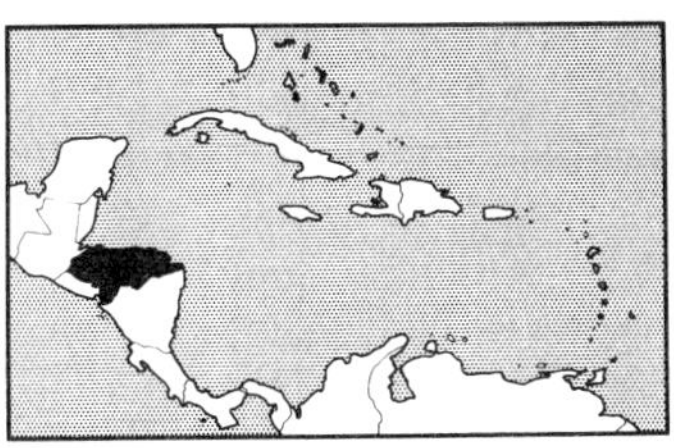

Honduras

During the year Amnesty International received an increasing number of reports of human rights violations, involving both Salvadorian refugees and Honduran citizens, including arbitrary arrests, torture, kidnappings and killings, allegedly committed by both Salvadorian and Honduran security forces and paramilitary groups.

The armed forces have been in power since a 1972 coup, and President General Policarpo Paz García has ruled the country directly since a bloodless coup in 1978. Domestic and regional tensions threatened a planned return to civilian rule, and it was within this unsettled context that Amnesty International followed reports of human rights violations: including the forcible repatriation of Salvadorian refugees back into El Salvador with the aid of Honduran security units; joint Honduran-Salvadorian military operations along the border to stop refugees entering Honduras; and the arrest, torture and extrajudicial execution of both Salvadorian refugees and Hondurans, including political activists, trade unionists, *campesinos* (peasant farmers), religious workers, and Hondurans working with Salvadorian solidarity groups and refugee assistance committees. Reports have also been received that paramilitary squads have emerged and issued death lists.

Amnesty International was gravely concerned about reports that people trying to escape fighting in El Salvador and seek refuge in Honduras had been massacred. During 1980 there were moves towards settlement of the long-standing border dispute between El Salvador and Honduras, and these moves coincided with reports that the security forces of the two countries had cooperated in preventing refugees entering Honduras and in forcibly returning refugees. In May 1980 hundreds of refugees were reported killed at the Sumpul River during a joint operation by Honduran and Salvadorian troops (see El Salvador). Amnesty International directed appeals to both governments expressing alarm at the reports of the indiscriminate killings by security forces and members of the Salvadorian rural paramilitary group ORDEN and called for a full investigation into the incident.

In October appeals to the Honduran Constituent Assembly were renewed: Salvadorian church sources had reported that Honduras had closed its border to refugees fleeing counter-insurgency operations in Morazán, El Salvador, where napalm and white phosphorus were allegedly being used, and that refugees were being returned.

Similar reports continued to reach Amnesty International although foreign priests, doctors and representatives of international refugee organizations apparently managed to limit the death toll by helping refugees to safety and insisting that people taken into custody be produced alive at recognized detention centres. Eye-witness accounts of incidents in March and April 1981 indicated that although members of ORDEN could cross the border at will, peasants fleeing certain areas, particularly the Salvadorian province of Chalatenango, were killed on the spot.

An unknown number of peasants died at the Rio Negro on 15 March in an unsuccessful bid to cross into Honduras; on 18 March two refugees were killed at the Rio Lempa by Salvadorian helicopters; and in mid-March 11 children were drowned, 15 reported missing and 22 others reportedly killed by the Honduran army on Honduran territory during another entry attempt by Salvadorian peasants. Twenty others were reported detained without charge, and the Honduran army was said to be limiting access to the area, interrogating and searching all those who attempted to enter, including representatives of refugee organizations. Some weeks earlier the Committee for Aid to Salvadorian Refugees in Honduras had alleged that women and children were being expelled from Honduras and pushed into the Rio Lempa on flimsy improvised rafts. The committee had also claimed that a joint military operation was being prepared in the region.

In early April 1981 Honduran troops were reported to have opened fire on a number of Salvadorians trying to enter Honduras near Ocotepeque. Those who were wounded but not killed were reportedly turned over to the Salvadorian National Guard. On 2 January 1981 Honduran troops near Mercedes, Ocotepeque, allegedly handed over a young refugee named Ernesto Hernández to members of a Salvadorian "death squad" who murdered him on Salvadorian territory. On 30 March 1981, 17 Salvadorians were allegedly handed over by Honduran troops to the Salvadorian National Guard; all were presumed dead. In another incident, Honduran police allegedly forcibly entered the hospital at Santa Rosa de Copán, removed six gravely wounded Salvadorians from their beds, and turned them over to the Salvadorian army.

On 14 April 1981 Amnesty International expressed its grave concern to the Inter-American Commission on Human Rights (IACHR) and the United Nations High Commissioner for Refugees (UNHCR) at reports of human rights violations of refugees from El Salvador seeking asylum in Honduras. It urged the IACHR to "take all measures to ensure full investigation into such incidents".

Earlier, on 19 August 1980, Amnesty International had written to the UNHCR to express its concern about the many thousands of Salvadorian citizens forced to flee their country and to ask the UNHCR to intervene with the governments of the region to urge them to protect these refugees. In particular it pointed out that more than 30,000 were estimated to have fled to Honduras, where they were not welcome.

On 26 February 1981 Amnesty International's testimony to the Committee on Migration, Refugees and Demography of the Council of Europe about Salvadorian refugees included reports of the alleged cooperation between Salvadorian and Honduran troops.

Those who have tried to help refugees have themselves suffered. Since local priests and the Honduran Bishops Council denounced the Sumpul River killings, residency permits for religious workers in the departments of Copán, Santa Bárbara and Ocotepeque have been inordinately delayed. A public communiqué accused all priests working in the Copán area of "international subversive connections", and the government announced that it was studying the possibility of expelling priests and nuns who had denounced the massacre.

In December two priests from Santa Bárbara and a seminarian, Antonio Bú, were accused of having murdered Dr René Perdomo Paredes. Antonio Bú and another seminarian were detained, interrogated and reportedly tortured. After the family of the dead man had spoken in their defence, they were released and the charges dropped. Fausto Milla, a priest working in Cópan, was arrested on 13 February as he returned from a conference on Salvadorian refugees held in Mexico. He was charged with transferring money and arms to El Salvador, although most observers agreed that he was detained because he had denounced the massacre at the Sumpul River. Amnesty International joined many organizations in appealing on his behalf, and he was freed on 18 February. At the mass celebrating his release several participants were detained and questioned about priests working in Copán.

Amnesty International appealed on behalf of Facundo Guardado Guardado, leader of the *Frente Democrático Revolucionario* (FDR), the Democratic Revolutionary Front, arrested on 18 January 1981 after visiting Salvadorian refugee camps on the border. Former Secretary General of the *Bloque Popular Revolucionario* (BPR), the Popular Revolutionary Bloc, Guardado had earlier been arrested in El Salvador in May 1979 at which time Amnesty International had similarly appealed on his behalf. The Salvadorian authorities had initially denied his arrest, but they eventually released him after an international campaign. After his arrest in January 1981 in Honduras, Guardado was reportedly seen in detention, and had allegedly been tortured, but the authorities repeatedly denied that he had been detained. A little-known guerrilla group hijacked a Honduran airliner on 17 March 1981 and demanded the release of 15 political prisoners, including Guardado, in exchange for the passengers' lives. Ten prisoners were freed by the Honduran government, including Guardado, who reportedly took refuge in Panama. His brother Sixto Francisco and his sister Teresa de Jesús and her child, who were living in exile in Honduras, were arrested. Earlier, another brother, José Antonio, had also been arrested. Their detention has been denied by the Honduran authorities and despite Amnesty International's appeals there has been no further information about them.

As the pace of agrarian reform has slowed in recent months, there have been confrontations between the authorities and Honduran *campesino* organizations. Trouble flared once again at the Isletas banana cooperative, where controversy has been raging since 1974. There have been reports of: death lists threatening the cooperative leaders; their harassment by the secret police; their periodic detention; and isolated incidents of torture. In January 1981 reports indicated that the army had once again imposed its own leadership upon the cooperative and militarized the zone.

On 21 January 1981 Amnesty International appealed on behalf of Felipe Viera, leader of a cooperative in Lean in the department of Atlantida, arrested on 10 January by the National Investigation Department, and taken to the army barracks in Tela. Friends who inquired there were told that he had been transferred to an army military base at Tamara, 45 kilometres north of the capital, Tegucigalpa. In response to Amnesty International inquiries, the Commander General of the Armed Forces, Colonel Gustavo Adolfo Albávez Martínez, denied Viera's detention and stated that he had been seen alive at the beginning of February 1981.

Two policemen were killed who had been involved in the 1975 Olancho incident, when seven leaders of the National Union of *Campesinos* and two priests were murdered. In February 1978, after an extended trial, two army officers were convicted of the murders. Eight others, including one of Olancho's largest land-owners on whose property the incident occurred, were acquitted. The two convicted men were later released before they had served their sentences. In February 1981 one was "killed while trying to escape", together with another former officer connected with the case. Reports suggest that they had been silenced to prevent them revealing information about other soldiers involved in the Olancho killings.

In March 1979 Amnesty International had appealed on behalf of 150 striking trade unionists including Tomas Nativi, who had reportedly been detained after a fire at the Bemis Handal textile factory in San Pedro. In and out of detention on several occasions since then, Tomas Nativi alleged that while in custody in December 1980 he had been tortured in a variety of ways including beatings, poisoning and simulated executions; he was left with swelling in his chest, stomach and arms, nerve damage to his hands, broken ribs, multiple bruising and internal injuries to his spleen and liver.

Mexico

The concerns of Amnesty International continued to be irregular arrest, detention and trial procedures, including the use of confessions obtained under torture as the only evidence to convict people on criminal charges, when the real reasons for arrest were political, trade union or peasant activities. Deaths in custody, in some instances as a result of torture, and the killing and "disappearance" of former prisoners shortly after release have also been reported during the year. It has also been alleged that former prisoners reported to have been released have merely been transferred from one prison to another, or have been rearrested.

On 23 September 1980 Amnesty International issued an urgent appeal on behalf of eight people detained by the authorities in Guadalajara. Among them was Armando Renteira Castillo, who had been released from prison the previous year after having served six years for alleged guerrilla activities. He allegedly "disappeared" for some days after his rearrest, and was tortured.

Throughout the year Amnesty International received reports of regular security forces and paramilitary units in the service of landowners and manufacturers collaborating to repress peasants and workers; one security unit frequently cited was the so-called *Brigada Blanca* (White Brigade), the 9th Army Brigade, based in *Campo Militar Número 1* in Mexico City. Although some "disappeared" people who later reappeared have given highly detailed information about their detention and ill-treatment by this unit, the government has continued to deny its existence.

In early 1981 one such paramilitary group, the *Frente Patriótico Anticomunista Nacional* (FPAN), National Patriotic Anticommunist Front, claimed responsibility for the killing of Ismael Núñez, an activist in the teachers' union in the Valle de Mexico. In April 1981 another unofficial paramilitary group, the so-called *Liga 16 de septiembre,* 16 September League, said to be part of FPAN, issued death threat leaflets directed at leaders of the *Partido Revolucionario de los Trabajadores* (PRT), the Revolutionary Workers' Party, one of the minority parties represented in Parliament as a result of the new electoral system introduced by the government of President López Portillo. One of those named on the list was Rosario Ibarra de Piedra, president of the *Comité Nacional pro-Defensa de Presos, Perseguidos, Desaparecidos y Exiliados Politicos* (CNPDPPDEP), the National Committee for the Defence of Prisoners, the Persecuted, Disappeared and Political Exiles, who was under consideration by the PRT as their candidate for the 1982 elections. On 22 April Amnesty International called on President López Portillo to guarantee the physical safety of Rosario Ibarra, whose son was among the "disappeared" the CNPDPPDEP was trying to locate. Throughout the year the CNPDPPDEP punctuated requests for investigations into the whereabouts of the "disappeared" with hunger-strikes and occupations of churches and embassies. Demonstrators were sometimes forcibly dislodged by the security forces.

Amnesty International continued its inquiries into the fate of the estimated 300 to 400 people taken into custody in recent years whose whereabouts were unknown. On 9 April 1981 during a meeting with the *Frente Estatal contra la Represión*, State Front against Repression, another group pressing for an official investigation, the new governor of the State of Guerrero reversed the stand of his predecessor that the "disappeared" must be considered dead, and stated that there was evidence that some of the missing persons were alive and held in secret cells. Others however were feared dead, and are believed to have been buried in secret cemeteries, particularly in the State of Guerrero. One such clandestine burial place was apparently found by workers digging under the Mexico City police headquarters in June 1980 who uncovered at least 10 bodies, believed to have been buried for at least five years.

The possibility that some of the "disappeared" might be held in secret jails, and the difficulty of obtaining details of mass arrests reported in remote rural areas where *indígenas* (indigenous people) and *campesinos* (peasants) were held in provincial jails, made it difficult to estimate the number of political prisoners held in Mexico. This was compounded by the authorities' frequent insistence that as Mexican law did not provide for political crimes there were no political prisoners, but only people detained in connection with ordinary criminal offences. For example the former governor of the State of Hidalgo denied that there were any political prisoners held in the state, despite allegations by local peasant leaders that conflicts over land had led to the murder or "disappearance" of 200 peasants and the detention of approximately 370 others over the last four years. However, in February 1981 the newly elected governor of Hidalgo stated that he had been informed that there were more than 100 political prisoners in that state alone.

Amnesty International has been following land conflicts in the State of Hidalgo, particularly in the Huasteca area, for some time. Here and throughout Mexico, control of the land has been an explosive issue since the revolution of 1910 to 1917, one aim of which was to divide up the large estates. However despite the fact that the constitution stipulates that all families are entitled to own land, it has been estimated that some four million rural families remained landless, and many of the human rights abuses reported to Amnesty International during the year have involved land tenure disputes. Some disputes date back to the agrarian reform which followed the struggle of 1910 to 1917, when officials working in the capital did not clearly delineate the lands in the provinces classified as *"ejidos"* (common land). More recent confrontations have been attributed to the fact that officials work from Mexico City to try and settle disputes between claimants who have titles of different dates showing possession of the same lands. Land whose value has been increased by development projects has been wrested from peasant farmers who have been working the land for years, but do not have official titles. A number of peasants who have occupied land in dispute for many years have been killed by paramilitary units in the service of large landowners. In some instances these units were reportedly helped by official military personnel, both in uniform and in plain clothes. It has also been suggested that reports of violent land occupation by peasants have been fabricated in order to justify attacks on peasant leaders and organizations who were trying to develop independent peasant movements outside the control of the ruling government party, the *Partido Revolucionario Institucional* (PRI), the Institutional

Revolutionary Party.

Amnesty International received reports of conflict in the Huasteca area throughout the year; peasants objected particularly to the presence of military units stationed at strategic points to prevent further land occupations by the peasantry. Reports also suggested that the *Policía Judicial* (Judicial Police) had arrested a number of local peasants to extort payments or force them to sell their land in return for their release. There has been no further word of two people from the area detained in February 1980.

In the State of Morelos, controversy has flared over plots of land awarded to local residents in 1947 by presidential decree, but subsequently illegally sold to a foreigner, who fell into tax arrears. It was then acquired by the state governor who registered it in the name of his children. To defend their right to the land, the local residents established a *colonia* (communal settlement) but were forced off by a combined police and army invasion in 1973. In the following years, leaders of this group and other *colonias* have been repeatedly harassed, arrested and tortured. Amnesty International has been investigating a number of these cases for several years; although the prisoners, held in Cuernavaca prison, have confessed to criminal offences, it has been alleged that their convictions were based solely on confessions extracted under torture, and that the real reason for their prosecution was their activities as peasant leaders. Over the year several of the Cuernavaca prisoners were released. However state and federal amnesties have been unevenly applied, and some prisoners have been released, while others accused of and tried on exactly the same charges were still held. Three of the Cuernavaca group were retried in late 1980, and resentenced to terms of 36 years in prison.

Alfredo Nava Mesa, a prisoner held at Cuernavaca whose case was being investigated by Amnesty International, was killed in prison on 29 January 1981 by another inmate who had already murdered three people. The killer was reportedly released later. It was also reported that shortly before Nava's murder, the judicial department of the federal police had concluded a study of his case, and had called for his release on the grounds that his continued imprisonment was unjustified.

Two deaths in custody were reported to Amnesty International in April 1981; those of Miguel Hernández Pérez who died after an incident in a Oaxaca prison allegedly provoked by the police, and student Ignacio Yañez García, who reportedly died under torture by police in San Miguel de Allende, Guanajuato.

Throughout the year Amnesty International received reports denouncing torture and ill-treatment in prisons. In October 1980 the

Attorney General of the State of Mexico was accused before Congress of ordering the detention, torture and assassination of young people, and of running secret jails in that state. Residents of San Pedro Xalostoc alleged that 17 people, mostly minors, were held in secret jails in San Miguel Xalostoc and Tepotzotlán, and that they had been tortured to make them confess to crimes they had not committed. In February 1981 the CNPDPPDEP protested against the systematic ill-treatment of prisoners in the State of Jalisco. In April 1981 the bishop of Cuernavaca, Sergio Méndez Arceo, ordered the excommunication of torturers in his diocese, and stated that the general public was convinced that "the police are not a protection, but a source of terror because of the maltreatment and torture which they use to extort, intimidate and obtain information from detainees".

During the year the bishops of the southern pacific region of Mexico spoke out against the involvement of the security services in the repression of peasants in their area. On 5 June 1980 Amnesty International appealed for an investigation into a clash on 30 May between landowners, allegedly aided by the army, and peasants on the Bolanchon Estate, Yahalón, in the southern state of Chiapas, during which an unknown number of peasants died. On 15 June soldiers returned to the area and after using teargas fired upon a group of peasants, killing 12 and wounding many more. A total of 723 families, some of whom had been awaiting settlement of land claims for 28 years, were evicted from their lands. Officials announced that leaders of the peasant families would be tried for criminal offences. Similar clashes between peasants and the private armies of large landowners, often led by decommissioned military officers and aided by official security forces, have been reported throughout Mexico during the year.

Clashes have been reported between the security services and trade unionists in a number of sectors including the oil industry. Conflict was particularly acute in the education sector, where the *Coordinadora Nacional de Trabajadores de la Educación* (CNTE), the National Coordinating Committee of Education Workers, led pressure for a wage rise and government guarantees of trade union freedom. The government also clashed with the *Sindicato Nacional de Trabajadores Universitarios* (SUNTU), National Union of University Workers, which was trying to create a national university workers' union. Violence flared several times as trade unionists organized demonstrations throughout the country. On 11 February 1981 Amnesty International appealed for information on the whereabouts of Fernando Medina Ramírez, a student teacher and trade union activist at the University of Baja California, who was forcibly detained by men in plain clothes at midday on 8 February 1981. The authorities initially refused to acknowledge Medina's detention, but he was eventually located in custody and flown to Mexico City where he was released. However, he has not been permitted to return to the University of Baja California.

On 23 March 1981 Mexico deposited instruments of accession to the International Covenants on Economic, Social and Cultural Rights and on Civil and Political Rights with the Secretary-General of the United Nations, subject to a number of interpretative statements and reservations.

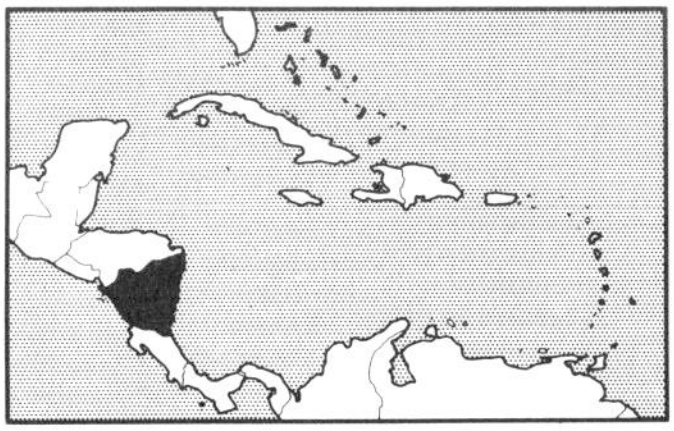

Nicaragua

Amnesty International concerns centred on the trials of former National Guardsmen and others charged with criminal offences committed under the authority of the government of General Anastasio Somoza Debayle that was overthrown in July 1979. A further concern has been the situation of prisoners held for contravention of the Law of the Maintenance of Public Order and Security (Decree No. 5 of 20 July 1979).

From 19 to 27 August 1980 an Amnesty International mission visited Nicaragua to observe trials, examine new legislation, and study the cases of individual prisoners. This was the second of a series of missions to observe trials following invitations extended to Amnesty International by the new government of Nicaragua.

In December 1979 Decree 185 established *Tribunales Especiales de Justicia* (special courts) to try National Guardsmen and others associated with the previous government detained after the revolution. These special courts were to apply the terms of the penal code in force at the time of the prisoners' alleged crimes.

In the first months of the new government an estimated seven to eight thousand prisoners were held in prisons, command posts and improvised jails. One year later, in August 1980, the number was estimated to be about six thousand. In October 1980 the authorities provided Amnesty International with a list — believed to be complete — of 5,598 prisoners held under the authority of the special courts including those held in the headquarters of the State Security police, *Departamento de Seguridad del Estado,* Department of State Security. Since then 573 prisoners have been pardoned, 503 of them on 10 December 1980, International Human Rights Day (Decree

589). Several hundred others are believed to have been released on expiry of their sentences.

On 19 February 1981 the special courts were dissolved and 160 prisoners whose trials were still pending were ordered to be released; 15 others were transferred to the jurisdiction of the ordinary courts.

Although a list of the sentences passed by the special courts has apparently not yet been made public, the authorities announced that 4,331 of the 6,310 prisoners held under the special courts' jurisdiction were sentenced to prison, and that 28 per cent, or about 1,213, received terms from 21 years to the maximum of 30 years.

Amnesty International's concerns in these cases was largely with trial procedures. Although none have been adopted as prisoners of conscience, significant trial irregularities have occurred. In some cases the defendant was charged with no specific criminal act. Some prisoners were convicted of murder (*asesinato*) although the prosecution had not named an individual victim, or the victim was said to have been "the Nicaraguan people" *("el pueblo nicaraguense")*. Members of National Guard units which inflicted torture or summary executions — murder under Nicaraguan law — were held to be responsible for crimes committed by the unit. Former National Guardsmen who had been stationed in the rural northeast of the country where thousands of *campesinos* (peasant farmers) were tortured and murdered by guardsmen between 1974 and 1979 generally received the maximum 30-year prison sentence for "atrocious murder" (*asesinato atroz*). Others considered less responsible were generally charged with "criminal association", for having been members of a criminal organization — the National Guard.

The special court system established both courts of first instance and appeal courts completely separate from the ordinary judicial system. In some cases severe sentences passed by the lower courts were reduced and convictions overturned by the appeal courts. Seized documents showed that Salvador Baltodano Conrado had been a collaborator of the *Oficina de Seguridad Nàcional* (OSN), Office of National Security. The prosecution told the court that there were "thousands and thousands of Nicaraguans murdered by the agents of death of the OSN" and that the prisoner's "conscious and voluntary" membership of the OSN was proof of guilt of criminal association and complicity in murder, for which he was sentenced to 30 years' imprisonment. The judgement was overturned by the appeal court which accepted the defence that no specific crime had been shown, and that the defendant had only served the OSN as a draftsman after a period of unemployment; and the sentence was reduced to one year for "criminal association" which was completed on 18 February 1981.

Although a not entirely ineffective appeals procedure existed within the special courts system, verdicts confirmed by the special appeals courts could not go to appeal before an ordinary court; the 4,311 prisoners sentenced by special court had no further legal remedy against alleged miscarriages of justice. Amnesty International was examining a number of cases heard by the special courts and pressing for a procedure of judicial review of verdicts where the trial before the special courts appeared to have been unsatisfactory.

A wide range of offences related to national security are punished with imprisonment under recent special penal legislation: notably the *Ley Sobre el Mantenimiento del Orden y Seguridad Publica*, Law for the Maintenance of Public Order and Security, (Decree No. 5 of 20 July 1979), the public order law. Categories of offences against public order and security include the illegal possession of firearms, explosives or "war materials" and crimes against morals. The public order law outlines broad categories of crime which encompass conspiracy and violent opposition to the state. Article 4 of the law as modified by Decree No. 488 of 9 August 1980 makes certain oral or written "expressions, proclamations or manifestos" punishable by 10 days to two years of detention and public works. These include statements intended to undermine national security; the economy; public order; health; morals; the judicial power; and "the dignity of persons, the reputation and rights of others".

The public order law was originally decreed as an extraordinary measure to meet an extraordinary national crisis; it was to remain in force only so long as Nicaragua remained in a state of national emergency. Despite this, Decree 383 of 29 April 1980 declared that the public order law would remain in force, even though the state of emergency had been lifted, and that it would be incorporated into the ordinary penal legislation.

The definitions of crimes provided by the law are imprecise, relating to conspiracy and the freedom of expression, and they are therefore open to arbitrary interpretation. Although the ordinary courts have jurisdiction in cases under the public order law a special truncated procedure is prescribed for public order law trials. The defence is allowed only two days' preparation after an accusation has been made to the court. After the trial has lasted three days, sentence must be passed within 48 hours (Article 5, Decree No. 34). Courts hearing public order cases are also exempted from the normal rules of evidence (Article 2, Decree No. 149).

About 100 prisoners are believed to have been convicted of serious offences under the public order law. Several were prosecuted for involvement in recent political violence; from armed clashes with the army and the militia in the Honduran border area and some parts of the Pacific coast to the murder of several teenagers taking part in the national literacy campaign.

Amnesty International has made inquiries about several public order cases of prisoners convicted of conspiring to carry out acts of violence, who were not accused of specific violent actions. Alejandro José Salazar Elizondo, Leonardo Somarriba González and six other Nicaraguan businessmen were convicted in December 1980 of conspiring to form an armed group to overthrow the government, and sentenced to one to nine years' imprisonment. According to trial documents almost the only evidence was the statements allegedly made by three of the accused while in the custody of the State Security police. These statements were made without the presence of a lawyer and were disavowed in court. Defence lawyers pointed out during an appeal that the court had accepted these written statements prepared by the State Security police rather than sworn statements by the accused made directly to the court, and had refused to insist on the presence in court of the responsible officers of the State Security police.

In a further appeal pending before the Supreme Court of Justice the defence has contended that while the eight were convicted on arms charges, no arms were produced in evidence and that the charge of having "disseminated orally or in writing proclamations or manifestos that undermine public security and the national economy" was not substantiated as no material evidence of such writings or testimonies of such statements had been produced.

The defence alleged that it had been hampered by the court's refusal to make proper arrangements for calling defence witnesses, in part because of the summary procedure used in the trial. The accused were notified of the general nature of the charges on a Tuesday (2 December 1980), had to name a defence lawyer and prepare their defence within 48 hours, and were sentenced the following Wednesday (10 December). The defence claimed that the sole basis for prosecution was "severe criticism [of the government] made during a social gathering".

Colonel Bernardino Larios Montiel and 12 alleged accomplices were similarly convicted of having organized an armed opposition group and having planned the abduction or killing of government leaders. Colonel Larios was a former National Guard officer who was jailed and exiled by the Somoza government, and later joined the revolutionary forces; he served as Minister of Defence from July to December 1979. The prisoners were detained in September 1980, and convicted in October; Colonel Larios received a sentence of seven years' imprisonment. Amnesty International has not yet determined whether Colonel Larios and others convicted in similar cases could be considered prisoners of conscience, but concern has been expressed over irregularities in trial procedures in these cases, and appeals were being followed closely.

José Esteban González, National Coordinator of the unofficial Permanent Commission on Human Rights of Nicaragua, and Vice-President of the *Partido Social-Christiano*, a Christian Democratic Party, was detained on 19 February 1981 by order of the First District Criminal Court of Managua on charges under Article 4 of the public order law. He was accused of having made public statements that were "intended to disrupt national security and integrity, public safety, and the national economy" and to abuse the "dignity of persons, and the reputation and rights of others". He had visited Europe, met political groups and international organizations, and had an audience with Pope John Paul II. He was accused of "slandering" the Nicaraguan people when press reports quoted him as claiming that "torture and repression" in Nicaragua was as bad as under President Somoza — statements he later claimed had been misinterpreted.

On 20 February 1981 Amnesty International expressed its dismay at the arrest of José González, whom it considered a prisoner of conscience, and two days later was informed that he had been detained on a court order and that his trial would be rapidly concluded. On 3 March José González was acquitted and released after a two-hour hearing.

During preceding months leading members of the government had accused the Permanent Commission on Human Rights in the press of orchestrating a campaign against Nicaragua for political purposes. On 12 February 1981 Nicaraguan police had occupied the commission's building, after the Ministry of Justice ordered the organization "suspended" on the grounds that it was not legally registered.

The following day Amnesty International cabled the five members of the Nicaraguan executive, the *Junta de Reconstruccion Nacional,* to deplore the ruling of the Justice Minister and to urge the *junta* to overturn the decision. An international press release was issued on the same day, emphasizing that measures by governments to obstruct or repress human rights organizations were incompatible with international standards for freedom of expression.

Amnesty International was informed the following day that the Justice Ministry decision had been reversed, and that the commission would be permitted to reopen immediately to continue its work in "the promotion of human rights". No further government harassment has come to the attention of Amnesty International.

Since 21 August 1979 the *Estatuto sobre Derechos y Garantias de los Nicaraguenses,* Law of the Rights and Guarantees of the Nicaraguans, has abolished the death penalty, and prohibited torture, and cruel, inhuman and degrading treatment. Although the use of torture was endemic under the government of President Somoza (see *The Republic of Nicaragua; an Amnesty International Report,* 1976), Amnesty International has received no convincing accounts alleging systematic ill-treatment or torture of prisoners under the present government.

A memorandum detailing Amnesty International's concerns was in preparation for submission later in 1981, incorporating the findings of its missions.

Paraguay

Amnesty International concerns have been irregular detention procedures, detention without trial, torture and "disappearances".

Most prisoners of concern to Amnesty International were detained either under state of siege legislation or under the anti-subversion Law 209, Defence of Public Peace and Liberty of Persons, passed in 1970. A state of siege has been in force in Asunción, the capital, ever since General Alfredo Stroessner took power in 1954, having been lifted only six times to coincide with elections.

Amnesty International knows of at least 25 political prisoners. Twelve have been adopted as prisoners of conscience or allocated to groups for further investigation. The trials of Amnesty International adopted prisoners of conscience Alfonso Silva Quintana and his wife María Saturnina Almada de Silva, which began in 1979, continued slowly. The couple were accused under Law 209 of subversive activities which carry a maximum penalty of six years' imprisonment. They had already spent 10 years in detention without trial from 1968 to 1978. Amnesty International adopted prisoner of conscience Constantino Coronel was released on 5 September 1980 and forced into exile. He had been charged with a criminal offence but independent observers believed that it was his position as a peasant leader that led to his imprisonment.

Short-term detentions have been used to control political opposition. Nicaragua's ex-President Anastasio Somoza, who had been living in

Paraguay since August 1979 after his government's defeat, was killed on 17 September 1980 in Asunción in a machine-gun and bazooka attack. The Paraguayan authorities announced that the attackers were Argentine guerrillas from the Marxist group the People's Revolutionary Army (ERP) collaborating with Nicaraguan Sandinistas. After the killing security forces searched homes, confiscated private papers and personal effects and arrested hundreds of citizens. Many of those arrested were Argentines and other foreigners. About 150 foreign nationals were expelled, mostly Argentine, including people married to Paraguayans and parents of Paraguayan children. Many reported ill-treatment while in detention. Pedro and Zulema Igón, both Argentines, were arrested on 11 October 1980 in Asunción. Pedro Igón's name later appeared on a list in an Argentine newspaper of people arrested in Argentina. Also detained at this time was leading opposition politician and economist Domingo Laíno. Personal documents were taken from his home on the morning of 30 September 1980. Later in the day some 12 men in civilian clothes arrested him. He was held until 15 October 1980. This was Domingo Laíno's third spell of short-term detention in just over two years.

In March 1980 a large number of peasants had been arrested after a small group of peasants had held up a bus to draw attention to problems over land (see *Amnesty International Report 1980*). The group represented the hundred or so families who in the early 1970s had set up a new colony in Acaray, Department of Alto Paraná. Since then the peasants have been in constant conflict over ownership of the land, even though they had authorization from the Rural Welfare Institute (IBR) to settle there. After the hold-up 10 peasants were reportedly shot dead. Most of the arrested peasants were released after varying periods of detention. Several minors were imprisoned. Apolonia Flores Rotela was 13 at the time of her arrest in March 1980. She was accused of several common crimes, including assault and robbery, and held until September 1980 when she was released after appearing before a judge. Her 15-year-old brother Arnaldo was held until January 1981. Apolinaria González, 16 and mentally retarded, was pregnant at the time of her arrest and gave birth in detention. She was released in January 1981 on the advice of a psychiatrist. Her husband and nine other peasants were still in prison in April 1981 and were being tried for several common crimes including assault, robbery and resisting the authorities. Sources have indicated that four of the peasants did not take part in the hold-up of the bus and Amnesty International has adopted these four as prisoners of conscience. The organization was also concerned about the trials of the others, especially since it appeared that these arrests were part of a general repression of peasants and the *Ligas Agrarias,*

Agrarian Leagues, a church-supported peasant organization.

A number of urgent appeals were issued, mostly concerning irregular detention procedures and incommunicado detention. On 27 August 1980 Antonio Maidana, Secretary General of the banned Paraguayan Communist Party, and Emilio Roa Espinosa, also a Communist Party and trade union leader, were abducted in Buenos Aires, Argentina. It is thought they were transferred from Argentina to Paraguay. Emilio Roa was 64 and suffered from a heart condition which required constant medical supervision. He had lived in Argentina for 22 years after being forced to leave Paraguay because of his trade union activities. Antonio Maidana, 69, had previously been adopted by Amnesty International as a prisoner of conscience until his release in March 1977 after over 18 years' imprisonment. The whereabouts of the two men were not known.

Amnesty International submitted information on Paraguay to the Secretary-General of the United Nations under the procedure set up to consider "a consistent pattern of gross violations of human rights". A statement was made to the General Assembly of the Organization of American States which met in Washington between 19 and 28 November 1980, in which Amnesty International outlined its concerns on human rights in Paraguay. The Inter-American Commission on Human Rights in its annual report to this Assembly recommended the lifting of the state of siege in Paraguay, restoration of independence to the judiciary, guarantees of trade union rights and freedom of expression and fair trial or release for all existing prisoners. It also urged the government to set a date for a visit by the commission which had been agreed in principle back in 1977.

Peru

On 28 July Peru's first civilian president was inaugurated after 12 years of military government, and the constitution of 1979 came into force. These major developments affected the human rights situation directly. The major concerns of Amnesty International had previously included the periodic short-term detention of thousands of civilians each year for political or trade union activity, their trial by military courts, and the death penalty. After the political and constitutional changes, Amnesty International was concerned about reports of arbitrary arrests linked to anti-terrorism operations, allegations of ill-treatment or torture, and the failure of prison conditions to improve.

The new constitution abolished the death penalty except for treason in time of external war (Article 235). It also ended the jurisdiction of the military courts over civilians, declaring that the *Código de Justicia Militar,* Code of Military Justice, would no longer apply in civilian cases (Article 285). This change in the law was accompanied by an end to the periodic mass arrests of trade union activists and political opponents.

Shortly before the change of government four Argentine citizens in exile in Peru were abducted in what was later shown to have been a combined operation by agents of the Argentine army and members of *Servicio de Inteligencia del Ejército* (SIE), Peruvian army intelligence. On 12 June 1980 Julia Ines Santos de Acabal was detained by men in civilian clothes in the Lima suburb Miraflores; the detention was witnessed and reported by Naomi Esther Gianetti de Molfino, the mother of two children who had "disappeared" after detention in Argentina. The next day Naomi Gianetti and two other Argentines living in Lima were abducted. Although Peruvian authorities initially denied any knowledge of the detentions, the four were reportedly held in the *Centro Recreacional del Ejército,* an army recreation centre, at Playa Hondable north of Lima, and Amnesty International made an urgent appeal on 17 June 1980 for the Peruvian authorities to guarantee their safety.

In October 1980 the weekly magazine *Equis-X* published an interview with Peruvian Army Captain Wilfredo Jacinto Cesare Zárate, who, it said, was the SIE doctor present during the interrogation of the Argentines at Playa Hondable. *Equis-X* quoted Dr Cesare as insisting that he "did not participate in the torture", but admitting his responsibility "to determine the limits of resistance of the victims" in order to prevent deaths during interrogation. Dr Cesare and other sources identified the torturers as members of Argentine military intelligence, assisted by officials of Peruvian SIE. On 17 June 1980 the Peruvian Ministry of the Interior said in a press release that three Argentines described as "subversive criminals" had been detained on 12 and 13 June, but had been expelled and handed over to immigration officials of Bolivia; this was immediately denied by the Bolivian Government.

An open letter to Amnesty International was published by president-elect Fernando Belaúnde Terry on 29 June 1980 in response to requests for him to use his good offices on behalf of the four "disappeared", in which he stated that he had asked for a full explanation, and had "clearly and definitely expressed fear for the safety of these people . . .".

In his inaugural address on 28 July 1980 President Belaúnde declared his government's intention to implement fully the new constitution and to promote the full observance of human rights. A general political amnesty bill was approved by Congress on 28 July that called for the release of all political detainees and the reinstatement of public employees dismissed by the previous government on political grounds. However several prisoners were excluded.

Shortly after the change of government a series of dynamite explosions were reported in the capital city area and in several departments. A wide variety of targets were attacked: public buildings, electricity pylons, the homes of provincial opposition leaders and the editor of a left-wing magazine, factories, and commercial premises. In most cases only property was damaged. Security authorities have attributed the bombings to a little-known group called *Sendero Luminoso,* Luminous Path, purportedly on the extreme political left. Leaders of the *Izquierda Unida* (IU), United Left, the coalition which groups most of Peru's left-wing political parties, have condemned the bombings and questioned whether such widespread attacks could be the work of one extremist group.

Vice-President Javier Alva Orlandini, a leader of President Belaúnde's party *Acción Popular,* said that despite the efforts of the security forces it was still unclear who was responsible for the terrorism and suggested that Peru's powerful narcotics smugglers might be trying to divert police attention from their criminal activities. Whoever was behind the attacks, they brought about special anti-terrorist laws that extended the penal code by defining and punishing crimes of terrorism. Decree 46 of 10 March 1981, issued by the executive while congress was in recess, defines "terrorism" as acts that have the "intent to provoke or maintain a state of anxiety, alarm or terror", and are "capable of causing great destruction", or "affecting state security". Actions causing "considerable" damage to private or public property are punished with no less than 15 years' imprisonment, and should death or serious injury be caused, no less than 20. Membership of an organization deemed to support terrorist methods may be punished by two to four years' imprisonment. The law also provides for four to eight years' imprisonment for inciting any of these crimes through "the press, radio, television or other means of social communications" and three to five years' for justifying or defending any act of terrorism publicly, or defending the actions of anyone imprisoned for terrorism.

Amnesty International was investigating the cases of several local government officials from IU opposition parties held on "terrorism" charges, including Isidro Quiroz, a city councillor in the Lima district of Carabayllo and a leader of the IU affiliate, *Union de Izquierda Revolucionaria* (UNIR), Union of the Revolutionary Left, who was detained in March 1981. In Puno province, where both the congressional deputy and local government leaders were members of IU, seven leaders of the UNIR were detained in April 1981 including its provincial vice-president Ronald Bustamente.

Eight leaders of the Cuzco department union of construction workers detained on 10 April 1981 on terrorism charges told a court that they had been severely tortured by the investigative police *Policia de Investigaciones del Peru* (PIP). Their allegations included near drowning, beatings while wrapped in wet cloths, burns with cigarettes, and a threat by a senior PIP officer that their houses would be blown up. The arrests came one day after a general strike in Cuzco department protesting against central government policies. The legal situation of the eight was unknown. Amnesty International has called for a full inquiry into the case.

Three hundred people were believed to have been detained in anti-terrorism operations in the highland departments of Ayacucho, Lambayeque, Puno and Cuzco, after special counter-insurgency forces of the *Guardia Civil* (Civil Guard), notably the *Batallón Sinchi*, and of the PIP were called in. In April 1981 trade union and political organizations in the departments of Cuzco, Puno and Lambayeque organized general strikes to protest against the detention of regional political leaders and against abuses by counter-insurgency forces including the arbitrary detention of peasant farmers and torture.

Prison conditions were a major concern of Amnesty International in the past year. In August 1980 Minister of Justice Felipe Osterling Parodi visited the largest prison, the *Centro de Rehabilitación y*

Adaptación Social (CRAS) of Lurigancho, in the outskirts of Lima, and was quoted as describing conditions as "truly Dantesque" and requiring radical reform. Lurigancho prison opened in 1968 with facilities for 1,800 prisoners and by 1981 housed over 6,000. In November 1980 the Lurigancho prisoners went on hunger-strike in protest at arbitrary beatings, and unprovoked shootings of prisoners by prison guards of the *Guardia Republicana*, and at the lack of adequate food, water, and medical attention. There has been no noticeable improvement since an Amnesty International mission visited Lurigancho prison in 1978.

Similar overcrowding and poor conditions marked the Lima prison *Centro de Sentenciados El Sexto*, which housed over 1,000 prisoners although it was built for 190. There have been prison mutinies and unexplained killings in both prisons. A fight among prisoners in the badly overcrowded El Sexto prison on the night of 4 March 1981 led to 31 deaths, with many prisoners burned to death while locked in cells.

On 3 October 1980 Peru ratified the Optional Protocol to the International Covenant on Civil and Political Rights which provides for individual complaints to be heard by the Human Rights Committee.

Suriname

Amnesty International's concerns were detention without trial; the establishment of special courts; retroactive legislation; and the alleged ill-treatment of prisoners.

After the overthrow of the government in February 1980 by non-commissioned army officers, some former government ministers and officials were detained without charge and without access to their families and lawyers. Amnesty International received reports that some of the detainees had been ill-treated. These allegations were raised by Amnesty International on 27 June 1980 in a letter to the Prime Minister Chin A Sen (who was subsequently appointed President), together with an inquiry as to whether the detainees would be tried. On 31 July 1980 Amnesty International asked Prime Minister Chin A Sen about the reported ill-treatment of Johannes Cornelius Krol, detained in May 1980 in connection with an alleged plot to overthrow the government.

In January 1981 an Amnesty International mission visited Suriname to discuss Amnesty International's concerns with the authorities, including the introduction of retroactive legislation and the establishment of a special court for cases of alleged corruption, both apparently intended to secure the conviction of former government ministers and officials. The first judge appointed to head the special court resigned because his efforts to ensure a fair trial were defeated by the behaviour of the prosecutors. Defendants and their lawyers were informed of the charges only a few days before the trial and were, therefore, unable to prepare an adequate defence.

After the return of the mission Amnesty International wrote to President Chin A Sen criticizing Decree B-9 in detail, in particular its retroactive effect; its wording, which lends itself to "the most arbitrary interpretation and application"; the creation of special courts, which "frequently results in proceedings and judgments which reflect the dilution of those safeguards afforded by the ordinary courts"; and the new provision for long periods of imprisonment partly or wholly in isolation. Allegations of ill-treatment of prisoners were also raised and specific mention was made of the death of Frits Ormskerk, said by the government to have been killed during an attempted coup in May 1980, but allegedly beaten to death.

In February 1980 an Amnesty International observer attended the trial of John Thijm, former Director of the Planning Bureau who was tried by the special court on charges of corruption, under Decree B-9. In his report to Amnesty International the observer pointed out that the acts with which the defendant was charged were not crimes at the time when they were said to have been committed and that: "Given the nature of the substantive criminal law to be applied, one may say, from the outset, that the trial was unfair, whatever the outcome . . ." The report stressed that the retroactive application of the criminal law did not accord with Article 15 of the International Covenant on Civil and Political Rights, of which Suriname is a State Party.

At the end of April 1981 all detainees known to Amnesty International had been brought to trial or released pending trial.

United States of America

Work for the abolition of the death penalty and against impending executions was Amnesty International's major concern during the year. On 20 April 1981 there were 794 people under sentence of death in the United States of America (USA).

In March and April 1981 appeals were sent to members of the US Senate Judiciary Committee considering a federal death penalty bill (No. S.114). They were urged to reject the reintroduction of the death penalty for certain crimes committed under federal jurisdiction.

Amnesty International wrote several times to state and federal prison authorities asking for information about alleged ill-treatment of prisoners. In August 1980 an Amnesty International mission visited Marion Federal Penitentiary in Illinois to investigate allegations that conditions and treatment in the "Control Unit" of the prison were inhuman and degrading, and that inmates had been physically ill-treated. Marion Federal Penitentiary is the highest security prison in the federal system; the "Control Unit" (strictly speaking a separate unit from the prison) houses prisoners who are regarded as extreme security risks.

In order to assess the prison regime and the allegations that it constituted a "behaviour modification program", the mission interviewed prisoners and collected medical data. No evidence was found to show that the existing regime harmed the physical or mental health of prisoners. Nor could the Amnesty International delegation find evidence of abuse of psychotropic drugs. However the mission recommended that certain aspects of the regime be investigated in detail by prison experts.

On 29 August 1980 Amnesty International wrote to Rose Bird, Chief Justice of the California Supreme Court, supporting the request of the State Public Defender for the conviction of Johnny Larry Spain to be reviewed. Johnny Spain, one of six defendants who became known as the San Quentin Six, was sentenced to life imprisonment in 1976. He was convicted of conspiring in an escape attempt from San Quentin prison in August 1971, during which his fellow Black Panther, George Jackson, and two other inmates were killed. Three prison guards were also killed. Amnesty International pointed out that it was not pronouncing on the guilt or innocence of Johnny Spain, but was concerned that: "... particularly in cases with political overtones, the fairness of the trial should be beyond reproach." Points of concern mentioned in the letter were the shackling of Johnny Spain throughout the trial and a juror's conversations with the trial judge. The petition to the California Supreme Court for Johnny Spain's appeal to be heard was denied.

A special study was completed of several cases of American Indians and Blacks who alleged that their prosecution on criminal charges was politically motivated. The report examined cases of political activists who were the targets of domestic intelligence programs and who alleged that there had been irregularities in the bringing of prosecutions against them. The report was scheduled for publication later in 1981.

In addition to this study Amnesty International investigated many cases of prisoners who maintained that although convicted on criminal charges, the real reason for their imprisonment was political, but no new prisoners of conscience were adopted during the year. Amnesty International continued to urge the authorities to grant Gary Tyler and Elmer "Geronimo" Pratt new trials or to release them (see *Amnesty International Report 1980*).

Uruguay

Amnesty International's concerns were the large number of prisoners of conscience; prison conditions which fell short of internationally recognized standards; the lack of legal safeguards for detainees; torture; and the trial of civilians before military tribunals whose procedures did not conform to recognized standards for a fair trial.

A plebiscite on a new constitution was held on 30 November 1980. Amnesty International was concerned that the proposed constitution would legitimize practices which have encouraged human rights violations in recent years, such as the lack of an independent judiciary and the wide powers of the armed forces, and further erode the legal safeguards in the previous (1967) constitution.

The new constitution was drafted by the Political Commission of the Armed Forces (COMASPO) in secrecy. In June 1980 a number of politicians who had called for political parties to be included in the constitutional process were arrested and briefly detained. The three political parties concerned, the traditional *Blanco* (National) and *Colorado* parties and the Christian Democratic party, were banned from political activity in 1973 for 15 years. Around 57 per cent of the electorate voted against the new constitution despite the fact that military officials had made it clear that a "no" vote would be interpreted as support for the government's measures and would delay plans to restore limited democracy.

There were over 1,200 political prisoners in Uruguay. A number of prisoners were released during the year, either on expiry of their sentences or in some cases shortly before, including more than 40 prisoners on whose behalf Amnesty International had worked. Approximately 350 prisoners have been adopted as prisoners of conscience or were being investigated by Amnesty International.

In August 1980 Amnesty International interviewed Hugo Walter García Rivas, a former private in the army who had sought refuge in Europe earlier in the year. Hugo García testified that he had been made to study torture techniques as part of his training in the Counter Intelligence Company of the army in Montevideo. In the classes prisoners were used for demonstrations and students practised torture on them. Hugo García had taken part in the torture of detainees to gain information. He had been present at the interrogation and torture of Humberto Pascaretta, a trade unionist who died in custody in June 1977 shortly after his arrest. Hugo García also testified to Amnesty International that he had taken part in the kidnapping in Brazil of Lilian Celiberti and Universindo Rodríguez Díaz in November 1978. He reported that the Brazilian and Uruguayan security forces had cooperated in taking Lilian Celiberti, Universindo Rodríguez and Lilian's young children from their flat in Porto Alegre, Brazil and transferring them across the border to Uruguay. Lilian Celiberti and Universindo Rodríguez were later accused of entering Uruguay with illegal material and were sentenced to prison. They have been adopted by Amnesty International as prisoners of conscience.

The extent of torture was confirmed by Daniel Rey Piuma, a former naval rating who sought refuge in Europe in October 1980. He has publicly stated that he witnessed the torture of prisoners by the navy and that doctors were present.

Amnesty International issued 22 urgent appeals during the year. Most concerned prisoners who were seriously ill, or who had been removed from prison to unknown destinations. Amnesty International received persistent reports of deteriorating conditions in the *Penal de*

Libertad, the main military prison for men, officially called *Establecimiento Militar de Reclusión no. 1* and in the *Penal de Punta de Rieles,* the main military prison for women, officially named *Establecimiento Militar de Reclusión no. 2.* In particular, Amnesty International has been concerned at reports of increased harassment. Several prisoners are reported to have been held in solitary confinement and others to have been removed from prison. Between 26 and 30 November 1980 a number of prisoners in the *Penal de Libertad* staged a hunger-strike in protest against the harsh conditions.

One of the prisoners taken from the *Penal de Libertad* was Mario Alberto Teti Izquierdo, who was removed at the end of September 1980 after being held in isolation for one month. His whereabouts remained unknown. In April 1981 Amnesty International learned that new trial proceedings were being opened against him. José Félix Martinez Salgueiro, in prison since March 1971, and believed to be the longest serving prisoner of conscience in Uruguay, was serving a sentence of 15 years plus three to seven years' security measures, which meant that he was not entitled to apply for release on parole and had to spend between 18 and 22 years in prison. He faced a new accusation: he was alleged to have used violence against an armed prison guard who was forcing him to change cells, which would have meant his sharing a cell with a mentally ill prisoner. Amnesty International took a serious view of the initiation of new trial proceedings against prisoners, which meant that prisoners could be kept in detention indefinitely.

Amnesty International medical groups have appealed to the Uruguayan authorities on behalf of ill prisoners who were denied adequate medical attention. Gladys Yánez, who had been adopted by Amnesty International as a prisoner of conscience, died in custody in September 1980, having suffered from a serious kidney disease. With specialized medical care her life might have been saved.

Other deaths of prisoners in custody have occurred in suspicious circumstances. Jorge Antonio Dabó Rebelo, a former long-distance swimmer of about 40, was said by officials to have died of a heart complaint. Other sources have claimed that his body bore marks of torture. Hugo Dermit, a student, had completed his eight-year sentence and was preparing for release when, according to the authorities, he committed suicide.

In December 1980 three prisoners serving sentences in the *Penal de Libertad*, Raúl Martínez, Orlando Pereira and Conrado Giurkovitz, three other prisoners who had been released earlier and were rearrested in December 1980, and several relatives of prisoners in the *Penal de Libertad* were accused of an alleged plot against the government. Teresa Gómez, a medical professor, was arrested on her return from the Peace and Justice Service in Argentina. Her husband, Jorge Voituret Pazos, has been held in the *Penal de Libertad* since April 1975 serving a sentence for "subversive association". Stela González, wife of prisoner Julio Fregeiro, was arrested on 26 November 1980. She had been active in denouncing conditions for her husband and other prisoners in the *Penal de Libertad,* and was accused of participation in the plot. Also detained was Guillermo Dermit, a 28-year-old doctor and brother of Hugo Dermit who was reported to have committed suicide around the time of his brother's arrest. Amnesty International expressed concern about the treatment of these prisoners.

Amnesty International submitted information on Uruguay to the Secretary-General of the United Nations under the procedure set up to consider "a consistent pattern of gross violations of human rights".

The Human Rights Committee established under the International Covenant on Civil and Political Rights took decisions on several Uruguayan cases. The Uruguayan Government was declared responsible for a number of violations of the covenant, including torture. For example in the case of adopted prisoner of conscience Ismael Weinberger Weisz the committee resolved in December 1980 that the covenant had been violated and declared that the government was "under an obligation to provide the victim with effective remedies including his immediate release . . ." Alberto Grille Motta, who was living in exile, named several torturers and interrogators whom he alleged took part in his interrogation, in evidence to the committee. These allegations have not been investigated by the Uruguayan authorities. The covenant obliges governments to submit a report within one year of its coming into force. Uruguay's report was due in 1977 but has not yet been produced despite a number of requests from the committee.

Amnesty International outlined its concerns in Uruguay to the General Assembly of the Organization of American States which met in Washington between 19 and 28 November 1980.

Venezuela

Amnesty International was concerned about the alleged ill-treatment of detainees by civil and military political police. Wilmer Ramos, said to have been a member of the Venezuelan Communist Party, was detained without warrant by the *Direccion de los Servicios de Inteligencia y Prevencion* (DISIP), the civilian political police, and died in custody two days later. He was detained on 23 December 1980 without violence or injury, but was taken from the DISIP headquarters in Portuguesa the next day with serious internal injuries; he died in hospital one day later, and his death was attributed to injuries caused by severe beatings. The Attorney-General, Dr Pedro J. Mantellini, responsible for the government response to abuses by security forces, appointed a special investigator to examine the case.

Six Colombian citizens whose small private plane made an unauthorized forced landing inside Venezuela in November 1980 were held for five days by the *Direccion de Inteligencia Militar* (DIM), military intelligence, at San Cristobal, Apure state. After the six returned to Colombia, pilot Ernesto Gaviria alleged that they had been tortured with electric shocks during an interrogation in which they had been charged with both spying and drug trafficking. It is not known whether the charges have been investigated by the Attorney General.

In December 1980 several officials commented on the *Amnesty International Report 1980.* Although they recognized the organization's impartiality they stressed that abuses reported in Venezuela were not government policy. Attorney-General Mantellini said measures had been taken to investigate abuses cited in the report and to punish the guilty. Dr Mantellini said that he would "not deny" that "there have been tortures and there have been disappearances", but he stressed these were generally cleared up and "their authors submitted to the action of justice".

However the fate of two people cited in the 1980 report remained unknown. Angel Rodriguez Perez, a member of the *Partido de la Revolución Venezolana* (PRV), Party of the Venezuelan Revolution, headed by former guerrilla leader Douglas Bravo, "disappeared" in February 1980 when he was allegedly seen in the custody of the *Policia Tecnica Judicial,* the national detective corps. Former political prisoner

Nicolas Montes Beltran, reportedly seen in DIM custody after visiting prisoners in the Caracas *Carcel Modelo* (model prison) in March 1980, has also "disappeared". Security officials have denied that the two were ever detained, and investigators from the Attorney-General's office have failed to provide satisfactory explanations.

Asia

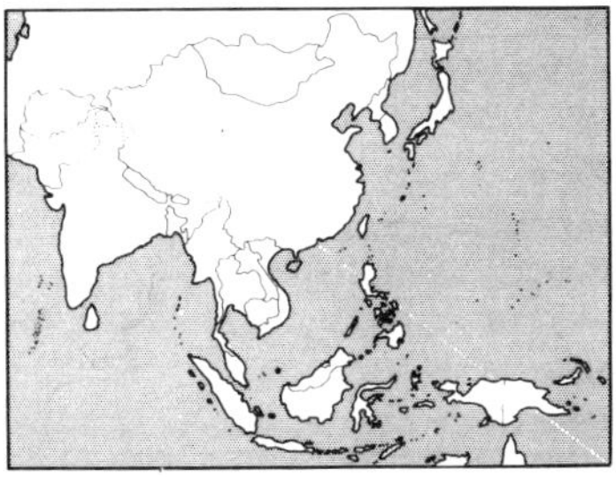

Respect for human rights improved to a limited extent in several countries in Asia with the release of considerable numbers of political prisoners in some, notably Viet Nam, the Philippines, Burma and Laos. However in other respects, for example preventive detention and prolonged political detention, the human rights picture has deteriorated in the last year. Although martial law was abolished in the Philippines and in the Republic of Korea, in both countries the government retained extraordinary powers of arrest and detention and used them extensively against critics.

Prolonged political imprisonment, in some cases without trial, is a major concern of Amnesty International in several Asian countries; especially Taiwan, Indonesia, Malaysia, Brunei and Singapore. In Taiwan (Republic of China) Amnesty International knows of at least 20 prisoners of conscience detained since 1950 in the infamous prison on Green Island. Fourteen other prisoners are believed to have been detained for the last 30 years, and Amnesty International continues to investigate their cases. All the prisoners were summarily tried during the period of emergency after the evacuation of the *Kuomintang* (Nationalist) government from mainland China to the island of Taiwan. In Indonesia Amnesty International estimates that at least 300 political prisoners arrested in connection with the 1965 coup remain in prison. Although the prisoners have all been tried, Amnesty International considers that their trials took place in circumstances which did not permit adequate legal safeguards.

In several Asian states preventive detention without trial is extensively used. In Brunei, which is still nominally British protected, Amnesty International worked for the release of nine prisoners who have been held without trial for alleged involvement in the rebellion of December 1962. The nine men have been in detention for up to 18 years, held under a state of emergency declared in 1962 and still in force. In Malaysia and Singapore political prisoners are held without charge or trial under the Internal Security Act (ISA), and some have been held since the early 1960s. Despite the release of several prominent political prisoners, at least 800 people are still detained in Malaysia without charge or trial under the ISA. The system under which they are detained does not allow the detainees any judicial recourse, nor does it afford them a fair review of their cases. Regrettably the Indian Government reintroduced preventive detention under the provisions of the National Security Act, and by the end of April 1981 Amnesty International had received reports that in certain Indian states political prisoners were being detained under the act.

Detention for the purpose of "re-education" remains a problem in the Socialist Republic of Viet Nam and in the People's Democratic Republic of Laos. In a memorandum submitted to the Vietnamese Government in May 1980 Amnesty International recommended the abolition of "re-education" camps. The detainees, held for the most part since 1975, have not been charged or tried and they are still imprisoned more than six years after the end of the war. Detainees have been freed over the last year but Amnesty International is concerned that the government has announced no timetable for future releases. In both Viet Nam and Laos adequate legal provisions providing minimum safeguards against arbitrary arrest and detention appear to be lacking.

Throughout the year armed hostilities involving foreign troops continued in three territories — Afghanistan, Kampuchea and East Timor. In each, human rights violations of concern to Amnesty International have been reported, in some cases involving both sides in the fighting. However the nature of these conflicts has critically hampered investigation of human rights abuses.

In East Timor, as well as in the Philippines, Amnesty International has been dismayed by the "disappearance" of people after their arrest and detention by security authorities. In October 1980 Amnesty International submitted a report on the "disappearance" of 22 people after their arrest by Indonesian military authorities in East Timor to the Working Group on Enforced or Involuntary Disappearances of the United Nations Commission on Human Rights. In September 1980 Amnesty International submitted to the working group five "disappearance" cases in the Philippines on which it had been working for several years. In the five years between 1975 and 1980 Amnesty International received reports of more than 230 "disappearances" in the Philippines. In the same five-year period Amnesty

International learned of more than 300 extrajudicial killings by military units or by irregular units believed to be acting under the instruction of government officials.

Political trials took place within the region which fell short of internationally agreed standards for a fair trial. For example in the People's Republic of China the trial opened in November 1980 of five former prominent political figures and five former senior military officers. Many of the charges were of a purely political nature and from the outset an assumption of the defendants' guilt was evident in official pronouncements. Amnesty International expressed its concern to the Chinese authorities and after the announcement on 25 January 1981 that two of the defendants, Jiang Qing and Zhang Chunqiao, had been sentenced to death with a two-year reprieve of execution Amnesty International appealed for the commutation of the sentences.

In the Republic of Korea a number of major political trials took place including that of former presidential candidate Kim Dae-jung and 23 other defendants, all of whom Amnesty International considered prisoners of conscience. The defendants were tried before a military tribunal and severe restrictions were placed on the defence. In September Kim Dae-jung was sentenced to death, and other defendants to long terms of imprisonment. In January 1981 the death sentence was commuted to life imprisonment.

In Pakistan political prisoners including prisoners of conscience were frequently tried before military tribunals without any provision for defence lawyers, or for appeal against sentence. In Bangladesh civilians have been tried before military courts on political charges and an Amnesty International delegate was denied access to one major trial.

The death penalty continued to be a major concern of Amnesty International. In the past year Amnesty International compiled dossiers on the death penalty in the People's Republic of China and in Japan. In Malaysia the government resumed executions after a 12-month interval, and executed nine men in seven days. Amnesty International also appealed on behalf of a prisoner sentenced to death in Australia; the death sentence was later commuted. The death penalty was a major concern of Amnesty International in Bangladesh and Pakistan where hundreds of people are executed each year. Others countries where executions took place were the Republic of Korea, Taiwan, Singapore and Thailand.

Amnesty International published a report on human rights violations in the Republic of Korea in February 1981. During the year submissions relating to human rights violations in Afghanistan, Indonesia, the Philippines, Republic of Korea, Singapore, Sri Lanka and East Timor were presented by Amnesty International to the

United Nations and other intergovernmental and non-governmental organizations.

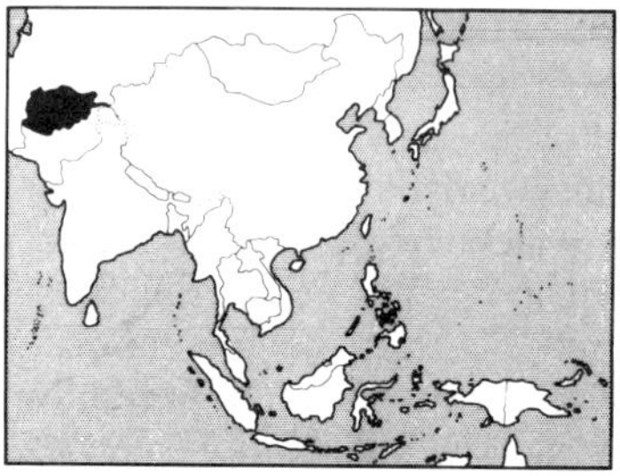

Afghanistan

Amnesty International was concerned about the arrests of several hundred political detainees during the year and the executions of several former government officials following trial *in camera.* It was concerned that no steps were taken by the government to investigate human rights abuses such as torture and "disappearance" which many thousands of political prisoners suffered between April 1978 and December 1979 when the present government came to power. In the absence of the detailed information about political prisoners arrested under previous administrations which the government had promised, Amnesty International continued its investigations into the fate of the "disappeared" prisoners. Amnesty International's efforts were directed towards pressing the government to implement the recommendations for the effective protection of human rights which it set out in a March 1980 memorandum, and to adhere to the assurances which the President gave Amnesty International when its mission visited the country in February 1980.

On 10 December 1980 the government stated that it "aimed at ensuring the social, economic, cultural, political and civil rights of the people as set out in the covenants on human rights". However it has taken no steps to ratify the two international covenants, a major recommendation of the March 1980 memorandum.

On 21 April 1980 the Revolutionary Council proclaimed the Fundamental Principles of the Democratic Republic of Afghanistan (DRA), pending the adoption of a constitution. The Fundamental Principles proclaim the right "to lead a secure life" (Article 29, section 1), the right to express opinions freely and openly (Article 29, section 7), the right not to be arrested without a warrant or outside the provisions of law valid at the time of committing the offence, the right to be presumed innocent unless found guilty and the right to legal defence (Article 30). Article 54 provides for "Special Courts" to assess "specific cases according to law" and Article 56 proclaims that "Judges are entitled to assess cases independently". The same article permits trials *in camera:* the "circumstances under which cases shall be discussed *in camera* will be anticipated by law". Verdicts are final and executions have to be approved by the Revolutionary Council Presidium (Article 58). Amnesty International has no independent information on the application of the Fundamental Principles to political prisoners arrested and tried during the year.

In the week of 26 April 1980 demonstrators, mainly school pupils and students, protested in Kabul against the presence of Soviet troops in the country. Sixty students including six girls were reported to be among those shot in the ensuing violence. On 12 May 1980 Kabul radio reported that 620 people had been arrested in connection with these demonstrations and that 96 would be tried. Amnesty International wrote to President Babrak Karmal on 14 May 1980 to express its concern at the reports of the killings, urging the government to investigate the deaths and asking it to confirm the number arrested. It recalled the assurances it had received during its February 1980 mission that political trials "would be open to the public and to Amnesty International", and asked for confirmation that Amnesty International could attend their trials, and for notice of trial dates.

The government informed Amnesty International on 31 March 1980 that the majority of those arrested in connection with the February disturbances in Kabul had been released and that "those remaining in custody would stand a fair trial". However Amnesty International was not informed by the government of the trial dates nor did it receive other details requested.

The *Kabul New Times* of 8 July 1980 reported that the Special Revolutionary Tribunal had "prosecuted a number of people arrested on charges of legal offences ranging from undermining the gains of the Saur Revolution to damaging national independence and sovereignty". The government stated that they were charged with: "espionage, distribution of news and false statements, membership in treacherous groups" and "perfidious activities such as instigating the people to counter-revolutionary actions such as the February 21 and 22 1980 incidents". The report specified the articles in the Criminal Procedures Law and the Criminal Law and added that "the accused were sentenced to various terms of imprisonment". A few others were apparently released "due to lack of incriminating evidence". On 29 July the Presidium of the DRA announced it had commuted the death sentences imposed by the Special Revolutionary Court on two of the accused — Shir Mohammad and Qorban Ali — to 15 years' imprisonment. Their trial had taken place "in public session", and the accused had participated in the 21 and 22 February disturbances "armed with weapons". Nine others — Barat Ali Jafari, Ali Jafar, Ain Ali, Haji Ali, Sayd Mohammad Bashir, Mohammad Daud Bakhtyari, Dad Mohammad, Khan Mohammad and Mohammad

Most were sentenced to terms of imprisonment ranging from five to 16 years.

Amnesty International cabled President Karmal on 1 August 1980 to express its concern that the prisoners had not been tried before an ordinary court nor granted the possibility of appeal to an independent tribunal as specified in Article 14(5) of the International Covenant on Civil and Political Rights.

The head of the Afghan mission to the United Nations (UN) told Amnesty International on 23 October 1980 that between 6,000 and 7,000 people had been arrested in connection with the April 1980 disturbances, of whom all but 60 or 70 had been released. The remainder were awaiting trial. Amnesty International has not received any further details.

On 8 June 1980 Kabul radio announced that 11 men had been executed. The government said they had been executed on charges including murder, mass killings, torture and "conspiracy against the government and the revolution". Ten were officials of the former government, including some prisoners Amnesty International had interviewed in February 1980. The government also executed Abdul Majid Khalakhani, a left-wing guerrilla leader known for his opposition to Soviet troops in Afghanistan. On 10 June 1980 Amnesty International wrote to President Karmal that it was deeply concerned about the 11 executions, adding that they appeared to violate the safeguards for open trial proclaimed in Article 56 of the Fundamental Principles of the DRA. The head of the Afghan mission to the UN told Amnesty International that among those executed were officials responsible for past human rights violations and confirmed that they had been tried *in camera.*

The government announced that three more officials of the previous government had been executed on 14 June 1980. Amnesty International cabled President Karmal on 19 June 1980 saying it was deeply concerned to learn of the further executions and urging the government to stop them immediately. The trial of these prisoners *in camera* by a Special Revolutionary Court contravened the assurances Amnesty International had received in February 1980. Amnesty International deeply regretted that the government had not informed it of the charges or the trial date. It also expressed concern that there had been no possibility of appealing to an independent tribunal. "The government's failure to adhere in these cases to the requirements of international law and to implement assurances given to Amnesty International is particularly disturbing as the trials resulted in the application of the death penalty".

On 2 August 1980 Amnesty International received a detailed reply to its cables of 10 and 19 June. The government said: "we hope that the time will come when the death penalty will be abolished in Afghanistan but at present the laws of the DRA, proceeding from realities of existing conditions provide for the death penalty". The government maintained that the trials had been held in accordance with Article 56 of the Fundamental Principles of the DRA and that "the trial in question was *in camera* for security reasons".

On 8 October 1980 Amnesty International replied in detail to President Karmal, clarified its position on political imprisonment and the death penalty, and reiterated its grave concern at not being allowed to attend the trials. It deplored the reported executions of four former government officials in late August 1980. It again called upon the President to halt further executions and attached a list of 35 names of former government officials held in Pule Charchi prison. There were no further reports of executions for several months but on 8 February 1981 Kabul radio announced that three members of the *Hezbi Islami* group which opposes the government had been sentenced to death by a Revolutionary Court. On 12 February it reported that four members of the *Mujahiddin* (Islamic guerrilla fighters) had been sentenced to death and executed. That day Amnesty International cabled President Karmal and appealed to him to halt further executions. It stressed that it was opposed to executions of prisoners whether carried out by the government or by groups engaged in armed opposition to the government. Amnesty International has received a number of reports that prisoners taken by such groups have been executed. One report of 2 March 1981 stated that 14 Afghan soldiers and the nephew of a DRA government minister were executed by an Islamic resistance group, the *Harhat-e-inquilib-e-islami,* after "trial by Islamic tribunal".

Statistics published in the *Kabul New Times* between 16 March 1980 and 8 December 1980 showed that the government had announced the release of at least 4,231 prisoners whom it described as "political prisoners" or "persons deceived by the enemies". Reports of political arrests included the arrests of university students at Kabul University for alleged membership of the banned Muslim Brotherhood during the late summer, arrests of several former government officials and university professors in December 1980, and arrests of suspected Islamic guerrillas and dissident members of the government reported in February and March 1981.

On 13 August 1980 the government stated that it had freed several hundred prisoners including: 140 untried prisoners during Ramadan; 240 prisoners released from Herat in September; 136 political prisoners from Kandahar in late November 1980; 86 people accused of "political offences" on 27 December 1980; and on 27 April 1981, 706 political detainees "to mark the third anniversary of the Saur

Revolution". Amnesty International welcomed these releases and asked President Karmal for details of the categories of political prisoners it had released and the place where they had been held. It urged the government to publish the names of the released political prisoners as recommended in the March 1980 memorandum. Amnesty International received no reply to these requests and government announcements of releases in the *Kabul New Times* remained unsubstantiated by details of individual political prisoners.

In February 1980 the government said that there were 41 political prisoners in Pule Charchi prison, and other official sources told Amnesty International that 91 political prisoners were "under investigation". On 12 April there were 385 political and security detainees in Pule Charchi prison according to a visiting delegation of the International Committee of the Red Cross (ICRC). Their number has reportedly further increased since then and international organizations have not been allowed to visit prisons holding political prisoners. Amnesty International was investigating several reports that political prisoners have been beaten during interrogation. Amnesty International has also received reports of political prisoners held in prisons in Jalalabad, Herat, Aibah in Samangan province, Kunduz, Kandahar, Nangarhar, Baghlan, Badghis, Mazar-e-Sharif and Jauzjan, but has been unable to obtain details on individual political prisoners.

Pursuing its statement to the United Nations Commission on Human Rights of May 1979, which had described a pattern of gross violations of human rights under the former government of President Amin, Amnesty International submitted supplementary information about human rights in Afghanistan on 30 May 1980. Amnesty International noted that the government had not fully investigated the whereabouts or fate of "disappeared" people. Amnesty International had submitted to the government a list of 450 people arrested before 27 December 1979, at least 100 of whom it believed to be among the "disappeared", but had not been given the details it requested. It had also urged the government to establish responsibility for past torture and "disappearances" and to ensure that those responsible were brought to justice. Amnesty International remained concerned that no systematic review of past human rights abuses appeared to have taken place and that former officials, named by authoritative sources as responsible, continued to hold official government positions.

According to a report from the ICRC the government had agreed that the ICRC and the Afghan Red Crescent should establish a tracing agency with a mandate which included the "search for missing persons". However since the summer of 1980 the authorities have opposed the establishment of such a tracing agency.

On 19 December 1980 Amnesty International supplied supplementary information to the United Nations Commission on Human Rights about human rights in Afghanistan, reiterating its deep concern that the government had not implemented its recommendations in respect of the thousands of "disappeared" and that their families continued to live in uncertainty about their fate, some believing their relatives were still alive and detained in Kabul's Pule Charchi prison and elsewhere.

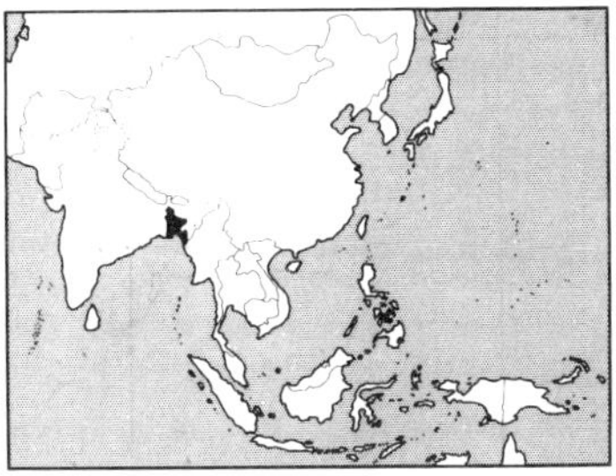

Bangladesh

Amnesty International was concerned about the continued imprisonment of political prisoners under special legislation; the trial of prisoners on charges of "anti-state activities" by military courts applying summary procedures; the inadequate protection of political prisoners in jail; prison killings; and the large number of executions, including those of people convicted by military courts without the right of appeal.

Arrests of politically active workers, students and trade union leaders continued to be reported, but details about individual prisoners of conscience seldom reached Amnesty International. In several cases the Supreme Court ruled that the detention of political prisoners was illegal and ordered their release, and the government has declared several amnesties, some of which have been of benefit to a small number of political prisoners.

On 22 April 1981 the Deputy Minister of Home Affairs stated in the *Jatiya Sangsad* (parliament) that 403 people were detained without trial. He said the government "reviews the cases from time to time and releases those who are considered eligible to be freed". Amnesty International continued to work for the release of several adopted prisoners of conscience held for many years without trial; one of them, Habibullah Khan of Pathuakhali, has now been detained for more than eight years.

The statement did not specify under which laws the 403 prisoners were held, but it is presumed to be the Special Powers Act which provides wide powers to detain political prisoners. In addition, an unknown number of political prisoners were still imprisoned after conviction by martial law courts under the provisions of the Fifth Amendment to the Constitution. This specifies that convictions passed by military courts remain valid despite the lifting of martial law in April 1979. It was not known how many of the estimated 1,000 prisoners convicted by martial law courts since 1975 were still in detention.

Amnesty International continued its exchanges with the Home Ministry about the political detainees it has adopted as prisoners of conscience. Of the 383 political prisoners detained under special legislation whose names were given to Amnesty International by the government of Shaikh Mujibur Rahman in 1975, the government has now released all but six. In response to its letter of 3 April 1980 and a cable of 27 May 1980 to the Home Minister inquiring about the arrest of 53 members of the Bangladesh Communist Party (see *Amnesty International Report 1980*) Amnesty International was informed that all members of the Communist Party were released in June 1980 except the Secretary General, Mohammad Farhad, who the government said was awaiting trial on a charge of "criminal conspiracy and waging or attempting to wage war". Amnesty International continued to investigate his case. It had adopted as prisoners of conscience the other members of the Communist Party detained under the 1974 Special Powers Act without specific charges.

On 13 August 1980 the government announced the release of 331 prisoners, including 17 political detainees whose names were given to Amnesty International by the government on 19 September 1980. On 7 November 1980 the government announced a further amnesty for prisoners on the occasion of National Revolution and Solidarity Day, according to reports in the Bangladesh press "as part of the government's efforts to remove congestion in jails as well as expediting trial cases". (In April 1980 the government announced that more than 83,000 cases were pending before the Bangladesh courts.) The government said it expected 1,500 prisoners would benefit from the amnesty but political prisoners held for "anti-state" activities would not be released. On 26 March 1981 the government announced another amnesty of 194 prisoners of whom 35 were said to be political detainees. Amnesty International has not received details of their identity.

On 4 November 1980 Amnesty International wrote to President Ziaur Rahman to reiterate its grave concern about the inadequacy of measures to protect political prisoners. Killings of political prisoners in jail have been reported particularly since 1975, and, in those rare instances where inquiries have been instituted by the government, their findings have not been publicized. In September and October 1980 there were violent incidents in Rangpur, Mymensingh and Magura jails. On 12 October 1980 prisoners took control of Khulna District jail holding 24 warders hostage and reportedly demanded the release of all prisoners detained for more than three months without trial. They demanded the abolition of the death penalty and improved prison conditions, including regular visits by High Court judges to the jails. On 21 October armed police entered the prison and the number of prisoners killed in the ensuing fighting was officially put at 39. Two hundred others were reportedly seriously injured, of whom 117 were police, according to the government. An opposition source put the number of prisoners killed as far higher.

On 4 November 1980 Amnesty International wrote to President Ziaur Rahman expressing grave concern about the incident and urging the government to set up an independent investigation to establish responsibility for the killings, and publish the findings. The government said that the prisoners were killed in fighting between two opposing groups of prisoners but public reaction in Bangladesh reflected a widespread belief that the police had killed them. On 22 October 1980 the government announced it had ordered a judicial inquiry by the district and sessions judge of Jessore but the findings have not been published. At the time of the incident the government admitted to serious prison overcrowding and that conditions were "awful": there were then 911 prisoners in the jail, which had an official capacity of 245.

On 27 November 1980 the Jail Reforms Committee, headed by Justice Munim of the Supreme Court, submitted its final report to the government. The committee was established on 4 November 1978 with a mandate to recommend prison reforms and changes in the prison code. The Home Minister, A. S. M. Mustafizur Rahman, said the government would "try to base its proposed improvements in the jails on the recommendations of the Jails Reforms Committee", but, as far as is known, the government did not publish the committee's report or its recommendations. On 24 November the Home Minister announced plans to build a separate prison for political detainees outside Dacca.

On 12 January 1981 it was reported that a prisoner awaiting trial, Jheru Karmaker, had died in Khulna Jail hospital. According to the superintendent of the jail he had been admitted from police custody to the jail hospital with "marks of physical torture".

Torture has also been reported in the Chittagong Hill Tracts, an area in south-eastern Bangladesh inhabited by a tribal population many of whom are Buddhists or Christians. They have opposed the settlement of Bengalis from the plains, a policy encouraged by successive Bangladeshi governments, and have demanded a return to a greater degree of autonomy. Particularly since 1975, the political demands of the tribal population have been accompanied by acts of violence. Amnesty International has received an increasing number of allegations that members of the armed forces and police as well as tribal people have been killed in guerrilla activities. There have also been continuing reports that the security forces were responsible for mass arrests, torture and forced expulsion of tribal people in the Hill Tracts. The allegations were difficult to assess particularly since official permission is required to enter the area.

On 4 November 1980 Amnesty International asked the government to investigate the events of 25 March 1980 when up to 300 tribal people were reportedly shot by the defence forces, and which had been reported widely in the press. It urged the government to set up an independent inquiry and asked for details of the number of people arrested in the Chittagong Hill Tracts in connection with political activities, and the charges against them. So far the government has not replied.

Fighting in the Chittagong Hill Tracts persisted and on 1 December 1980 the government introduced the Disturbed Areas Bill in the *Jatiya Sangsad.* The bill was strongly opposed by political parties and the Supreme Court Bar Association, and has been referred to the Standing Committee on Law and Parliamentary Affairs. It empowers the government to declare any part of Bangladesh a "disturbed area" by simply giving notice in the government gazette. Specified military, paramilitary and police personnel may, if in their opinion "it is necessary for the maintenance of public order", "fire upon or otherwise use force, even to the extent of causing death, against any person engaged in any unlawful activity", which the bill defines widely as activity "prejudicial to the sovereignty or territorial integrity of Bangladesh" or to Bangladesh's "security or public order". The bill allows for the arrest and detention of prisoners without trial, apparently indefinitely. People committing or advocating "unlawful activity" can be sentenced to imprisonment or death by hanging or shooting.

Amnesty International wrote to President Ziaur Rahman on 2 February 1981, saying it was concerned that the bill would authorize official personnel to shoot to kill people on mere suspicion. It drew the government's attention to the United Nations Code of Conduct for Law Enforcement Officials. Amnesty International also expressed concern that the wide powers to arrest and detain people suspected of committing "unlawful activity" would allow people to be arrested or killed for the non-violent exercise of human rights. An Amnesty International observer visiting Dacca in April 1981 learned that the bill was still before parliament and was assured by the Vice-President and Minister of Law that Amnesty International's views "would be taken into consideration".

On 9 March 1981 the trial of Colonel (Ret'd) Abdul Aziz Pasha,

Colonel Didarul Alam, Colonel (Ret'd) Norunnabi Choudhury and two civilians, Kazi Munir and Mosharraf Hussain, opened before the Dacca Field General Court Martial. They were charged with holding secret meetings and inciting armed personnel to military rebellion. The accused were alleged to have planned to stage a coup on 17 June 1980.

On 17 March 1981 Amnesty International cabled President Ziaur Rahman expressing concern that, despite the lifting of martial law, two civilians were among the accused on trial before a military court, whose summary proceedings Amnesty International had previously described as "falling far short of international standards" (*Report of an Amnesty International Mission to Bangladesh, 4-12 April 1977)*. It urged the government to grant a fair and public trial to all the accused but no reply was received. Amnesty International sent an observer to the trial and to hearings of the petition submitted by Mosharraf Hussain, one of the five accused, to the Division Bench of the Supreme Court, challenging the military courts' jurisdiction to try civilians. The observer arrived in Dacca on 9 April 1981 and left on 20 April 1981 after finally having been informed that he would not be allowed to attend the Field General Court Martial proceedings. During his stay he met the Deputy Attorney General (Criminal), defence lawyers, the Vice-President and Minister of Law, Justice Sattar, and the Joint Secretary of the Home Ministry. He discussed Amnesty International's concerns about the trial and about provisions in the Disturbed Areas Act. After his departure Amnesty International cabled the President to explain why the delegate had left Dacca: "His inability to attend the trial greatly heightens concern about the standards of fairness and openness adopted by the Field General Court Martial. The rule of law requires that justice must not only be done, but must also be seen to be done". Although appreciating that defence facilities were apparently available to the accused, Amnesty International feared that the trial fell short of internationally recognized standards. Amnesty International understood that the entire prosecution evidence was based on statements by two of the five accused who had turned state witness, and that some confessions were allegedly obtained under duress. It said trial standards of independence and impartiality were not met by judges who were career army officers and therefore part of the executive. It added its belief that the trial of civilians before such courts would appear to be against the spirit of the constitution. Amnesty International said it was disturbed that no reasons for the court's decision were required and that there were no provisions of appeal, as required by Article 14(5) of the International Covenant on Civil and Political Rights. Amnesty International appealed to the President to transfer the trial to an independent court where full legal safeguards, including the right of appeal, were observed. The government was also asked to investigate allegations that confessions had been obtained under duress.

The number of executions was high and included prisoners executed for "political and anti-state activities". On 27 May 1980 the Home Minister stated that 424 people had been executed over the past five years. Many of these death sentences were apparently passed by military courts with no appeal. The sentence has to be confirmed by the President.

Only rarely did details of individuals sentenced to death reach Amnesty International. In its letter of 4 November 1980 Amnesty International asked the government to give the names of all people under sentence of death but this information has not been received. It also expressed grave concern about the hanging in Dacca Central Jail on 4 June 1980 of four members of the Awami League, reportedly convicted by a Special Military Court on charges of murdering political opponents. The executions were apparently carried out without the accused being granted the minimum safeguard of the right of appeal.

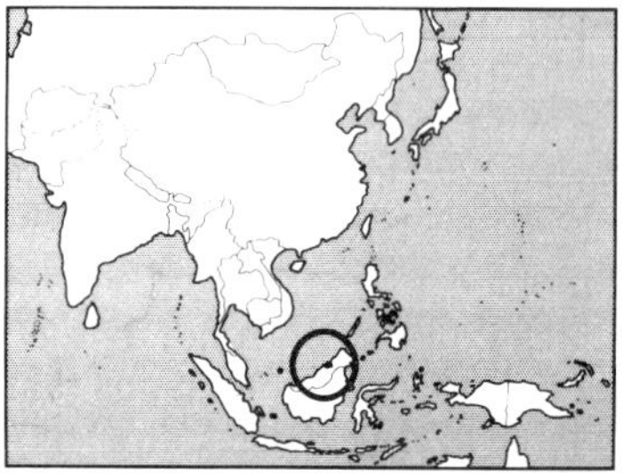

Brunei

Amnesty International was concerned by the continued use of emergency legislation to detain people without trial for extraordinarily long periods.

All the detainees held under emergency orders about whom Amnesty International has received information were former members of the banned *Partai Rakyat Brunei* (PRB), Brunei People's Party. In August 1962 the PRB had won all the elected seats in the Legislative Council. Sultan Sir Omar Ali Saifuddin called in British troops to suppress a rebellion launched by the PRB after the Legislative Council had failed to meet.

After the defeat of the rebellion, approximately 2,500 members of the PRB and its military wing, the *Tentera Nasional Kalimantan Utara* (TNKU), North Kalimantan National Army, were arrested. Almost all have been released. Section 83 of the 1959 constitution permits the Sultan to proclaim a state of emergency whenever it appears to him that a public danger exists. Under Section 83(3), the Sultan is empowered to issue any orders he considers desirable subject only to the provision that "no such order shall confer any right to punish without trial, by death, imprisonment or fine". The Sultan issued the Emergency Orders of December 1962 under Section 83(3) authorizing the Chief Minister to issue two-year detention orders renewable indefinitely. The Sultan and his successor, Sir Hassanal Bolkiah, have maintained the state of emergency ever since 1962, and have used the Emergency Orders to detain political prisoners for many years without trial.

Since November 1974, 40 detainees who had been adopted by Amnesty International as prisoners of conscience have been released. The remaining nine adopted prisoners of conscience have spent between 15 and 18½ years in detention. Amnesty International understands that there have been further arrests of alleged associates of the PRB under the Emergency Orders since the initial wave after the rebellion. Amnesty International believes that approximately 30 detainees were held under the Emergency Orders but could not be sure of the precise number. The government would not disclose the figure even to members of the Legislative Council.

Amnesty International was concerned by the conditions in which the detainees were held. After eight prisoners escaped in July 1973, the remaining detainees were transferred from the relatively liberal conditions of Berakas detention camp to the much stricter regime of Jerudong prison, where they were believed to be held in isolation and denied regular visits and correspondence. Amnesty International received reports that a number were in declining physical and mental health. Several were of advanced years, two being in their sixties.

Amnesty International believes that those still detained were not being held because they individually constituted a threat to the security of Brunei. This conclusion was suggested both by the fact that most detainees have been released and by consideration of the background of those still detained. Of those still in detention, four were farmers, two foremen, one was a fitter, one a teacher and one a fisherman. All except one were ordinary members of the PRB, the exception being Othman bin Haji Karim who was a branch committee member; he was a 66-year-old farmer and featured as a prisoner of the month in the *Amnesty International Newsletter* in September 1980.

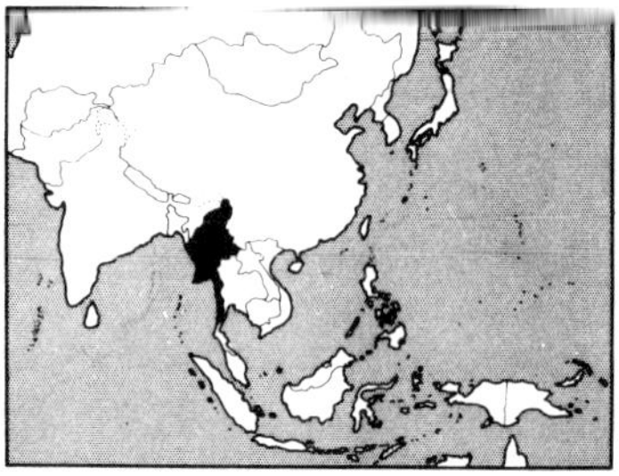

Burma

Amnesty International's concerns were political imprisonment and the ill-treatment of detainees. Although some political detainees have been released, Amnesty International continued to receive reports of ill-treatment and torture which have proved difficult to substantiate. The government of General Ne Win enforced strict censorship and observers were not allowed into the country.

On 28 May 1980 the government proclaimed an amnesty stating that no action would be taken against "those engaged in insurrection against the State" for offences committed earlier, if they returned "to the legal fold" within 90 days. The amnesty applied to political and criminal prisoners.

A considerable number of political opponents of the government took advantage of this amnesty. Some had been in exile and others had associated with insurgent groups within Burma. Amongst those who returned from exile abroad was U Nu, the former Prime Minister, whose government was overthrown in a coup by General Ne Win in 1962.

Amnesty International received reports that all those detained in mass arrests during former United Nations Secretary-General U Thant's funeral in December 1974, and student demonstrations in June 1975, were released. Also released under the amnesty was Thakin Soe, former Chairman of the Burmese Communist Party's "Red Flag" faction, whose death sentence had been confirmed on 19 March 1974 by the State Council and who had been held on death row ever since. Some 4,000 political prisoners were reportedly released under the amnesty.

Many of the allegations of arrests and ill-treatment of political detainees concerned minority peoples such as the Karens and the Rohingya Muslims of Arakan. Amnesty International was investigating reports that Htun Myint Kyu, the former Secretary-General of the Burma Muslim Organization, had once more been arrested and held in detention.

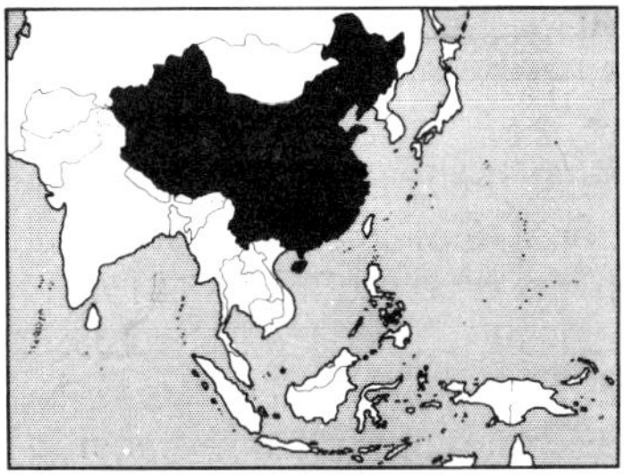

China

The main concerns of Amnesty International were political imprisonment, unfair trial procedures, and the use of the death penalty. In the past year there has been a noticeable deterioration in the human rights situation marked by a number of arbitrary arrests and increased restrictions on civil liberties.

On 27 September 1980 the Chief Procurator, Huang Huoqing, announced that the case of "the Lin Biao - Jiang Qing counter-revolutionary clique" had been investigated and sent to the Supreme People's Court for prosecution. The defendants, 10 former leading officials, were described as "10 major criminals" and included the so-called "gang of four": Jiang Qing (Mao Zedong's widow), Zhang Chunqiao, Yao Wenyuan and Wang Hongwen. A fifth civilian defendant, Chen Boda, was to be tried with the "gang of four" by a civilian tribunal. The other five defendants — all former military commanders — would be tried by a military tribunal. Both tribunals would be part of a special division of the Supreme People's Court formed especially for the occasion with over 30 judges.

The civilian defendants were charged with "counter-revolutionary" offences including "conspiring to overthrow the political power of the dictatorship of the proletariat and splitting the nation", "organizing and leading a counter-revolutionary clique", "framing and persecuting party and state leaders and usurping party and state power" and "torturing people to extract confessions". The five military defendants were also charged with "plotting to murder Chairman Mao and instigating counter-revolutionary armed rebellion". This charge referred to the attempted coup by former Defence Minister Lin Biao, who disappeared in September 1971. By the time the trial started the five former commanders had already spent more than nine years in detention.

In announcing the forthcoming trial, the Chief Procurator indicated that trials of alleged followers of the "gang of four" would be held throughout the country during the following months. The indictment, which became available later, named 60 other people allegedly involved.

On 13 October 1980 Amnesty International wrote to the Chief Procurator, Huang Huoqing, urging a full and fair trial for all political defendants and stating that in its experience when former political officials were prosecuted on charges connected with their actions when in office, there was an inherent danger of internationally agreed standards for a fair trial being jeopardized by political considerations. It cited principles such as the right of the accused to be presumed innocent until proven guilty, guaranteed in the Universal Declaration of Human Rights and the International Covenant on Civil and Political Rights, and asked for clarification of the facilities for the defendants to present their defence. Referring to the Chief Procurator's statement that as well as the 10 "principal defendants", others would soon be tried separately, Amnesty International urged the government to make public full details of the people concerned, the charges against them and relevant legislation, and the dates of their trials.

The trial of the 10 started in Peking on 20 November 1980. The defendants were offered a number of leading Chinese jurists as defence counsel, but several refused. Only chosen "representatives of the masses" were admitted in court. Selected extracts were shown on television and published in the official press. A few unofficial reports of the proceedings showed that the selective reporting by the official news media was politically biassed against the defendants. For instance statements implicating Mao Zedong which were said to have been made by Jiang Qing in her defence were not reported. During the last hearing on 29 December 1980 the prosecution demanded the death sentence for Jiang Qing, but the penalties it requested for the other defendants were not disclosed. The court then adjourned to decide its verdict.

After the announcement on 25 January 1981 that two of the defendants, Jiang Qing and Zhang Chunqiao, had been sentenced to death, Amnesty International appealed to the authorities to commute the death sentences. In both cases the sentences were passed with a two-year stay of execution and, according to the law, execution depends on the prisoner's behaviour during that period. In a news release on 25 January 1981 Amnesty International pointed out that in some other cases prisoners who had been given a suspended death sentence had eventually been executed. Furthermore the procedures instituted for the trial meant that the decision of the special court was final and none of those convicted would have the right to appeal.

Amnesty International declared that the proceedings had failed to meet internationally agreed standards for a fair trial. From the outset an assumption of the defendants' guilt was evident in official statements and press reports. No witnesses were reported to have been called for the defence during the trial, which was surrounded by secrecy and of which only selected extracts were published. It was also evident from the indictment that some of the charges were of a purely political character and unrelated to actions that might be reasonably regarded as criminal.

Amnesty International reiterated these concerns in a letter to the Prime Minister, Zhao Ziyang, on 30 April 1981 saying in particular that the standards applied at the trial of the 10 former officials might have an adverse effect on the conduct of other political trials. These concerns had been reinforced by statements made after the trial by jurists including the President of the Supreme People's Court, Jiang Hua. In early March 1981 he said in a report to the Standing Committee of the National People's Congress that the trial had set an example for judicial work and that the judgement would "withstand the test of time and strengthen China's socialist legal system."

Amnesty International also raised other cases which had come to its attention, including that of a group tried for political offences in January 1981 in Kunming, Yunnan province. They were officially described as a "counter-revolutionary clique plotting to overthrow the government and topple the proletarian regime". According to Kunming radio on 23 January 1981 the alleged leader of the group, Wang Yongkun, had "actively followed the Jiang Qing counter-revolutionary clique" and gathered a group of more than 10 people who from March 1967 "held many meetings" and "secretly plotted criminal activities to topple Premier Zhou Enlai". However the report gave no information on any such "criminal activities" except for the accusation that, in May 1976, Wang Yongkun and his group, "thinking that the chance for counter-revolution had come", wrote posters and slogans "slandering and levelling false charges against party and state leaders" which they posted in the centre of Kunming and other places. In its letter, Amnesty International expressed concern that Wang Yongkun and eight others tried with him were sentenced to penalties ranging from 15 years' imprisonment to three years' surveillance on the basis of accusations which appeared to be purely political. The letter asked for information on the precise charges, on the nature of the evidence on which the charges were based, and on the facilities for defence at the trial.

While noting official measures to restore proper legal process over the past years and official comments indicating that increased attention should be paid to the rights of citizens, Amnesty International also raised several cases of people who appeared to have been denied the most fundamental protection and who were held for the peaceful exercise of basic human rights. Ren Wanding, formerly chairperson of the defunct unofficial group, the "Chinese Human Rights Alliance", was arrested in Peking on 4 April 1979 while putting up a poster criticizing the restrictions on unofficial publishing imposed a few days earlier by the Peking municipal authorities. Since then no information has been disclosed on the charges against him and his whereabouts. Despite many appeals his fate remained unknown and he has now been detained for two years, apparently without charge or trial.

Liu Qing, an editor of the dissident magazine *April Fifth Forum,* was arrested in Peking on 11 November 1979. He had distributed an unauthorized transcript of the trial of Wei Jingsheng, the former editor of the unofficial magazine *Exploration,* who was sentenced to 15 years' imprisonment in October 1979 on political charges. Nothing was heard of Liu Qing for several months after his arrest and his family was neither informed of any charges against him nor allowed to see him. It is reported that in August 1980 the Peking Public Security Bureau informed his relatives that he had been sent to Shaanxi province for three years of "re-education-through-labour". This punishment can be imposed by a simple recommendation by the police, without the person concerned being charged or tried. Liu Qing has received an administrative punishment amounting to detention without trial for the peaceful exercise of his human rights.

Another editor of the *April Fifth Forum,* Xu Wenli, and one of his associates, Yang Jing, were reported to have been arrested in Peking on 10 April 1981. It was also reported that their relatives were neither told of the reasons for their arrest nor informed of their whereabouts. This contradicts the provisions of the Arrest and Detention Act adopted by the National People's Congress in 1979, which stipulated that the family should be informed of the reason for arrest and the place of detention within 24 hours (Article 5) and that the person arrested should either be formally charged or released within three to seven days (Article 8). Amnesty International urged the Prime Minister to look into these and other similar cases so that the detainees might be promptly released or brought to a fair and open trial.

Until his arrest Xu Wenli worked as an electrician in a Peking factory. He was the founder of the *April Fifth Forum,* which is thought to be the first unofficial magazine to have appeared in Peking in the autumn of 1978. By June 1979, when unofficial journals were banned, the group publishing the magazine consisted of about 20 people, mainly young workers and some members of the Chinese Communist Youth League. The group decided to cease publication in March 1980 after strong warnings from the authorities. Since then the group has circulated a private newsletter and joined in appeals with other similar groups calling for the release of imprisoned dissenters. According to sources in Hong Kong on 10 January 1981 Xu Wenli appealed to the authorities about Liu Qing, asking for his relatives to be informed of his whereabouts and conditions and for him to be granted a proper trial or released if innocent. Xu Wenli was reported to have been taken away from his house at midnight on 10 April 1981 by the police who also confiscated his tape recordings and personal papers. No further information has been received on his or Yang Jing's detention.

These arrests followed a series of warnings in the official press in early 1981 against people considered too critical of the government or who "attacked the party leadership and socialist system". An unpublished Communist Party document is reported to have called for a total ban on "illegal publications and organizations" and to have named several potential victims of disciplinary action.

Other supporters of unofficial groups and magazines were reported to have been arrested in several cities during the year. In some cases detention lasted only a few days, and in others the detainees were sentenced. Three printing workers from Taiyuan, Shanxi province, were tried in February 1981 for "organizing a counter-revolutionary group". The three, Wang Jianwei, Zhang Jianxin and Chen Yuming, were accused of forming an independent party, the "Chinese Democratic Party", which had published a manifesto criticizing the one-party rule of the Communist Party and demanding a "government of union". They are believed to have been arrested in 1980 in Taiyuan. According to an official press report, Zhang Jianxin and Chen Yuming were sentenced to three years' and Wang Jianwei to two years' imprisonment by Taiyuan Intermediate People's Court.

A 78-year-old Roman Catholic priest, Father Stanislas Shen, was reported to have been arrested on 6 May 1980 in Shanghai on charges of "hampering production and modernization", after a pilgrimage of several thousand people near Shanghai. Despite his age and a heart condition Father Shen was sent to the Beimaoling labour camp in Anhui province, where he had apparently already spent 20 years in detention. He had been released from there two years previously. Despite appeals on his behalf, he was still held there in late 1980.

Hao Ming, an art critic and journalist from Hong Kong, has been detained incommunicado without charge since his arrest in Shanghai on 7 October 1980 during a trip to China. Hao Ming, better known under his pen-name Fang Dan, had emigrated from China to Hong Kong in 1974 but had returned on several short visits since then. His sister in Peking was officially informed of his arrest by the police on 5 November 1980, but was not told the reasons for his detention or where he was being held. By mid-January 1981 his whereabouts were still unknown and no charges had yet been made public against him. His wife, who lives in Hong Kong, had received no answer from the government departments in Peking to which she had written inquiring about her husband's arrest. Fang Dan was thought to have been arrested because of his close personal contacts with certain intellectuals, artists and high-ranking cadres in China. The purpose of his last trip to

China was to attend an unofficial art exhibition in Urumqi (the capital of Xinjiang province, in the northwest).

Amnesty International continued to be concerned about the use of the death penalty for a wide range of criminal and "counter-revolutionary" offences. As part of its work for the abolition of the death penalty around the world, it published a dossier on the death penalty in the People's Republic of China, and appealed for commutation of death sentences on humanitarian grounds in all cases which came to its attention.

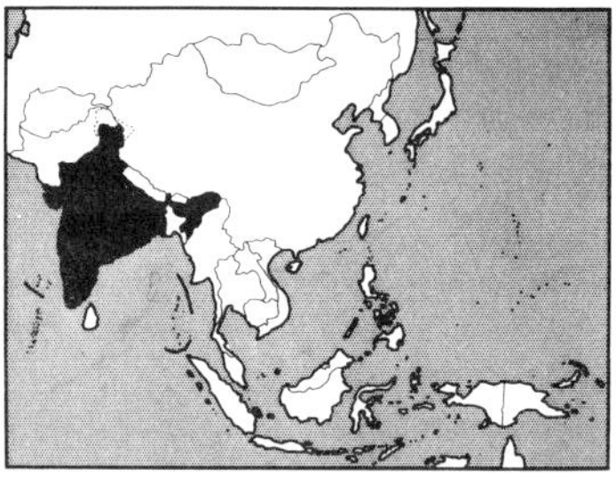

India

Amnesty International concerns were the reintroduction of statutory provisions for preventive detention, widespread police brutality, torture, persistent reports of deaths in police custody, and killings of political activists by the police. It was also concerned that executions have resumed since the Supreme Court upheld the constitutional validity of the death penalty.

India ratified the International Covenant on Civil and Political Rights on 10 April 1979, but the government made a declaration before signing which included an important reservation on the applicability of the safeguards against arbitrary arrest and detention: "With reference to Article 9 of the International Covenant on Civil and Political Rights, the Government of the Republic of India takes the position that the provisions of the Article shall be so applied as to be in consonance with the provisions of clauses (3) to (7) of Article 22 of the Constitution of India. Further, under the Indian legal system, there is no enforceable right to compensation for persons claiming to be victims of unlawful arrest or detention against the state". (Article 22 of the constitution provides the constitutional basis for preventive detention.)

In a letter of 4 November 1980 to Prime Minister Indira Gandhi Amnesty International expressed its belief that the declaration rendered void the text and meaning of Article 9 of the covenant and recommended its withdrawal. On 30 April 1980 Amnesty International had urged the government to ratify the Optional Protocol to the International Covenant on Civil and Political Rights, which allows individuals to petition the Human Rights Committee for alleged breaches of the covenant after all domestic legal mechanisms have been exhausted. On 4 November 1980 the Joint Secretary, Ministry of Home Affairs, replied that "the government of India are of the view that complaints by individuals against any executive action should be dealt with only by national courts and not by an International Organisation. It is, therefore, not considered necessary to ratify the Protocol."

On 23 September 1980 the President of India announced the National Security Ordinance (NSO), which was replaced by the National Security Act (NSA) on 23 December 1980. Like the ordinance, the act gives wide powers of arrest and detention without trial to both the central and state governments. Detention may be ordered for three months initially and the orders may be renewed for up to 12 months. The grounds for detention are widely defined; officials may order people to be detained to prevent them "from acting in any manner prejudicial to the security of the state . . . the maintenance of public order . . . or the maintenance of supplies and services essential to the community". Detainees have to be informed of the reasons for detention normally within five and not more than 10 days after arrest and within three weeks the grounds for detention have to be put before an Advisory Board consisting of three active or retired High Court judges. The opinion of the Advisory Board is binding upon the government. However detainees have no right of legal representation before the Advisory Board, and if the board does not confirm the grounds for detention, a fresh detention order can be made upon release.

Strong opposition to the reintroduction of statutory provisions for preventive detention was expressed in the press and in parliament. Some Indian states were entirely opposed to detention without trial but others said they would use it to detain critics of the government. At the end of April 1981 the Supreme Court was still hearing a petition challenging the constitutional validity of the NSO. The petition was brought by a member of parliament of the Communist Party of India (Marxist) from Bihar who had been detained under the NSO despite the state government's earlier assurance it would not be used against political opponents.

Amnesty International wrote to the Prime Minister on 4 November 1980 to reiterate its long-standing concerns about the use of preventive detention. It said that the proposed statutory detention laws bypassed long-established legal procedures according to which charges have to be brought in an independent court, the accused has the right to a defence lawyer and the right of appeal. Amnesty International said the provisions of the NSO negated fundamental legal safeguards laid down in the Universal Declaration of Human Rights and the International Covenant on Civil and Political Rights. It expressed concern at the departure from these international human rights standards in peace-time without due regard for the provisions of Article 4 of the covenant, which lays down specific limits for derogation from provisions of the covenant in "time of public emergency which threatens the life of the nation". Amnesty International expressed the fear that the wide powers for detention in the ordinance would enable central and state government officials to hold people of dissenting views in prolonged detention without trial. Amnesty International members around the world wrote to the government reasserting the organization's concerns about preventive detention. However the Home Ministry's letter of 4 November 1980 to Amnesty International stated: "You have suggested that provisions relating to preventive detention should be deleted from the Constitution of India. In the totality of the circumstances obtaining in this country, the Government of India does not consider it necessary to amend the Constitution in order to dispense with the provisions relating to preventive detention".

On 6 December 1980 the government said 207 detainees were held under the provisions of the NSO, with the largest numbers in Uttar Pradesh (65) and Madhya Pradesh (63). Prime Minister Gandhi assured opposition members on 10 January 1981 that the act was not intended to curb political dissent. India's Home Minister, Zail Singh, gave similar assurances when introducing the National Security Bill in the *Lok Sabha* (parliament) on 12 December 1980 but added that the government would not hesitate to use preventive detention "to put down violent forces trying to sabotage democracy". The provisions of the NSO appear to have been used on a relatively small scale in a few states to detain some hundreds of detainees suspected of minor criminal acts and some on apparently political grounds. However reports indicated that the NSA had been used in most states and that detainees included critics or suspected critics of the government held on vaguely defined grounds of national security.

Students, trade unionists, members of political parties and others have been arrested under the NSA and the NSO for engaging in non-violent political activities. Reports included the arrest of members of the Communist Party of India and the Communist Party of India (Marxist) in Andhara Pradesh; sympathizers with the Communist Party of India (Marxist-Leninist), known in India as "Naxalites", in the Punjab and Tamil Nadu; members of the Muslim League in Uttar Pradesh; and members of the Congress (I) Party, the *Jammat-e-Islami* (Party of Islam), and the People's League in the state of Jammu and Kashmir, which has its own preventive detention law, the Public Safety Act. Arrests have also been reported from the states of Rajasthan, Gujarat, Karnataka, Madhya Pradesh and Orissa. Many arrests under the NSA resulted in short-term detentions as the Advisory Boards and the state High Courts ordered the release of some detainees ruling that there were insufficient grounds for detention. For example Shankar Guhar Niyogi, a well-known labour leader from Bhopal, was one of the first arrested under the NSA on 11 February 1981, but his release was ordered by the Madhya Pradesh Advisory Board on 19 March, which found the grounds for his detention "flimsy".

Civil disobedience protests continued in Assam against immigrant workers, mainly of Bengali origin. On 5 April 1980 the state was declared a disturbed area, and the 1955 Assam Disturbed Areas Act and Armed Forces (Assam and Manipur) Special Powers Act, 1958, came into force. Section 4 allows army officers to "resort to firing, even causing death" to prevent a "breach of the peace". Between September 1979 and December 1980 more than 290 people were reported to have died in violent clashes over demands for the eviction of the non-Assamese population. Several hundred students have been detained under the provisions of the Assam Preventive Detention Ordinance, promulgated on 18 April 1980. Eight leaders of the opposition movement were ordered to be released by the Gauhati High Court on 9 June 1980, which found that the detention orders were "bad in law and void". The court observed that "the vagueness of the grounds infringed the fundamental rights of the detainees under Article 22(5) of the Constitution". In addition several thousand people have been arrested under the NSA and NSO in connection with large-scale peaceful political protests, but most were released within days of their arrest.

On 26 May and 23 June 1980 the Joint Secretary, Ministry of Home Affairs, replied to Amnesty International's request for information about six political prisoners. Five had been released. Amnesty International continued to investigate the imprisonment of the sixth, Binod Kumar Sharma, who had been arrested on 4 March 1975 in Bihar for alleged left-wing activities, charged with offences under the penal code, but not tried. The High Court was hearing a petition for the withdrawal of his case. Amnesty International also investigated the cases of two political prisoners in Andhra Pradesh: Ch. Venkati and G. Venkatyya, who have been detained without trial for three and four years respectively.

After presenting an aide-mémoire in April 1980 (see *Amnesty International Report 1980*) Amnesty International wrote to the Prime Minister on 28 August expressing deep concern at reports of frequent deaths in police custody. Most were poor people, including *Harijans* (untouchables); in several instances they had been taken into custody without charge. The Indian press reported at least 27 deaths in police custody between January and September 1980 and formal inquiries in no more than 12. Official reports often stated the cause of death to be "disease or suicide" but unofficial reports alleged torture and police brutality. Police officers appear only rarely to have been suspended pending inquiry, and the Supreme Court of India in a judgment of 12 March 1980 expressed surprise at this. Where police officers have been prosecuted, they have rarely been convicted.

In its letter of 28 August 1980 Amnesty International said that the right to life and freedom from torture was not effectively protected in India. It urged the government to establish an independent body to investigate complaints of ill-treatment, torture and deaths in police custody; specific legal measures to protect suspects from ill-treatment and torture; full investigations of the record and conduct of responsible police officials; and the incorporation of the United Nations Code of Conduct for Law Enforcement Officials and the United Nations Declaration on the Protection of all Persons from Torture and Other Cruel, Inhuman or Degrading Treatment or Punishment into the training of police personnel throughout India, and their translation into the various Indian languages.

On 3 September 1980 Amnesty International wrote to the Governors and Chief Ministers of India's 22 states with the text of the aide-mémoire asking them to take similar steps. It asked the Chief Ministers of Bihar, West Bengal, Madhya Pradesh, Uttar Pradesh, Karnataka, Gujarat, Maharashtra, Rajasthan, Haryana, Tamil Nadu, Tripura and the Lieutenant Governor of New Delhi to investigate specific deaths in police custody which had occurred in their states. During November and December 1980 Amnesty International undertook a campaign urging the central and state governments to implement the Amnesty International recommendations. On 29 October 1980 the Chief Minister of Tripura, Nripen Chakraborty, replied that a magisterial inquiry had been instituted into the death in police custody of Renu Rai Deb Barma. The government said the inquiry had established that the cause of death was a stroke, but the report was not included in the reply. Amnesty International wrote to the Chief Minister on 28 November 1980 asking him to investigate the death of another prisoner, Chaitra Mohan Jamaitia. According to a report in the *Hindustan Times* of 12 February 1981, the Lieutenant Governor of New Delhi, Mr Jagmohan, asked the Federal Home Minister Zail Singh to investigate immediately the deaths in police custody of three men: Emmanuel, Raegeria and Laxman Singh. Amnesty International received no replies from the other 10 states it wrote to about the allegations of deaths from police brutality and torture. Reports of deaths in police custody continued in 1981.

Acts of serious police brutality and atrocities continued throughout the year. The pressing need for police reform was confirmed by the Prime Minister herself when commenting on widely publicized reports that at least 36 suspected criminals had been deliberately blinded with needles and acid in the state of Bihar between October 1979 and November 1980. Two men described how they had their eyes pierced and soaked in acid. One man said that after his eyes had been punctured with a bicycle spoke they were covered with acid soaked pads and bandages. Amnesty International cabled the Chief Minister of Bihar on 28 November calling for an independent investigation whose findings would be published.

The Indian parliament called for a report and an inquiry and for the suspected police officers to be charged. The Bihar government announced on 30 November that an inquiry had been ordered and suspected police officers charged with "negligence". The Supreme Court sent two officers to Bhagalpur jail to investigate the reports, and ordered 31 of the prisoners to be examined in a New Delhi hospital. It also ordered the Bihar government to provide detailed information on the arrest and detention of the prisoners, and the steps taken to prosecute policemen who had blinded prisoners. However of the 15 policemen originally suspended at least 12 have since been reinstated. At the end of April 1981 hearings before the Supreme Court were continuing, but the press reported that the Bihar Government had failed to provide the Supreme Court with documentation as requested.

On 29 December 1980 the All India Police Federation urged the government to create an "independent" police force free from "illegal executive orders". The Secretary General of the Federation, Mahendra Singh Adit, said there were thousands of instances where subordinate officers had to obey such orders which were often "verbal and secret", and if they refused to obey they would later be harassed and victimized. He added that the blindings of arrested men in Bhagalpur must have occurred through such executive orders and urged the government to institute an "in-depth inquiry".

Further evidence of police atrocities during interrogation was reported. Nine men were interviewed out of 12 who alleged their legs had been broken by the Varanasi police. Krishna Murari Singh, 29 years old, stated that, on 21 July 1979:

> "I was stretched on the floor . . . two people were standing on my thighs and stamping. Then two persons caught hold of my left foot and began lifting it upwards. One person kicked my knee joint viciously, breaking the kneecap. Then a policeman's boots repeatedly pounded my damaged left knee . . . Somebody again lifted my leg and rotated it in a clockwise direction."

Three of the 12 men developed serious gangrene infections and had a leg amputated. The police denied the charges and the Senior Superintendent of Police in Varanasi was reported on 5 February 1981 as saying: "The injuries might have been caused during the course of lawful arrest".

Amnesty International remained concerned that no effective measures have been taken to prevent police brutality and torture. On 4 November 1980 the government informed Amnesty International that Indian laws contained adequate provision for safeguarding human rights and sufficient safeguards against police brutality and torture. "Furthermore, the terms of reference of the National Police Commission set up by the government of India include enquiry into the system of investigation, use of improper methods, the extent of their prevalence and suggestions as to how the system may be modified or changed and made an efficient and scientific one consistent with human dignity and how the related laws may be suitably amended. The recommendations of the National Police Commission would be examined carefully and appropriate action taken by the government". Although six reports are believed to have been submitted so far by the commission, only one was put before parliament in 1980.

The Supreme Court continued to hear petitions from prisoners complaining of "overcrowding", "inhuman conditions" and ill-treatment in jail. More than half of them were in the states of Uttar Pradesh and Bihar. On 4 February 1981 the Supreme Court expressed concern at the "disturbing state of affairs with regard to the administration of justice in Bihar". Eight prisoners held for eight years and more without trial had applied to the Supreme Court. It directed that all prisoners held for more than two years without trial should be provided with free legal aid and should be released on bail, or their trial should be started within two months.

Amnesty International was gravely concerned by persistent reports that alleged members of the Communist Party of India (Marxist-Leninist), known as Naxalites, and their sympathizers, had been killed in incidents which the police officially described as "encounters". Relatives alleged that they were deliberately shot by the police after arrest, and that some had been tortured.

On 18 December 1980 the Minister of State for Home Affairs, Yogendra Makwana, said that in the state of Andhra Pradesh 216 Naxalites had been killed by the police in encounters since the start of the Naxalite movement in 1968. Seven of them had been killed during 1980. The State Minister said such killings have also occurred in the states of Maharashtra, Tripura, Tamil Nadu, West Bengal and Orissa. In the North Arcot and Dharmapuri districts of the state of

Tamil Nadu 13 alleged Naxalites were killed between August and December 1980, after a bomb exploded in the area on 6 August 1980. The *Statesman* of 8 March 1981 reported that after the incident 1,000 villagers, many of them *Harijans,* were arrested. Between 100 and 120 of them were still reportedly detained in March 1981. On 28 March 1981 in the state assembly the Tamil Nadu Finance Minister, V. R. Nedumchezhiyan, denied opposition charges that all 13 men killed had been taken by the police and shot. However as far as Amnesty International is aware no inquiries have been instituted into these cases. Press reports confirmed that official inquiries into such incidents were rarely instituted and then only under intense public pressure; when policemen were suspended in connection with murders they were usually reinstated shortly afterwards.

Amnesty International was concerned that the recommendations in its aide-mémoire of April 1980 were not implemented. It had recommended that official impartial commissions inquire into alleged killings by the police, that the government publish the outcome, and that full investigations be made into the record and conduct of police officials named in such incidents, in line with the United Nations declaration against torture.

On 9 May 1980 the Supreme Court of India dismissed a petition brought by Mal Singh and others challenging the constitutionality of the death penalty in India. On receiving the petition, the Supreme Court had stayed all executions. Of the 130 prisoners awaiting execution at the time of the Supreme Court's judgment, 15 had exhausted all appeal procedures and had their clemency petitions rejected. On 14 May 1980 Amnesty International cabled President Neelam Sanjiva Reddy and Prime Minister Gandhi to urge clemency for all the condemned prisoners who were again facing immediate execution. It stressed that the hopes of the condemned men had been raised by the Supreme Court's earlier staying order and urged clemency on humanitarian grounds. Amnesty International learned that one prisoner was executed on 29 July 1980.

On 4 September 1980 Amnesty International urged the President to use his powers of clemency to prevent further executions. During the following three months Amnesty International members wrote to the President, the Prime Minister, and the Governors and Chief Ministers of the 22 states appealing for clemency. In response the Chief Ministers and Govenors of several states replied that no executions had taken place in their states, and the Government of West Bengal voiced its opposition to the death penalty altogether. Amnesty International made further appeals for individual prisoners facing execution. On 23 April 1981 Amnesty International members cabled the government to urge clemency for Ranga and Billah. The

Supreme Court on 23 April had ordered them to be executed as soon as possible.

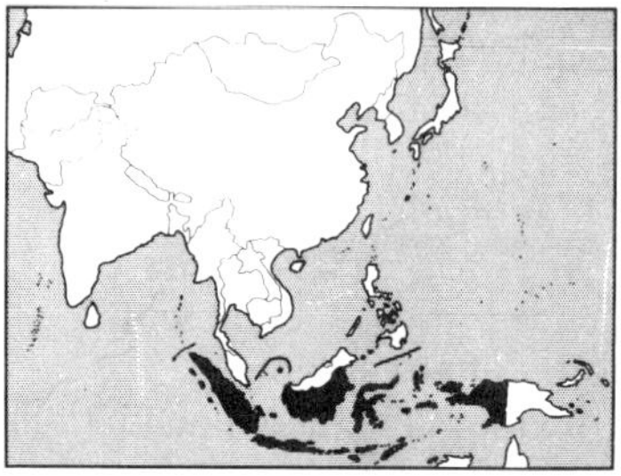

Indonesia and East Timor

Amnesty International was concerned about the treatment of people arrested in connection with the 1965 coup attempt, both those still in detention and the several hundred thousand who had been released but still suffered restrictions on their civil and political rights. Amnesty International was also concerned about the prolonged imprisonment without trial of Muslim political activists, some of whom might have been detained for their religious and political beliefs; and about violations of human rights in areas where secessionist movements were active. Amnesty International continued to receive reports that East Timorese who opposed the Indonesian occupation of that territory have "disappeared", been imprisoned without trial in deplorable conditions and summarily executed. Amnesty International was concerned that a number of people were under sentence of death, most of them for offences allegedly connected with the 1965 coup.

Amnesty International's principal concern in past years has been the treatment of people arrested and detained in connection with the coup attempt of October 1965 and its aftermath. The government had moved towards resolving the long-standing problem of political detention created by the mass arrests that followed the 1965 coup attempt by completing the "phased release program" of untried political prisoners in December 1979. It had also issued a decree in November 1979 making tried political prisoners eligible for remission of their sentences on the same basis as convicted criminals. Amnesty International welcomed these steps but expressed its continuing concern at the restrictions imposed on released prisoners and at the apparently arbitrary application of the remission decree.

Some restrictions on released prisoners, such as the requirement that they report regularly to the authorities, have been eased in the past year but most remain in force, severely curtailing the civil and political rights of former detainees and preventing their reintegration into society. Amnesty International continued to receive reports that released prisoners were restricted in their movements, had marked identity cards identifying them as ex-detainees, and were excluded from employment in the public sector and in "vital industries". These restrictions contributed to their most frequent problem: that of finding employment. Informal restrictions apparently extended to the private sector, despite government assurances that released prisoners would be free to seek employment in private industry. Amnesty International understood that private employers were requested to report regularly to the authorities on the behaviour of employees who were ex-detainees. Restrictions on freedom of movement also affected opportunities to seek employment.

In September 1980 the Minister of Home Affairs, General Amir Machmud, announced that the government had uncovered plans by released prisoners to revive the *Partai Kommunis Indonesia* (PKI), Indonesian Communist Party. Although no evidence was publicly produced the Minister stated that more intensive measures to control and monitor released prisoners would be introduced at all levels down to the village. It was reported that the government was requiring released prisoners to register with the authorities between January and March 1981. In April 1980 Amnesty International launched a year-long special action on behalf of these released prisoners. Appeals were made to national and local officials, employers and other groups urging them to ease the reintegration of released detainees.

Amnesty International was also concerned about approximately 350 prisoners who had been tried for alleged offences in connection with the 1965 coup and did not benefit from the remission decree of November 1979, some of whom were adopted prisoners of conscience. Under the decree political prisoners may have their sentences reduced each year; at the discretion of the authorities they may be released on parole. Amnesty International was disturbed by the many obstacles to the uniform application of the decree including: the levying of "administrative costs" on applicants for remission or parole, pending appeals by prosecutors, and the requirement that applications for remission or parole be endorsed by the court which originally tried the applicant's case. Another problem was that prison sentences often ran from the date of sentence, which in some cases was several years after arrest. Ubed Djubaedah, who has been detained in Tanggerang prison near Jakarta and adopted by Amnesty International as a prisoner of conscience, was arrested in December 1965 but not sentenced until September 1974. She has been detained for more than 15 years but because her sentence of 14 years ran from the date the court handed down its verdict she may not be released until 1988.

On 22 July 1980 Amnesty International appealed to President

Suharto on behalf of five named political prisoners, Suparman, Majid, Djadiwirosubroto, Yohannes Parsidi and Sulami, as well as other tried political prisoners who had not been granted remission. It urged him to grant remission and parole on 17 August, Indonesian Independence Day, which is traditionally the date on which the President has granted remission to criminal prisoners. Amnesty International later learned that Djadiwirosubroto was released in August 1980, Yohannes Parsidi was granted four years' remission and Sulami received three months' remission. Yohannes Parsidi, a former civil servant and member of the regional assembly (DPRD) detained in Nusakembangan Camp, Central Java, was arrested in 1965 but was not tried until 1976 when he received a 13-year sentence. Sulami, formerly third secretary of the PKI-affiliated women's association *Gerwani,* was arrested in 1966 and was sentenced in 1975 to 20 years' imprisonment to run from the date of her arrest.

Amnesty International was also concerned that among the 350 prisoners tried for alleged involvement in the 1965 coup were approximately 50 people under sentence of death who were not eligible for remission. It wrote to President Suharto on 29 April 1981 pointing out that although members of the government had unofficially indicated that none of these prisoners would be executed, there was no possibility of their being rehabilitated. It also submitted a list of 58 people it believed had been sentenced to death for involvement in the 1965 coup attempt and its aftermath. It asked for clarification in view of statements made by officials that only 31 people were under sentence of death on these charges.

Since 1977 large numbers of people identified as Muslim political activists have been arrested in Jakarta, North and South Sumatra, and West, Central and East Java. Several have been charged with being members of the *Kommando Jihad* (Holy War Command), allegedly an organization dedicated to the violent overthrow of the government and the institution of an Islamic state. However statements by officials have indicated that the name *Kommando Jihad* has been applied to a variety of armed Islamic groups acting independently of each other. Since many of those detained on charges of involvement with the *Kommando Jihad* had been active members of the legal Muslim opposition party, the *Partai Persatuan Pembangunan* (PPP), United Development Party, and since a number were held without trial, Amnesty International was concerned that they might have been detained for the legitimate exercise of their political and religious beliefs. Most were arrested in 1977 and 1978 in the period of the general elections, in which the PPP constituted the chief opposition to the government-backed organization *Golkar,* and the subsequent presidential election.

Amnesty International has also noted with concern the detention for short periods of people who challenged government policies limiting their right to freedom of expression. Haji A. M. Fatwa, a Jakarta religious leader, had been adopted by Amnesty International as a prisoner of conscience in 1978. Since his release after eight months' imprisonment in 1978, he has been detained briefly at least three times. He was arrested in August 1980 when he tried to preach a sermon at a service celebrating *Idul Fitri*, the close of the month of Ramadan, and again on 19 October 1980 during the feast of *Idul Adha*. On the second occasion he and a number of companions were reportedly severely beaten by soldiers at an army district headquarters and at the Jakarta branch of the state security agency KOPKAMTIB (Command for the Restoration of Security and Order). Amnesty International also learned of the short-term detention of two newspaper editors in Bandung and Medan in March 1981, who had published reports of an armed attack on a police station near Bandung.

Amnesty International was concerned by reports from Aceh in North Sumatra that in its campaign to suppress the secessionist movement known as the Aceh National Liberation Front (ANLF) the Indonesian army has not only violated the fundamental human rights of people allegedly involved, but also of the wider population. Prominent members of the Acehnese community who were believed not to be associated with the ANLF have been arrested, tried and sentenced to long periods of imprisonment. They included Ahmad Arif, formerly head of religious education in the Department of Religion in the district of Pidie, and Muhammad Nuh Usman, formerly Chairman of the District Assembly of Pidie, both sentenced to 13 years' imprisonment in mid-1977 on charges of being sympathetic to the ANLF. Amnesty International has been investigating the cases of both these men. Several people related to leading ANLF members, including wives and children not associated with the ANLF, have been held without trial, presumably to induce their relatives to surrender to the authorities. Amnesty International was investigating five of these cases. Amnesty International was also concerned about people arrested for alleged involvement with the ANLF who have been held for up to four years without trial and about reports that people held by the authorities, whether associated with the ANLF or not, have been ill-treated and tortured. It has received reports of the extrajudicial killing of two leading members of the ANLF. Dr Zubair Machmud, a leading member of the Central Committee of the ANLF, was shot and killed by Indonesian troops on 25 May 1980, and Dr Muchtar Husbi, first Vice-Chairman of the ANLF, was shot and killed by Indonesian troops on 15 August 1980.

Amnesty International continued to work on behalf of three people from Irian Jaya, formerly West Irian. The three were serving sentences for having signed the so-called Serui declaration, issued in 1975, which called for the independence of Irian Jaya. Amnesty International learned of further arrests of people engaged in non-violent pro-independence activities as well as of people associated with the secessionist movement, *Organisasi Papua Merdeka* (OPM), Free Papua Organization. On 4 August 1980 six women were arrested for having hoisted the Papuan flag in front of the office of the Governor of Irian Jaya. They were reported to be still in detention in March 1981. Prisoners arrested for alleged involvement with the OPM were believed to be held in the military headquarters (KODAM-KASAK) in Jayapura and in prisons in Biak, Manokwari and Serui.

Amnesty International has received reports of people dying after ill-treatment at the hands of the Indonesian army. One such report received during the year concerned Baldus Mofu, an outspoken Papuan nationalist. On the night of 8 December 1979 he was taken from his home, severely beaten, and then returned to his home where he died shortly afterwards.

Amnesty International has continued to be concerned about violations of human rights in the territory of East Timor, occupied by Indonesian forces since December 1975. It wrote to President Suharto on 28 April 1980 expressing its concern that large numbers of East Timorese had "disappeared", been summarily executed or been imprisoned without trial as a result of the actions of the Indonesian occupation forces. Amnesty International appealed for investigations into the fate of 22 people who had "disappeared" and into the conditions in which East Timorese were imprisoned. The letter also asked for the President's cooperation in ensuring that the International Committee of the Red Cross (ICRC) be permitted to expand its activities in East Timor to include tracing missing persons and prison visits. Amnesty International submitted its findings on East Timor to: the Foreign Operations Sub-Committee of the United States House of Representatives, in June 1980; the United Nations Special Committee on Decolonisation, in October 1980; and to the Working Group on Enforced or Involuntary Disappearances of the United Nations Commission on Human Rights. Although Amnesty International received no reply to its letter to President Suharto, the Indonesian Government did inform the UN working group that, as regards the investigation of "disappearances" in East Timor, the government had decided that its limited resources should be used for purposes other than tracing missing persons. It also asserted that those who had "disappeared" in East Timor were most probably victims of revenge killings by other East Timorese. Amnesty International found this reply difficult to accept since all of those known to Amnesty International who "disappeared" did so after being taken into custody. Moreover, Amnesty International has recommended that the ICRC should be enabled to trace missing persons in East Timor, even if the Indonesian Government was unable to undertake its own investigation.

Amnesty International continued to receive reports of "disappearances", summary executions and imprisonment without trial in East Timor. The most persistent were received after an attack by East Timorese on an Indonesian army post on the outskirts of the capital, Dili, on 10 June 1980. Amnesty International understands that approximately 400 people were arrested after this attack, some of whom were later released. However about 120 were taken to the island of Atauro, north of the main island of Timor, where they were believed to be still held at the end of the year. On 14 November 1980 Amnesty International appealed to the Indonesian authorities on behalf of David Ximenes, formerly a second lieutenant in the Portuguese army, who had been arrested after the June attack and subsequently "disappeared".

Under Indonesian law the death penalty may be imposed for a wide range of offences, including premeditated murder, subversion, treason, hijacking and drug trafficking, and there were, according to official figures, five people under sentence of death besides the approximately 50 sentenced to death in connection with the 1965 coup. It was not known whether this figure of five included Timsar Zubil who was sentenced to death in Medan in 1977 for a series of bombings allegedly carried out for the *Kommando Jihad*. Amnesty International received no reports of people being sentenced to death or of executions during the year.

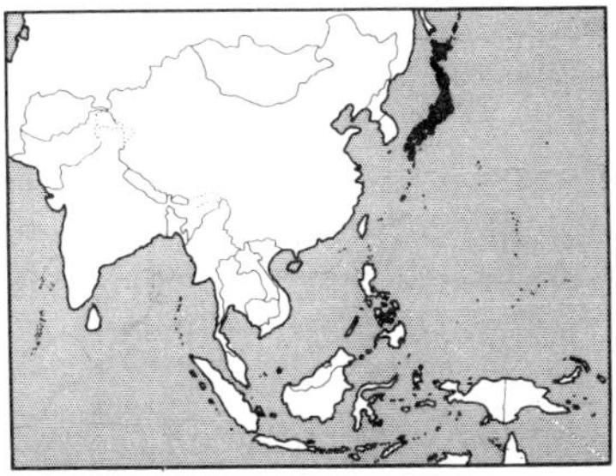

Japan

Amnesty International was concerned about the use of the death penalty as a punishment for criminal offences. On 18 November 1980 Amnesty International wrote to Prime Minister Zenko Suzuki and to Minister of Justice Seisuke Okuno expressing concern at the number of executions — 44 during the five-year period 1974 to 1978 — and at the large number of offences — 17 — for which the death penalty is provided in Japanese law. It urged the Prime Minister and Minister of Justice to support legislation to abolish the death penalty, and, pending abolition, to use their influence and authority to stop executions and commute death sentences.

Amnesty International has the names of 38 prisoners under sentence of death in Japan. A special appeal was made for the commutation of the death sentence on Hirasawa Sadamichi because of his age and deteriorating health. He was sentenced to death in 1950; by 1981 he was 89 years old. His third appeal for pardon was turned down in December 1980.

At least five death sentences have been pronounced for murder since May 1980. Amnesty International recently learned that one execution was carried out in December 1980.

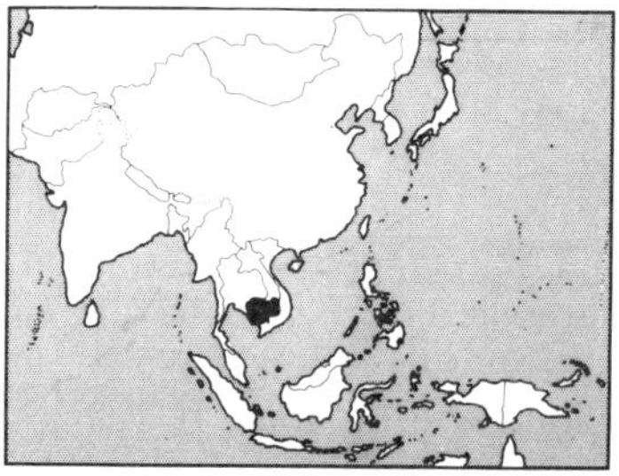

Kampuchea

Amnesty International was concerned about the forcible return in May 1980 of Kampuchean refugees in Thailand to Kampuchea where they risked possible imprisonment, ill-treatment or execution by either the Government of the People's Republic of Kampuchea (PRK) or by resistance groups along the Thai-Kampuchean border. Amnesty International was also concerned about reports of political imprisonment and of political trials in the PRK, and believed that some prisoners of conscience might be detained by the PRK authorities for "re-education".

The armed forces of the former Government of Democratic Kampuchea (DK) overthrown in January 1979 and the anti-communist resistance groups, the largest of which is the Khmer People's National Liberation Front (KPNLF) or *Sereika*, continued to fight the armies of Viet Nam and the PRK from bases along the Thai-Kampuchean border. The Government of the PRK, which controls the capital Phnom Penh and most of the country, held local elections in March 1981. On 10 March 1981 it circulated a draft constitution for public discussion.

In July 1980 the PRK authorities announced that between 23 June and the beginning of July they had captured 600 people among Kampuchean refugees repatriated from Thailand, who, they claimed, had been sent by resistance groups to conduct propaganda or sabotage.

Some were later released. "Treason" trials of partisans of the KPLNF took place in June and in November 1980. On 5 June 1980, 17 people, mostly PRK officials who had been arrested in August 1979, were tried under Decree Law No. 2-DL of 15 May 1980 "for treason against the revolution and other crimes". The charges against them under Articles 3(a) and 4(a) of Decree No. 2-DL included: propaganda against the political program of the Kampuchea National United Front for National Salvation (KNUFNS); opposition to the relations between the PRK and the Socialist Republic of Viet Nam; attempts to establish a political and military network; affiliation and contact with the KPNLF; and communications with Thai and United States intelligence agencies. They were sentenced on 7 June to terms of imprisonment ranging from three years to 20 years. Amnesty International was concerned at the delay between the prisoners' arrests and their trial, and at the retroactive application of legislation. It has not been able to assess whether the prisoners were given a fair trial. In November 1980 the trial took place of a group called "the nationalists", most of them reportedly public servants or soldiers under pre-1975 governments. They faced charges of plotting to overthrow the government in liaison with resistance groups on the Thai-Kampuchean border. They were sentenced to terms of imprisonment ranging between two and 20 years. Their leader, tried in his absence, was sentenced to life imprisonment.

In late 1980 the authorities of the PRK stated that their only prisoners were *Khmer Rouge,* that is supporters of the DK, and armed counter-revolutionaries. However Amnesty International received reports throughout the year that people had been detained on suspicion of criticizing the government or the Vietnamese or for attempting to leave the country. Some were apparently sent for "re-education" in accordance with a memorandum of the Interior Ministry of 29 November 1980 which gave instructions on the arrest and "re-education" of "any person carrying out propaganda campaigns to sabotage internal unity and Kampuchea-Vietnam-Laos solidarity". According to some reports hundreds of people were detained without trial in prisons in Phnom Penh for criticizing the government. Amnesty International was investigating these reports.

On 2 December 1980 and on 7 January 1981, the anniversaries of the foundation of the KNUFNS and of the overthrow of the DK, a number of prisoners who had "reformed" themselves were released or had their sentences reduced. Details were not known.

Decree Law No. 2-DL provides the death penalty for counter-revolutionary activities and treason, as well as for other criminal offences. Reports that seven civil servants were executed for "anti-Vietnamese activities" in October 1980 were denied by the PRK authorities.

The Government of Democratic Kampuchea, overthrown in January 1979 but still recognized by the United Nations, signed the International Covenant on Civil and Political Rights on 17 October 1980.

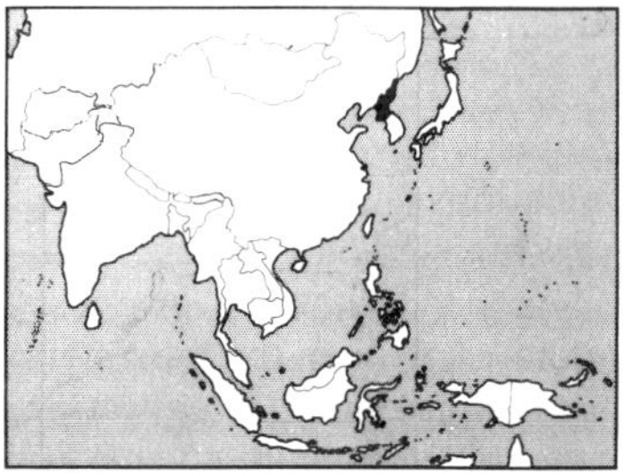

Korea (the Democratic People's Republic of)

Amnesty International continued to be concerned by the extreme reluctance of the authorities to make public any information about political imprisonment and other human rights violations.

Amnesty International has been particularly concerned over the years about the punishment of political offences and the imprecise definition of such offences. Article 20 of the "Law Governing the Organization of the Procuracy and Internal Affairs" may be applied to anyone considered untrustworthy by the authorities. This article provides for prosecution for such broadly defined crimes as subversive conduct and association with subversive intent. The legal procedure for "state crimes" comes under a special statute that is referred to in the Code of Criminal Procedure but is not known to have been made public. This procedure is reportedly the exclusive province of the Ministry of Public Security.

Although the law allows questioning by officials of the Public Security Office for up to two months after a person's arrest, this period may be extended twice by the provincial procurator's office or the Procurator-General. In practice it appeared that if the agreement of the Chief Prosecutor was obtained, the period of interrogation could be extended indefinitely. In the case of the Venezuelan communist and poet Ali Lameda, whose acount of imprisonment in North Korea Amnesty International published in 1979, this period of interrogation lasted for 12 months before he was charged.

Although Amnesty International received reports of several prisons holding political prisoners, only two specific prison camps were known to exist: Camp No. 8 in Chagang province and Camp No. 149 in Yanggang province. Camp No. 8 was reported to hold political offenders whom the authorities considered guilty of serious crimes. Detainees at Camp No. 149 were also held for "political offences" and were allowed to have their families live with them.

The existence of "re-education" camps was confirmed to a visiting delegation from the American Friends Service Committee (AFSC) in 1980 but they were not allowed to visit a camp.

Amnesty International has also received reports of the banishment of political offenders. In September 1980 it was reported that individuals allegedly opposed to the growing political power of Kim Chong-il, the son of President Kim Il-sung, had been banished. Residents of Pyongyang, Hamhung, Wonsan and Hwanghae province were reported to have been forcibly evacuated to areas bordering the Yalu and Tuman rivers near the frontier with the People's Republic of China.

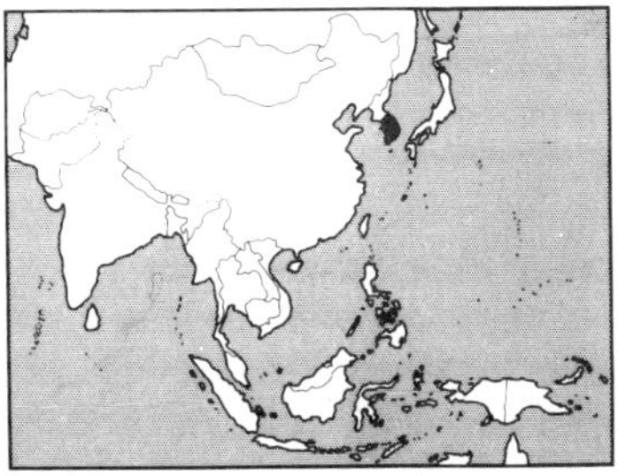

Korea (the Republic of)

The concerns of Amnesty International were the arrest and detention of prisoners of conscience, frequent and serious irregularities in the judicial process, the ill-treatment and torture of political prisoners and the use of the death penalty for political and criminal offences.

On 2 March 1981 Amnesty International launched a worldwide campaign to publicize its concerns in the Republic of Korea and to persuade the authorities to stop using political imprisonment, torture, unfair trial and the death penalty. These concerns were described in *Republic of Korea: Violations of Human Rights,* an Amnesty International report published at the beginning of the campaign.

Martial law had been imposed on most of the country after the assassination of President Park Chung-hee on 26 October 1979. On 17 May 1980 it was extended to the whole country. The martial law command issued Regulation No. 10 (MLR 10) which banned all political activities, tightened press censorship, prohibited strikes and made it illegal to criticize present or former presidents or to "spread rumours". The arrest, detention and search of anyone violating MLR 10 were permitted without warrant. The declaration of nationwide martial law was followed within hours by the detention of student leaders and others known to be critical of the government. In the capital, Seoul, hundreds of people were detained by the military authorities for investigation, some of whom had formerly been adopted by Amnesty International as prisoners of conscience. In the

Kwangju area more than 500 people were detained, the majority of them after the army had quelled disturbances in the city on 27 May. On 18 May a student demonstration ended in violence when paratroopers intervened. Continuing clashes during the following days culminated in the demonstrators taking control of the city. On 27 May the army regained control.

In July 1980 Amnesty International sent a mission to South Korea to discuss its concerns with the government and to investigate reports of mass arrests and torture since 17 May and the legal situation and treatment of prisoners detained before that date. The authorities refused to allow the delegates to enter the country. The Embassy of the Republic of Korea in Tokyo told the Amnesty International representatives that the timing of the mission was inconvenient because the issue of human rights was "too sensitive in South Korea at this time".

On 15 August 1980 Amnesty International submitted a number of recommendations to the government. These included appeals for the release of prisoners of conscience detained since before 17 May 1980; the release or trial of all those detained since that date, and the publication of a full list of detainees; the end of incommunicado detention and the investigation by an independent body of prisoners' claims of ill-treatment and torture; fair and open trials and in particular the exclusion from evidence of incriminating statements made under duress and respect for the principle that a defendant is presumed innocent until proved guilty.

Amnesty International remained concerned at the use of laws other than the martial law regulations which allowed people to be detained for the non-violent exercise of their right to freedom of expression and association. Detention and arrests continued under provisions of the Anti-Communist Law, 1961, rescinded in January 1981, concerning activities allegedly benefiting the People's Democratic Republic of Korea; the National Security Law, 1960, concerning "anti-state organizations"; Articles 87, 90 and 98 of the Criminal Code, concerning subversion and espionage; the Public Security Law, 1975, on preventive custody; and the Law on Assemblies and Demonstrations, amended in November 1980.

A new constitution was promulgated on 27 October 1980, guaranteeing freedom from torture, freedom of speech, press, assembly and association and the exclusion of forced confessions from evidence in court. However, these rights may be restricted constitutionally "when necessary for national security, the maintenance of law and order or for public welfare" in violation of the International Covenant on Civil and Political Rights. Martial law was partially lifted in September 1980 and completely rescinded on 25 January 1981, although the martial law courts continued to process cases until 24 February 1981. A presidential amnesty was granted to 5,221 criminal and political prisoners on the inauguration of President Chun Doo-hwan on 3 March; another presidential amnesty was granted on 3 April to 83 prisoners convicted on charges related to the Kwangju disturbances. Thirteen prisoners adopted by Amnesty International as prisoners of conscience were released under these amnesties.

In a letter to President Chun Doo-hwan on 27 February 1981 welcoming the lifting of martial law, Amnesty International recommended that the government consider ratifying the International Covenant on Civil and Political Rights. It also urged it to review the cases of all political detainees including those imprisoned under the previous government, as many had reportedly been convicted on the basis of confessions obtained under duress and sometimes torture.

On 2 May 1980, 73 people were sentenced by Seoul District Criminal Court under the National Security and Anti-Communist laws in connection with an allegedly pro-communist group, the South Korean National Liberation Front (SKNLF) (see *Amnesty International Report 1980*). The court sentenced four defendants to death; 44 to terms of imprisonment ranging from three years to life; and 25 others received suspended sentences. On 2 May 1980 Amnesty International urged President Choi Kyu-hah to commute the death sentences and expressed its concern at reported irregularities in the trial. In September the appeal court commuted two of the death sentences to life imprisonment but confirmed those on Lee Jae mun and Shin Hyang-shik; it also reduced some sentences. On 24 December the Supreme Court confirmed both death sentences. At all stages of these legal proceedings Amnesty International urged the commutation of the death sentences, expressed concern at irregularities in the trial and called for a retrial. It received reports that the prisoners were ill-treated and tortured and had made confessions under duress. Several defendants had had limbs broken and one his spine. Amnesty International continued its investigation as it believed some of the prisoners might be prisoners of conscience. Among them were two prisoners of conscience who had already been arrested on other charges when accused of being members of the SKNLF. Lee Jae-oh, a high school teacher and Secretary General of the Executive Committee of Amnesty International in the Republic of Korea, was arrested on 6 August 1979 and charged with violations of Emergency Regulation No. 9 for criticizing the government in a speech at a prayer meeting (see *Amnesty International Report 1980*). At the time of his arrest in March 1979 Im Tong-kyu was working at the Labour Affairs Research Institute of Korea University. While in prison he was indicted in the SKNLF case and given a second life sentence.

On 19 May 1980 Amnesty International cabled President Choi Kyu-hah and martial law commander General Lee Hui-song, appealing for the release of Kim Dae-jung, the opposition leader, and requesting assurances that the 43 other people arrested on 17 May would be granted full legal safeguards, and that the charges against them would be made public if they were not immediately released. Kim Dae-jung and the 23 people who stood trial with him were held incommunicado until a few days before their trial began. On 31 July Kim Dae-jung was charged with having made speeches considered by the government to be beneficial to the People's Democratic Republic of Korea and with financing and instigating student disturbances in Kwangju on 19 to 27 May 1980 in an attempt to overthrow the government and seize power. Twelve of his co-defendants were charged with participating in a meeting which was illegal under martial law regulations and with conspiracy to subvert, under the criminal code. The others were charged with violations of martial law regulations. The trial before a military tribunal started on 14 August, and all were found guilty on 17 September. Kim Dae-jung was sentenced to death, the others to terms of imprisonment of between two and 20 years. Amnesty International considers that their trial failed to fulfil internationally recognized legal standards. All the defendants but one denied the charges and claimed that they had been beaten, intimidated and deprived of sleep to make them confess. Severe limitations were placed on the defence. The defendants were not allowed counsel of their choice: a number of civil rights lawyers were taken into custody and others were intimidated into not taking up the cases. Restrictions were put on the defendants' testimonies in court; no witnesses were called in the case of those charged only with violations of martial law; some witnesses were reportedly intimidated and witnesses for the defence not allowed to give evidence; confessions were accepted as evidence without proper examination of their validity or of the defendants' claims that they had been improperly obtained.

Amnesty International cabled President Chun Doo-hwan on 24 September 1980 urging him to commute the death sentence on Kim Dae-jung if upheld by the appeal courts. Amnesty International repeatedly appealed for the immediate and unconditional release of Kim Dae-jung and his co-defendants, or for their retrial in an open court with full legal safeguards. On 2 December 1980 it appealed to the heads of government of the 43 member countries of the United Nations Commission on Human Rights in an effort to prevent the execution of Kim Dae-jung. The sentences on Kim Dae-jung and some of his co-defendants were confirmed by the Supreme Court on 23 January 1981. After worldwide expressions of concern Kim Dae-jung's death sentence was commuted to life imprisonment by the

President and the sentences on 11 co-defendants were reduced to five to 15 years. On 23 January 1981 Amnesty International wrote to President Chun Doo-hwan to welcome his decision to commute the death sentence on Kim Dae-jung, and urged him to exercise his presidential power of clemency to commute all death sentences submitted to him. Among those sentenced with Kim Dae-jung for whose release Amnesty International continued to appeal were: Reverend Moon Ik-hwan, a Presbyterian minister adopted twice before by Amnesty International as a prisoner of conscience; Reverend Lee Moon-young, formerly a professor at Korea University, dismissed for political activity, who had been adopted as a prisoner of conscience twice before in 1977 and 1979; Ye Chon-ho, a former member of the National Assembly; Koh Eun, a poet, previously adopted as a prisoner of conscience after his arrest in 1979; Cho Song-oo, a student at Korea University; and Sul Hun, also a student adopted as a prisoner of conscience after his arrest in 1977 (see *Amnesty International Report 1977* and *1980*).

Amnesty International also adopted as prisoners of conscience several of Kim Dae-jung's associates after they were arrested on 17 May 1980. They were tried by the Capital Garrison Court Martial in September 1980 for holding a meeting in violation of martial law regulations. The Supreme Court reduced their sentences to terms of imprisonment ranging from one and a half to three years. They included Han Hwa-gap, press secretary to Kim Dae-jung (see *Amnesty International Report 1980*), Kim Ok-doo and Han Yun shik, secretaries of Kim Dae-jung.

Amnesty International called for the release of a number of students arrested after demonstrations in May 1980 in Seoul and in provincial cities. These demonstrations were largely peaceful and Amnesty International received no information to suggest that these students had used or advocated violence. Two of them, Kim Bong-wu, a student at Kyunghee University, and Cho Tae-won, a student at Pusan University, were sentenced to three years' imprisonment for violation of MLR 10. Both had previously been adopted as prisoners of conscience when arrested in 1978 and 1979 respectively.

Amnesty International was concerned about the reported ill-treatment and torture of the people detained in connection with violent disturbances in Kwangju in May 1980. Several prisoners were reported to have died while under interrogation. Prisoners were reportedly beaten, deprived of sleep and subjected to long periods of continuous interrogation to make them confess. Amnesty International was concerned also about irregularities in proceedings against 390 people sentenced on 25 October 1980 by a Kwangju martial law court on charges including liaison with Kim Dae-jung, and attempted insurrection. The defendants were not allowed lawyers of their choice.

On 27 October Amnesty International cabled President Chun Doo-hwan and martial law commander General Lee Hui-song deploring the imposition of five death sentences and urging the defendants' retrial in an open court with full legal safeguards. Two prisoners had their death sentences commuted by a military appeal court on 31 December 1980. The Supreme Court rejected the appeals of the three others on 31 March but their sentences were commuted by President Chun Doo-hwan on 3 April 1980. Among the defendants sentenced to prison on 25 October a number had their sentences suspended by the appeal courts. A few others benefited from the presidential amnesty on 3 March 1981, and 57 of the 83 whose sentences were confirmed by the Supreme Court at the end of March were released by presidential amnesty on 3 April 1981. Amnesty International appealed for the release of some of these prisoners whom it had adopted as prisoners of conscience. Among them were Hong Nam-soon, a prominent civil rights lawyer, Professor Myong No-keun, from Chunnam University and Father Kim Sang-yong, who were prominent members of the Citizens' Committee to Seek Solutions to the Kwangju Disturbance. The committee wrote to the President asking for a government apology for its handling of the disturbances.

Amnesty International learned of 37 journalists detained during the year. It adopted as prisoners of conscience three members of the Journalists' Association of Korea, including its President. On 17 May 1980 the association complained to the military authorities about censorship and threatened to stop work. Kim Tae-hong, the President of the association, was arrested on 27 August after several months in hiding. Details of his trial and his sentence are not known. Eight journalists who protested against the tightening of press censorship under MLR 10 and were charged under the Anti-Communist Law and MLR 10 with "spreading false and malicious rumours" about the army's actions during the Kwangju disturbances were also adopted as prisoners of conscience. Four of them were reportedly released on 13 February 1981.

Amnesty International has been investigating reports of arrests of journalists, students and trade unionists during the last three months of 1980.

When student Kang Jong-kon's five-year sentence on political charges expired on 14 February 1981 he was reported to have been detained under the Public Security Law. Amnesty International appealed for his release in the belief that he was detained because of his refusal to change his political views.

Amnesty International investigated the arrests of students in March and April 1981 after demonstrations at several universities. They were charged under the Law on Assemblies and Demonstrations. According to information received they had neither used nor advocated violence, and Amnesty International appealed for their release.

Amnesty International continued to appeal for the release of prisoners of conscience detained for many years. Among them were 16 prisoners tried in the "People's Revolutionary Party" case in 1974 (see *Amnesty International Report 1980*). In August 1980 it launched a special appeal for the release of Soh Joon-shik and Soh Sung, who have been detained since 1971. Soh Sung was serving a sentence of life imprisonment; Soh Joon-shik was still held in detention under the Public Security Law, although his sentence had expired in May 1978.

On 11 December 1980 the poet Kim Chi-ha was released from prison. The life sentence he had received on account of his writings had already been commuted to 20 years' imprisonment (see *Amnesty International Report 1978, 1979, 1980*). Also released on that date were Professor Yu In-ho, a co-defendant of Kim Dae-jung, and six defendants in the Young Women's Christian Association (YWCA) case of November 1979 (see *Amnesty International Report 1980*). Five more defendants in this case were reportedly released in the 3 March 1981 presidential amnesty. Amnesty International also welcomed the release under the 3 March 1981 presidential amnesty of Lee Bu-yong, a reporter, adopted by Amnesty International after his arrest in December 1979 (see *Amnesty International Report 1980*).

During the year Amnesty International worked on behalf of 140 prisoners of conscience and other political prisoners, and appealed for a fair trial for many more.

Amnesty International continued to appeal for the commutation of death sentences for political and criminal offences. During the year 10 death sentences were imposed for political offences, eight of which were later commuted by the President. There were, to Amnesty International's knowledge, seven political prisoners on death row. Two had their sentences confirmed by the Supreme Court in December 1980: Lee Jae-mun and Shin Hyang-shik, both sentenced in the SKNLF case. An application for retrial by the other five was rejected on 25 July 1980. In a letter to President Chun on 23 January 1981 in which it welcomed his decision to commute the death sentence on Kim Dae-jung, Amnesty International urged the commutation of the death sentence on four prisoners, expressing its belief that they had been convicted after unfair trials. Five people convicted in December 1979 of the assassination of President Park and sentenced to death were executed on 24 May 1980.

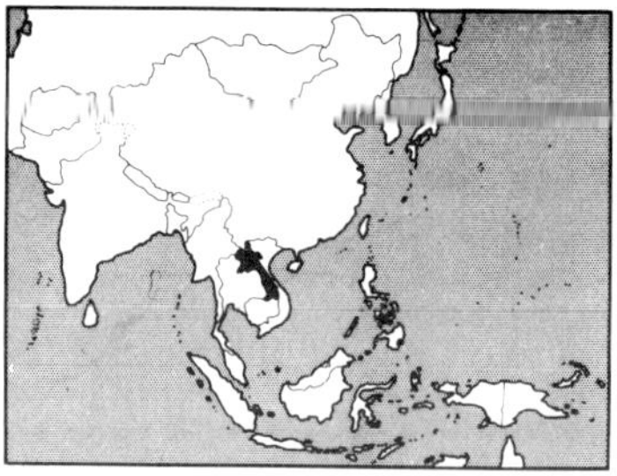

Laos (the Lao People's Democratic Republic)

Amnesty International's main concern was the continuing detention without charge or trial of thousands of people held in "re-education" camps since 1975. It was also concerned by new arrests and the lack of legal safeguards for those detained on political grounds. However a significant number of people were freed in late 1980 and, although precise figures and details were unavailable, there were further releases in early 1981.

Since the publication in April 1980 of its report *Political Prisoners in the People's Democratic Republic of Laos,* Amnesty International has continued to work on behalf of 80 political detainees whose cases had been taken up by Amnesty International for adoption as prisoners of conscience or for investigation. Many were former civil servants (including a few military officers), and professional people, who had been detained in camps without trial since the change of government which marked the end of the "neutralist" coalition in Laos in 1975. Most high-ranking civil servants and military officers who were assigned to "re-education" at that time were sent to camps in Houa Phan (Sam Neua) province, in the northeast of the country along the border with Viet Nam.

Among the prisoners of conscience for whom Amnesty International renewed its appeals was Baliene Khamdaranikorn, the former Director of Civil Aviation and reportedly a member of a small "neutralist" party, the *Neo Thang Noum,* Youth Party. In March 1981 Amnesty International learned that Baliene Khamdaranikorn had been recently released and had returned to the capital, Vientiane.

His release was one of a number that have taken place since the autumn of 1980. It was reported that about 200 people had been released from camps in Houa Phan province by the end of November 1980, and it appeared that released detainees were returning to Vientiane in small groups. A number attended the celebrations of National Day in Vientiane in December 1980. Among those known to Amnesty International whose release was later confirmed were Oudong Souvannavong, the 64-year-old former Director of the National Bank of Laos, and his brother Ouday; Soukpraseuth Sithimolada, a 48-year-old former diplomat and *chef de cabinet* in the Ministry of Foreign Affairs; and Chansamone Voravong, a 50-year-old cartographer-engineer and former Director of the National

Agricultural Institute of Laos on whose behalf appeals had been made for proper medical treatment.

Those released were held in various camps in Houa Phan province, including camps 04, 05 and 06. Some were reported to have been reintegrated into the civil service and others to have applied for administrative posts. Still others were said to have been released because of their old age or ill-health. The releases were reported to have been based on an official assessment, in each case, of whether the detainee could be reintegrated into society in view of the degree of "re-education" attained and the technical skills possessed. Although detainees continued to be released from the northeast in small groups during the first four months of 1981, it was not known how far this process would continue and what would happen to those not considered sufficiently "re-educated". Amnesty International was concerned that they might be held indefinitely although they had already been detained for nearly six years without charge or trial.

In a letter to Prime Minister Kaysone Phomvihane on 17 March 1981, Amnesty International welcomed the releases, and asked whether they were part of a long-term process which would affect everyone detained in "re-education" camps because of their opinions or functions under the former government. Inquiring about two groups released in January and February 1981 reportedly containing more than 100 people, Amnesty International asked the government to make public the names and circumstances of all the people involved. It submitted a list of 99 people who had been adopted or investigated by Amnesty International. Amnesty International stressed that there seemed to be no justification for continuing to detain them without charge or trial. They included Khamchanh Pradith, a 50-year-old diplomat and former Ambassador to Australia who has been held in northeast Laos since November 1975; and Viboun Abhay, Phom Bounlytay, Houmphan Norasing and Vannavong Rajkhoun, all former members of the National Coalition Consultative Council who in November 1975 were asked to go to Viengsay in Houa Phan province for a meeting of the council, but were then held there. A few members of the council were released from the northeast in 1976 but the others have been detained since then. The list included detainees of whom nothing has been heard for several years or who have been rumoured to be dead. Prasongsith Boupha, a fifth-year medical student in his mid-twenties at the time of arrest, was sent for "re-education" at the Chinaimo military camp in Vientiane in October 1976. Despite many inquiries no official information has been disclosed about Prasongsith Boupha or other medical students sent for "re-education" at the same time.

Amnesty International has also been concerned about the fate of

Tiao Souk Bouavong, a 77-year-old former member of the National Assembly, who is reported to have been arrested on 15 October 1975 in Vientiane and accused of planning a coup. According to information received by Amnesty International, these accusations were unfounded. After his arrest he was first held in Samkhé prison, near Vientiane, and later moved to an unknown destination. Concern increased because of his age and poor health. As far as is known, he has not been tried or charged with any offence.

Amnesty International was concerned by the absence of any legislation providing safeguards against arbitrary arrest and detention despite statements made by the Prime Minister Kaysone Phomvihane in a report to the Supreme People's Council (SPC) on 26 December 1979 in which he called on the Justice and Interior Ministries to draft laws on arrest and detention for adoption by the SPC, and stressed that "those arrested with complete evidence should be brought to court for trial immediately" and "those arrested without valid evidence must be freed". Since then governmental decrees and regulations have been reported, but have not been published, and their nature and content are not known. Although a National Congress of People's Representatives appointed the SPC to draft a new constitution, this task has not been completed and no new laws have been adopted since 1975.

In its letter to Premier Kaysone Phomvihane on 17 March 1981 Amnesty International referred to these statements and asked about reports that between 200 and 400 people were arrested in Vientiane in October 1980 in a political purge within the administration.

Observers in Vientiane noted that these arrests came shortly before the anniversary celebration on 2 December of the establishment of the present government in 1975. A similar wave of arrests had taken place before the celebrations in autumn 1979. Those arrested in October 1980 were reported to have been mainly junior civil servants, but students and teachers were also held. It was later reported that a large number of those arrested were released during the following weeks and that most of the civil servants detained were charged with corruption. However it appeared that a few remained in detention on political grounds. Amnesty International urged the government to make public the names of all those held and the precise charges against them, but no further information has been received.

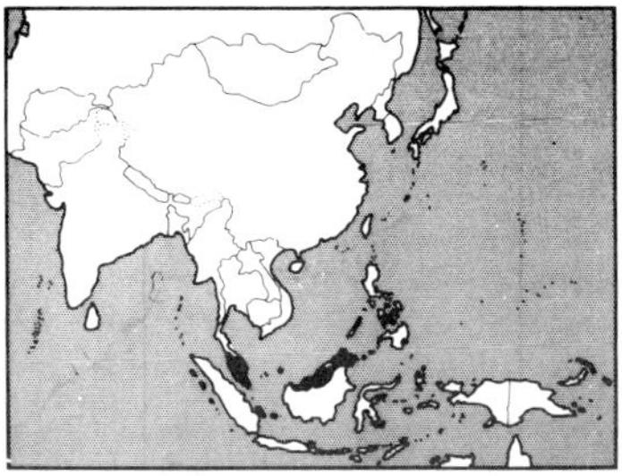

Malaysia

Although a number of prisoners have been released since the beginning of 1980, Amnesty International was still concerned about the indefinite detention without trial of several hundred Malaysians under the Internal Security Act 1960 (ISA). It was also concerned about the sudden resumption of executions in February and March 1981.

About 80 prisoners have been adopted as prisoners of conscience or were being investigated by Amnesty International. These prisoners were held under the ISA, which permits the detention without charge or trial, for renewable two-year periods, of people regarded by the Minister of Home Affairs as a threat to the security of Malaysia. As noted in the *Report of an Amnesty International Mission to the Federation of Malaysia*, published in August 1979, the ISA has been used to detain members of the legal opposition, as well as trade unionists engaged in legitimate trade union activity. Tan Hock Hin, former Assistant Secretary General of the Labour Party of Malaysia, has now been detained for 14 years without trial because of his political activity. Like all political prisoners held under the ISA, Tan Hock Hin has never been formally charged, but was served with a two-year detention order which has been repeatedly renewed since his arrest in 1967. He was held in the Batu Gajah Special Detention Camp.

In June 1980 Amnesty International renewed its appeals for the release of Abdul Samad bin Ismail, the former managing editor of the *New Straits Times* and one of Malaysia's leading intellectuals, who had been detained since 1976 for alleged involvement in "communist subversion". Unlike most people detained under the ISA, Samad Ismail was held at an undisclosed Special Branch Holding Centre in Kuala Lumpur, where he was kept in solitary confinement. Fears for his health were expressed on many occasions in view of these conditions. Samad Ismail was released in early February 1981 after making a statement on television renouncing his previous beliefs.

Amnesty International was particularly concerned by the condition of Yong Ah Chit, formerly a teacher and President of the Chinese Language Society of the University of Malaya, who was arrested in 1975 under the ISA and detained at the Taiping Detention Camp. In September 1979 Amnesty International issued an appeal on his behalf after learning that he was showing signs of severe mental stress resulting from his four-year detention. It was feared that continued detention would lead to further, possibly irreversible, deterioration. Later reports indicated that Yong Ah Chit's condition was worsening, aggravated by the considerable pressure being exerted on him to make a public "confession" of his alleged subversive aims. This pressure was reported to have continued even after he agreed to sign a pledge to refrain from all future political activity. He was in a state of acute depression at the time he was released, and Amnesty International learned later that he committed suicide in July 1980 shortly after his release. Amnesty International renewed its appeals to the government to improve medical facilities for people held under the ISA and to abandon the common practice of requiring "confessions" as a condition of release.

These concerns were again raised in April 1981 in a letter to the Prime Minister, Datuk Hussein bin Datu Onn, in which Amnesty International also welcomed the releases which had taken place since 1980. Among those released were Samad Ismail; Dr Syed Hussein Ali, 44, an associate professor of sociology at the University of Malaya before his arrest in 1974, who was released in September 1980; and Encik Abdullah Majid, a former Deputy Minister who had been arrested in November 1976 together with Encik Abdullah Ahmed, another former Deputy Minister, after an intense power struggle within the ruling United Malays National Organisation. Abdullah Majid was released in February 1981 after publicly denouncing his own previous pro-communist feelings.

In its letter to the Prime Minister Amnesty International cited figures given in a recent letter from Tan Sri D. B. W. Good, the Chairman of the Advisory Board responsible for reviewing detainees' cases and making recommendations to the Minister of Home Affairs. According to Tan Sri Good, of 740 detainees whose cases were reviewed by the Advisory Board between January and October 1980, 200 were released. Amnesty International welcomed these releases and asked for a list.

Noting that several recently released prisoners had made public confessions and statements renouncing their beliefs, and recalling the case of Yong Ah Chit, Amnesty International again urged the government not to require "confessions" as a condition of release. It also called on the government to stop serving renewable restriction orders on released detainees. Stringent restrictions were placed on most detainees at the time of release, limiting where they might live, travel and work, banning political activities and requiring them to report regularly to the police. Such constraints amounted to a continued serious curtailment of their civil and political rights.

Amnesty International said it understood that most prisoners held under the ISA in the Batu Gajah and Taiping Detention Camps were arrested because they were regarded by the Ministry of Home Affairs as a threat to the security of the country, and not because they had committed criminal offences or engaged in acts of violence. Amnesty International stressed that the system did not afford any chance of a fair review of their cases, as the periodic reviews by the Advisory Board appeared to rely largely on reports made by the Special Branch officers who were also responsible for advising the Minister of Home Affairs on detentions. Most detainees refused to attend interviews. Amnesty International asked for clarification of the criteria used by the Advisory Board, and for detainees to be allowed legal representation during reviews by the board, as the first steps towards preventing arbitrary decisions.

Amnesty International also asked about conditions at the Batu Gajah Special Detention Camp, where regulations enforced since 1977 have imposed a severe regime on the 100 or so prisoners held there. The prisoners are held in isolation most of the time. In principle they are allowed out of their cells for a weekly bath and a daily walk, but the frequency and duration depend on the goodwill of the camp's staff. In addition mail and family visits are severely restricted. Amnesty International was concerned that the mental and physical health of detainees was likely to deteriorate under such conditions, and urged the government to repeal the Internal Security (Detained Persons) (Amendment) Rules 1977.

Amnesty International was seriously concerned by the resumption of executions in February and March 1981. Nine young men were executed in the seven days to 4 March 1981, after being convicted of illegal possession of firearms under the ISA. The ISA prescribes a mandatory death sentence for murder or illegal possession of firearms. These latest executions brought the number of people hanged since March 1980, when executions resumed after a lapse of 11 years, to 20.

One of those hanged on 4 March, Teh Cheng Poh, a 31-year-old carpenter, was sentenced to death by the Penang High Court in November 1976 after being convicted under the ISA of possessing a home-made pistol and five rounds of ammunition. His appeal to the Federal Court was dismissed in March 1977, but the Privy Council in London upheld the appeal in December 1978 when it ruled that Teh's trial was null and void, as the regulations under which he had been tried were outside the authority of the constitution. The Federal Court ordered a retrial before the High Court at which he was again found guilty. His last appeal to the Federal Court was dismissed in January 1980.

About 50 other condemned prisoners were awaiting execution in Pudu Prison in Kuala Lumpur. By the time executions were resumed

11 had exhausted their legal appeals, and their one hope lay with Malaysia's Pardons Board. Only five death sentences are said to have been commuted in the past two years.

A 31-year-old Singaporean, Tan Chay Wa, was sentenced to death in January 1981 after being convicted under the ISA of possessing a pistol. After his arrest in 1979 he was served with a two-year detention order for alleged involvement in underground political activities and it was only later that he was charged with possession of the pistol.

Amnesty International cabled the Prime Minister on 27 February and 4 March expressing deep concern at the resumption of executions. It wrote again on 9 March 1981 urging the government, on humanitarian grounds, to commute the sentences of all those still awaiting execution.

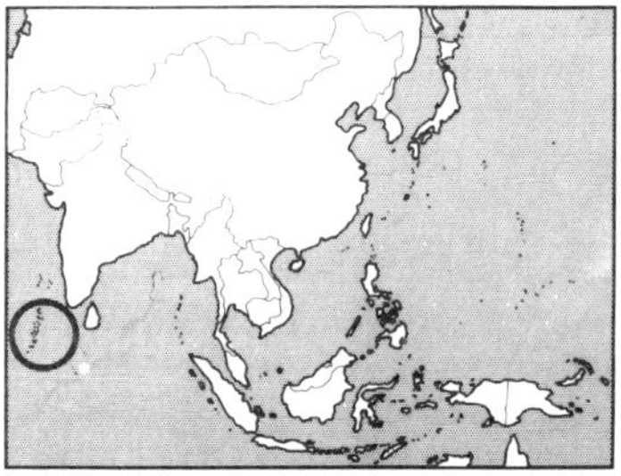

Maldives

Amnesty International was concerned about procedures in the trials of a number of detainees held in connection with an alleged conspiracy to overthrow the government of President Maumoon Abdul Gayoom.

The coup attempt which was uncovered in February 1980 was alleged by government officials to have been master-minded by former President Ibrahim Nasir, living in Singapore. The government arrested and detained a number of people said to have been involved, and at the same time members of families associated with the former President, including wives and children, were placed under house arrest. Amnesty International understands that at least three people were sentenced on charges of having associated with former President Nasir. One of these, Mohamed Ismail Manniku Sikku, formerly Director of Civil Aviation, whose case was being investigated by Amnesty International, was banished to an atoll in May 1980 for 10 years and a day, under a law applied retroactively making it an offence to associate with an enemy of the state.

In February 1981 the three alleged leaders of the coup attempt, Ahmed Nasseem, Kuwa Mohamed Maniku and Maisam Ali Maniku, were brought to trial charged with treason, a crime punishable by death under the penal code. In a cable sent on 6 February 1981 Amnesty International appealed to President Gayoom to ensure that trial procedures conformed to internationally recognized standards of fairness. On being informed by the Maldivian Government that it regarded the case as involving "planned acts of terrorism", Amnesty International explained in a cable of 17 March 1981 that it was concerned that the accused had been held incommunicado without access to family or legal counsel for nearly a year before being brought to trial, during which time they might have been subjected to undue pressure; that the accused did not have access to legal counsel during trial proceedings; and that they faced the death penalty. On 27 April 1981 they were sentenced to life imprisonment.

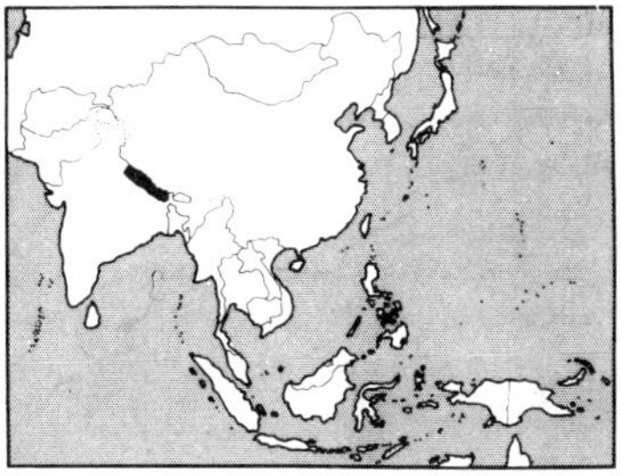

Nepal

Amnesty International continued to be concerned at the imprisonment, in some cases without trial, of political opponents including people detained for the non-violent expression of their views.

Shortly after a referendum on 2 May 1980 the government adopted the highly restrictive Freedom of Speech and Publication Ordinance, which among other things prohibited the formation of associations, organizations or unions motivated by party politics. Some provisions of the ordinance, including the requirement that district administrators approve all public meetings, posters or wall writing, were removed after widespread protests but were later incorporated into the Local Administration (Amendment) Act of September 1980. Under this act, Zonal Commissioners and Chief District Officers are empowered to declare areas under their administration "disturbed areas", shoot "lawless elements" on sight, ban meetings and demonstrations and arrest people under the preventive detention provisions of the Public Security Act (PSA). Alternatively prison terms of up to three months may be imposed after summary proceedings. As in previous years, several hundred people engaged in political activities were arrested under the PSA, which allows preventive detention under renewable nine-month detention orders up to a maximum of three years. Some of these were subsequently reported to have been released. Others were arrested under the Treason (Crime and Punishment) Act, (the Raj Kaj Act), which covers rebellion and treason, for which the maximum penalty is death, and sedition, for which the maximum penalty is three years' imprisonment. Amnesty International received reports of a number of arrests during the referendum campaign under the Arms and Ammunition Act. Seventeen of these people were later reported to have been acquitted and released.

A series of student-organized demonstrations, beginning in September 1980, focused on a number of issues, including the continued detention of political prisoners despite the amnesty of 13 April 1980 (see *Amnesty International Report 1980*). The demonstrations led to the arrest of several hundred students, workers and peasants. In April 1981 the President of the newly-formed Political Prisoners Release Committee said that his organization had recorded the names of 128 political prisoners throughout the kingdom. Amnesty International was informed of the names of 146 teachers, political activists and students arrested in the two months preceding the national assembly elections. Other sources reported between 400 and 600 arrests in this period, including election candidates whose manifestos were deemed to contain objectionable material and political activists who had called for a boycott of the elections.

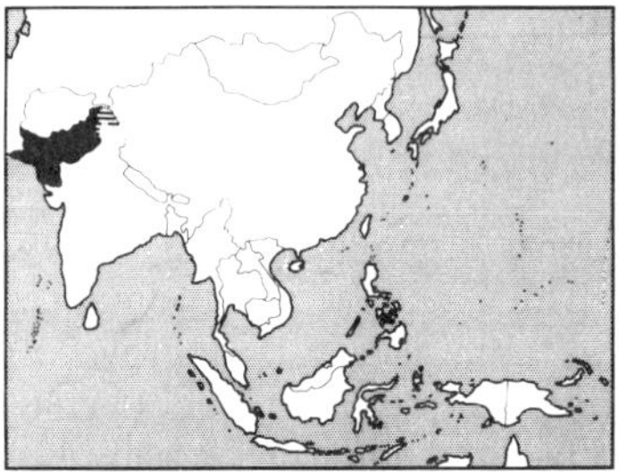

Pakistan

The concerns of Amnesty International continued to be the wide powers of arrest and detention without legal safeguards which were used to detain many hundreds of prisoners of conscience and the trial of political prisoners by military tribunals applying summary procedures without the right of defence by a lawyer or the right of appeal. Amnesty International was concerned about incommunicado detention, police brutality during interrogation, and the deaths of several prisoners, including two political prisoners, in police custody allegedly as a result of torture. The practice of flogging people for non-violent political activity was resumed. Amnesty International remained deeply concerned by the large number of executions, many following sentences by military courts applying summary procedures without the right of appeal.

Under martial law, political parties were dissolved and all political and trade union activity banned. Strict censorship was enforced and since October 1979 elections have been indefinitely postponed.

On 27 May 1980 President Zia-ul-Haq issued Presidential Order No. 21 of 1980 amending Article 199 of the constitution. The Presidential Order prohibited the High Courts and the Supreme Court from reviewing the legality of martial law orders and regulations adopted by the government, and from reviewing the legality of martial law itself. The High Courts were no longer allowed to hear any petitions from political prisoners challenging the legality of their detention, or their trial or conviction by a military court. The government simultaneously issued two martial law orders. Martial Law Order No. 77 extended the jurisdiction of the military courts at the expense of the civilian courts by empowering military courts to try cases of "treason, subversion, sedition, sabotage, prejudicial activity and seducing members of the armed forces". Martial Law Order No. 78 incorporated the provisions of Martial Law Order No. 12, permitting prisoners to be detained without trial for a maximum of 12 months, but removed the existing right to be informed of the grounds of detention.

Amnesty International cabled President Zia-ul-Haq on 30 May 1980 to express its concern about these constitutional and legal changes saying it believed they were a "further serious departure from the rule of law in Pakistan". It urged the government to repeal the legislation, to restore the supervisory jurisdiction of the civilian courts and to release all prisoners of conscience. Despite the constitutional amendments the High Courts continued to hear some petitions from political prisoners, set aside several sentences of floggings imposed by military courts and stayed the executions of several civilian prisoners sentenced to death by military tribunals.

On 24 March 1981 the President promulgated the Provisional Constitutional Order 1981. It effectively annulled the 1973 constitution, seriously impaired the independence of the judiciary, and gave the President power to change the constitution at will. The order reaffirmed the May 1980 constitutional amendments and required all High and Supreme Court judges to take an oath to uphold the new constitutional order. The Chief Justice of Pakistan, two Supreme Court judges and at least nine High Court judges refused to take the oath. The government did not allow several High Court judges to take the oath, effectively removing them. The March 1981 order removed the remaining legal safeguards protecting the basic human rights of political prisoners.

On 19 June 1980, 80 lawyers were arrested in Lahore for taking part in a demonstration calling upon the government to hold elections and to withdraw the May 1980 constitutional and martial law amendments. Ten lawyers were among 12 people arrested in Karachi on 22 August 1980, under martial law provisions banning all political activity, for organizing a procession "urging the government to restore the constitution and the rights guaranteed by it". Although the lawyers were released shortly after their arrest, many other prisoners of conscience faced detention without trial or trial by military courts under martial law provisions prohibiting all political activity (in particular Martial Law Regulations 13 and 33). Many leaders of political parties, including Begum Bhutto and Benazir Bhutto of the Pakistan People's Party (PPP) and Air Marshal Asghar Khan of the centrist party *Tehrik-i-Istiqlal,* were rearrested during the year. In early August 1980 the government arrested more leaders of the PPP and the *Tehrik-i-Istiqlal* under the provisions of Martial Law Order No. 78. During the summer students and trade union officials were arrested under the same order. Charges included the writing and distributing of political pamphlets, prohibited under martial law.

Amnesty International wrote to President Zia-ul-Haq on 26 September 1980 urging the government to release all prisoners of conscience, to abolish the practice of detaining political prisoners without trial and of trying political prisoners before military courts applying summary procedures.

Political arrests continued and their number increased sharply during the first months of 1981. In the first week of January some 40 people, many of them students, were arrested in Karachi in connection with plans to observe the birthday of former Prime Minister Bhutto. On 3 January 1981 Irshad Rao, the editor of the pro-PPP paper *Al Fatah,* was arrested together with five other journalists. The police said they had discovered a "clandestine publication group" which was "printing and publishing anti-state subversive literature".

Also arrested during the first weeks of January were a number of rank and file members of the PPP, allegedly on suspicion of "passing secrets to a foreign country". The government later said that the arrests had been made under the Army Act. Several of those arrested were reportedly taken to Attock Fort, where they were held incommunicado for up to six weeks without being told the grounds for their arrest.

Between 16 and 26 February 1981 more than 200 people were arrested in Multan and Lahore after the formation on 6 February 1981 of the Movement for the Restoration of Democracy, a nine-party alliance of all the major opposition parties, including the PPP, the *Tehrik-i-Istiqlal,* the Pakistan Democratic Party, the pro-Islamic *Jamiat Ulema Islam* and the Muslim League. The government arrested nearly all its leaders and officers, as well as members and sympathizers. They included students supporting the movement's demands for the immediate lifting of martial law and the resignation of the government until the establishment of a civilian government to supervise elections.

Amnesty International cabled President Zia-ul-Haq on 26 February 1981 to express its concern at the arrests of approximately 100 leading members of opposition parties, and urged the government to release them and others arrested on 16 February.

On 2 March 1981 a Pakistan International Airlines plane was hijacked. The hijackers demanded the release of political prisoners in Pakistan, and 54 political prisoners were released on 15 March 1981. According to press reports, the hijacking was carried out by the *Al Zulfikar* organization, which the government claimed later to be the armed wing of the PPP, but without providing any evidence. In the weeks after the hijacking hundreds of PPP members and sympathizers were arrested throughout the country. Amnesty International has estimated that by mid-March 1981 at least 1,000 political prisoners were added to the several hundred already held at the beginning of 1981, and numerous arrests continued to be reported of members of all major opposition parties.

Amnesty International continued to be concerned about the procedures under which political prisoners were tried by military courts. Summary military courts do not allow defence lawyers at the trial, and there is no appeal. Hundreds of political prisoners have been tried by such courts during the year under the provisions of Martial Law Regulations 4, 15, 18, and in particular 13 and 33, for participating in demonstrations, for possessing political literature, and for organizing or attending political meetings. They were sentenced to terms of imprisonment of up to one year. About 60 have been adopted as prisoners of conscience.

Amnesty International was concerned at several reports that political prisoners had been tried *in camera.* On 5 March 1981 Amnesty International cabled the Minister of Home Affairs, Mahmoud A. Haroon, and the Home Secretary for the Sindh province to express concern about reports that Jam Saqi, Badar Abroo, Shabir Shah, Jamal Naqvi, Kamal Warsi and Amar Lal were being tried by a special military court in Karachi Central Jail. After their arrest the government had announced on 29 August 1980 that it had discovered "a secret cell working underground . . . producing and disseminating clandestine subversive literature calculated to erode the ideological foundations of Pakistan . . .", but did not publish specific charges. Amnesty International urged the government to allow all the accused a lawyer of their choice, to transfer the trial to an open court, and to give full rights of appeal as guaranteed in the constitution. Amnesty International has taken up these cases for investigation.

In its letter of 26 September 1980 Amnesty International expressed its deep concern about reports that at least five prisoners had been tortured and died in police custody in the 12 months from November 1979. Nazir Abbasi, President of the Sind National Students Federation, reportedly died in custody in Karachi on 9

August 1980, 11 days after arrest. Family members alleged that Nazir Abbasi had died as a result of torture, and said they had seen wounds on his body when they received it for burial. On 13 August 1980 Amnesty International urged President Zia-ul-Haq to order an independent inquiry, and to publish its findings in full. The government has instituted formal inquiries into only three of these five deaths, one of them being a judicial inquiry. On 26 September 1980 Amnesty International urged the government to establish judicial inquiries into all five cases, to publish the findings in full and to investigate fully the record and conduct of police officials against whom there was evidence of involvement in such practices. Amnesty International also urged the government to review police training methods and said that the inclusion of the United Nations Code of Conduct for Law Enforcement Officials in police training would be an important step towards preventing torture.

In its letter of 26 September 1980 to President Zia-ul-Haq Amnesty International urged the immediate abolition of floggings and amputations saying it considered them "cruel and inhuman" punishments and as such prohibited under international law. During the first seven months of 1980 summary military courts ordered the flogging of at least 76 people convicted on criminal charges. The sentences ranged from three to 15 lashes each. Amnesty International was glad to note that although several people were sentenced to have their hands amputated the punishment had not been carried out as far as Amnesty International was aware. During the year Amnesty International launched urgent appeals on behalf of Mohammed Dutta, Lateef Ullah, Ghulam Ullah, Hussain Mahesar and Ali Asghar, who were sentenced to amputation, and expressed concern that flogging was still often being imposed by summary military courts and *Shari'a* (Islamic law) courts for offences including political offences. There has been a sharp increase in the incidence of flogging for political offences since the beginning of 1981.

Amnesty International's letter of 26 September 1980 was released to the press on 3 November 1980, and during the following months Amnesty International members throughout the world wrote to the government urging it to take immediate steps to halt torture, floggings and executions in Pakistan, and to release all prisoners of conscience. Amnesty International did not receive a direct reply to its letter. However in a public response to the publication of the letter on 3 November 1980, the government was quoted on 6 November as saying that "there were only two political detainees in Pakistan". It denied reports that five prisoners had died during the year in police custody as a result of torture. It said all five men had died "by natural causes" (*Dawn,* 7 November 1980). It specified that Nazir Abbasi (who was 25 years old at the time of his death and had no known medical history of heart disease) had died of a "heart attack". The government said this was the conclusion of a report drawn up by a medical board, but it did not release the text. On 10 October 1980 Amnesty International cabled the President to deplore a report that another political prisoner, trade union leader Inayat Masih, had died in hospital on 6 September while in custody. It urged the government to establish an independent inquiry.

On 13 April 1981 Amnesty International cabled the Minister of the Interior to express concern about reports that two members of the PPP, lawyer Qamar Abbas and former Attorney General Yahya Bakhtiar, who had been sentenced to five years' imprisonment by a special court on charges of election-rigging in Quetta constituency, had been assaulted in police custody in Peshawar and Quetta jail respectively. Amnesty International urged the government to provide full medical treatment immediately, to conduct a public inquiry into both incidents and to take appropriate measures to establish responsibility.

The number of executions continued to be of profound concern. Among those sentenced to death were civilians convicted by special military courts against whose verdict there was no appeal, although executions had to be confirmed by the Chief Martial Law Administrator, President Zia-ul-Haq. Statistics given by the government to the United Nations on the period to 1978 confirmed a rise in the number of executions in Pakistan since martial law. A man was sentenced by a special military court in Faisalabad on 13 July 1980 to be executed in public; and on 9 April 1981 two men were executed in Kot Lakhpat jail, Lahore, after being convicted of murder by a special military court. One of the accused, Wajid, was 18 years old at the time of his hanging. Throughout the year Amnesty International appealed for clemency for 18 civilians sentenced to death by military courts, nearly all without being allowed to appeal. In its September 1980 letter Amnesty International had appealed to the President to commute all death sentences as a step towards abolishing the death penalty. Amnesty International does not know of a single case in which the President granted clemency out of the hundreds of prisoners who have been sentenced to death since the military government took power in June 1977.

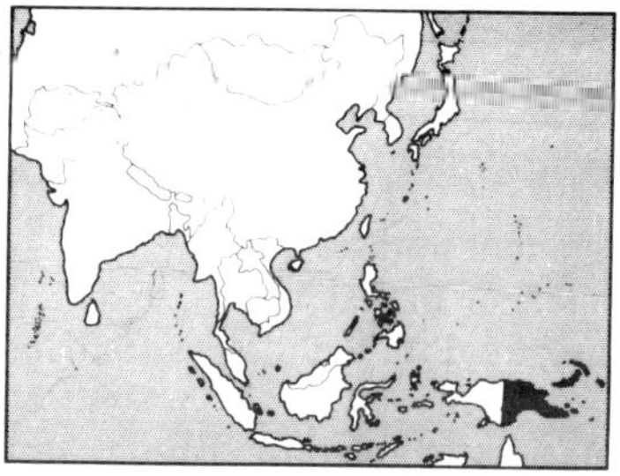

Papua New Guinea

A private member's bill to restore the death penalty as a discretionary punishment for wilful murder was defeated in parliament on 13 November 1980. The bill was opposed by leading members of the government, including the Prime Minister, Sir Julius Chan, and the Minister of Justice, Paul Torato. Papua New Guinea abolished the death penalty for wilful murder in 1974. Amnesty International had launched an appeal to officials urging that the death penalty not be reintroduced.

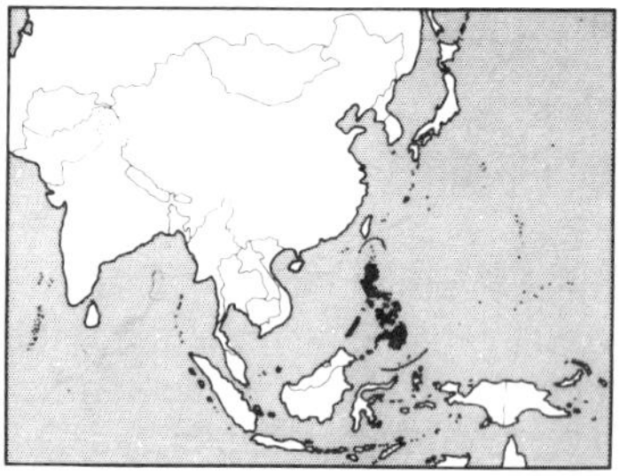

Philippines

On 17 January 1981 President Marcos lifted the state of martial law in force since September 1972. Amnesty International's concerns since the imposition of martial law have been: the arrest and detention of prisoners of conscience; the detention of political prisoners for long periods without trial; the trial of political prisoners before military tribunals under procedures which do not conform to internationally recognized standards; the extra-legal practices of military personnel including arrest and detention without charge or trial, "disappearance", torture and killing of people considered opponents of the government; the imposition of the death penalty by civil and military courts and the extension of the range of offences for which the death penalty may be imposed. Amnesty International was concerned that the pattern of human rights violations established during the period of martial law did not end with its lifting. The grounds for such concern were the wide-ranging emergency powers retained by the President, particularly regarding arrest and detention, the prominent role still assigned to the armed forces and continuing reports of human rights violations.

Under the martial law powers the armed forces were authorized to arrest and detain for prosecution or preventive detention anyone suspected of conspiring "to seize political and state power". During the period of martial law approximately 70,000 people were detained under these provisions. Amnesty International believes that in recent years approximately 1,000 political detainees were held under martial law at any one time. Many of these were held for short periods so that the total number of arrests in one year was considerably higher than 1,000.

Amnesty International continued to receive regular reports of torture after arrest. Prisoners have frequently been tortured during "tactical interrogation" immediately after arrest by a unit of the intelligence and security forces. They were often held incommunicado in secret holding centres known as "safe houses". Some who "disappeared" into "safe houses" were released later or reappeared in a military detention centre. Others never reappeared and their fate or whereabouts after abduction was never ascertained. Other victims were later found dead and mutilated in isolated areas. In the period 1975 to 1980 Amnesty International received reports of more than 230 cases of "disappearance". Five such cases on which Amnesty International had been working were referred to the United Nations Working Group on Enforced or Involuntary Disappearances in September 1980.

Large numbers of people believed to have engaged in non-violent protest against government policies were arrested during the year. On 20 and 21 May 1980, 22 people, mostly students associated with the Student Christian Movement, were arrested in Cebu City after protests against a government slum clearance project. They were later charged with subversion and Amnesty International investigated their cases. In Manila, between June and the end of September 1980, at least 60 students were arrested for what the government called "preventive reasons", after taking part in demonstrations focusing on educational issues and the continued imposition of martial law. On 2 and 3 September 1980 a number of trade unionists were arrested. They were associated with the Philippine Alliance of Labor Organizations, the National Federation of Labor and the *Kilusang Mayo Uno* (KMU), First of May Movement, which were jointly planning a labour rally for 25 September. Although most were released within days, three, including Ernesto Arellano, Executive Secretary of KMU, who was adopted as a prisoner of conscience, were not released until 9 April 1981. Demonstrations against martial law which took place in September, around the anniversary of the proclamation of martial law, prompted further arrests in Manila, Cebu City, Davao City and elsewhere.

Amnesty International also received reports of individuals being arrested for exercising their right to freedom of expression. Father Pepito Bernardo, a priest from the diocese of Cabanatuan who has worked among tribal peoples in the Philippines and is a board member of the Episcopal Commission on Tribal Filipinos (ECTF), an organization founded under the auspices of the Catholic Bishops' Conference of the Philippines, was arrested on 26 September 1980 in Ilagan, Isabela, for allegedly being in possession of "subversive materials". He was later served with an Arrest, Search and Seizure Order (ASSO) and taken to Bicutan Rehabilitation Centre. He was adopted as a prisoner of conscience.

As a result of widespread arrests in the Manila area between June and October 1980, the number of people held in the chief military detention centre in the Metro Manila area, the Bicutan Rehabilitation Centre (Camp Bagong Diwa), more than trebled. Compounding the problem of overcrowding was an instruction issued in June 1980 which gave the President sole authority to approve the release of people arrested by ASSO, which slowed the release process. On 29 September 1980 the detainees in Bicutan went on a three-day hunger-strike in pursuit of a number of demands including: abandonment of the new release procedures; the immediate release of 54 detainees recommended for release by the Ministry of National Defense; and an increase in the food allowance. A second hunger-strike for the same demands, involving 132 detainees, was held between 3 and 21 November. On 6 November Amnesty International launched an appeal urging the authorities to improve conditions in Bicutan and to review release procedures. It also urged the authorities to ensure that no reprisals would be taken against those participating in the hunger-strike, as had happened after previous hunger-strikes. On learning that five detainees, including Father Bernardo, were seriously ill as a result of the hunger-strike and that two others, José Luneta and Saturnino Ocampo, had been punished by being removed from Bicutan to the Military Security Unit (MSU), Fort Bonifacio, Amnesty International launched a further appeal on 18 November 1980. The appeal called for all necessary medical treatment for the ill, for the release of Father Bernardo, and for no reprisals to be taken against those on hunger-strike. On 21 November, after receiving assurances that a number of detainees would be released, the prisoners ended their hunger-strike. Between October and December 1980 Amnesty International also learned of hunger-strikes for improved conditions and release of detainees in Camp Alagar (Cagayan de Oro), Camp Bagong Ibalon (Legaspi City) and Camps Lahug and Sergio Osmena Sr (Cebu City).

In the period around the lifting of martial law the authorities announced the release and amnesty of large numbers of detainees and former detainees. Between 29 November 1980 and 18 January 1981 the amnesty and temporary or permanent release of 3,762 detainees and former detainees were announced. The majority were alleged members of the guerrilla New People's Army (NPA) and the

Muslim secessionist Moro National Liberation Front (MNLF) who had already been released, and who were now granted amnesties. Others had been convicted by military tribunals of common crimes such as gambling, illegal firearms possession, robbery and murder. Amnesty International believes that no more than 129 of those released between 29 November and 17 January were political detainees. Amnesty International understands that 12 prisoners were released from Bicutan on 18 January 1981.

On 17 January 1981 it was announced that 341 prisoners, 159 of whom were said to be charged with public order and national security offences, would be released. Between 5 March and 20 April 1981 a further 13 detainees were released from Dorm 9-C, New Bilibid Prisons, Muntinlupa, where they had been transferred on the lifting of martial law. Amnesty International also learned of individual releases of detainees in the period after the lifting of martial law. On 5 December 1980, 24 December 1980, and 20 January 1981, Amnesty International wrote to President Marcos to welcome reports of the release and amnesty of 232, 1,200, and 159 detainees respectively. On each occasion it asked for full lists of those released. No such lists were provided, but it would appear that fewer than 200 detainees held for national security and public order offences were freed. Moreover, it appears that all were granted "temporary release": their cases were still pending before the courts, and they were still subject to restrictions on their freedom of movement and association and had to report regularly to the authorities.

Eleven prisoners whose cases had been taken up by Amnesty International were among those released. Most had been held in detention centres in the Manila area. Three women detainees, Marietta Socorro Briones, Luminada Malingin and Linda Angel Rentillosa, who had been held in Camp Lahug, Cebu City, and were among the 22 charged with subversion, were released in January 1981. Eduardo Quitoriano, an adopted prisoner of conscience held on charges of subversion since December 1978, was released from Camp Alagar, Cayagan de Oro City, Misamis Oriental, on 14 February 1981. On 24 December 1980 Father Pepito Bernardo and Father Jeremias Aquino were released (see *Amnesty International Report 1980*). On 13 December 1980 Leoncio Co, who had been detained without trial on subversion charges since March 1970, before the declaration of martial law, was released. Four other detainees facing charges of rebellion or subversion or both — Eduardo Lingat, Fernando Tayag, Delfin Delica and Hermengildo Garcia — were released between 29 November 1980 and 6 April 1981.

Despite the lifting of martial law, the powers retained by the

President are extensive. They are set forth in: Amendment 6 to the 1973 Constitution ratified in the referendum of October 1976; the Public Order Act (Presidential Decree (PD) No. 1737); and the National Security Code (PD No. 1498). Amendment 6 allows the President to exercise emergency powers short of declaring a state of martial law. PD No. 1737 specifies the emergency powers to be exercised by the President under Amendment 6, among them the power to take whatever measures he may deem necessary to meet an emergency "including but not limited to preventive detention". The National Security Code is a compilation of orders and decrees issued under martial law relating to national security and public order, including General Order (GO) No. 2 as amended which authorizes the Minister of National Defense to arrest, detain and release people believed to have committed specified security and public order offences. In addition, Proclamation No. 2045 lifting the state of martial law provides that the suspension of the privilege of the writ of *habeas corpus,* which had been introduced with the imposition of martial law, would continue in areas in Mindanao where the MNLF were active, and with respect to people detained for public order and security offences. The only martial law decree or order known to have been revoked on the lifting of martial law was GO No. 8 of 27 September 1972, which had created military tribunals with jurisdiction over specified offences which included security and public order offences.

Despite the revocation of GO No. 8 Proclamation No. 2045 provided for military tribunals to continue to hear cases pending before them. It appeared that the effect of revoking GO No. 8 was to reaffirm Letter of Instruction (LOI) No. 772 of November 1978 in which President Marcos had ordered all new cases over which military tribunals had previously held jurisdiction to be referred in future to the civil courts. The implementation of LOI No. 772 was uneven, with some new security and public order cases still being referred to military tribunals and others to civil courts. In 1980, for example, at least three major political cases were referred to military tribunals: those of Olaguer *et al,* Kalaw *et al* and Pinguel *et al.* The Supreme Court is understood in January 1981 to have rejected *habeas corpus* petitions in three major martial law cases. One of these cases, that of Aquino *et al,* was reported to have been reopened before a military tribunal in April 1981.

During the period of martial law the military tribunals were challenged on a variety of grounds including their denial of defendants' rights to due process. Military tribunals were constituted not as part of the judiciary but as agencies of the executive; their members were career officers ultimately responsible to the President in his capacity as commander-in-chief. Moreover, very few trials started before military tribunals and even fewer were completed both because pre-trial and trial proceedings were subject to inordinate delays and because cases were suspended for long periods awaiting decisions from the Supreme Court on defendants' petitions. Amnesty International knows of no cases of a political nature decided by military tribunals during the year.

A small number of detainees were transferred from military detention centres to civilian prisons on the lifting of martial law. Thirty-three were transferred from the Bicutan Rehabilitation Centre to Dorm-9C, the National Penitentiary, Muntinlupa. Amnesty International also learned of transfers from military detention centres in Benguet, Pangasinan and Davao City to city and provincial jails. However at the end of April 1981 a number of military camps were still being used as detention centres, including Camp Olivas in Pampanga, Camp Bagong Ibalon in Legaspi City and Camp Lahug Detention Centre in Cebu City. Detainees were also still being held in places administered by branches of the intelligence and security services such as 4th Regional Security Unit (RSU-4), Camp Crame, Quezon City and the MSU, Fort Bonifacio. Prisoners transferred to Muntinlupa faced worse prison conditions and the 33 detainess held there went on a three-day protest hunger-strike on 16 February 1981. In the following two months 12 prisoners were released from Muntinlupa and six transferred back to the Bicutan Rehabilitation Centre. The centre had been reopened earlier to accommodate three detainees transferred from the MSU. The three included Saturnino Ocampo and Sixto Carlos Jr, whose cases have been taken up by Amnesty International.

Amnesty International was concerned by continuing evidence of torture and ill-treatment, "disappearances" and extrajudicial killings. Amnesty International knows of cases where detainees, having suffered severe torture during interrogation, were subsequently held incommunicado in a detention centre for an indefinite period. Approximately 20 prisoners were still detained in restrictive conditions, including in some cases total isolation, in the MSU, Fort Bonifacio, at the end of April 1981. Among them were alleged leaders of the Communist Party of the Philippines and the NPA, including the alleged Communist Party Chairman José Maria Sison and his wife Juliet Delima Sison, who have been held in solitary confinement since their arrest in November 1977. Bernabe Buscayno, a former commander of the NPA, has been detained in isolation in RSU-4, Camp Crame, since shortly after his arrest in August 1976. Benigno Aquino, the former leader of the Liberal Party and regarded as President Marcos' chief political rival before martial law, was released from the

MSU on 8 May to have heart surgery in the United States of America. He was charged in his absence, together with 86 others, of complicity in the urban bombing campaign undertaken by the so-called April 6 Movement between August and October 1980. Also alleged to be involved in the April 6 Movement were a number of prominent exiled politicians, and former Senator Jovito Salonga, still resident in the Philippines, who was arrested on 11 October 1980 and detained in the MSU until 30 November when he was placed under house arrest.

In April 1981 it was reported that Maria Milagros Lumabi-Echanis was also being held in the MSU. On 16 August 1980 she had been taken with her two-month-old son by men in plain clothes from her uncle's house in Manila. Her parents' attempts to discover her whereabouts from the authorities proved fruitless. On 11 March, after learning that she had been seen in the MSU, Amnesty International appealed to the authorities to confirm that she was being held there and urged that she be released or, if charged, be transferred to a regular detention centre.

Two other cases of "disappearance" — those of Romeo Crismo and Petronilo Torno — were investigated by Amnesty International. No information has been received on their whereabouts or fate. Romeo Crismo, a public accountant and former leader of the Methodist Youth Fellowship, "disappeared" in Cagayan province on 12 August 1980. Petronilo Torno, a trade unionist, was taken from his home in Quezon province, reportedly by members of the Philippine Constabulary, in June 1980, shortly after being released from detention together with a number of fellow trade unionists.

Amnesty International has received frequent reports in recent years of extrajudicial killings by military units, by irregular units believed to be acting as agents of the armed forces, or by other officials. This practice is known in the Philippines as "salvaging". Amnesty International received reports of more than 300 cases of "salvaging" between 1975 and April 1980. The number of reported cases grew each year. Many were reported from Davao and Maguindanao in Mindanao, Quezon province and the Bicol region in Luzon, and Samar and Negros Occidental in the Visayas. Two instances of "salvaging" — the killing of Macli-ing Dulag in Kalinga-Apayao, northern Luzon, and the killings of nine people in Negros Occidental — received wide publicity. In August 1980 the Minister of National Defense, Juan Ponce Enrile, announced that four army personnel had been charged in connection with the killing of Macli-ing Dulag, but Amnesty International has received no further information about the trials. Nineteen people including the Mayor of Kabankalan, Negros Occidental, were charged with murder after the "disappearance" of 14 residents between 29 March and 7 May 1980. However none of the people charged were in detention at the end of April 1981 and no reports have been received indicating any progress in their trial. Amnesty International received further reports of "salvaging" from the Bicol region in southern Luzon; Quezon, Cagayan and Isabela provinces in eastern Luzon; and Nueva Ecija, central Luzon. It has also received reports of killings by private armies, allegedly operating with official sanction. One such case involved the death on 13 April 1981 of Father Godofredo Alingal, priest of the parish of Kibawe, Bukidnon, Mindanao.

Amnesty International believes that more than 800 people were under sentence of death, most in the National Penitentiary, Muntinlupa. They included Sabiniano Contreras, sentenced to death in March 1972 when he was 15 years old. Amnesty International wrote to President Marcos on 30 October 1980 urging him to do everything in his power to intervene and remove him from death row. Almost all those under sentence of death were awaiting review of their sentences by the Supreme Court. Eleven people have been under sentence of death since the 1950s. On 29 January 1981 it was learned that the Supreme Court had rejected the final appeal against the death sentence of Exequiel Angeles, a former policeman sentenced in 1969. Amnesty International appealed to President Marcos for clemency and in March 1981 learned that President Marcos had commuted the sentence to life imprisonment. Others under sentence of death were convicted for offences allegedly committed while they were members of the NPA or its predecessor the *Hukbong Mapagpalaya ng Bayan*, People's Liberation Army, (popularly known as the Huks). Executions have been carried out infrequently in recent years. Amnesty International understands that no executions took place during the year under review.

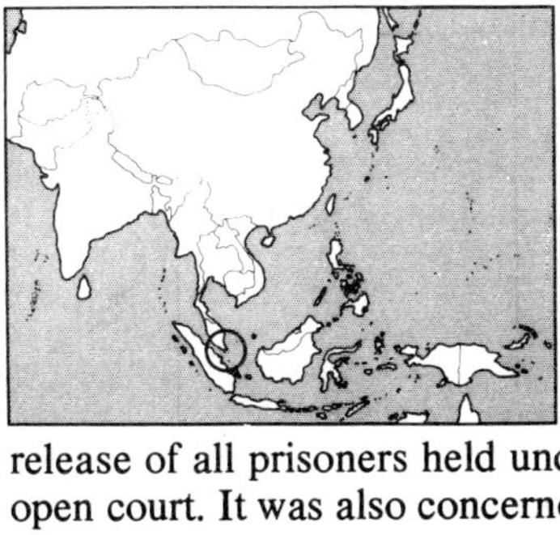

Singapore

Amnesty International was concerned about the prolonged detention without trial of political prisoners under the Internal Security Act 1961 (ISA). Some prisoners have been held for 18 years. It appealed for the immediate and unconditional release of all prisoners held under the ISA or for their early trial in open court. It was also concerned about the use of the death penalty and appealed to President Benjamin Sheares to commute all death sentences.

Under Section 8(1)(a) of the ISA, a person may be detained if the President believes it is necessary "with a view to preventing that person from acting in any manner prejudicial to the security of Singapore or any part thereof or to the maintenance of public order or essential services therein". These preventive detention orders cannot be challenged in the courts; they are valid for up to two years and may be renewed indefinitely. A press statement issued by the Prime Minister's Office on 31 March 1980 declared that a condition for the release of prisoners held under the ISA was "a public undertaking disowning the Communist Party of Malaya's use of force and terror to overthrow the Government". Amnesty International was concerned that the prisoners' alleged connections with the CPM were never proved in open court, and believed that many were imprisoned for the peaceful exercise of their right to freedom of expression and association. The same statement from the Prime Minister's Office allowed the prisoners voluntary exile as an alternative to release. Prisoners who refused these conditions would be released only "when they [were] assessed to be of no danger to Singapore".

Amnesty International believed that these conditions had created a situation where prisoners were pressurized to make the undertaking. Instances of torture and ill-treatment of detainees held under the ISA were described in the *Report of an Amnesty International Mission to Singapore, 30 November to 5 December 1978,* published in January 1980. On 1 July 1980 Amnesty International wrote to Prime Minister Lee Kuan Yew about the commission of inquiry he had appointed to look into allegations of ill-treatment in interrogation and detention centres. It pointed out that the commission's conclusion that "the process of interrogation does involve psychological stress" but not torture was apparently based solely on interviews with prison doctors and examination of medical records in only three cases. The commission did not appear to have investigated fully the findings of the Amnesty International report which detailed the ill-treatment of 21 detainees, including the case of Ho Piao, whose sworn affidavit testified to assault and repeated dousing with water in refrigerated rooms, and the cases of Chai Chong and Chow Tien Pao who were allegedly beaten after their hunger-strike in 1978. It appeared from the press statement that the commission had not interviewed the detainees. Although the press statement stressed the opportunities for detainees to draw the attention of their lawyers, families, doctors and officials from outside the internal security department to torture and injuries inflicted upon them, Amnesty International noted that in practice these opportunities were severely restricted. Amnesty International reiterated its recommendation that a public commission of inquiry be set up to investigate all allegations of ill-treatment cited in the report.

Amnesty International did not know of any recent arrests under Section 8(1)(a) of the ISA. It continued to appeal on behalf of three prisoners of conscience held without trial since 1963, amongst the longest detentions for political prisoners anywhere in the world. They were Ho Piao, a former secretary of the National Seamen's Union, Dr Lim Hock Siew, the former Secretary General of the *Barisan Sosialis,* (Socialist Front), and Lee Tze Tong, a trade union leader and Member of Parliament for the *Barisan Sosialis.* Another prisoner, Dr Poh Soo Kai, detained under the ISA from 1963 to 1973, was rearrested in 1976 and has been adopted as a prisoner of conscience. All four men had been active in the opposition and Amnesty International believed that they were detained for expressing views opposing government policies. Dr Lim Hock Siew and Lee Tze Tong have been living in enforced exile on small islands off the main island of Singapore since October 1978 and February 1980 respectively. Both were served with restriction orders under Section 8(1)(b) of the ISA which imposes restrictions on residence, travel, association and activities and prohibits them from addressing public meetings. Amnesty International continued to urge their unconditional release.

Chia Thye Poh, a former Member of Parliament for the *Barisan Sosialis,* editor of the party's newspaper and an assistant lecturer at Nanyang University, has been detained without trial since October 1966 and has been adopted by Amnesty International as a prisoner of conscience. Before his arrest under the ISA, Chia Thye Poh had been fined in May 1966 for publishing a "seditious article" in the *Barisan Sosialis* newspaper *Chern Sien Pau.* The article criticized the government's treatment of another *Barisan Sosialis* Member of Parliament then held in detention under the ISA. Tan Kim Oh has also been detained under the ISA since 1966, when he was an undergraduate student at Nanyang University. Tan Kim Oh was known to have been a leading opponent of "suitability certificates", which the government had introduced as a requirement for entry into institutions of higher education. Amnesty International has adopted him as a prisoner of conscience. Kuo Pao-kun, aged 41, who at the time of his arrest in March 1976 was the secretary of the Chinese Chamber of Commerce and the director of a theatrical troupe, was released on 1 October 1980 but Amnesty International has the names of 32 detainees believed to be detained under the ISA.

On 15 October 1980 Amnesty International urged President Benjamin Sheares to commute the death sentences on Ong Ah-chuan and Koh Kai Cheng after the failure of their appeal to the Judicial

Committee of the Privy Council in the United Kingdom. They had been given a mandatory death sentence for a drug trafficking offence. Ong Ah-chuan was executed in February 1981. In a cable to President Sheares on 6 March 1981 Amnesty International expressed its grave concern at this execution and reiterated its appeal to the President to commute the death sentence on Koh Kai Cheng and all death sentences submitted to him in the future. Ten people were believed to be on death row for drug trafficking offences.

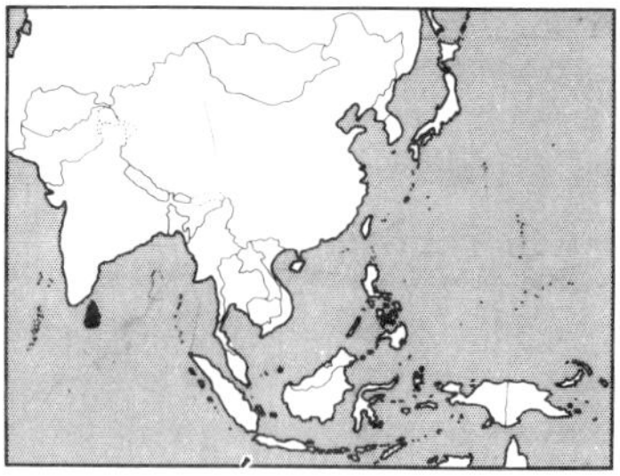

Sri Lanka

Amnesty International was concerned about the wide powers of arrest and detention under the Prevention of Terrorism Act (PTA) and about people arrested under its provisions and held incommunicado. The fate of three Tamils who "disappeared" in 1979 has still not been clarified.

A major development in 1980 was the government's decision to sign and ratify the International Covenant on Civil and Political Rights. The government acceded to the covenant on 11 June 1980 and made a declaration under Article 41 of that covenant recognizing the competence of the Human Rights Committee to hear interstate complaints about violations of the covenant. On 3 June 1980 Amnesty International cabled President J. R. Jayewardene welcoming the government's decision. In a letter of 17 September 1980 Amnesty International expressed the hope that this important initiative would be followed by an early decision to ratify the Optional Protocol to the International Covenant on Civil and Political Rights, as Amnesty International had recommended in its memorandum submitted to the government in May 1980. The government has not yet ratified the Optional Protocol.

Amnesty International said it was encouraged to note that the Proscription of Liberation Tigers of Tamil Eelam and Other Similar Organizations Law had lapsed in May 1980, a law which Amnesty International had criticized. It expressed concern however that the PTA remained in force, which similarly suspends legal safeguards. Several arrests were reported under the PTA, which allows for detention without trial for up to 18 months "in such place and subject to such conditions as may be determined by the Minister". Under the PTA detainees need not be produced before a magistrate within 24 hours of arrest as is the normal rule, and there are no safeguards against incommunicado detention. Detainees have been denied any access to their lawyers and relatives for long periods.

On 5 June 1980 several opposition parties and trade unions organized a demonstration to protest against rising living costs exacerbating the earlier cut in the food subsidy program. Pro-government unions organized a counter-demonstration, and one man died in the ensuing violence. On 16 July the government imposed emergency rule and invoked the Public Security Act. It banned the general strike called by the Joint Committee for Trade Union Action for 18 July and then dismissed 40,000 public sector employees who went on strike nevertheless. Officials said opposition parties had planned the general strike to overthrow the government and obstruct its development program. Opposition sources claimed 150 people were arrested, but all were released shortly afterwards.

On 8 August 1980 opposition parties and trade unions demonstrated in Colombo Fort against the dismissals of workers who participated in the 18 July general strike. The demonstration ended in violence and the police arrested 32 trade union leaders and left-wing political leaders. On 17 September 1980 Amnesty International wrote to the President asking the government to confirm that the arrests made under the emergency imposed in July 1980 had been short-term and that those arrested were being released. It expressed concern about reports that some might face trial under the Emergency Regulations, despite the fact that the emergency had been allowed to lapse on 15 August.

Amnesty International later learned that all those arrested had been released within two months of their arrest except G. I. D. Dharmasekera, the General Secretary of the Lanka Democratic Front. Amnesty International has not been able to establish under what legislation he was being held and what the specific charges were against him. It is investigating his case.

Thirty members of the Tamil minority were reported to have been arrested in April and early May in connection with an armed robbery at Neerveli in the northern region on 25 March 1981. Two policemen were killed in the incident. Amnesty International wrote and cabled to President Jayewardene on 30 April 1981 to verify reports of the arrests and to urge the government to meet the minimum standards laid down in the International Covenant on Civil and Political Rights. While acknowledging that those responsible for violent incidents should be brought to justice, Amnesty International expressed concern that the arrested people were apparently held incommunicado, and that relatives were not informed about their whereabouts. It stressed that the removal of safeguards against incommunicado detention by the PTA facilitated human rights violations. Amnesty International named seven people reportedly arrested and asked the government to publish the names of all those arrested, to allow them immediate access to a lawyer of their choice, to inform the relatives of the place of detention and allow them immediate and regular visits to the prisoners. It urged the government to publish the charges against the 30, or to release them.

The effective provision of minimum legal safeguards to detainees was one of the main concerns outlined by Amnesty International in its memorandum presented to the government on 23 May 1980 (see *Amnesty International Report 1980*). The memorandum dealt with events in the northern Jaffna region after the declaration of an emergency on 11 July 1979. Many young Tamils were arrested under the Emergency Regulations, the PTA or other special legislation. It detailed allegations of torture and reports that six Tamils had died in the custody of the police. The memorandum was sent to the President, the Prime Minister, the Minister of Foreign Affairs and the Minister of Justice, asking for the government's comments and observations, and was also sent to the Minister of Trade and Shipping who is the Chairman of the Parliamentary Select Committee inquiry into the six deaths, the Inspector General of Police, the Military Commander for the Jaffna district and the Deputy Minister of Defence, the officials met by the Amnesty International delegate visiting Sri Lanka in August 1979.

In its letter of 17 September 1980 Amnesty International expressed concern that it had still not received the government's comments on the memorandum submitted in May. On 25 November 1980 Amnesty International discussed the memorandum with the Acting High Commissioner in London. Amnesty International was told that it would receive a full reply from the government. It was informed that the Parliamentary Select Committee, set up to inquire into the allegations that six Tamils had died in the custody of the police after allegedly being arrested in July 1979, was expected to finalize its report in January 1981, and that the report would be published. The bodies of two of the men were found on the morning of their arrest and one died later in the prison hospital. The Jaffna magistrate returned a verdict of homicide in the case of Iyathurai Indrarajah, one of the Tamils who died after his arrest, and found "evidence of police violence". The government denied that the other three, Ramalingam Balendran, Sellathurai Rajeswaran and Sellathurai Parameswaran, had been arrested. Their bodies have not been found although relatives have testified to their arrest and believe they subsequently died in police custody. Amnesty International was informed that the government believed the three men were in hiding afraid of interrogation in connection with criminal charges.

On 27 February 1981 Amnesty International wrote again to the government asking for the report of the Parliamentary Select Committee. It drew the government's attention to United Nations General Assembly Resolution 33/173 of 20 December 1978 requesting governments to undertake speedy and impartial investigations into all cases of "disappeared" people. Amnesty International has not received a reply and knows of no published information about the progress made in the Parliamentary Select Committee's investigations or about its findings. The fate of the three "disappeared" Tamils has not yet been clarified.

Amnesty International also asked the government for details of any proceedings against individual police officers implicated in torture. Amnesty International has not received a reply from the government nor any indication of proceedings being instituted against individual officials.

Although death sentences are known to have been passed since the United National Party (UNP) government assumed office in 1977, Amnesty International understands that no executions have taken place since that date.

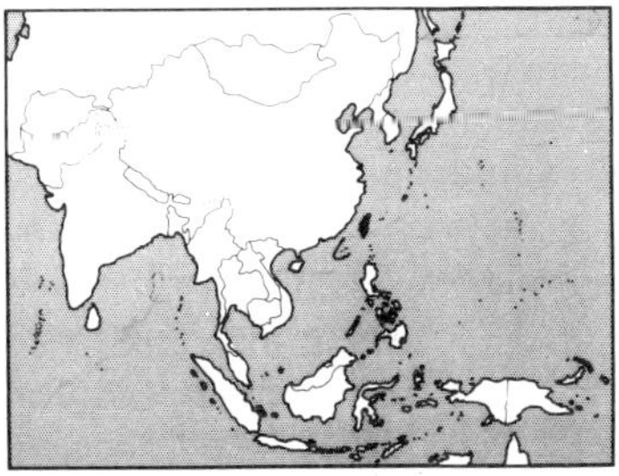

Taiwan

Amnesty International was concerned about the arrest and detention of prisoners of conscience. It continued to investigate a number of cases where it believed that political prisoners had been convicted of activities involving violence after unfair trials, and possibly for the non-violent expression of their political views. It remained concerned at the conviction of political prisoners on the basis of confessions made during incommunicado detention and at the number of death sentences for criminal offences.

The majority of political prisoners of concern to Amnesty International were convicted of sedition under the Statute for the Punishment of Sedition (1949). This statute is part of the provisions of the state of siege declared in Taiwan in 1949; it specifies a number of offences against the internal and external security of the state and gives jurisdiction to military courts. Amnesty International was also concerned about the use of the Public Officials Election and Recall

Law of May 1980, which prescribes a term of imprisonment for spreading seditious ideas in the course of an electoral campaign.

Among the prisoners of conscience for whose release Amnesty International appealed were people arrested in the early 1950s for alleged pro-communist activities, who were arrested in a period of emergency; many were given summary trials. At least 20 were known to be still in detention.

Amnesty International learned that Tseng Cheng-chin, a watch-dealer from Taipei, detained since 1976 and an adopted prisoner of conscience, was released in May 1980 on grounds of ill-health (see *Amnesty International Report 1978* and *1979*). A special appeal was made in January 1981 for the release of Li Ching-sun, a former newspaper editor, who received a life sentence for sedition in 1971 which was commuted to 15 years in 1975. Amnesty International believed that he was detained for having written articles critical of the government.

Amnesty International continued to urge the immediate and unconditional release of Li Ching-jung, the editor of the magazine *Fubao Chihsheng*. He was arrested on 26 December 1979 and held incommunicado for almost four months. He was tried by a military court and sentenced on 15 May 1980 to five years' imprisonment for writing articles advocating the peaceful reunification of Taiwan with the People's Republic of China and spreading propaganda beneficial to the communists.

Amnesty International adopted as prisoners of conscience eight members of the staff of the magazine *Formosa* whose trial by military court on charges of sedition in March 1980 had been observed by an Amnesty International delegate (see *Amnesty International Report 1980*). Huang Hsin-chieh, Shih Ming-teh, Yao Chia-wen, Chang Chun-hung, Lin Yi-hsiung, Lin Hung-hsuan, Lu Hsiu-lien and Chen Chu, all executives or editors of *Formosa* and involved in opposition to the government, were arrested in December 1979 and January 1980. They were convicted in April 1980 of attempting to overthrow the government by organizing a riot in Kaohsiung on 10 December 1979 (known as the "Kaohsiung incident"). The Taiwan Garrison Command announced on 30 May 1980 that their sentences, ranging from 12 years' to life imprisonment, had been confirmed by a military appeal court. Amnesty International believed that these prisoners were detained for their political beliefs and activities and that there was no evidence that they had used or advocated violence; it was concerned that confessions, which the defendants claimed in court had been obtained by illegal means including violence, threats, inducements and fraud, were admitted as evidence without a thorough investigation by the court. Amnesty International was concerned also that some sessions of the pre-trial hearings were held *in camera*: during these sessions the defendants reportedly stated that their confessions had been voluntary. The court later used this to dismiss the defendants' complaints about how their confessions had been obtained.

On 27 February 1981 Amnesty International submitted a memorandum to the government. It contained recommendations arising from the missions to Taiwan in February and March 1980, and from later developments in the cases of those arrested after the Kaohsiung incident. At the end of April 1981 the government informed Amnesty International that it would send its comments on the memorandum in the near future. These documents were to be published later in the year.

Thirty-three prisoners were tried on criminal charges in connection with the Kaohsiung incident. They had been arrested in late 1979 and early 1980 and interrogated by the Taiwan Garrison Command on suspicion of sedition. Their cases were transferred to a civilian court in late February 1980. On 31 March 1980 they were charged with either "inciting a group of people to commit or threaten violence" or "being accomplices in acts of violence". The full court hearings took place from 21 to 26 May 1980 and the verdict was announced on 2 June 1980. Three defendants were acquitted and one was given a suspended sentence. The sentences, ranging from 10 months' to six years eight months' imprisonment, were in many cases reduced on appeal. Amnesty International has adopted most of those still detained as prisoners of conscience because it believed they were detained either on account of their political activities and association with *Formosa* magazine or in violation of their right of peaceful assembly. Writers, local politicians and political activists received the longest prison sentences. Amnesty International believed that the charges of violence against them had not been substantiated: in most cases the only evidence for conviction was confessions and incriminating testimonies which the defendants claimed in court had been made under duress. On 18 February 1981 Amnesty International requested the Minister for Legal Affairs, Li Yuan-tzu, to order an inquiry into reports that this group of prisoners was held in solitary confinement, denied the right to work, not allowed outdoor exercise and that their reading material was extremely restricted. It also expressed its concern that their mental and physical health appeared to have been greatly impaired by their detention; it asked for a thorough inquiry into the complaints made by most of the prisoners about their treatment while detained for investigation.

Amnesty International adopted as prisoners of conscience six people charged with having helped Shih Ming-teh, the general manager of *Formosa* magazine, to escape arrest or with not having reported him to the police. They were tried by a military court on 16 May 1980 and sentenced on 5 June 1980 to terms of imprisonment ranging from two to seven years. Four co-defendants were given suspended sentences. Amnesty International believed they were detained for non-violent actions performed out of humanitarian concern and for conscientious reasons.

Yeh Tao-lei, a 30-year-old sociology graduate and a teacher at a junior college, was arrested by the Taiwan Garrison Command on 9 September 1980 on charges of sedition. She was reportedly held incommunicado for a two-month interrogation during which she confessed to the charges against her. On 17 November 1980 she was accused of having been recruited to work for the People's Republic of China while a student in the United States of America, and of having carried microfilms of communist books back to Taiwan. Yeh Tao-lei was tried on 6 January 1981 by a military court, found guilty and sentenced to 14 years' imprisonment. Amnesty International was concerned that the main evidence on which the verdict was based was her confession which may have been obtained under duress.

Amnesty International also investigated the case of Kao Huo-yuan, sentenced to 13 years' imprisonment on 18 December 1980 after a military court had found him guilty of participating in a seditious group advocating the independence of Taiwan while he was in the United States of America. Kao Huo-yuan was accused of having received instructions and money from this organization to carry out seditious activities on his return to Taiwan. Amnesty International was concerned that he was reportedly convicted on the basis of his confession. According to official but unconfirmed reports, other people were arrested at the same time on suspicion of advocating the independence of Taiwan. No details of their names or of the charges have been made public.

Amnesty International appealed for the release of Chang Chun-nan, a former member of the National Assembly and an active member of the opposition, who was arrested on 17 January 1981 and charged on 30 January with advocating the independence of Taiwan and calling on the people to overthrow the government, during the electoral campaign for the Legislative *Yuan* in December 1980. Amnesty International received information that he did not advocate the use of violence. Chang Chun-nan was sentenced by Taichung District Court on 3 March 1981 to three and a half years' imprisonment.

Amnesty International investigated the case of three other election candidates prosecuted for their speeches or for holding "unauthorized meetings" during the electoral campaign. Amnesty International adoption groups worked on behalf of 134 political prisoners in Taiwan.

Amnesty International remained concerned about the number of death sentences imposed by civilian and military courts and about the number of executions carried out every year. To Amnesty International's knowledge 25 death sentences were passed for murder, armed robbery, kidnapping and embezzlement between September 1980 and April 1981 and eight executions were carried out during the same period. It expressed its concern to the authorities and urged the commutation of all death sentences.

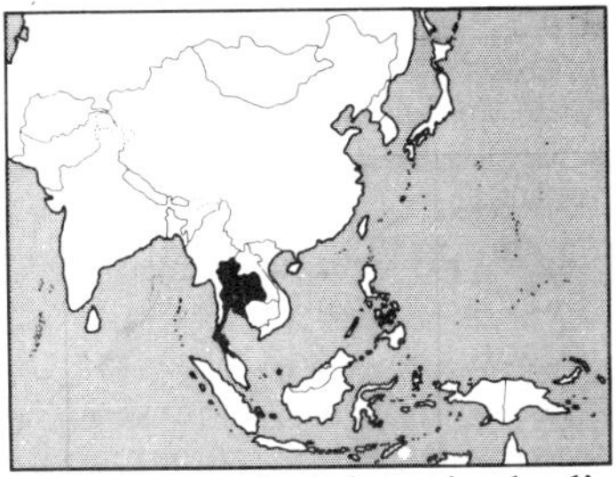

Thailand

Amnesty International's main concerns were political imprisonment, the prison conditions of political prisoners, and the death penalty.

The constitution of 1978 (chapter 3, section 27) guarantees the presumption of innocence, access to courts or administrative bodies to seek redress, and the right to legal counsel in all cases before a court. However, the right to legal counsel may be denied during the pre-trial period which diminishes legal protection.

Furthermore, provisions of the Anti-Communist Activities Act of February 1979 allow people accused of communist activities to be detained for up to 210 days with the approval of the police Director-General, and for up to 480 days with the permission of a military or criminal court. The number of people held under this act was not available, but it appeared that arrests were few and concentrated in southern and northeastern Thailand.

More than 200 people were reportedly still held without trial since their arrests between 1976 and 1978 under previous governments. They had been sentenced administratively without trial under Martial Law Decrees 21 and 22. Twenty-eight of the prisoners were believed to have received life sentences and a further 89 were sentenced to 10 years' or more imprisonment.

In a letter to the Prime Minister of Thailand, General Prem Tinsulanond, in April 1981 Amnesty International pointed out that the continued detention of these individuals contravened the United Nations Declaration of Human Rights and the International Covenant on Civil and Political Rights. Amnesty International noted with regret that although the government had abolished the relevant decrees over 200 people were still detained under these provisions. Amnesty International urged that their cases be reviewed immediately, and that they be released or charged and brought to an early trial.

Following reports that refugees were being coerced into returning to Kampuchea to fight, Amnesty International cabled Prem Tinsulanond, Prime Minister of Thailand, on 23 May 1980 urging his government to continue to grant the right of first asylum to people trying to flee Kampuchea for fear of political reprisals and to further guarantee that Kampuchean refugees who did not wish to return for fear of such reprisals from any of the contending forces in Kampuchea be given all facilities to apply for resettlement in a third country. In June 1980, and in spite of opposition from the authorities of the People's Republic of Kampuchea, the United Nations High Commissioner for Refugees supervised a voluntary repatriation scheme.

In December 1980 the government released a group of 186 prisoners, largely Chinese and Vietnamese, who had been in detention for up to 20 years awaiting deportation on charges of illegal immigration. Most were over 50 years old and one man was 83. They complained of inadequate medical conditions in prison and of frequent beatings by guards. Amnesty International believes that some 56 prisoners, also accused of illegal immigration, remained in detention at Bangkhen Temporary Prison in Bangkok.

Prison conditions continued to concern domestic civil rights groups and Amnesty International. In June 1980 the Lawyers Association of Thailand and the Coordinating Group for Religion in Society published a study criticizing overcrowding and ill-treatment of detainees in prisons. Amnesty International also continued to receive reports of persistent human rights violations including killings in southern Thailand, which it has not been able to substantiate.

According to recent reports four executions took place in 1980.

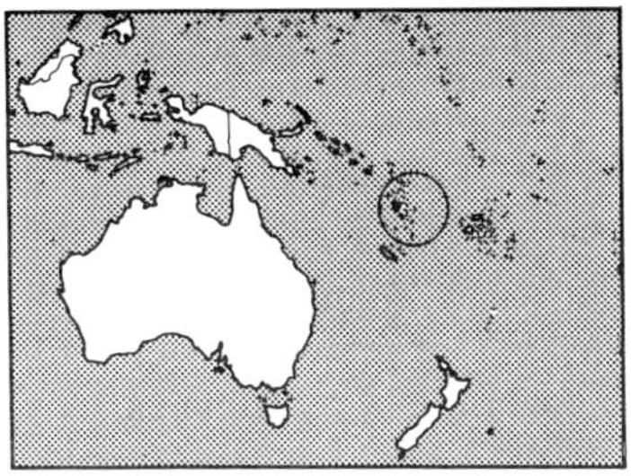

Vanuatu

Amnesty International received reports of widespread arbitrary arrests and ill-treatment after the suppression in August 1980 of the secessionist Vemerama movement based on the island of Espiritu Santo. Amnesty International learned of the arrest of approximately 1,000 people in the period August to October 1980, most of them francophone Melanesians. On 22 October 1980 Amnesty International expressed its concern at reports of arbitrary detention and ill-treatment, and appealed to the government of Vanuatu to investigate reports of ill-treatment, to improve prison conditions and to ensure adequate medical treatment for prisoners. At the same time the Public Prosecutor was urged to bring to trial those charged with offences and to release those being held without charge.

On 21 November 1980 it was reported that a series of trials of people involved in the rebellion which had begun in mid-September had ended with the sentencing of Jimmy Stevens, the rebel leader, to 14 years' imprisonment on 11 charges including incitement to rebellion, training an army, and illegal arms possession. Approximately 700 people were reportedly tried between mid-September and 21 November 1980. About 550 were found guilty of offences connected with the rebellion and 130 were sentenced to terms of imprisonment ranging from four weeks to 14 years.

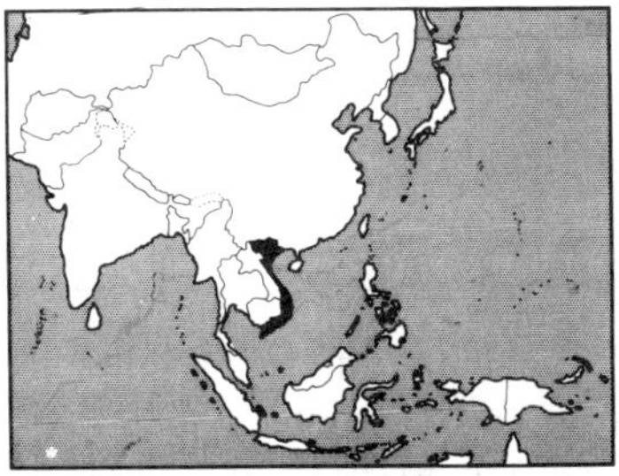

Viet Nam

Amnesty International's main concerns were the continuing detention without charge or trial of tens of thousands of members of the pre-1975 South Vietnamese administration and armed forces; arrests on political grounds and the absence of adequate legal safeguards; the lack of proper medical care for detainees in need of specialized treatment; the psychological and physical effects of long-term detention for an indeterminate period; and the death penalty.

Following a mission to Viet Nam in December 1979 Amnesty

International submitted a memorandum outlining its concerns to the government in May 1980. The memorandum focused upon Amnesty International's long-standing concern for the thousands of prisoners held without charge or trial in "re-education" camps after the end of the war in 1975. Although the transfer of power in Viet Nam in April 1975 took place without summary trials and executions Amnesty International was concerned that thousands of prisoners were still detained with no indication from the government as to when they could expect to be released.

The policy of the Provisional Revolutionary Government of South Viet Nam, which ruled from the end of April 1975 until the reunification of the country on 2 July 1976, towards personnel of the former government was outlined in a policy statement of 25 May 1976. This decree stated that "re-education" would last three years and that those individuals charged with criminal acts would be tried. However in discussions with the Amnesty International delegation the Vietnamese authorities stated that the 26,000 prisoners acknowledged to be in "re-education" camps were detained under the provisions of Resolution 49 NQ/TVQH of 1961 which stipulates that although the period of detention for "re-education" is three years, this may be extended.

In its memorandum to the government in May 1980 Amnesty International pointed out that it had consistently opposed prolonged administrative detention without trial throughout the world. Such detention was incompatible with internationally recognized standards of human rights and basic principles of justice; it led inevitably to a severe curtailment of civil liberties and deviations from normal procedural safeguards. Amnesty International recommended that the system of compulsory detention without trial for the purpose of "re-education" be abolished. It advised as a first and urgent step the establishment of an independent commission with full power to examine the grounds of detention in each individual case. Where there were not sufficient grounds for specific criminal charges the individual should be immediately released, and the decisions of the commission should be binding on the executive.

In September 1980 the government replied in writing to the memorandum. In its reply, and in the course of further discussions between Amnesty International and Vietnamese officials in London, the government argued that the policy of "re-education" which it had pursued was more humane than resorting to trials and judicial condemnation. Moreover those still detained in "re-education" camps were held to be guilty of "national treason" and to "have committed acts detrimental to public security".

In its reply the government announced that some 6,000 detainees had been freed between December 1979 and September 1980 leaving 20,000 prisoners remaining in "re-education" camps. It said that "the Socialist Republic of Viet Nam is thinking about measures to encourage those of the former regime who are still in camps to actively reform and re-educate themselves . . . to open ways for those who would show real repentance to go back to their families and to society." The government also promised to "examine seriously the problem of ratification of international covenants suggested by Amnesty International".

Amnesty International sent an aide mémoire to Prime Minister Pham Van Dong in January 1981 welcoming the news of further releases of detainees from "re-education" camps and the repeated assurances of the strict prohibition of torture and ill-treatment of detainees, which was reflected in Article 69 of the new 1980 Vietnamese Constitution. However Amnesty International pointed out that most prisoners in "re-education" camps had spent some five and a half years in detention without charge or trial. Amnesty International maintained that individuals should not be detained indefinitely merely because of their rank or position in a former administration. Nor could it be said that all those who had formerly held high positions were by that very fact "guilty of national treason". This was particularly true since many of the cases known to Amnesty International were people whose positions could not be said to have involved them in the prosecution of the war. The aide mémoire cited several examples including adopted prisoners of conscience Buu Huong and Dr Vu Quoc Thong. Buu Huong was a diplomat whose entire career had been spent in the financial branch of the Foreign Service of South Viet Nam. Dr Vu Quoc Thong had been Dean of the Faculty of Law in Saigon University; not only had he not occupied an official position in the former administration but he had openly criticized it. Dr Vu Quoc Thong and Buu Huong have since been released from detention.

Amnesty International's aide mémoire pointed out that the detainees had been deprived of the right to presumption of innocence. Detainees had to accept the need for their own "re-education" as a precondition for their release. Since they had not been convicted by a court of any offence this could not be reconciled with respect for the right to be presumed innocent until proved guilty, proclaimed in Article 11 of the Universal Declaration of Human Rights and guaranteed in Article 14 of the International Covenant on Civil and Political Rights. In addition, the retroactive application by the Vietnamese Government of legislation violated an important principle of international law that no one should be penalized for an act which was not designated a crime at the time it was committed. This principle finds clear expression in Article 11 of the Universal Declaration of Human Rights. In view of these factors Amnesty International recommended that detainees in "re-education" camps against whom there were no grounds for specific criminal charges should be released as speedily as possible.

Amnesty International also raised in the aide mémoire the cases of several prisoners of conscience who had no connection with the former administration of South Vietnam and who were arrested after 1975. Among these were the lawyer Trieu Ba Thiep; Duyen Anh, a well-known Vietnamese writer (see *Amnesty International Report 1980*); Pham Van Tam, a former senator and Secretary-General of the Vietnamese League of Human Rights; and Cao Giao, a journalist. Trieu Ba Thiep and Cao Giao have since been released from detention.

In March 1981 the Vietnamese Government replied by citing historical precedents such as the Nuremberg Tribunal of 1946, the Tokyo international tribunal of 1948 and the trial of Adolf Eichmann in 1961 to justify its retroactive appliction of "laws punishing counter-revolutionary crimes". The "application of DRV (North Vietnamese) law against those Vietnamese in the South who collaborated with the enemy with a view to consciously betraying their homeland is both legitimate and legal."

Although the Vietnamese reply spoke of an increased rate of releases no definite commitments were made. In December 1980 there had been unconfirmed reports from Hanoi that most of the 20,000 prisoners still held by the government would be released in 1981. No further details have been forthcoming although there has been a steady stream of individual releases throughout the year.

Amnesty International worked on behalf of more than 150 prisoners in Viet Nam. Among them were Do Lai Ky and Dr Truong Van Quynh. Do Lai Ky, 56 years old, was a professional diplomat and at the time he was sent to a "re-education" camp in 1975 a senior civil servant in the Ministry of Foreign Affairs. He has been detained for more than six years and was being held in the camp at Nam Ha, Ha Nam Ninh province in northern Viet Nam. Dr Truong Van Quynh was a distinguished Vietnamese physician and former director of the Nhi Dong Children's Hospital in Saigon and of the Cho Quan Psychiatric Hospital. He is believed to have been detained because he was a member of the *Viet Nam Quoc Dan Dang* (VNQDD), the Vietnamese *Kuomintang* or Nationalist Party.

Other detainees who have been adopted by Amnesty International as prisoners of conscience were arrested months and even years after the end of military conflict in April 1975. Amnesty International believes that many were detained for the non-violent expression of views critical of the present government, for example Nguyen Sy Te and Vu Ngoc Truy. Nguyen Sy Te was a writer and formerly a Professor of Education at Saigon University. His writings are believed to have been classified as "reactionary". At the time of his arrest in February 1976 Nguyen Sy Te was reportedly writing an essay entitled "A Humanist Ideology" critical of the policies of the government. He was detained for two years in Chi Hoa prison in Ho Chi Minh City and then transferred to a camp in Gia Trung in the central highlands where he remained a prisoner. He was reportedly in extremely poor health. Vu Ngoc Truy was a lawyer detained, Amnesty International believes, for his anti-communist views. Arrested in June 1978 he has now been held for more than three years without charge or trial.

The cases of Nguyen Sy Te and Vu Ngoc Truy illustrate the inadequacy of legal safeguards for people arrested in Viet Nam. Under Article 5 of the Provisional Revolutionary Government Decree No. 02/SL/76 of 23 March 1976, a person may be detained for up to 12 months for interrogation and investigation by the security authorities. Even this long period has been exceeded by the Vietnamese security authorities. For example the journalist Cao Giao was detained for more than two and a half years without charge or trial before being released in February 1981. In its memorandum of May 1980 Amnesty International pointed out that this lengthy period of investigation was not compatible with accepted standards of human rights because it allowed a person to be deprived of liberty without any judicial proceedings and without being charged. Amnesty International urged the government to limit the period for interrogating people suspected of political offences.

A major concern of Amnesty International during the year has been conditions in "re-education" camps and in particular the inadequacy of medical care for prisoners needing specialized treatment. Despite shortages of both medical personnel and drugs the government has an obligation to ensure that medical conditions in "re-education" camps at least match those recommended in the United Nations Standard Minimum Rules for the Treatment of Prisoners. Amnesty International brought several cases of sick or aged prisoners to the attention of the authorities and urged their release on humanitarian grounds.

Amnesty International has received reports of prisoners detained in "re-education" camps after the prison authorities knew they had terminal diseases. Truong Van Truoc died in August 1980 of cancer of the stomach in detention camp 90A TD 63/TC, Thanh Hoa. Writer Ho Huu Tuong, whose case had been raised by the Amnesty International delegation in December 1979, was transferred from

Xuyen Moc "re-education" camp to the hospital of Ham Tan in Thuan Hai province on 2 June 1980. Only three weeks later he died, just after he was finally given permission to return to his family in Ho Chi Minh City. Truong Van Truoc and Ho Huu Tuong died after having been chronically ill for several months. Amnesty International recommended to the Vietnamese Government in January 1981 that it undertake an urgent review of medical conditions in all "re-education" camps, and of the cases of all sick prisoners.

Amnesty International was concerned that the right to visits and correspondence seemed to depend on detainees' progress in "re-education" and general good conduct. Amnesty International pointed out in its May 1980 memorandum that these basic rights should be seen as minimum standards and all detainees should be entitled to them without discrimination. Amnesty International recommended that a system should be set up for regular inspection of prisons and camps by an independent body.

Viet Nam retains the death penalty although few executions have taken place. Most death sentences that have come to the attention of Amnesty International appeared to be of people convicted of murder while attempting to flee the country.

A report was in preparation detailing Amnesty International's concerns for publication in 1981.

Europe

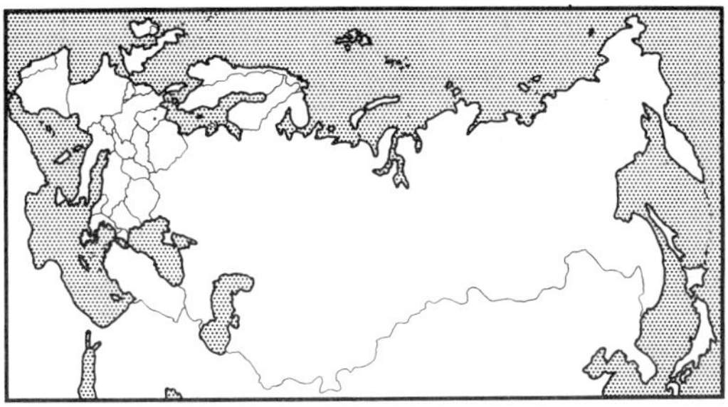

Amnesty International was concerned about human rights issues in many countries in Europe. In several people were imprisoned for the non-violent expression of their beliefs. In many countries trials with a political background fell short of internationally recognized standards for a fair trial. In some prisoners were tortured, beaten or otherwise cruelly treated. In a few countries all these violations took place.

As in previous years most of the people adopted by Amnesty International as prisoners of conscience were imprisoned for the non-violent exercise of their rights in countries in Eastern Europe. Many were imprisoned under vague provisions of criminal law which explicitly restrict freedom of conscience in contravention of international law, or which are so widely interpreted by the prosecuting authorities and the courts as to have that effect. In several countries of Eastern Europe people were charged or convicted of crimes they had not committed, and in two, the USSR and Romania, people were confined in psychiatric hospitals without medical justification, for political reasons.

In the USSR the severe repression of all forms of dissent continued. Political tension in Poland and Yugoslavia contributed in varying degrees to the arrest and imprisonment of prisoners of conscience; and in Bulgaria, Czechoslovakia, and Romania too, dissent was punished with arrest, prosecution and imprisonment. Hundreds of people were imprisoned in the German Democratic Republic (GDR) for trying to leave the country without official permission, or for persisting in seeking permission to emigrate.

The legislation of many countries of Europe — both Eastern and Western — allows conscientious objectors to military service to be imprisoned and such prisoners were adopted by Amnesty International as prisoners of conscience in France, Switzerland, Italy, Greece and several states of Eastern Europe. An organization which aims to spread information about conscientious objection in France was itself held to be illegal because of this aim.

In the Federal Republic of Germany (FRG), some 200 people were arrested and about 50 held in detention for expressing support for the demands of hunger-striking prisoners. Some were released after a few days; others spent several weeks in pre-trial detention. By the end of April 1981 most had been granted provisional liberty pending trial. Although the hunger-striking prisoners were members of violent political groups, many of those detained had expressed support for the demands of the hunger-strike without using or advocating violence. In Northern Ireland emergency legislation appears to have been used at least once during the year to detain a batch of people against whom there was no reasonable suspicion of involvement in violence, contrary to the provisions of the law.

In Spain and Turkey anti-terrorist measures and emergency legislation have been used to detain people for their opinions. Amnesty International's main concern about such legislation in Western Europe was the risk that prisoners would be ill-treated after arrest. The Government of Spain did not comment on the *Report of an Amnesty International Mission to Spain 3-28 October 1979* which stated Amnesty International's concern that ill-treatment amounting to torture had taken place and which describes cases from 1979. Events have since confirmed that these practices have persisted. In Turkey widespread and systematic torture continued after the September 1980 coup. The authorities did not deny that torture took place, but claimed that it was limited and happened without official knowledge or approval. Amnesty International believes that torture could not be so widespread without the knowledge of the authorities.

Amnesty International was concerned by reports that prisoners of conscience had been beaten in Poland, Czechoslovakia, Romania and the USSR, and by the treatment of prisoners of conscience confined to psychiatric hospitals in the USSR and Romania. Prison conditions for people suspected or convicted of politically motivated crimes in the FRG were not altered by the authorities as Amnesty International had recommended, even though the authorities did not deny Amnesty International's findings that they could damage the prisoners' health. Prison conditions for prisoners of conscience fell far short of internationally accepted standards in many countries in Eastern Europe, notably the USSR, Romania and Albania.

Amnesty International assessed not only the substance of legislation that affected human rights, but also the interpretation of the law by courts and procedural aspects of trials with a political background. To this end Amnesty International sent observers to trials in France, Italy, Northern Ireland, Poland, Republic of Ireland, Spain and Yugoslavia. An observer nominated to attend a trial in Czechoslovakia was refused access to the country. In other countries secrecy surrounding trials of prisoners of conscience prohibited independent observation altogether. In a submission to a Council of Europe conference on terrorism, Amnesty International warned of the erosion of the criminal justice system by emergency and anti-terrorist measures in Western Europe, saying that such legislation "has tended to make inroads on precisely those legal structures which are crucial to the fairness of the particular criminal justice process." In particular long periods of incommunicado detention without independent (judicial) control have been conducive to the ill-treatment of detainees in Spain and Turkey, and in the past in Northern Ireland and the Republic of Ireland. Amnesty International trial observers also noted deficiencies in the procedures in the Court of State Security in France.

Amnesty International continued to be concerned about the fate of people missing in Cyprus since the hostilities of 1974. On 22 April 1981 the United Nations Secretary-General's special representative in Cyprus announced that agreement had been reached on the terms of reference for a committee on missing persons to investigate cases of missing people from both the Greek Cypriot and Turkish Cypriot communities.

The death penalty is retained in all Eastern European countries. Amnesty International learned of death sentences in Bulgaria, Hungary, Romania, USSR and Yugoslavia but fears that there were others about which it did not know. In Western Europe the trend towards abolition continued. In the process of revising the constitution the Netherlands strengthened its abolitionist position, and in the Republic of Ireland, the Roman Catholic Commission on Justice and Peace spoke out against the death penalty. However four executions took place in Turkey, the first since 1972, and four people were sentenced to death in France and seven in the Republic of Ireland.

On the eve of the follow-up conference in Madrid to the Conference on Security and Cooperation in Europe Amnesty International wrote to the states who had signed the Helsinki Final Act (1975) saying that in several of the participating states people were still imprisoned because of their conscientiously held beliefs, in violation of Principle VII of the Final Act. Amnesty International called on the governments to consider developing methods to evaluate the extent to which Principle VII had been respected.

As in previous years Amnesty International submitted information on human rights questions within its mandate to the Council of

Europe. Amnesty International's submissions included: evidence to committees of the Council of Europe's Parliamentary Assembly on refugees from El Salvador; information on human rights in Turkey; and a presentation of Amnesty International's concerns regarding anti-terrorist measures which many member states of the Council of Europe had introduced. In November 1980 the Parliamentary Assembly invited member states who had granted visas to Argentine political prisoners to bring pressure to bear on the Argentine authorities to allow them to leave the country as soon as possible. Before the 12th Conference of European Ministers of Justice Amnesty International members in Western Europe appealed to their own governments to support proposals in the Council of Europe for the abolition of the death penalty. The conference decided to defer the issue until its next session in 1982 but it noted, significantly, "that it has not been established that the total abolition of the death penalty by many member states had led to any negative consequences in the field of criminal policy".

Amnesty International also presented information on human rights violations to the Commission of the European Community and to members and committees of the European Parliament. In June 1980 it testified to the European Parliament's Political Affairs Committee during hearings on the implementation of the Helsinki Final Act. Amnesty International welcomed the decision of the European Parliament to set up a working party on human rights, and in June 1980 called on the European Parliament "to appeal to member states to codify the existing trend towards abolition of the death penalty in Western Europe and to amend their legislation accordingly". In November 1980, in an emergency resolution prompted by the sentencing to death of three French prisoners, the European Parliament asked member states of the European Community to suspend all executions until it had held a debate on the issue.

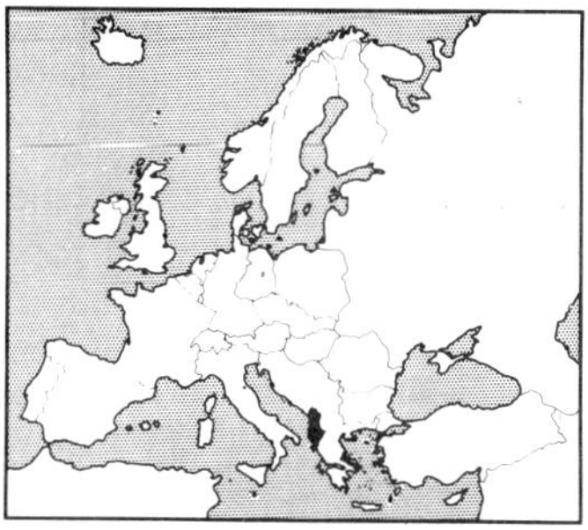

Albania

The concerns of Amnesty International were the existence and application of legislation punishing the non-violent exercise of human rights, the imprisonment and subjection to forced labour of prisoners of conscience, unfair trial procedures, harsh prison conditions and the death penalty.

Albania is a member of the United Nations; it has not, however, signed or ratified the international human rights covenants. Key provisions of the constitution, criminal and criminal procedure codes explicitly limit the exercise of certain human rights and stress the role of law in defending the socialist state and the Albanian Workers' Party from "socially dangerous acts", in particular, "manifestations of bureaucracy and liberalism". Amnesty International believes that the very broad formulation of Article 55 of the criminal code breaches international standards guaranteeing the freedom of conscience, belief, religion and expression. Article 55 defines as an offence:

> "Fascist, anti-democratic, religious, warmongering or anti-socialist agitation or propaganda, as well as the preparation, dissemination or the keeping for dissemination of literature with such a content as to weaken or undermine the state of the dictatorship of the proletariat."

The punishment is deprivation of liberty of from three to 10 years (in time of war or when "especially serious consequences have resulted" deprivation of liberty for not less than 10 years; or death).

The Albanian constitution does not guarantee the right to freedom of movement, and in practice travel abroad has been almost exclusively restricted to official delegations and officially authorized students. People who tried to leave the country without official authorization were liable under Article 127 of the criminal code to up to five years' deprivation of liberty for "illegal passage across the borders of the state". Amnesty International has been informed of several people sentenced in the 1960s to between 12 and 25 years' imprisonment for trying to leave Albania without official permission, under Article 64 of the former criminal code (1958). Under Article 47 the current criminal code retains the penalty of deprivation of liberty for from 10 to 25 years, or death, for:

"flight from the state and refusal to return to the fatherland on the part of a person sent on service or allowed temporarily to leave the state".

Information received by Amnesty International indicated that in the late 1970s up to 2,000 political prisoners were detained in the prison camps of Ballsh and Spaci alone, and that many had been convicted for expressing dissatisfaction with economic or political conditions in Albania. No information has since been received to indicate any substantial change. Since 1967 when Albania was officially proclaimed an atheist state all places of worship have been closed and religious leaders of the Moslem, Orthodox and Roman Catholic faiths prohibited from performing religious functions. Those who continued to do so have reportedly been severely repressed. Of three Roman Catholic titular bishops detained in the mid-1970s after privately conducting religious ceremonies, two — Bishops Fishta and Coba — were reported to have died in detention. The third, 65-year-old Nikoll Troshani, has variously been reported to be detained at Ballsh camp or at the camp of Tepelena. Reports received by Amnesty International alleged that Bishop Coba died in 1979 after being beaten by guards for trying to hold Easter mass for fellow detainees at a prison camp, Paperr, near Elbasan. Five other Roman Catholic priests have been reported to be detained in camps in southern Albania.

Amnesty International learned of two foreign nationals detained in a section of Ballsh camp reserved for foreigners; both had voluntarily left their own countries to live in Albania. One was reportedly arrested and convicted after he had applied to leave Albania, the other after he had criticized the authorities and listened to foreign radio broadcasts.

In past years Amnesty International has received reports alleging serious deficiencies in procedures during investigations and trials. There have been reports that psychological and sometimes physical pressure has been used to obtain confessions from the accused or testimony from witnesses. Some prisoners were held in solitary confinement without access to family or lawyer during pre-trial investigation for up to six months. Where defendants were permitted defence lawyers, counsel appeared to have always been state-appointed, and to have provided only nominal services. Some defendants did not see their defence counsel before the trial itself.

In April 1980 a new criminal procedure code came into force. The information available to Amnesty International was not sufficient to allow an assessment of its practical application, but certain of its provisions gave grounds for concern and were incompatible with internationally recognized standards for fair trial. The right of the accused to defence counsel of their choice is not guaranteed in all circumstances, and indeed the wording of the criminal procedure code appears to imply that defence counsel is "designated" by the court and not by the accused. Amnesty International continued to be concerned about decree No. 5912 of 1979, which allows administrative internment or banishment without trial (in contravention of Article 56 of the constitution) for unspecified periods, a measure which may also be used "against members of the family of fugitives living inside or outside the state" — that is as a reprisal against people who have not themselves necessarily broken Albanian law.

Reports have described conditions in labour camps in Albania during the 1960s and 1970s where political prisoners were employed on projects including the construction of factories and housing, marsh-drainage and mining. Conditions at Spaci camp, with a population estimated at over 500 political prisoners, appeared to be particularly harsh. Prisoners reportedly mined copper in eight-hour shifts, six days a week, with little industrial protection apart from helmets and cotton masks. Work targets were described as excessive and prisoners who failed to meet these targets risked extra work hours or solitary confinement. Conditions for the approximately 1,400 political prisoners at Ballsh camp, (there are also camps at Ballsh for ordinary criminals and for foreigners), if less harsh than at Spaci, also appeared to be very poor. Prisoners reportedly slept in unheated barracks, on straw mattresses laid out on wooden platforms. At both camps food was reported to be deficient in quality and quantity, needing to be supplemented by parcels from prisoners' families and by food bought from the prisoners' wages. Medical care, provided by staff mainly recruited from among the prisoners, was described as seriously inadequate. Prisoners punished by solitary confinement were reportedly kept in an unheated, concrete cell measuring approximately 2m by 1m, with neither bed nor mattress. It was also reported that guards have punished prisoners by stripping them to the waist and beating them with rubber hosing filled with sand or gravel.

The criminal code lists 34 crimes (of which 23 are political and military crimes) punishable by the death sentence.

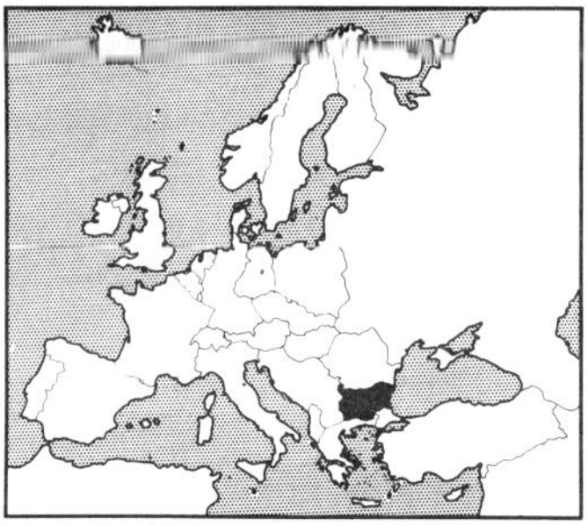

Bulgaria

The concerns of Amnesty International were the existence and application of legislation limiting the exercise of human rights, political imprisonment, violations of international standards with regard to pre-trial investigation and trial procedure, ill-treatment of detainees, poor prison conditions and the death penalty.

In April 1981 Amnesty International wrote to Todor Zhivkov, head of state and Secretary General of the Bulgarian Communist Party, appealing for an amnesty for all prisoners of conscience to mark the celebration of the 1300th anniversary of the founding of the Bulgarian State.

Despite guarantees of freedom of speech, of the press, of assembly and of association in the constitution, people who exercised these freedoms in a manner not approved of by the authorities, although non-violently, were liable to imprisonment under the criminal code. Ljuben Sobadschiev from Ruse, for whose release Amnesty International has worked since his conviction in 1978, was imprisoned under Articles 108, 109 and 113 of the criminal code for having distributed leaflets in a local supermarket in which he criticized official economic policy and complained of food shortages. He was sentenced to four and a half years' imprisonment. Article 108 makes "anti-state agitation or propaganda" an offence punishable by up to five years' imprisonment; Article 109 prescribes three to 12 years' imprisonment for "forming or being a member of an organization whose activities are aimed at committing offences against the state"; Article 113 makes people who commit these offences against another workers' state liable to the same penalty.

Emigration is severely limited by the government and, as in past years, Amnesty International has worked on behalf of those imprisoned for attempting to leave the country without official authorization. Under Article 279 of the criminal code people convicted of this offence may be punished by up to five years' imprisonment and a fine of 3,000 levas. In November 1980 Amnesty International began investigating the case of Sotir Iliev, a 33-year-old builder-architect from Plovdiv, who in March 1980 applied for political asylum in Vienna after having left Bulgaria without official authorization. On 11 April he disappeared from Vienna; he was subsequently tried in Bulgaria and sentenced to 18 months' imprisonment. The Austrian authorities instituted legal proceedings against persons unknown held responsible for his disappearance; it has been alleged that he was kidnapped in Vienna by Bulgarian state security agents. Sotir Iliev was reportedly serving his sentence in Sofia central prison.

Amnesty International has learned that Dimiter Kolev, an adopted prisoner of conscience convicted of having sought to leave Bulgaria without official permission, was released in May 1980 in very poor health.

Amnesty International continued to work on a number of cases of people sentenced to long terms of imprisonment for espionage, including both adopted prisoners of conscience and cases under investigation. Typically these were people with friends or relatives living abroad, with whom they maintained contact, or with foreign acquaintances living in Bulgaria.

Amnesty International continued to work on the cases of three Pomaks (ethnic Bulgarians of the Moslem faith) — Bajram Gaitov, Jumer Ilanski and Mr Bunzev — who were sentenced to up to 20 years' imprisonment in 1973 after protesting against an official policy of forced assimilation by which Pomaks were required to change their Moslem names for Bulgarian ones.

Amnesty International was concerned about continued reports of ill-treatment of detainees during preliminary investigation in the investigation department of the Razvigor Street State Security Centre in Sofia. Under Bulgarian law, a person may be held in custody for up to 10 days before being formally charged. During preliminary investigation, which may last up to six months, the accused has the right of access to defence counsel only if the Procurator permits. Several former prisoners have reported that attempts were made to extort confessions from them. They alleged that they had been threatened, subjected to violence, such as punching and beating with rubber truncheons, interrogated for long periods and deprived of sleep; in two cases they were reportedly taken to the "Fourth Kilometre" psychiatric hospital in Sofia and forcibly given drugs.

Many political prisoners have had only minimal access to defence counsel, who were generally state-appointed, and there have also been complaints that political prisoners or their defence counsel were given their dossiers only days before the trial and were thus unable to prepare an adequate defence. Political trials were usually heard *in camera,* although the verdict was pronounced in open court.

Conditions in Sofia central prison, where some prisoners of conscience have been held, were reported to be crowded, unhygienic and well below internationally recognized standards.

The majority of adopted prisoners of conscience have served their sentences in the high security prison of Stara Zagora. Former prisoners have stated that the prison population of Stara Zagora varied in the past decade between 900 and 1,400, and estimated the number of political prisoners at about 250. It has also been claimed that about 15 per cent of all prisoners in Stara Zagora were serving sentences for having attempted to cross the border without authorization, but Amnesty International could not verify this. Reports have frequently referred to overcrowding in Stara Zagora prison; political prisoners were reportedly detained in units 1 and 6, in cells measuring approximately 4m by 2m, and housing four people. Prisoners have complained of the noise of loudspeakers in the cells broadcasting radio and alleged that these loudspeakers concealed listening equipment. Although conditions at Stara Zagora appeared to be generally better than at Sofia central prison, prisoners have complained of difficult working conditions. Food has been described as poor and prisoners had to supplement it with food from a prison shop and from their families. Medical care consisted of twice-weekly visits of two hours by a qualified doctor and dentist. This was quite inadequate and at other times prisoners could obtain only the most basic medical care. Prisoners have reported being punished for minor breaches of prison rules by solitary confinement with greatly reduced food rations in an unheated cell, without toilet or washing facilities. By allowing prisoners to spend a night in their own cells before returning them to solitary confinement, prison authorities have at times prolonged this punishment well beyond the maximum of two weeks.

The criminal code retains the death penalty for 29 crimes. Amnesty International learned of two executions during the year. A press report on 27 August 1980 stated that Anton Dimitrov Andreev, sentenced to death by the District Court of Kardzhali for the "particularly cruel" murder of his pregnant, 18-year-old wife, had been executed. On 20 November 1980 the execution of Tsano Nikolov Petrov was reported. He had been sentenced to death by the District Court of Vidin for the "premeditated and particularly cruel" murder of a young woman.

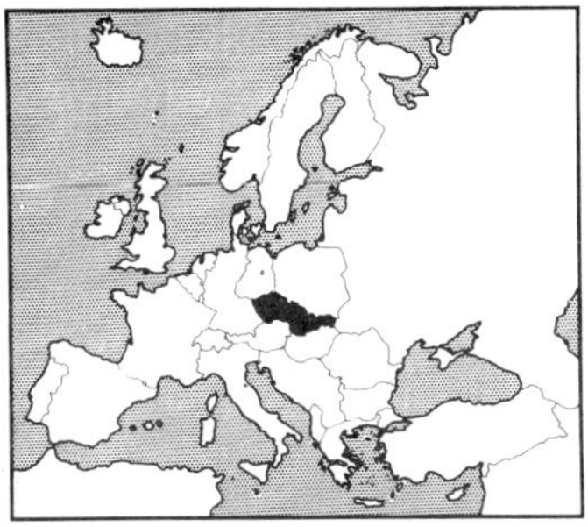

Czechoslovakia

Amnesty International continued to be concerned about: the imprisonment of people expressing views disapproved of by the authorities; trial procedures that fall short of internationally recognized standards; poor conditions of detention for political prisoners; harassment and ill-treatment of dissenters; and the retention of the death penalty. At the end of April 1981 Amnesty International was working on behalf of 29 adopted prisoners of conscience and investigating six further cases, but it believed that there were many more prisoners of conscience about whom it did not have definite information.

On 8 May 1980 the CSSR proclaimed an amnesty to mark the 35th anniversary of the liberation of Czechoslovakia from German occupation by the Soviet army but only one prisoner adopted by Amnesty International benefited from it.

The Czechoslovak weekly *Tribuna* on 25 June 1980 accused Amnesty International of focusing its activities against the Soviet Union and other socialist countries and of interfering in the internal affairs of socialist states. In a letter to *Tribuna* dated 21 October 1980 Amnesty International drew attention to its public record which showed that it worked impartially on human rights issues within its mandate throughout the world. The letter was not published.

The Czechoslovak Penal Code (1973) includes a number of articles which explicitly restrict the exercise of human rights by people whose views and beliefs are disapproved of by the authorities. These articles contravene the International Covenant on Civil and Political Rights and are used to imprison people who have criticized the policies of the government and the Communist Party.

Vaclav Umlauf, a miner aged 20 preparing for theological studies, was arrested on 19 March 1980, and on 23 May 1980 sentenced by the district court in Brno to three years' imprisonment on charges of "incitement" and "damaging the interests of the Republic abroad". He had complained at work that the equipment in the mines was inadequate and had openly condemned the Soviet military intervention in Afghanistan. The court also found him guilty of having distributed an unspecified "anti-state" text and of having sent a letter to a priest in the United Kingdom in which he criticized the trial in October 1979 of six members of the Committee for the Defence of the Unjustly Persecuted (VONS). Pavel Santora, a 25-year-old worker, was remanded in custody on 12 March 1980 after the state security police had searched his home and confiscated various unofficial texts. On 22 July 1980 the district court in Usti nad Labem found him guilty of "distributing among his co-workers and friends written materials of anti-state and anti-socialist content . . . of tendentiously informing about the criminal proceedings against VONS members . . . and of acting out of hostility to the socialist, social and state order of the CSSR" and sentenced him to one year's imprisonment. He appealed against the verdict, but the appeal court in Usti nad Labem increased his sentence to 18 months on the grounds that his activities were highly dangerous to society.

Jiri Cernega, a 25-year-old worker and Charter 77 signatory who had been repeatedly harassed, was remanded in custody on 3 November 1980 for "detracting from the dignity of the President of the CSSR". He was accused of having taken a portrait of the President off a wall, of making insulting remarks, and of allowing a photograph to be taken of himself and his friends holding the portrait. On 27 January 1981 he was sentenced by the district court in Klatovy to six months' imprisonment, and at an appeal hearing on 12 March the regional court in Plzen increased his sentence to one year.

Amnesty International has received information about continued arrests, prosecutions and imprisonment of religious believers. Oskar Formanek, a 66-year-old Jesuit priest who had been barred from exercising his office and had retired, was sentenced on 25 June 1980 by the district court in Presov to 18 months' imprisonment suspended for four years for "obstructing state supervision of the church" and for "incitement". He was accused of holding prayer meetings in private homes and of declaring before a witness that the church in the CSSR was under state control. The court also accused him of disseminating religious literature. His co-defendant Maria Kozarova was sentenced on similar charges to 12 months' imprisonment suspended for three years. Another Roman Catholic priest from Slovakia, Jozef Labuda, was sentenced on 30 October 1980 by the district court in Rimavska Sobota to six months' imprisonment for saying mass and for holding prayer meetings with a group of young people in a mountain hut without state permission. At the same trial Emilie Kesegova, a librarian, was given a four-month prison sentence for organizing the meeting. Josef Barta, a 59-year-old Franciscan priest barred from exercising office was arrested on 18 November 1980 during a police raid on members of the Franciscan order in Liberec, North Bohemia, and charged with "obstructing state supervision of the church". His home was searched on 28 January 1981, and a number of people were interrogated in Liberec and Prague. Father Josef Barta was released from pre-trial detention on 20 February 1981, but judicial proceedings against him were continuing.

Amnesty International was concerned that many dissenters trying to exercise their human rights in non-violent ways have been arrested, tried and imprisoned on criminal rather than political charges. In all these cases the criminal charges were preceded by a long history of harassment and detention.

Two musicians, Karel Soukup and Jindrich Tomes, both Charter 77 signatories, were arrested in mid-1980 and on 5 November 1980 sentenced by the district court in Usti nad Labem to 10 months' and 12 months' imprisonment respectively for singing songs with "anti-socialist content and using vulgar expressions" at a private wedding party. The court ruled that they had committed a breach of the peace. Karel Soukup had been detained in March 1976 on a similar charge and although released from pre-trial detention later that year, he has not been officially informed that criminal proceedings against him have stopped. Engineer Rudolf Battek, a sociologist, Charter 77 spokesperson and VONS member, with a history of harassment and imprisonment for political activities going back to 1969, was arrested on 14 June 1980. In the year leading up to his last arrest the police took action against him nine times, with repeated house searches, short-term detentions, interrogations and surveillance. After two sessions of interrogation he was driven a long way from Prague and abandoned. On 14 June 1980 he was called to the local police station about the theft of his car. When no one attended to him he left the police station and a police officer ran after him and dragged him back. He was detained and charged with "assaulting a policeman". This charge was later changed to one of "causing bodily harm". On 12 January 1981 the Procurator informed his wife that in addition to the charge of causing bodily harm he had been charged with subversion. In April 1981 Rudolf Battek, who suffers from a serious asthmatic condition, was still awaiting trial. In the 10½ months of pre-trial detention he was denied almost all contact with his wife and his lawyer.

Amnesty International drew attention to two prisoners of conscience who faced new charges before they had completed their sentences. Jiri Wolf, whose three-year sentence was to expire in February 1981, was charged on 18 June 1979 with "false accusations" and on 20 June 1980 brought to trial before the district court for Prague 2. The new charge refers to a statement he made during his first trial in October 1978 (see *Amnesty International Report 1979*). At the trial on 20 June 1980 Jiri Wolf again stated that during the investigation after his arrest in February 1978 he had been forced to change his evidence and that he admitted his guilt under physical and psychological pressure. He claimed that when he refused to cooperate the police had threatened and insulted him, punched his stomach and face, and threatened that his pregnant wife would be imprisoned. The court held that this allegation constituted "grossly insulting a public agent" and extended his sentence by a further six months. Petr Cibulka was brought to trial in January 1980 for "obstructing the purpose of custody" while serving a two-year sentence for "incitement". In 1979 he went on hunger-strike to protest against unacceptable working conditions and repeated physical attacks on him by ordinary prisoners. For this he was sentenced to a further six months and at an appeal hearing in March 1980 his sentence was increased to one year. On 27 January 1981, shortly before the expiry of his second sentence, he was brought to a third trial before the district court in Plzen and given a 10-month prison sentence for "insulting two prison guards". He stated in court that the guards forced him to remove official newspapers and journals he was allowed to have in his cell. He appealed against the verdict and the regional court in Plzen on 12 March 1981 set aside the sentence on the grounds that the two prison guards had exceeded their authority and that the accused had already been punished for making insulting remarks. On 16 March 1981 Amnesty International wrote to the President of the CSSR welcoming the outcome.

Trials of dissenters continued to violate internationally accepted standards for a fair trial; in particular defendants were sometimes denied access to a lawyer at the pre-trial stage.

Amnesty International was concerned at reports that conditions of detention of prisoners of conscience in Mirov prison fell short of internationally recognized standards. Petr Uhl, serving a five-year sentence in the second (stricter) prison category in Mirov prison, has been repeatedly harassed and punished. He was punished three times in November 1980 after making complaints to the prison director about the lack of hygiene and frequent discrimination against political prisoners.

Amnesty International issued urgent appeals on behalf of the prisoners of conscience Jaromir Savrda, Otta Bednarova and Rudolf Battek whose poor state of health was giving cause for particular concern.

Throughout the year Amnesty International received information about the harassment, intimidation and short-term detention of active dissenters for the non-violent exercise of their human rights. The police broke up numerous meetings of Charter 77 signatories and VONS members, searched their homes, detained them for questioning and released them within 48 hours. Petr Pospichal, a Charter 77 signatory and a former prisoner of conscience, alleged that he had twice been taken into custody and beaten in September and October 1980. Vaclav Maly, a Charter 77 spokesperson and VONS member, was taken on 10 December 1980 from a VONS meeting to the police headquarters in Prague where he was handcuffed, beaten, threatened and interrogated about the meeting. He was released after 50 hours in detention.

According to figures provided by the CSSR to the United Nations, in the period 1974 to 1978, 22 people were sentenced to death and 16 were executed; two were sentenced for offences against the state and the rest sentenced and executed for offences against the person. Amnesty International did not learn of any death sentences or executions during the year.

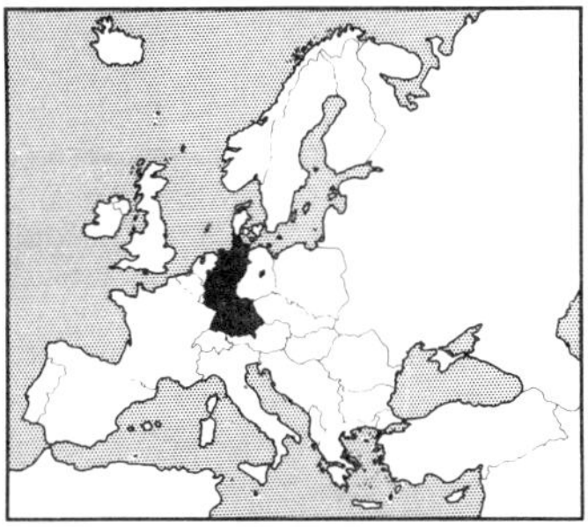

Federal Republic of Germany

Amnesty International continued to be concerned about aspects of high-security detention, and it became increasingly concerned about the way in which anti-terrorist legislation was applied against the exercise of freedom of expression. Amnesty International also worked on behalf of people imprisoned for being conscientious objectors to military service.

In May 1980 Amnesty International published a dossier: *Amnesty International's Work on Prison Conditions of Persons Suspected or Convicted of Politically Motivated Crimes in the Federal Republic of Germany: Isolation and Solitary Confinement.* The dossier contained Amnesty International's findings that strict isolation of prisoners in high-security detention could seriously affect their physical and mental health, and had done so in a number of cases (see *Amnesty International Report 1980*). The prisoners concerned had all been charged with or convicted of politically motivated acts of violence. None was adopted by Amnesty International as a prisoner of conscience; its sole concern was that prisoners should not be subjected to conditions that threaten their health.

In the dossier Amnesty International called for the abolition of strict forms of isolation and, pending this, for the health of the prisoners to be properly monitored by doctors trusted by both prisoners and authorities. Amnesty International recommended remedial action if medical examinations conducted with the full cooperation of the prisoners showed damage to health.

Amnesty International's conclusion that the conditions imposed on these prisoners had serious effects on their health has never been disputed by the authorities, and has been explicitly confirmed by the courts. However the authorities rejected Amnesty International's recommendations and continued to impose strict isolation on many prisoners. The authorities and the courts argued that the prisoners, because they were so dangerous, forced the authorities to impose security measures which damaged their health, and were therefore themselves responsible for the regime. Although the authorities expressed in general terms a willingness to reduce the isolation imposed on prisoners this led to no improvements in practice.

Such conditions have been imposed not only on prisoners who were members of groups such as the Red Army Fraction (RAF) or the 2 June Movement, but also on others regarded as high security risks, especially if there were political aspects to the case. They have also been imposed on people in investigative detention suspected of "making propaganda for a terrorist association", without it having been alleged that they had been involved in any acts of violence.

In early January 1981 lawyers and doctors from all over the world wrote to federal and *länder* (state) authorities urging them to reconsider Amnesty International's recommendations. They pointed out the obligation of the authorities under international law to exercise their custodial authority to safeguard the health and well-being of all prisoners. They rejected the argument that the prisoners were so dangerous that the authorities were relieved of this obligation.

From early February 1981 a number of politically motivated prisoners went on hunger-strike. A large proportion of them were detained in the kind of conditions about which Amnesty International had expressed concern. Their demand that politically motivated prisoners should be held in groups extended to issues outside Amnesty International's mandate, which it therefore could not address or support. However in a letter of 13 March 1981 Amnesty International again urged the authorities to abolish solitary confinement and small-group isolation as regular forms of imprisonment, and to implement, until then, the recommendations it had made as far back as October 1979. In view of the poor health of a number of hunger-strikers Amnesty International on 8 April 1981 called for the implementation of its recommendations as a matter of urgency. On 16 April 1981 Sigurd Debus, one of the hunger-strikers, died in a hospital in Hamburg. The prisoners ended their fast shortly afterwards.

The authorities replied that the hunger-strike was seen by the prisoners as part of their violent actions against the Federal Republic of Germany (FRG), as was their demand to be held in groups made up only of politically motivated prisoners. The prisoners' isolation was largely because they had rejected association with ordinary prisoners;

the so-called "small-group isolation" was to avoid stricter forms of detention. The prison authorities saw to it that the prisoners received medical attention, including visits by doctors from outside the prison system.

Although some prisoners have rejected contact with non-politically motivated prisoners, Amnesty International knows of others who have been willing to accept such social contact, but have been denied it. Amnesty International also believes that the general lack of trust between the prison doctors and the prisoners has led to the health of politically motivated prisoners not being adequately monitored.

In its letter of 13 March 1981 Amnesty International had expressed concern about the arrest and indictment on criminal charges of people supporting the hunger-striking prisoners' demands. The letter referred to allegations "that the mere support of the prisoners' demands and of the hunger-strike as a means of obtaining them, is treated by the prosecuting authorities as 'support of a criminal association' in the sense of paragraph 129a of the FRG Criminal Code". Amnesty International's letter continued:

> "It is said that individuals are prosecuted in cases in which no advocacy is involved of the violent aims of groups to which some of the prisoners claim allegiance. These cases are said to include a number of defence lawyers. Amnesty International is concerned that people may be prosecuted and imprisoned for the non-violent expression of their political beliefs, without advocacy of violence".

In his reply the Federal Minister of Justice said that he "shared Amnesty International's opinion that a criminal prosecution solely because of support of the hunger-strike and the demands connected with it should be out of the question". Solidarity with the demands became criminal only when they were connected to propaganda for a specific terrorist association and its violent aims.

However in Amnesty International's opinion the arguments in indictments and judicial decisions against supporters of the hunger-strike constitute a threat to the non-violent exercise of the freedom of expression. Judge Kuhn, a judge at the *Bundesgerichtshof* (federal court), who is responsible for the pre-trial proceedings in virtually all these cases, has argued in many cases that the "ultimate aim" of the hunger-strike was the continued existence of the Red Army Fraction. Supporters of the hunger-strike who he felt "knew and wanted" this "ultimate aim" therefore supported the terrorist organization, even though the opinions they expressed related only to the direct demands of the hunger-strikers. Many supporters of the hunger-strike were consequently held in investigative detention charged with "making propaganda for a terrorist association" (Article 129a of the criminal code) because of "ultimate aims" which Judge Kuhn held to be apparent from, for example, the use of a red five-pointed star. Amnesty International was collecting information on these cases.

Arrests and investigative detentions of this kind became widespread during the hunger-strike; yet in October 1980, before the hunger-strike, a number of people had already been charged under Article 129a for putting up a banner in a square in Munich with the words "For the grouping together and self-determination of prisoners from the RAF" and a red five-pointed star. They were found guilty of "making propaganda for a terrorist association" in January 1981 and were given suspended sentences.

On 19 May 1980 Albert Mayr, a stonemason, was sentenced by the *Amtsgericht* (district court) Bruchsal to six months' imprisonment for refusing to obey orders and desertion. The prisoner, who served his sentence in Rottenburg, had applied twice on religious and moral grounds for recognition as a conscientious objector. On both occasions, in 1977 and 1979, the *Prüfungsausschüsse* (examination boards) of Kempten and Augsburg respectively turned down his application. After his application had been refused a second time Albert Mayr wrote to the military authorities to say that he would not submit to further tests of conscience because he believed them unjust. At the time of his trial Amnesty International told the President of the court, Herr Zimmermann, that it believed Albert Mayr to be a genuine conscientious objector, and requested his immediate release. He was adopted by Amnesty International as a prisoner of conscience.

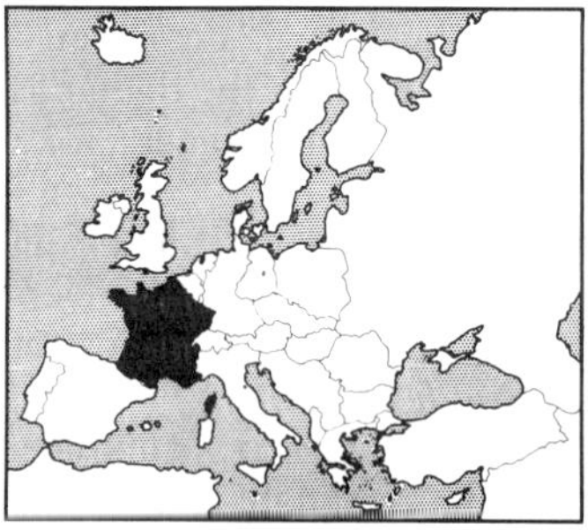

France

The concerns of Amnesty International related to the prosecution and imprisonment of conscientious objectors to military service, the limitation of the right to freedom of expression, trial procedures in special courts and the death penalty.

In the past year Amnesty International worked on 43 cases of conscientious objectors sentenced to short prison terms. Laws on conscientious objection fall short of internationally recommended standards by limiting exemption from military service to those who "are opposed unconditionally to the personal use of arms because of religious or philosophical convictions" (Article 41 of the *Code du service national,* National Service Code).

Amnesty International considers that both the letter and the application of the law do not meet the standard adopted by the Parliamentary Assembly of the Council of Europe calling for exemption from armed service "for reasons of conscience or profound conviction arising from religious, ethical, moral, humanitarian, philosophical or similar motives" (Resolution 337 of the Parliamentary Assembly of the Council of Europe 1967).

Amnesty International has adopted as prisoners of conscience people who have been called up who have had their applications for conscientious objector status rejected, and people charged with desertion who have declared their objection to military service after joining their regiments.

During the year under review conscientious objectors have generally received heavier sentences than in previous years. Some received long prison sentences even though declared *réformé* (unfit for, and exempt from, military service) between arrest and trial; in the past such people usually received suspended sentences of a few months only. Jehovah's Witnesses received the maximum sentence of two years.

On 4 December 1980 Amnesty International wrote to Dr Solange Troisier, an official at the Ministry of Justice with responsibility for medical services in prisons, expressing concern about an adopted conscientious objector François Rodriguez, who was then on the 34th day of a hunger-strike. Amnesty International had received reports of his worsening condition and allegations that after his transfer to Fresnes prison he had been denied the small amount of sugar usually given to hunger-strikers when taking liquid. François Rodriguez had been sentenced to six months' imprisonment on 31 October 1980 on a charge of *insoumission* (insubordination) although he had been previously declared *réformé définitivement* (permanently unfit for and exempt from military service) after a hunger-strike during an earlier period of arrest for *insoumission*. Like all conscientious objectors who are *réformé*, he was serving his sentence in a civilian prison, since he was no longer in the army. Dr Troisier replied to Amnesty International saying that the case was receiving very close medical attention and that his health gave no cause for concern. On 23 December 1980 François Rodriguez was released from prison after 57 days of hunger-strike by order of the Minister of Defence on a recommendation from the civilian prison authorities.

A number of conscientious objectors have been sentenced to additional terms of imprisonment on charges of wilful self-mutilation as a consequence of going on hunger-strike.

Article 50 of the *Code du service national* prohibits the dissemination of propaganda in any form which is "likely to incite potential conscripts to benefit from the provisions of the law recognizing conscientious objection". This effectively prohibits people from giving information about the laws on conscientious objection. Amnesty International believes the law limits the non-violent exercise of freedom of expression and deprives people of information about their legal rights.

There have been several prosecutions under Article 50 during the past year. In March 1981 Amnesty International sent a telegram to the President of the *Tribunal correctionel* (magistrates' court) of Paris, expressing concern at the trial of Damien Thébault for having published a booklet giving information on laws concerning conscientious objection and on the legal consequences of refusing military and alternative service. Amnesty International said it would adopt Damien Thébault as a prisoner of conscience if he was sent to prison. The trial was adjourned until 12 May 1981.

Amnesty International works for a fair trial within a reasonable time for prisoners of conscience and political prisoners. Article 6 of the European Convention on Human Rights guarantees this right to all defendants. Amnesty International considered that the procedures in the *Cour de sûreté de l'Etat* (Court of State Security) were not consonant with the spirit of Article 6 of the European Convention on Human Rights because of the discrepancy between the powers given to the prosecution and the defence (see *Amnesty International Report 1980*). Amnesty International was also concerned by the political nature of the court. Two of the five judges are military, and only the Minister of Justice, a politician, may initiate proceedings, not the prosecution. The court tries all cases where in the opinion of the Minister there has been an action aimed at substituting an illegal authority for the authority of the state. An extended period of six days for interrogation by the police is allowed and the court has its own investigating judges. Suspects may be held in preventive detention for an unlimited period while the case is under judicial investigation and no appeal is possible.

On 14 January 1981 in the Court of State Security the trial opened of 17 Corsicans, some of whom had been on hunger-strike for up to 60 days. They were charged with participating in an armed group intending to create a disturbance against the state by invading public and private property, and with kidnapping. All the defendants were members of Corsican independence movements.

On 6 January 1980 three heavily armed men who were allegedly members of an anti-independence group called *Front d'action nouvelle contre l'indépendence et l'autonomie* (FRANCIA) were stopped at a road block outside Bastelica in Corsica by "autonomists" armed with hunting rifles. The autonomists claimed that the FRANCIA members were going to murder an autonomist who lived in the village and that they had acted in self defence. No one was hurt but the autonomists took the three men hostage and announced a news conference to publicize the violent activities of the anti-autonomists. After three days some of the autonomists left Bastelica with the hostages and took over a hotel where they took further hostages. The days up to 13 January were spent in negotiations between the autonomists and the police. All the hostages were eventually released unharmed.

The prosecution accepted that there were important mitigating circumstances. The court condemned them to sentences ranging from six months' suspended imprisonment to four years'.

An Amnesty International observer attended this trial in the Court of State Security. He criticized the use of this special court with the attendant risks of political interference and pointed out that he considered it incorrect to try the autonomists under special jurisdiction although the anti-autonomists were allowed to stand trial in a normal court. He repeated the criticisms of the procedures of the Court of State Security regarding the discrepancy between the powers of the prosecution and the defence and concluded that it was doubtful whether in this case the use of special courts had allowed for the proper administration of justice or a fair trial *(une bonne justice et d'un procès vraiment équitable.)*

In February 1981, after full parliamentary discussion, a law "reinforcing the security and protecting the liberty of persons" was introduced. This changed the law in two areas of concern to Amnesty International. First, it replaced the summary courts' procedure known as *flagrant délit* with a similar procedure which will effectively apply to a wider range of cases. In the past Amnesty International has criticized the prosecution of people arrested during demonstrations in summary courts under the *loi anti-casseurs* (anti-wreckers law) using the *flagrant délit* procedure. In Amnesty International's opinion the use of summary courts to give rapid judgments could prevent a fair trial where the facts were in dispute. The new procedure may be used to prosecute offenders where the maximum sentence is less than five years' imprisonment.

Second, Amnesty International drew attention to the new power given to the police to verify a person's identity. Where people cannot or will not identify themselves they may be detained in a police station for up to six hours.

Amnesty International wrote to every member of the Senate on 2 October 1980, before they had considered the draft law, expressing its concern about the new law. Amnesty International wrote again on 17 December 1980, before the final voting by the two assemblies, to

President Giscard d'Estaing, the Prime Minister, the Minister of Justice and the leaders of all the parliamentary groups because, even with minor amendments to the original bill, the elements of concern to Amnesty International remained.

Crimes which carry the death penalty are tried in the Assize Courts *(Cours d'assises)*. Judgments of the Assize Courts may be appealed against to the *Cour de cassation,* the highest court, whose sole function is to determine whether any judgment referred to it is in accordance with the law. If the *Cour de cassation* decides to set aside a judgment, a new trial in another Assize Court is ordered. If, however, the verdict of the Assize Court is upheld, the only recourse available to the convicted person is to petition the President to exercise his right of clemency under Article 17 of the French Constitution of October 1958. If clemency is granted, the sentence of death is normally commuted to life imprisonment.

France was again a major target of Amnesty International's program against the death penalty. The European Parliament adopted an emergency resolution on 21 November 1980 calling on all members of the European Community to suspend the use of the death penalty pending a full debate. Additionally, the Parliamentary Assembly of the Council of Europe on 22 April 1980 urged that the death penalty be abolished for offences in peacetime.

There have been no executions in France since September 1977. However, in the year under review, death sentences were passed on seven people. A retrial has been ordered in two cases, and five prisoners were under sentence of death at the end of April 1981.

On 10 April 1981 Amnesty International wrote to all the candidates in the forthcoming presidential elections outlining the areas where French law concerned the organization, because it contravened the standards of international law. Amnesty International pointed out that France does not allow individual complaints to be brought under Article 25 of the European Convention on Human Rights or the Optional Protocol of the International Covenant on Civil and Political Rights. France did, however, ratify the International Covenant on Civil and Political Rights on 4 November 1980.

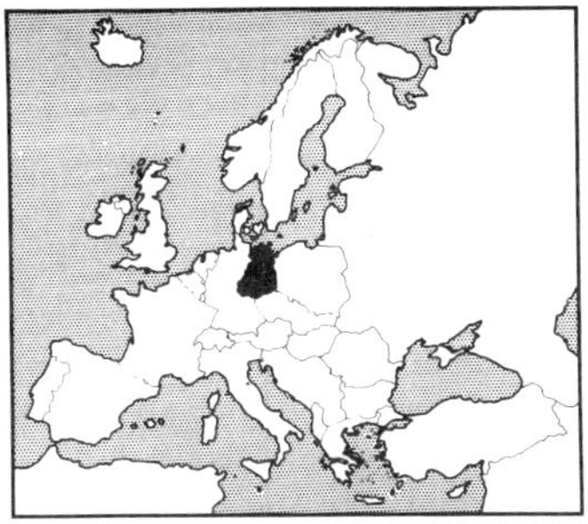

German Democratic Republic

Amnesty International's main concern continued to be the arrest of GDR citizens for the non-violent exercise of human rights, in particular the right to freedom of expression and the right to leave one's country. On 4 February 1981 Amnesty International published *German Democratic Republic (GDR),* a revised version of its briefing paper first published in October 1977.

During the year Amnesty International worked on behalf of 190 prisoners of conscience or people thought likely to be prisoners of conscience. The majority of these were would-be emigrants, imprisoned either for attempting to leave the country without permission or for persisting in efforts to obtain permission. Others included a conscientious objector to military service, and a number of people arrested for expressing critical views.

The GDR has ratified a number of international human rights instruments, including the International Covenant on Civil and Political Rights, but the exercise of some of these rights is severely restricted by articles in the penal code, in particular Articles 99 ("treasonable passing on of information") and 106 ("incitement hostile to the state"). Article 99 proscribes "handing over, collecting or making available" information "not categorized as secret" (the handing over of secret information is proscribed elsewhere in the penal code) "to the disadvantage of the interests of the GDR" to a "foreign power, its institutions or representatives . . . or to foreign organizations as well as their helpers". Amnesty International considers that this article of the penal code restricts the right "to seek, receive and pass on information regardless of frontiers" (Article 19 of the International Covenant on Civil and Political Rights) in a way that goes well beyond the restrictions allowed by the covenant. The offence carries a prison term of from two to 12 years and has been used against a number of would-be emigrants who have asked foreign organizations to help with their efforts to emigrate legally. Siegfried Domeier, a baker, and his wife Steffania, a waitress, were typical. After applying repeatedly but without success for permission to emigrate they contacted organizations in the Federal Republic of Germany (FRG) for help. As a result their story was publicized in the FRG. They were arrested in April 1980 and each sentenced in September to three years six months' imprisonment for "treasonable passing on of information". They were released on 2 April 1981.

The exercise of the right to freedom of expression is further restricted by Article 106 of the penal code, "incitement hostile to the state", which proscribes discrediting "social conditions, representatives or other citizens of the GDR because of their state or social activity" and importing, producing, disseminating or displaying "writings, objects or symbols" for this purpose. Amnesty International sought the release of a number of prisoners convicted under this article, including Simone Langrock, a 23-year-old bank employee. She was arrested on 22 April 1980 after taking part in dissident activities including distributing leaflets appealing for the release of political prisoners in the GDR. She had also applied for permission to emigrate. On 15 May she was sentenced to five years' imprisonment for "incitement hostile to the state". Several members of her family have been imprisoned for political reasons, including her grandfather, Albert Mainz, as a communist under the Nazis, and her father, Rolf Mainz, recently imprisoned in the GDR on the same charge of "incitement hostile to the state".

In February 1981 Amnesty International sent a copy of the revised briefing paper to Erich Honecker, Chairman of the State Council, and appealed to him to initiate a review of the penal code to ensure that it conformed, both in substance and application, with the GDR's international commitments to respect human rights. Until the outcome of such a review Amnesty International urged that prosecutions under articles of the penal code which explicitly restrict the exercise of human rights, including Articles 99 and 106, be suspended.

Amnesty International has received no reply to this letter, but on 6 February Erich Honecker, commenting on the briefing paper, described Amnesty International as "one of the many organizations in the West, funded by shady sources, whose task it is to slander respectable states". He also said that since 1979 there had been no political prisoners in the GDR. The interview was carried in a number of publications including the *Berliner Zeitung,* a GDR newspaper, and the FRG weekly magazine *Stern.* Amnesty International wrote again to Erich Honecker informing him fully about its policies on the acceptance of funds and explaining that the organization seeks to end human rights violations falling within its mandate, irrespective of where they take place. The letter noted his statement that there were no political prisoners in the GDR and enclosed a list of people, including Simone Langrock, whom Amnesty International believed to be prisoners of conscience, urging that their cases be examined.

Following the publication of the briefing paper Amnesty International groups as part of a campaign wrote to the authorities urging the release of all prisoners of conscience and the repeal of laws resulting in their conviction.

Prisoners of conscience continued to be released to the FRG, before completing their sentences, in exchange for money paid by the FRG Government. This is commonly known as the "buying out" scheme. Although many prisoners have gained their freedom in this way, Amnesty International does not endorse prisoner exchanges, and calls upon governments to release prisoners of conscience without conditions. The FRG authorities hold that the "buying out" scheme is the only effective help for prisoners of conscience in the GDR and that action by others on behalf of the prisoner, particularly publicity, could only hinder their efforts. They discouraged relatives and others with information about prisoners of conscience from seeking publicity or contacting other organizations. During the year they urged a number of organizations in the FRG to stop publicizing information about prisoners of conscience in the GDR. Amnesty International has repeatedly urged the FRG authorities to provide examples where publicity has had an adverse effect on prisoners, as this has not been borne out by its own observations, but they have not done so. Amnesty International was concerned that the withholding of information about prisoners of conscience in the GDR from the public might impede efforts to combat human rights violations in this country. These concerns were raised in a meeting between Amnesty International and the FRG Ministry responsible for the "buying out" scheme in West Berlin in September 1980.

The death penalty is retained for a number of offences including political ones. In October 1980 Hans-Joachim Heusinger, the Minister of Justice, stated that no death sentences had been passed or carried out during the past few years, but that the death penalty would nonetheless be retained for the time being. As part of the campaign Amnesty International groups wrote to the authorities urging them to consider whether the time had not come to abolish this form of punishment, in view of the fact that it had not been used in recent years.

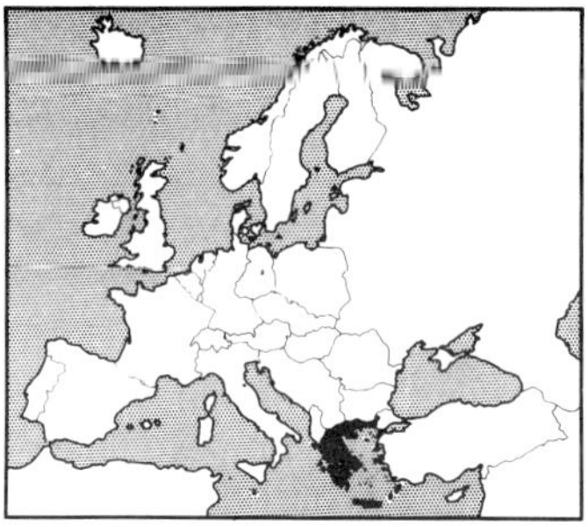

Greece

Amnesty International continued to be concerned about the imprisonment of conscientious objectors. According to Greek law all men between the age of 18 and 40 years are liable for military service. Since October 1977 Law 731/77, amending conscription Law 720/70, has allowed conscientious objection to armed military service on religious grounds only, and alternative unarmed military service of twice the duration — four years. There is no provision for alternative civilian service outside the military system. All the conscientious objectors adopted by Amnesty International as prisoners of conscience were Jehovah's Witnesses, who refused unarmed as well as armed military service. Consequently they were tried for disobedience by a court martial and were usually sentenced to four and a half years' imprisonment plus deprivation of civil rights for five years. After the military court proceedings, they served their sentences in the agricultural prison of Kassandra, where each day spent on farm labour counted as two days of the sentence served. Upon release prisoners were given a certificate to present to the military authorities in order to be discharged from the army. They were then exempt from further military duties. The practice of repeated sentencing appears to have ceased since the introduction of Law 731/77. Only one repeated sentence became known to Amnesty International during the year: the initial three-year sentence of Joel Karavitsis had been reduced to two years on appeal, and a further sentence of two years' imprisonment was imposed to complete four years.

In April 1981 Amnesty International was working for the release of 75 imprisoned conscientious objectors.

In November and December 1980 Amnesty International members took special action urging the abolition of the death penalty. The penal code provides the death sentence for treason and certain crimes connected with high treason as well as for murder under particularly aggravating circumstances. The last execution was carried out on 25 August 1972 for murder. Since then death sentences have been passed on two occasions, against two Palestinian terrorists and three former leaders of the Greek military *junta*. These were all commuted to life imprisonment.

Amnesty International received a number of allegations of ill-treatment in prison. One case was raised in a letter to Minister of Justice George Stamatis of April 1981, asking if any investigation into these allegations, which were reported in the national press, had taken place.

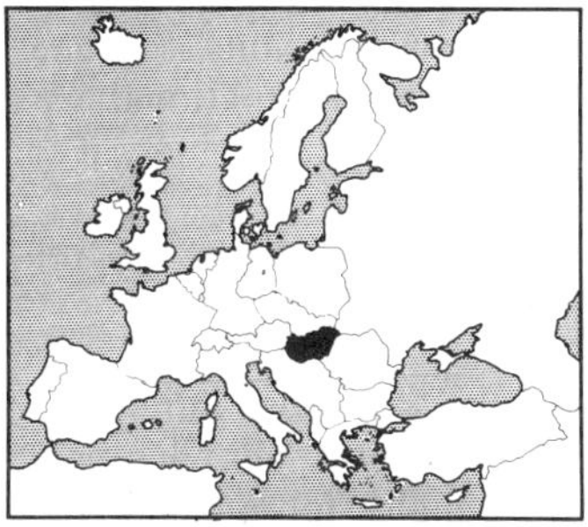

Hungary

The concerns of Amnesty International were the existence and application of legislation restricting freedom of expression and movement, and the death penalty.

In July 1980 the Human Rights Committee set up under the International Covenant on Civil and Political Rights examined a report from the Hungarian Government (supplementing its 1977 report) on its implementation of the covenant. Information received by Amnesty International in recent years has indicated that people who publicly criticize official policies or the political system are liable to imprisonment of up to eight years under Article 148 of the criminal code, dealing with "subversive activity", including "incitement against the constitutional order".

Statements by officials in the past year have confirmed that among political prisoners serving sentences were people convicted of incitement against the constitutional order. Amnesty International feared that some of them were prisoners of conscience.

According to press reports Dr Imre Markoja, Minister of Justice, said in a phone-in program on Hungarian television on 16 October 1980 that prisoners convicted of political crimes in Hungary formed only 0.2 per cent of all prisoners and that there were under 50 of them. He stated that this figure included war criminals, convicted spies and people convicted of incitement against Hungary's constitutional order. The Chief Public Prosecutor, Karoly Szijarto, in a statement on 25 February 1981 said that in 1980 there had been 65 criminal offences against the state, peace and mankind, and that a "large majority" of these had taken the form of verbal incitement, very often under the influence of alcohol. However for lack of specific information on individual cases, Amnesty International did not adopt any prisoners of conscience.

Emigration is restricted by the government. Because of these restrictions some would-be emigrants, after having tried all legal avenues in vain, have attempted to leave the country without authorization. Those who attempt to do so may be punished with up to three years' imprisonment. Preparations for an unauthorized crossing of the border are also punishable.

Amnesty International has received reports that a former prisoner of conscience, Sandor Rudovics, was sentenced in May 1980 to a year's imprisonment by a court in Szombathely after having spoken in a restaurant of his plans to leave Hungary without official authorization. He had already served at least two previous sentences for attempting to leave the country. Amnesty International was investigating the cases of Peter Oszvath (aged 20) and Mihaly Rudi (aged 19), who were sentenced by Gyor County Court on 24 February 1981 to three years' and 20 months' imprisonment respectively. Together with a friend, Gabor Baksa, they had attempted to cross the border near Sopron into Austria in a stolen lorry but were stopped by border guards. Gabor Baksa, who succeeded in reaching Austria, was sentenced in his absence to four years' imprisonment.

The criminal code retains the death penalty for a number of political and military offences as well as for aggravated cases of murder. During the year Amnesty International learned of three executions. Amnesty International learned of the imposition of one death sentence before it was carried out, that on Lajos Nagy, and appealed to the Chairman of the Presidential Council to commute it.

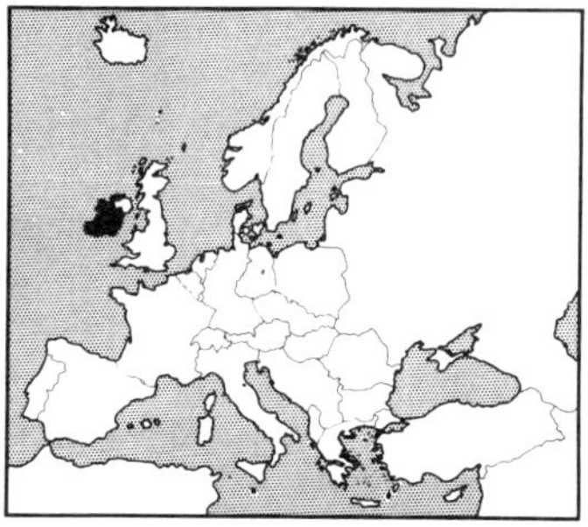

Ireland

Amnesty International had no adopted prisoners of conscience during the year, nor was there a pattern of allegations of ill-treatment in police custody (see *Amnesty International Report 1977* and *1978*). However Amnesty International sent an observer to assess the fairness of a trial which raised important issues linked to these earlier allegations.

In May 1980 an Amnesty International observer attended the appeal hearing of Osgur Breatnach and Bernard McNally. The two members of the Irish Republican Socialist Party had been convicted on 13 December 1978 of armed robbery in the Special Criminal Court in Dublin, a non-jury court set up to try politically motivated offences affecting the security of the state. Both defendants, who denied involvement in the robbery, had been convicted solely on the basis of confessions which they alleged were the result of ill-treatment during prolonged incommunicado detention in police custody in April 1976.

Amnesty International collected information on their cases during its 1977 mission to Ireland to investigate allegations of ill-treatment by police of detainees held on suspicion of politically motivated crimes. Information included medical reports noting injuries found on the accused on their last day of police custody and on their subsequent admission to prison.

The Special Criminal Court ruled at the trial that the injuries had been self-inflicted and that it was satisfied beyond reasonable doubt that their confessions were voluntary (in law only purely voluntary confessions may be used as evidence). Amnesty International's observer, who attended only the part of the appeal hearing related to Osgur Breatnach, said in his report:

> "In the light of the numerous injuries which the accused had sustained, some of which, according to expert witnesses, were incapable of self-infliction and/or were consistent with assault, it was unreasonable of the court to hold that no such doubt existed. Moreover, on the evidence the court could not have found beyond all reasonable doubt that Breatnach was not subjected to brutalities and/or oppressive circumstances of both a physical and psychological nature which rendered him incapable of the exercise of his free will for legal purposes."

On 22 May 1980 the Court of Criminal Appeal quashed the convictions in both cases and ordered the release of the prisoners. In its judgment, published only on 16 February 1981, the appeal court held that the Special Criminal Court should not have admitted the confessions in evidence; since this was the only evidence against the accused, their convictions and sentences were set aside.

A third defendant in the same trial, Edward Noel ("Nick") Kelly, who had been convicted in his absence, returned to Ireland in July 1980 and surrendered himself to the police. His conviction too was based solely on a statement he made to the police during a prolonged period of incommunicado detention. However on 18 December 1980 the Court of Criminal Appeal refused his application for appeal on grounds including the fact that he had not presented any evidence to support his allegation of ill-treatment in police custody, and that he had not substantiated the allegation that his statement had not been made voluntarily. Kelly applied for permission to appeal to the Supreme Court. The Court of Criminal Appeal has reserved its judgment on this application. Amnesty International was concerned that the judgment of the Court of Criminal Appeal in the case of Breatnach and McNally had still not been made public at the time of Kelly's appeal seven months later, especially since it contained important considerations of law regarding the circumstances under which statements made in police custody should be excluded in evidence.

The death penalty in Ireland is retained under the Criminal Justice

Act 1964 for several categories of crime, including a mandatory death sentence for the murder of a police officer in the course of duty.

Four prisoners were sentenced to death during the year. On 27 November 1980 Peter Pringle, Colm O'Shea and Patrick McCann were sentenced to death by the Special Criminal Court for the murder of a policeman after a bank robbery in July 1980. Their convictions were upheld by the Court of Criminal Appeal on 22 May 1981, but their sentences were later commuted to life imprisonment by the President of the Republic. Peter Rogers was sentenced to death by the Special Criminal Court on 11 March 1981 for the murder of a policeman in October 1980. At the end of April 1981 his appeal was still pending. Amnesty International appealed for the commutation of all death sentences.

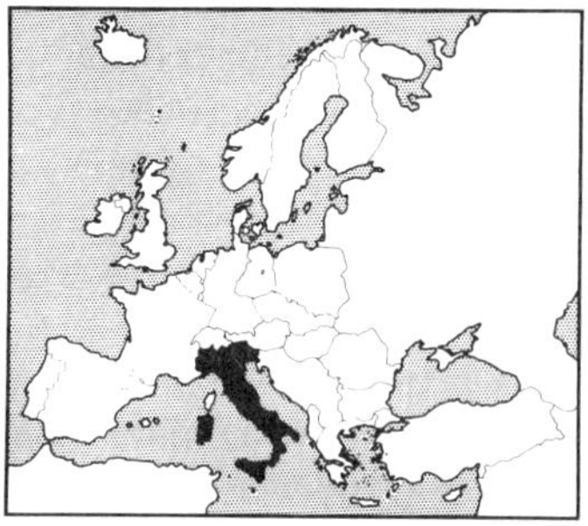

Italy

Amnesty International's main concerns in the past year have been the length of detention of people held pending the investigation of politically motivated crimes, and the imprisonment of conscientious objectors.

Italian law permits people suspected of serious crimes to be held for two years and eight months at each judicial stage from arrest to the outcome of the final appeal. Amnesty International considers that suspects have been held for judicial investigation for excessive periods, especially as many suspects were released after prolonged detention without ever having been brought to trial. Amnesty International was therefore concerned that where people were held awaiting trial for these extended periods, there was a risk of detention on political grounds rather than on reasonable suspicion.

Most detentions with which Amnesty International has been concerned during the year were of people suspected of crimes of subversive association (Article 270) and participation in an armed band (Article 306). Amnesty International was concerned at the unclear and tenuous nature of the evidence which was frequently held to justify their prolonged detention. In many instances the original charges were dropped only to be replaced immediately with new charges. This enabled the judicial authorities to keep people in what amounts to preventive detention for lengthy periods while remaining within the law.

The main focus of this concern was the continued detention without trial under judicial investigation of groups of people arrested on 7 April 1979 and after in connection with the political movement known as *Autonomia Operaia Organizzata,* Organized Workers' Autonomy. Since December 1980 the charge against a number of defendants in the "7 April" case of involvement in the kidnapping and murder of former Prime Minister Aldo Moro has been withdrawn. However all the defendants faced charges of subversive association and forming or participating in an armed band. A third charge, "armed insurrection against the powers of the state", (Article 284), has been brought against some of the defendants. It carries a life sentence and its use was unprecedented.

The major part of the judicial investigation, based in Rome, into the *Autonomia Operaia Organizzata* has been completed and 69 alleged "autonomists" have been committed for trial. However the trial date has not yet been announced, even though the defendants have been in custody for up to 25 months.

Mario Dalmaviva, arrested on 7 April 1979, began a hunger-strike in Fossombrone maximum security prison on 12 January 1981. After a period of 20 months in detention he was demanding to be put on trial and to be transferred from a "special" to an ordinary prison. He described himself as a "communist without adjectives and without a party", and expressed his opposition to armed struggle.

On 2 February 1981 Amnesty International wrote to Adolfo Sarti, Minister of Justice, urging a fair and prompt trial. Amnesty International acknowledged the gravity of the charges against Mario Dalmaviva and that it could not at that stage evaluate all the evidence; however its preliminary investigations had not established any substantive evidence against Mario Dalmaviva and it pointed out that the defendant had denied involvement in terrorist activity. Amnesty International was concerned that Mario Dalmaviva and his co-defendants, including Luciano Ferrari-Bravo and Lauso Zagato, had been in detention for nearly two years without trial. Furthermore Ferrari-Bravo had not even been interviewed in the previous 19 months by the investigating judge. The Minister was asked for information about the health of Mario Dalmaviva and the judicial position of all three prisoners. No reply has been received.

Among a group of "7 April" cases investigated by Amnesty International were those of Luciano Ferrari-Bravo, Alisa Del Re, Alessandro Serafini, Guido Bianchini and Massimo Tramonte. These last four were rearrested in January 1981 and subjected to a separate judicial investigation based in Padua. These four prisoners had been released in 1979 by order of the investigating judge of Padua because of lack of evidence. In some cases the judge referred to the mass of evidence that had been gathered as "largely favourable" to the defendants, and he stated "that they had never been involved in specific acts of violence". In others he observed that no proof could be found of links between the defendants and the acts of violence that had been carried out in the Paduan region. However the release orders were contested by the prosecuting authorities who appealed to the *Corte di Appello,* the Court of Appeal, arguing that evidence against the defendants existed, and their appeal was upheld. The defence appeal against the verdict was rejected by the *Corte di Cassazione,* the highest court, and the defendants were rearrested in January 1981 and imprisoned. Dr Carmela di Rocco, a fifth defendant rearrested in January 1981 after having been released for lack of evidence in July 1979, was again released by the investigating judge because of ill health and her need for special hospital care. However a third warrant for her arrest has since been issued by the Deputy Prosecutor of Padua.

On purely humanitarian grounds Amnesty International intervened in the case of another "7 April" defendant, Oreste Scalzone, and asked the judicial authorities for information about his health. He was not adopted as a prisoner of conscience but Amnesty International was concerned about several specialist reports which stated that his medical condition had gravely deteriorated since his arrest. Amnesty International received no reply. However shortly afterwards it learned that Oreste Scalzone had been transferred from prison to a hospital in Rome and was then provisionally released on health grounds.

The special powers of search, surveillance and detention of Law No. 15 of 6 February 1980 remained in force (see *Amnesty International Report 1980*).

Amnesty International welcomed the virtual closure on 30 November 1980 by ministerial decree of the military prison of Gaeta. This medieval fortress in the region of Latina, scarcely modified for use as a prison, has been the subject of repeated complaints about insanitary conditions and inadequate facilities. Most of its inmates were Jehovah's Witnesses and other conscientious objectors. After the prison was closed they were released under a system of supervised liberty (*libertà vigilata*).

The campaign to close Gaeta because of its conditions resulted in serious charges being brought under military law against Sergio Andreis, an adopted prisoner of conscience held in that prison. Although President Pertini had pardoned him in July 1980 for his refusal to do military service, he was kept in prison under fresh charges. He was charged under Articles 89 and 93 of the *Codice Penale Militare di Pace,* the Military Penal Code in Peacetime, with revealing, and with attempting to reveal restricted information. The charges related to a small section of an article he had written about Gaeta prison. Although the text was confiscated by the prison authorities a letter with this information appeared in both an anti-militarist journal in Brescia and in a newspaper in the Federal Republic of Germany. The article described prison conditions in Gaeta and also cited cases in which prisoners had been denied adequate medical treatment. The passage which provoked the charges referred to the aerial and maritime defences of Gaeta.

Sergio Andreis was tried by the military tribunal of Rome on 10 October 1980. Amnesty International sent an observer to the trial. The defendant admitted that he had sent the intercepted material but claimed that he had neither intended to publish restricted information nor known that it was restricted. All the information had been obtained through conversations with conscientious objectors and ex-conscripts over 10 years and by observations from his cell and within the exercise yard. He maintained that his only aim in publishing the article was to make the public aware of the conditions in the prison which were then under scrutiny by parliament.

He was acquitted of revealing restricted information for lack of evidence. However he was convicted of attempting to reveal restricted information and sentenced to 10½ months' imprisonment, suspended for five years, and payment of costs. Referring to the constitution, the Amnesty International observer criticized the system which allowed Sergio Andreis, as a conscientious objector, to be treated as a *militare* (military personnel) and be judged under military law, but he did not criticize the procedural aspects of the trial, although he mentioned the "intense control of questioning by the court". Amnesty International believes that he was prosecuted for exercising his right to freedom of expression and that he did not procure or release any information that could reasonably be classed as secret. Sergio Andreis was appealing against the verdict.

Amnesty International worked on two additional cases where conscientious objectors adopted as prisoners of conscience were faced with further charges in connection with their imprisonment.

On 12 December 1980 Judge Giovanni D'Urso was kidnapped by the Red Brigades. At the time he was responsible for controlling movements of convicted or suspected terrorists between maximum security (special) prisons. One of the stated aims of the Red Brigades has been to force the closure of the maximum security prison of Asinara. After the kidnapping there were disturbances in several maximum security prisons and on 28 December a violent riot broke out at Trani prison where some Red Brigade prisoners were held. Hostages were taken. The riot affected a group of "7 April" defendants who were held separately awaiting trial. On 11 January

1981 warrants were issued against Luciano Ferrari-Bravo, Emilio Vesce and Antonio Negri, among others, on charges of collaborating in the kidnapping of Giovanni D'Urso by maintaining contacts outside the prison and by actively taking part in negotiations to obtain his release. These "7 April" defendants were among the signatories of a document in which they denied taking any part in the riot and which criticized the system of "special prisons" such as Trani. Amnesty International was investigating these charges in the context of its wider investigation of the case of the "7 April" suspects. Judge Giovanni D'Urso was released unharmed on 15 January 1981.

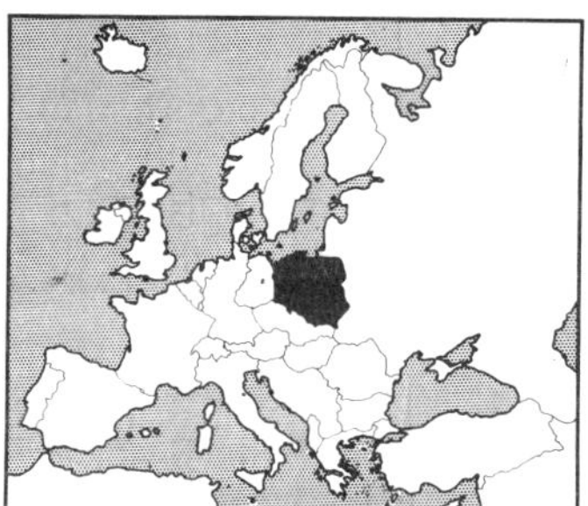

Poland

Amnesty International followed human rights developments during the year against a background of major social and political change. The outbreak of strikes in July 1980 led to an agreement on 31 August between the inter-factory strike committee in Gdansk and the authorities which included accepting independent trade unions, the release of all political prisoners and a commitment to end the persecution of individuals for their opinions. The independent trade union Solidarity, with a membership of some 12 million workers, was officially registered on 10 November 1980. The First Secretary of the Central Committee of the Polish United Workers Party, Edward Gierek, was replaced by Stanislaw Kania on 5 September 1980.

Until the Gdansk agreement the pattern of repression of previous years continued (see *Amnesty International Report 1980*). Members of the growing organized unofficial human and civil rights movement which began in 1976 were subjected to detention in police custody for up to 48 hours and to politically motivated arrests, trials, convictions on false criminal charges. The movement included groups such as the Committee for Social Self-Defence (KSS KOR), the Movement for the Defence of Human and Civil Rights (ROPCiO) and "Self-Defence Committees" founded by students, farmers, religious believers and other groups, as well as unofficial trade unions. In May 1980 Amnesty International appealed for the release of ROPCiO member Tadeusz Szczudlowski and Dariusz Kobzdej of the Young Poland Movement, another unofficial group. They were arrested on 3 May 1980 after speaking at an unofficial rally in Gdansk to mark the anniversary of the first Polish constitution of 3 May 1791. The rally was attended by some 4,000 people and a number of participants were alleged to have been physically assaulted by police. Tadeusz Szczudlowski and Dariusz Kobzdej were both allegedly beaten while being driven to police headquarters. On 5 May they were sentenced by a Tribunal for Petty Offences to three months' imprisonment on charges unknown to Amnesty International. This sentence was reportedly confirmed at an appeal hearing on 11 July.

On 12 June 1980 Miroslaw Chojecki, manager of NOWA, a publishing house printing works banned by the censor, and Bogdan Grzesiak, a NOWA printer, were convicted of appropriating state property after being given, by workers of a state publishing house, a duplicator which was to be scrapped. Amnesty International's observer was hindered from attending the trial. The defendants were sentenced to 18 months' imprisonment suspended for three years. Amnesty International was concerned by irregularities during their pre-trial detention. It adopted them as prisoners of conscience.

KSS KOR associate Marek Kozlowski was also adopted as a prisoner of conscience. In July 1979 he gave information to KSS KOR about Tomasz Koscielik, a worker from Slupsk, who had been permanently injured as a result of police assaults. The policemen concerned were later tried and convicted. According to reports Marek Kozlowski himself was later repeatedly beaten, threatened and interrogated by the security police. On 1 July 1980 he was found guilty of "threatening behaviour" and sentenced to 19 months' imprisonment. Amnesty International believes that the charge was false and that Marek Kozlowski was imprisoned for his activities for KSS KOR.

Amnesty International has been concerned at the detention of known activists for up to 48 hours in police custody. In most cases their houses were searched and possessions such as unofficial literature, typewriters and paper confiscated. This was the most frequent method of harassment during most of the year. Reports indicated that many members of human and civil rights groups were repeatedly arrested and held for 48 hours, but released without charge. Some alleged that they had been beaten and threatened during their detention, others were placed in a prison cell without explanation and released after 48 hours. Some were rearrested immediately after release.

The number of detentions appeared to increase about the time of unofficial meetings and demonstrations. For example over 70 people were detained for up to 48 hours at the time of the appeal hearing of adopted prisoner of conscience Jan Kozlowski on 26 May 1980. Jan Kozlowski, member of the Farmers' Self Defence Committee, had been sentenced to two years' imprisonment on 1 February 1980 for alleged assault. The verdict was upheld on appeal.

In June 1980 isolated detentions were reported to Amnesty International, including associates of the unofficial Roman Catholic journal *Spotkania* (Encounters) in Lublin on 25 June, collaborators with *Robotnik* (The Worker) near Rzeszow on 22 June, and members of KSS KOR and the Student Solidarity Committee in Poznan on 22 June 1980.

Following the outbreak of strikes in July 1980 which gradually spread throughout Poland, members of KSS KOR and other human rights activists collected and issued information about the strikes in order to by-pass the virtual official news blackout. As the strikes spread and strike committees were formed, isolated reports reached Amnesty International of activists being detained for up to 48 hours. Some alleged that they were beaten. The first known instance of a striker being detained was on 11 August.

On 20 August the Polish news agency PAP issued a first report about the strikes; shortly afterwards over 20 activists issuing information about the strikes were arrested in Warsaw, Poznan, Wroclaw, Szczecin and Krakow. Some were released after 48 hours while others were reportedly moved every 48 hours to different police stations, being rearrested each time to circumvent the law prescribing time limits on detention. After the news of their arrest Amnesty International appealed to the Polish authorities for their release on 21 August. Further appeals to release them, and adopted prisoners of conscience Edmund Zadrozynski, Marek Kozlowski and Jan Kozlowski, were sent on 27 August 1980 (see *Amnesty International Report 1980*).

On 31 August the government agreed to 21 demands made by an inter-factory strike committee at the Lenin Shipyards in Gdansk, committing itself to the release of all political prisoners; the release, pending review of their cases, of Edmund Zadrozynski, Jan Kozlowski and Marek Kozlowski; and an end to the persecution of individuals for their opinions. Within 24 hours all those detained on and after 20 August were released. Shortly afterwards Amnesty International learned of the release of the three adopted prisoners of conscience.

Protests continued after the Gdansk agreement, calling on the government to implement the agreement. Reprisals against activists continued. Amnesty International received numerous reports that dissidents involved in setting up the independent trade union Solidarity were detained and interrogated about their membership of Solidarity and in some cases of KSS KOR. By the end of 1980 these detentions appeared to have decreased.

Amidst growing attacks in the official news media on "anti-socialist forces" accused of disrupting the internal affairs of Poland, Leszek Moczulski, leader of a small, unofficial nationalist political group known as the Confederation for an Independent Poland (KPN) was arrested on 24 September and charged with "slandering the dignity of the Polish People's Republic and its organs" and "having participated in an organization with criminal objectives". His arrest followed the publication, in the Federal Republic of Germany, of an interview in which he described the KPN as an opposition party whose aims were "an independent sovereign Poland, free from Soviet rule and from the totalitarian dictatorship of the Polish United Workers Party". Two other KPN members, Tadeusz Stanski and Zygmunt Golawski, were arrested on similar charges. Also charged was Wojciech Ziembinski, a member of ROPCiO.

On 20 November following police searches in Solidarity's Warsaw offices Jan Narozniak, a volunteer worker in the office's print shop, was arrested and charged with betraying state secrets. A document had been found and was being reproduced in the Solidarity offices which came from the Procurator General's office and gave guidelines to local procurators for prosecuting dissenters. It appeared to confirm the pattern of repression of activists described by Amnesty International. On 25 November Piotr Sapelo, a worker in the duplicating centre of the Procurator General's office who had reportedly passed this document to Jan Narozniak, was arrested on similar charges. On 24 November, after the authorities had refused Solidarity's demand for the release of Jan Narozniak, workers occupied the Ursus factory near Warsaw. On 25 November they threatened a general strike in the Warsaw region unless Jan Narozniak, Piotr Sapelo, Leszek Moczulski, Wojciech Ziembinski, Tadeusz Stanski and Zygmunt Golawski were released. On 26 November Amnesty International appealed for their release and said that it regarded them as prisoners of conscience. On 27 November Jan Narozniak and Piotr Sapelo were conditionally released and the threat of a general strike was lifted.

On 10 December, in response to the continued reprisals against its members and members of the human and civil rights movement, in contravention of the Gdansk agreement, Solidarity announced its decision to establish a Committee for the Defence of Prisoners of Conscience.

In December three further members of KPN were arrested and charged: Tadeusz Jandziszak of Wroclaw, Krzystof Bzdyl of Krakow, and Jerzy Sychut of Szczecin.

On 9 January 1981 Amnesty International wrote to Stanislaw Kania appealing for the release of the seven people then in detention and setting out its concerns about the laws and practices by which people were arrested, detained, tried and sentenced to imprisonment for the non-violent exercise of their human rights.

On 24 January another KPN member, Romuald Szeremietiew was arrested in Warsaw and on 6 March KPN members Leszek Moczulski, Romuald Szeremietiew, Tadeusz Stanski and Tadeusz Jandziszak were indicted on charges under Articles 123 and 128 of the penal code, which make it an offence:

> "in agreement with other persons . . . [to] make preparations . . . with the purpose to deprive the Polish People's Republic of its independence, to detatch a portion of its territory, to overthrow by force its system or to weaken its defence capability".

Amnesty International has adopted all eight detained as prisoners of conscience and has been concerned that although they have not yet been tried the official news media have stated that KPN members had plotted the violent overthrow of the state. Available information indicated that none had used or advocated violence, and that they were arrested for expressing views disapproved of by the authorities.

Amnesty International welcomed the release of Wojciech Ziembinski from investigative detention on 13 March after a heart attack, and that of Jerzy Sychut on 23 April, but was concerned that proceedings against them continued.

Amnesty International was investigating six cases of people convicted of espionage; the defendants were reportedly denied proper legal safeguards and the trials held *in camera.*

Amnesty International continued to be concerned about deficiencies in the law dealing with investigative detention, in particular about the wide powers of detention granted to the state procurator and the police, and the suspect's limited right of access, before indictment, to lawyer and family. On 3 February 1981 the Minister of Justice, Jerzy Bafia, announced that the Justice Ministry was reviewing the criminal law. Regulations governing preliminary hearings, temporary detention and the scope and application of the death penalty were especially noted as being considered for revision.

The death penalty was still in force although Amnesty International did not receive any reports of any death sentences or executions during the year.

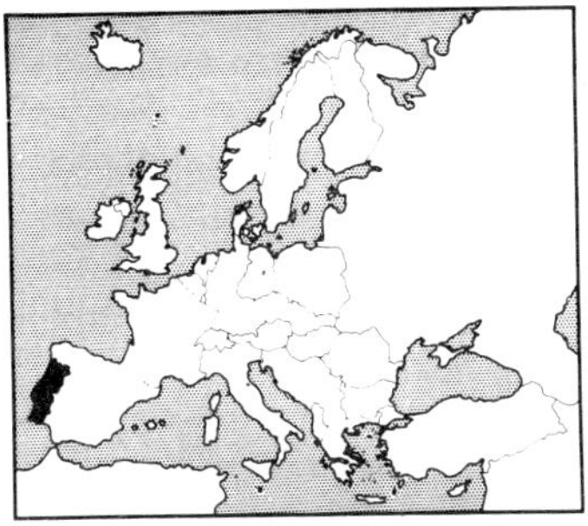

Portugal

Amnesty International's main concerns in the past year were the continued delay of the trials and appeals against sentence of alleged members of the *Partido Revolucionário do Proletariado* (PRP), Proletarian Revolutionary Party, and the failure of the courts to justify their decision not to apply the law of amnesty to those prisoners already sentenced. A final verdict has not yet been given in all PRP cases, even though the accused have been in detention for nearly three years.

In June 1978 Carlos Antunes and Isabel do Carmo, the leaders of the PRP, were arrested. Many other members of this party were arrested at the same time and detained in prison in connection with bank robberies and explosions allegedly carried out by the PRP. Carlos Antunes and Isabel do Carmo were never accused of being directly implicated in these acts. After a trial lasting three months on 9 April 1980 they were found guilty of responsibility for, moral complicity in, and receiving money in connection with, raids on banks and a bomb explosion. They were sentenced to 15 years' and 11 years' imprisonment respectively. A third defendant, Fernanda Fraguas, was sentenced to 10½ years' imprisonment for taking part in a bank robbery.

Amnesty International sent an observer to the trial. In his report he criticized the proceedings in court because: firstly, the court admitted hearsay evidence; secondly, no written transcript was made, which could inhibit the fairness of appeal proceedings; and thirdly, the defence was not allowed to call witnesses. An appeal was lodged with a higher court, the *Tribunal da Relação* of Lisbon, which upheld the verdict. A further appeal was lodged with the Supreme Court which had given no decision by the end of the year. An appeal for the application of the amnesty law was also before the Supreme Court.

The Public Prosecutor of Oporto began an investigation into allegations of ill-treatment of PRP detainees shortly after their arrest in June 1978. The results have not been revealed.

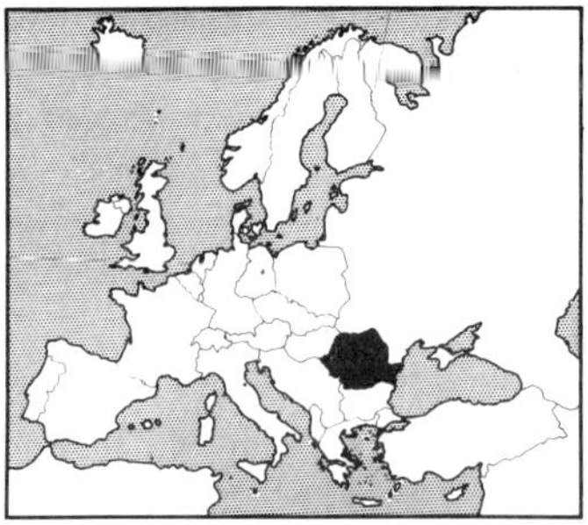

Romania

Amnesty International's main concern has continued to be the punishment by imprisonment or forced labour, sometimes on false criminal charges, of those who sought to exercise internationally accepted human rights in a non-violent manner. In June 1980 Amnesty International published *Amnesty International Briefing: Romania,* outlining its concerns and documenting human rights violations.

The majority of cases adopted by Amnesty International during the year were of people imprisoned as a result of their attempts to obtain official permission to emigrate. Some were members of Protestant sects who had previously been harassed for trying to practise their religion at places and times not authorized by the state. They have generally been sentenced to up to six months' imprisonment or forced labour, officially termed "corrective labour without deprivation of liberty", on charges of "parasitical" or "anarchic" conduct under Decree 153/1970. This decree allows for a summary trial without right of legal defence. In April 1980 Ene Chelaru, Valerian Palocoser, Vasile Bilanca and Dumitru Nemesneciuc, four Pentacostalists from Suceava and Radauti, were arrested when they went to militia offices to apply for passports to emigrate. Within 24 hours they were sentenced under Decree 153/1970 to imprisonment of from four to five months. Between 23 and 27 March 1981 Emil Dumitru, Solomon Sidea, Gabriel Culea, Manea and Dumitru Stancu and Petre Varvara, six members of a Protestant sect from Constanta, were arrested and sentenced to six months' corrective labour under Decree 153/1970 after they had declared that they would go on hunger-strike in Bucharest unless they were allowed to emigrate.

Decree 153/1970 also contains provisions against soliciting for prostitution. Amnesty International believes it was used to imprison Mia Berecz, a 19-year-old Baptist from Constanta on false charges. After several unsuccessful attempts to obtain permission to emigrate to the United States to join her parents, she travelled to Bucharest to make a further application. While drinking coffee in a milk-bar she was reportedly accosted by a young man, a foreign student. State security officers instantly appeared and accused her of offering sexual relations for payment. She was sentenced on 26 March 1980 to five months' imprisonment by the court of sector 3 in Bucharest.

Romanian citizens who publicly demonstrate in support of their human rights are liable to imprisonment under Article 321 of the criminal code for "disturbing the public peace". In September 1980 Gerhard Kloos and Doru Bodnariuc, two young men from Medias whose applications to emigrate had repeatedly been refused, demonstrated in the market-place of Medias. They carried banners and posters demanding that the Romanian authorities respect their fundamental human rights by allowing them to emigrate. It was reported they they were immediately arrested and shortly afterwards sentenced to five years' imprisonment by a court in Medias. The trial reportedly took place *in camera,* and the defendants were denied access to defence counsel. Both men were reportedly beaten by police after their arrest, and suffered from poor health in the prison of Aiud where they were detained.

A number of Romanians whose applications to emigrate have repeatedly been refused have tried to leave the country without official permission, an offence punishable under Article 245 of the criminal code with from six months' to three years' imprisonment. Amnesty International has adopted several such people as prisoners of conscience. In March 1981 two young women from Iasi, Silvia Tarniceru and Elena Boghian, were sentenced to 15 months' imprisonment for illegally crossing the border into Yugoslavia, where they were arrested by Yugoslav border guards and returned to Romania.

Amnesty International has adopted as prisoners of conscience a number of religious believers imprisoned in connection with the peaceful pursuit of religious activities. A group of Christians were arrested near Radauti in October 1980 while attempting to take Bibles across the border into the Soviet Union. They were then allegedly beaten by police to extract information and confessions from them. According to sources in Western Europe, a 26-year-old man died as a result of this beating; Amnesty International has not been able to verify this report. In January 1981 at least five of these Christians — Michael Kloos, Manfred Herberth, Gheorghe Hofman, Mathias Fackner and Paul Gross — were tried *in camera* by a court in Radauti and reportedly sentenced to prison terms of between one and a half and four years, and fined, on charges of illegal possession of foreign currency and smuggling. Amnesty International believes that the real reason for their conviction was their attempt to distribute Bibles despite the official restrictions on printing and distributing religious literature in Romania and the Soviet Union.

Amnesty International has sought the release of a number of Reformed Seventh-Day Adventists sentenced for insubordination to prison terms of three to four years for refusing, on grounds of conscience, to perform military service on their Sabbath (Saturday).

They included Ioan Maris, Mircea Dragomir, Ion Anghel, Viorel Ardeleau, Petre Anghelus and Lucian Bistriceanu.

Amnesty International received a detailed report on the arrest and confinement to a psychiatric hospital of Eugen Onescu, a 21-year-old worker from Bucharest. In spring 1979 he joined an independent trade union movement called the *Sindicatul Liber al Oamenilor Muncii din Romania* (SLOMR), the Free Trade Union of Romanian Workers. On 26 May 1979 he was forcibly brought to the Kula Annexe of the Dr Marinescu psychiatric hospital No. 9 where he was held for three weeks and given heavy doses of sedatives with painful side effects. Mihai Moise, a 45-year-old former teacher, returned to Romania in July 1980 after some years in France. On 15 August he stood before the building of the Central Committee of the Romanian Communist Party with a document complaining that assurances by the authorities that he would be provided with work and lodging had not been met. He was arrested, and after four days' detention without food or contact with anyone outside, forcibly confined in Constanta psychiatric hospital. Amnesty International appealed for his release which reportedly took place in December 1980.

Amnesty International did not learn of other such cases during the year and it is possible that this form of repression of dissent may have decreased. Amnesty International was keenly interested in the application of a new decree, No. 313/1980, dealing with "assistance to dangerously mentally ill persons", which replaced Decree 12/1965, under which a number of prisoners of conscience adopted by Amnesty International in the past had been forcibly confined to psychiatric hospital.

Amnesty International welcomed the release, before the expiry of their sentences, of prisoners of conscience Gheorghe Brasoveanu, Dr Ionel Cana, Gheorghe Rusu and Robert Damboviceanu. However despite appeals by Amnesty International Father Calciu, an Orthodox priest and former political prisoner, continued to be imprisoned. At Christmas and Easter 1980 his food rations were reportedly greatly reduced for 10 days. His health was believed to be extremely poor. On 11 November 1980 Father Calciu went on hunger-strike to demand a retrial in public. In December, despite forcible feeding, he had reportedly suffered a severe loss of weight and his life was in danger; he was transferred to Jilava prison hospital where he was believed to be at the end of April 1981.

Conditions of detention and trial procedures for prisoners of conscience have seriously infringed internationally accepted standards. Amnesty International has received many reports of prisoners of conscience being beaten and threatened during investigation to extort confessions. Some have been held incommunicado; others have had only minimal access to family and defence counsel. The right to defence counsel of the defendant's choice has frequently been denied. Defendants have complained of hasty, prejudged trials, and of being deliberately humiliated by the court. Amnesty International continued to be concerned at the use of Decree 153/1970 to imprison dissenters by means of summary trial without right of legal defence.

Prison conditions, as described by former prisoners of conscience, fell well below the United Nations Standard Minimum Rules for the Treatment of Prisoners. Over-crowding, poor diet and insanitary conditions have severely impaired prisoners' health. Medical care has been inadequate, a matter of particular concern to Amnesty International since many prisoners of conscience had health problems before being imprisoned. Prisoners of conscience were made to work in conditions which were often primitive and were punished if they failed to meet production targets. Amnesty International has received several reports that prisoners have been kept in chains in cells.

Under the 1969 criminal code 28 crimes carry a discretionary death sentence. The only death sentence known to Amnesty International was that of a murderer executed by firing-squad in Bucharest on 13 November 1980.

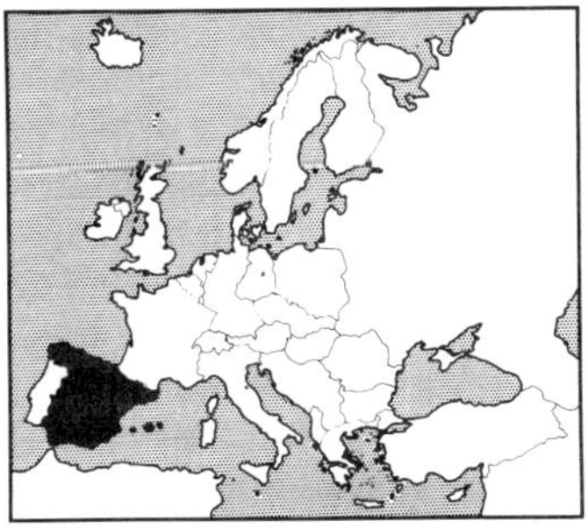

Spain

Amnesty International's main concern was the ill-treatment and torture of people detained under the anti-terrorist laws. Legal and political changes took place during the year which affected human rights in Spain. The armed confrontations between extremist forces of left and right, of autonomists and the police and the *Guardia Civil* (paramilitary police force) intensified in the past year, especially in the Basque country. On 24 March 1981 the armed forces were given an operational anti-terrorist role for the first time.

Prime Minister Adolfo Suárez, who had been in office since July 1976, resigned in February 1981. Major legislation, including a new constitution in 1978, was passed during his term of office. This new legislation was largely responsible for the improved human rights situation following the death of General Franco in November 1975. Leopoldo Calvo Sotelo became Prime Minister on 25 February 1981. Elements of the army and *Guardia Civil* attempted a coup on 23 February 1981 during the parliamentary debate about his nomination. During the coup attempt rebel Civil Guards under the command of Lieutenant Colonel Antonio Tejero Molina held members of the *Cortes* (parliament) prisoner at gunpoint. At the end of April 1981, an inquiry was taking place with a view to legal action against those responsible and Lieutenant-Colonel Tejero and other senior officers were in detention.

The chief legislative tools in combating the political violence were the powers of arrest and detention under the anti-terrorist laws (Law 56/1978 of 4 December 1978 and Royal Decree-Law 3/1979 of 26 January 1979). Under these laws the police can detain not only members of armed groups, but also people who publicly defend their activities or even associate with their members.

The detainee may be held incommunicado for interrogation in a police station, initially for three days, and for another seven days after extension by a magistrate of the *Audiencia Nacional* (National Court). Lawyers were generally denied access to detainees during the 10 days of incommunicado detention, in contravention of the right to legal assistance guaranteed in Article 17(3) of the constitution. Effective judicial supervision is lacking. Amnesty International considers these conditions conducive to ill-treatment and torture. Evidence collected during an Amnesty International mission in October 1979 supported this view, and allegations of ill-treatment and torture of people held under the anti-terrorist laws were still being received regularly at the end of April 1981.

In September 1980 Amnesty International presented its *Report of an Amnesty International Mission to Spain, 3-28 October 1979* to the government and invited its comments. The report was published in December 1980. No reply has been received. The mission delegates, who included two doctors, had interviewed 14 people who had been held under the anti-terrorist laws in Madrid, Barcelona and Bilbao. All had been held incommunicado for up to 10 days and subjected to exhausting interrogations and beatings, mock executions, electric shocks and other forms of ill-treatment and torture. The report contains details of the legislation then in force, of the cases examined, and the recommendations of the mission.

The recommendations, which were consistent with the human rights guarantees of the 1978 constitution, called for the abolition of 10-day incommunicado detention; access to lawyers for suspects detained for interrogation; and the introduction of *habeas corpus* legislation provided under the constitution. It recommended that judicial control over the interrogations should be strengthened, and that public prosecutors should intervene to protect the rights of detainees as well as take legal action against offenders. It recommended a system of recorded medical examinations for detainees after arrest and immediately before transfer from police custody, with a provision for intermediate examinations, and a legal right for detainees to see independent doctors.

The report condemned political murder by armed groups and said that Amnesty International opposed arbitrary arrest and detention as a violation of fundamental human rights, regardless of whether such acts were committed by governments or opposition groups. Amnesty International appealed publicly for the release on humanitarian grounds of José Maria Ryan, an engineer at the Lemoniz nuclear power station in the Basque country, who had been kidnapped by *Euskadi Ta Askatasuna-Militar* (ETA-m), Basque Homeland and Liberty, an autonomist group. José Maria Ryan was murdered and his dead body found on 6 February 1981. On the night of 19 February 1981 the three Honorary Consuls of Austria, El Salvador and Uruguay were kidnapped by *ETA Político-militar,* another Basque autonomist group. On 25 February 1981 Amnesty International appealed for their release on humanitarian grounds. They were released unharmed on 28 February 1981.

The anti-terrorist laws on arrest and detention were introduced as an interim measure until a new penal code and code of penal procedure were adopted. Law 56/1978 laid down the type of suspects who could be held and the procedures which should be adopted. Royal Decree-Law 3/1979 widened the range of offences for which suspects could be held. On 1 December 1980 Law 56/1978 was replaced by a new Organic Law 11/1980, which retained the powers under Law 56/1978 and also suspended three important constitutional rights. Article 55.2 of the constitution allows certain guaranteed rights to be suspended for the purpose of investigating armed groups and terrorists. Royal Decree-Law 3/1979 remains in force and complements Organic Law 11/1980. It did not however suspend the constitutional right to legal assistance which is continually denied by police to people held incommunicado for interrogation under the anti-terrorist laws. None of the criticisms of Law 56/1978 made by Amnesty International in its report have been answered by its replacement with Organic Law 11/1980.

The possible consequences of allowing unsupervised incommunicado detention for up to 10 days were illustrated by the death in custody on 13 February 1981 of José Arregui Izaguirre. He and a companion, Isidro Echave Urrestrilla, allegedly members of ETA-m, were captured in Madrid after a gun battle with members of the police and Civil Guard. They were held incommunicado for nine days before they were transferred to hospital where Arregui died. A post-mortem examination revealed injuries to his lungs, burns on his feet, bruises to his body, eye injuries and severe internal bleeding. The immediate cause of death was certified as pneumonia. Isidro Echave, who was shot and had a bullet in his shoulder, was only operated on several days after his removal from the police station and he had been badly tortured. A screw-driver had reportedly been manipulated in the gun-wound.

More and more people have been detained under the new anti-terrorist law. Since its introduction in December 1980, 815 people have been arrested and held under the two anti-terrorist laws 11/1980 and 3/1979. According to official statistics from the Minister of the Interior, 319 people were held in the same period last year. Amnesty International was concerned by the scale of these arrests, especially as most of the detainees were later released without charge.

On 10 October 1980 the trial began in the *Audiencia Nacional* in Madrid of José Orive Velez, on charges of abduction, attempted damage and illegal possession of arms and explosives. José Orive was interviewed by the Amnesty International mission, and details of his ill-treatment and torture were published in the report. He had been provisionally at liberty since the court released him in June 1979. Amnesty International sent an observer to his trial. The trial observer drew attention to, among other things, the fact that José Orive's complaint of torture while held incommunicado of 25 May 1979 had not been judicially investigated; and to the delay of nearly 20 months in bringing the case to trial. He also reported the negligence of the prosecution in failing to take account of the fact that José Orive was a minor until nearly the end of the trial and the inclusion in the summary of the two charges of attempted damage and possession of arms and explosives which were not based on substantial evidence. José Orive was found guilty of abduction and sentenced to four years and five days' imprisonment. He was acquitted on the other two charges. The trial observer believed that, in spite of the criticisms mentioned above, the trial had not been conducted unfairly and that, in the face of the evidence, the court could reasonably find as it did.

The trial of civilians before military courts, used to restrict freedom of expression, has long been a concern of Amnesty International. On 22 November 1980 a reform of the Code of Military Justice removed the powers of military courts to try civilians for offences such as damaging or insulting the army and a number of well-known cases were then quashed by civilian courts.

On 11 November 1980 the government announced its intention of ratifying Article 25 of the European Convention on Human Rights for an initial period of two years, beginning on 1 July 1981. This will permit individual applications to the European Commission on Human Rights.

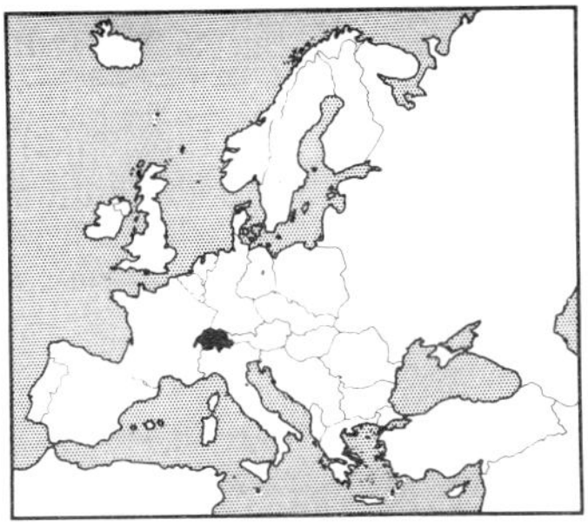

Switzerland

Amnesty International's concern was the imprisonment of conscientious objectors to military service.

Under Article 81 of the military penal code every conscientious objector is sentenced to prison, even where the military tribunal recognizes a severe conflict of conscience on religious or ethical grounds. If the objection to military service is considered to be primarily political a longer term of imprisonment is given.

According to official sources 354 people were convicted of refusing military service in 1980. Of 202 cases 96 were classified as refusing on religious grounds, 86 on ethical grounds and 20 on political grounds. Many conscientious objectors were sentenced to terms of imprisonment too short to make it practicable for Amnesty International to adopt them, even though it regarded them as prisoners of conscience.

During the year Amnesty International adopted two pacifists: Matthias Huber, a member of the board of the *Internationale der Kriegsdienstgegner* (the Conscientious Objectors' International) and an editor of its journal *Virus;* and Urs Geiser, a student of theology. They both received five months' imprisonment in the form of *arrêts répressifs*, which is given in cases where extenuating circumstances have been recognized. Although convicted conscientious objectors may be allowed to do prescribed work outside the prison boundaries, they are held in the prison in solitary confinement for the remainder of the time. Amnesty International considers this system amounts to imprisonment.

Amnesty International recognized as a prisoner of conscience Pierre-Alain Léchot, who was sentenced to four months' imprisonment in the form of *arrêts répressifs* by the military tribunal of Neuchâtel on 12 June 1980. His religious convictions were acknowledged by the court.

Nicolas Pythoud was considered a prisoner of conscience after being sentenced to eight months' imprisonment by the military tribunal of La Tour-de-Peilz on 24 April 1980. He received a relatively high sentence because, although the tribunal found that his pacifist convictions were partially founded on religious and moral principles, it also considered that he was motivated primarily by political beliefs.

The failure in 1977 of an amendment to the constitution to

establish an alternative civilian service has meant that every year hundreds of citizens are convicted for the exercise of their conscientiously held beliefs, contrary to internationally recognized norms, in particular Resolution 337 (1967) of the Parliamentary Assembly of the Council of Europe, of which Switzerland is a member.

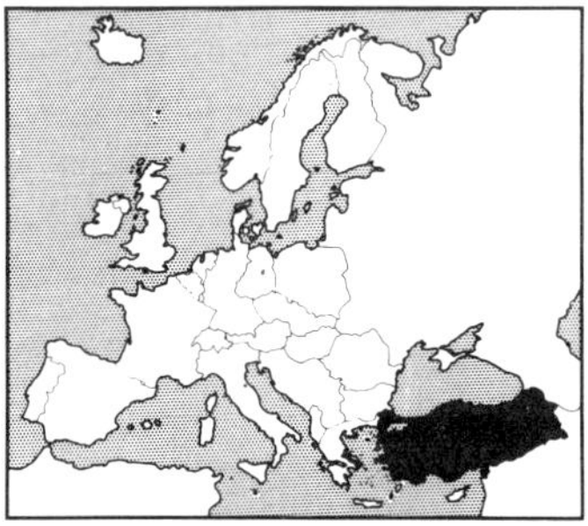

Turkey

The main concerns of Amnesty International were torture, executions and death sentences, and the holding of prisoners of conscience.

Political violence, which has resulted in thousands of deaths since 1975, continued. Martial law, imposed in December 1978 in 13 of Turkey's 67 provinces, had been renewed at two-monthly intervals and extended to cover 20 provinces, but assassinations by both right and left-wing groups had mounted to over 5,000 by 12 September 1980 when Turkey's military leaders abolished parliament after a coup and imposed martial law on the whole country. General Kenan Evren, the Armed Forces Chief of Staff, announced that legislative and executive powers would be held by the National Security Council headed by himself. Later in the month a government was appointed under a retired admiral, Bulent Ulusu.

Thousands of people were detained, including members of parliament, members of political parties and trade unionists. The duration of detention without charge under martial law was increased from 15 to 30 days and then in November 1980 to 90 days. All political and trade union activity was banned and three newspapers, *Aydinlik* and *Democrat* on the left and *Hergun* on the right, were closed down.

Subsequent changes in the martial law regulations extended the powers of martial law commanders, giving them control over mail, communications, press censorship and all labour and trade union activities. Under the new law people could be sentenced to six months' to two years' imprisonment for propagating "erroneous, unfounded or exaggerated information in a manner to create alarm or excitement among the public". The penalty would be doubled if the offence was committed through the news media and if a foreigner was involved the sentence was to be not less than a year. Another change made sentences of up to three years passed by military courts not subject to appeal.

In May 1980 (that is, before the coup) an Amnesty International mission visited Turkey to investigate the increasing allegations that political prisoners were being tortured. The mission interviewed people who had been tortured and talked to lawyers, doctors, members of political parties, trade unionists and journalists. On the basis of information from these meetings and from documents, including medical reports, Amnesty International published a news release on 9 June 1980 which reported that torture had become widespread and systematic and that most people detained by police and martial law authorities were subjected to torture, which in some cases was alleged to have ended in death.

Methods of torture included electric shocks, *falaka* (beating the soles of the feet), and violent assaults on all parts of the body, including the sexual organs. Some detainees — both men and women — were also subjected to a form of rape, with police truncheons or other objects inserted into the anus or vagina. Detailed information was given on three people who were alleged to have died after being tortured: Yasar Gundogdu, Osman Mehmet Onsoy and Oruc Korkmaz. Torture was reported by both right and left-wing political groups.

Allegations of torture continued and increased and by July 1980 Amnesty International had detailed information about 10 deaths alleged to have been caused by torture in the preceding six months. On 4 July 1980 Amnesty International wrote to the Prime Minister Sulcyman Demirel saying: ". . . we now have received a large amount of information, including medical reports, which make it quite clear that torture is extensive and that the cases referred to above are not isolated or unusual incidents." On 23 July the Turkish Ambassador in London, Vahap Asiroglu, informed Amnesty International that:

> "The martial law authorities have already looked into a total of 39 complaints concerning allegations of torture. The investigations of 14 complaints have been completed and since there was no evidence to substantiate them, the martial law authorities have decided to take no further action. The investigations in connection with the remaining 25 allegations are still continuing and I understand that a number of people are assisting the martial law authorities in their enquiries."

Amnesty International requested further information about these investigations and a list of all 39 complaints, but did not receive this.

On 25 July an appeal was sent to Prime Minister Demirel for an urgent investigation into allegations that Fikri Sonmez, the Mayor of Fatsa, and others detained with him were being tortured. It is not known whether these allegations were investigated.

On 17 September 1980, five days after the coup, Amnesty International wrote to the new head of state, General Evren, saying that while the organization was "sympathetic to the difficulties which any government is faced with in dealing with the political violence which has resulted in so many killings . . . there is never any justification for torture". Enclosed with this letter were the findings of the Amnesty International research mission and documentation detailing torture allegations.

Following the military takeover and the large number of people taken into custody (122,609 between 12 September 1980 and 10 April 1981, according to the Turkish newspaper *Milliyet,* 4 May 1981), even more allegations of torture reached Amnesty International. On 9 October Amnesty International appealed to General Evren for an inquiry into the death on 2 October of Ahmet Feyzioglu, a trade union lawyer, in Bursa Central Police Station. In November 1980 the organization published the names of eight people alleged to have died as a result of torture since 12 September, including Ilhan Erdost, a left-wing publisher who was beaten to death by soldiers at Mamak military prison in Ankara on 7 November. The Turkish authorities later announced that these deaths had been investigated and that some people would be prosecuted. On 1 December 1980 Amnesty International wrote again to General Evren expressing concern at reports of deaths in custody after torture. By the beginning of April 1981 Amnesty International had received the names of 20 people reported to have died in custody since 12 September, and believed that torture continued to be widespread and used as an administrative practice.

On 17 April an Amnesty International mission went to Turkey to discuss its concerns with the authorities. The delegates met General Necdet Oztorun, the Deputy Chief of Staff; General Recep Ergun, the Martial Law Commander for Ankara; General Nezet Bologirey, Commander responsible for coordination of martial law; Foreign Minister Ilter Turkmen; Minister of State Ilhan Oztrak; and Fahri Gorgulu, Director of the Turkish Police. All the concerns of Amnesty International were raised in these meetings, but particular emphasis was placed on the many allegations of torture. Amnesty International appreciated steps taken by the authorities to check torture, but urged further safeguards to protect prisoners from ill-treatment. Specific recommendations were that the government should issue public instructions to military and police personnel that torture is prohibited and constitutes a criminal offence; that the 90-day detention period should be drastically reduced and that access to lawyers and family should be accorded in all cases throughout the period of custody.

The mission also had talks with former Prime Ministers Bulent Ecevit and Suleyman Demirel, with the Presidents of the Turkish and Istanbul Bar Associations, with lawyers, journalists, relatives of detainees and released detainees.

On 28 April 1981 Amnesty International was invited to address the Political Affairs Committee of the Council of Europe's Parliamentary Assembly in Paris. The committee was told that the substantial information about torture in Amnesty International's possession made an "irrefutable case that torture is being practised on such a large scale in Turkey that it is impossible that it is carried out without official sanction." The committee was also told of Amnesty International's conviction that the actions taken by the authorities had not resulted in any lessening of torture, or made it any easier for people to make complaints about torture.

The imprisonment of people under Articles 141, 142 and 163 of the Turkish penal code continued during the year (see *Amnesty International Report 1980*). Article 141 prohibits forming organizations "aimed at establishing the domination of a social class over other social classes"; Article 142 prohibits "making propaganda for the domination of a social class over other social classes"; Article 163 is used to imprison anyone who "opposes secularism, forms or organizes, plans, manages or administers a society aiming, even partially, to impose religious principles on the basic social, economic, political or legal order of the state".

Journalists, writers and translators were sentenced to terms of imprisonment under Article 142, although some were permitted to pay a fine instead of going to prison. Of the thousands of people in prison in April 1981 accused of politically motivated offences, many were charged with crimes of violence, but many others were held for their non-violent political activities and beliefs. These included officials of DISK (the Confederation of Revolutionary Trade Unions), members of the Turkish Labour Party, members of the National Salvation Party (including former members of parliament), and members of the Turkish Workers' and Peasants' Party. Trials of all these people were scheduled to take place, but until these and other trials have been completed it is impossible for Amnesty International to make any estimate of the number of prisoners of conscience.

Many Kurds were also in prison, both before and after the coup of 12 September 1980. Trials of some Kurdish groups accused of terrorist activities had started by April 1981, but Amnesty International had also received information about Kurds who were reported to have been detained, tortured and released without charge. On 25 March Serafettin Elci, a former cabinet minister, was sentenced to 2 years and 3 months' imprisonment for "making

Kurdish and secessionist propaganda". He was convicted on the basis of published statements in which he was quoted as having said: "I am a Kurd. There are Kurds in Turkey." Amnesty International regards him as a prisoner of conscience.

Between 12 September and 13 December 1980 four men convicted of political killings were executed, the first executions since 1972. The last of the four to be executed was 19-year-old Erdal Eren who was sentenced to death in March 1980 after being convicted of killing a soldier during a demonstration. The death sentence was subsequently annulled on legal grounds by the Military Court of Appeal, but was reimposed by the Council of the Offices of the Military Court of Appeal in November 1980 and approved by the National Security Council on 12 December.

Frequent appeals have been made to the authorities for a stop to executions and the abolition of the death penalty. In its letter to General Evren on 17 September Amnesty International urged him "to consider that the best way for a government to demonstrate its belief in the inviolability of human life is to abolish entirely the use of the death penalty." The death penalty was one of the concerns raised with the authorities by the Amnesty International mission in April 1981.

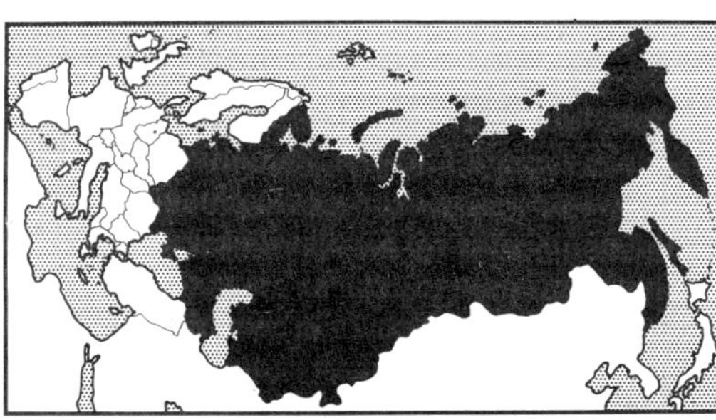

Union of Soviet Socialist Republics

Amnesty International remained concerned about the harassment, imprisonment and forcible confinement in psychiatric hospitals of people holding views — whether political, religious or nationalist — disapproved of by the authorities; frequent violations of internationally accepted standards for fair trial; the harsh conditions of detention of prisoners of conscience; and the use of the death penalty.

During the year Amnesty International learned of approximately 200 people arrested for the non-violent exercise of their human rights. Over 30 were forcibly confined in psychiatric hospitals without genuine medical grounds. It also learned of the harassment, intimidation, short-term detention and, in some cases, physical ill-treatment of many other dissenters. In the course of the year it worked on behalf of about 500 prisoners who had been adopted as prisoners of conscience, or who were being investigated as possible prisoners of conscience.

Even though the USSR has ratified a number of international human rights instruments, including the International Covenants on Civil and Political Rights and on Social, Economic and Cultural Rights, the authorities continued to convict prisoners of conscience under criminal law which prescribes imprisonment for the non-violent exercise of human rights: "anti-Soviet agitation and propaganda"; "circulation of fabrications known to be false which defame the Soviet state and social system", often referred to as "anti-Soviet slander", and "violation of the laws on separation of church and state and of church and school", which forbids teaching religion to children "in an organized way". The authorities also used the criminal law to convict prisoners of conscience on charges with no ostensible relationship to the dissenting activities of those convicted, and which Amnesty International believed to be without foundation and politically motivated.

On 27 June 1980 the Presidium of the Supreme Soviet of the USSR proclaimed an amnesty in connection with the Olympic Games in Moscow, but its provisions were not published. Amnesty International has learned that the amnesty benefited prisoners serving sentences of up to two years for "minor offences", and some war veterans, mothers, and decorated workers serving terms of up to five years' imprisonment. The amnesty excluded those convicted of political offences such as "anti-Soviet slander". A number of prisoners of conscience were released from corrective labour colonies and given a milder punishment known as "building up the national economy": they were sent to complete their sentences on construction sites often far from their homes.

On 22 June the authorities forcibly expelled Vladimir Borisov from the USSR. The long-standing dissenter, victim of political abuses of psychiatry and former prisoner of conscience had been rearrested on 30 May.

During the year the authorities continued the major drive against all categories of dissenters launched towards the end of 1979. In July 1980 Amnesty International issued a list of 144 people imprisoned during the preceding nine months. Arrests and trials of dissenters continued, and on 21 January 1981 it expressed concern in an international news release. The first four months of 1981 saw no apparent improvement. Heavy sentences were frequent: during the year at least 19 prisoners of conscience were sentenced to 10 or more years' imprisonment and internal exile for "anti-Soviet agitation and propaganda".

Forms of repression within Amnesty International's mandate have hit three types of dissenter especially hard: "Helsinki monitors", unofficial groups trying to monitor Soviet compliance with the human rights provisions of the Final Act of the 1975 Helsinki Conference on Security and Cooperation in Europe; critics of the Soviet nationalities policy in the non-Russian Soviet Republics and advocates of political independence for their nations, particularly Ukrainians, Lithuanians and Estonians; and religious believers, particularly Baptists, Seventh-Day Adventists, Pentecostalists and Russian Orthodox believers.

The authorities have continued to imprison Helsinki monitors. In the spring of 1980 Tatyana Osipova, a member of the Moscow Helsinki monitoring group, and Vasyl Stus and Ivan Sokulsky, both former prisoners of conscience and members of the Ukrainian Helsinki monitoring group, were arrested. The Armenian Helsinki monitor, Eduard Arutyunyan, was sentenced to two and a half years' imprisonment and the Ukrainian monitors, Petro Rozumny and Yaroslav Lesiv, to three and two years' imprisonment respectively. In June two Helsinki monitors and former prisoners of conscience were convicted of "anti-Soviet agitation and propaganda": Moscow group member Viktor Nekipelov and Ukrainian group member Vitaly Kalynychenko were given 12 and 15 years' imprisonment and internal exile respectively. Another Ukrainian monitor, Vyacheslav Chornovil, rearrested while in internal exile, was falsely convicted of attempted rape and sentenced to five years' imprisonment. In the same month, Oksana Meshko, a 75-year-old Ukrainian monitor and mother of the prisoner of conscience Oleksander Serhiyenko, was forcibly confined in a psychiatric hospital. In August the Lithuanian monitor, Dr Algirdas Statkevicius, was ruled mentally ill and unaccountable for his actions, and ordered by a court to be confined indefinitely in a special psychiatric hospital for the "especially dangerous". Olha Heyko Matusevych, a Helsinki monitor whose husband is serving a 12-year sentence for participation in the Ukrainian group, was sentenced to three years' imprisonment.

In the following months Vasyl Stus and Ivan Sokulsky were both given 15-year sentences of imprisonment and internal exile. In December the Lithuanian Helsinki monitor, Vytautas Skuodis, received 12 years' imprisonment and internal exile, and Dr Leonard Ternovsky three years' imprisonment. In the following month, Oksana Meshko was sentenced to six months' imprisonment and five years' internal exile. In March 1981 two Lithuanian monitors, Mecislovas Juravicius and Vytautas Vaiciunas and a Ukrainian monitor, Ivan Kandyba, were arrested. At the beginning of April Tatyana Osipova was sentenced to five years' imprisonment and three years' internal exile.

A number of those imprisoned during the year for peacefully exercising human rights were members of non-Russian nationalities. Most had protested against what they consider to be an official policy of "Russification" discriminating against national minorities, or had advocated the secession of their Union Republic from the USSR. They were imprisoned despite basing their activities on Article 36 of the USSR Constitution (1977) which proscribes discrimination on the grounds of race or nationality, and Article 72, which proclaims that "each Union Republic has the right freely to secede from the USSR". Many were charged with "anti-Soviet agitation and propaganda" and given sentences of up to 15 years' imprisonment and internal exile.

Those imprisoned for "nationalist" activities in Ukraine included Mykola Kraynyk, sentenced in August 1980 to 10 years' imprisonment and internal exile for organizing a clandestine group peacefully seeking to achieve Ukrainian political independence. Stepan Khmara, Vitaly Shevchenko and Oleh Shevchenko were given sentences of 12, 11 and eight years' respectively in December for circulating an unauthorized Urkainian journal. Vasyl Kurylo was reported to have been sentenced to a total of 15 years' imprisonment and internal exile for a similar offence. In Lithuania, Antanas Terleckas and Julius Sasnauskas were tried in September, convicted of "anti-Soviet agitation and propaganda" and sentenced to eight and six and a half years' imprisonment and internal exile respectively. Among a number of Lithuanian activists tried at the end of 1979 for circulating unauthorized journals were Gintautas Iesmantas and Povilas Peceliunas, who were sentenced to 11 and eight years' respectively. In Estonia, Mart Niklus, a leading activist, was sentenced in January to a total of 15 years' imprisonment and internal exile. Other imprisoned Estonian dissenters included Yuri Kukk (two years), who died in March in a corrective labour colony after a prolonged hunger-strike, Veljo Kalep (four years) and Viktor Niitsoo (four years). Several campaigners for national rights were also imprisoned in Armenia — A. Manucharyan, A. Navasardyan, A. Arshakyan — and in Georgia — N. Samkharadze, V. Shgenti, Z. Gogiya, V. Chitanava.

More than half of the prisoners of conscience arrested during the year were religious believers. Most were members of "dissenting" Baptist, Seventh-Day Adventist and Pentecostalist congregations which reject the restrictions imposed by the state on religious activity. The authorities regard these "unregistered" religious communities as illegal. Among those imprisoned were leaders of all three of these "dissenting" denominations.

Amnesty International learned of the imprisonment of almost 80

Baptists. Most members of their unofficial governing body known as the Council of Evangelical Christians and Baptists in the USSR have been imprisoned. These included Pastor Mikhail Khorev, who was almost blind, sentenced in May to five years' imprisonment; Pastor Nikolai Baturin, a former prisoner of conscience, given the same sentence in August; and Pyotr Rumachik sentenced in early 1981, also to five years' imprisonment. Another leading Baptist, Pastor Dmitry Minyakov, was arrested in January. On 26 March Amnesty International issued an urgent appeal for him after receiving reports that he was gravely ill as a result of a protest hunger-strike in Tallinn prison. In August four Baptists — Galina Yudintseva, Lyubov Kosachevich, Sergei Bublik and Tamara Bystrova — were given three-year sentences in connection with the discovery of an unofficial Baptist printing press in Dnepropetrovsk in central Ukraine. In June another seven Baptists were arrested in Krasnodar Territory in southern Russia for unofficially printing religious literature, and later sentenced to between three and four years' imprisonment.

Most of the Seventh-Day Adventists imprisoned during the year were accused of distributing unauthorized religious literature. Twenty-two "dissenting" Adventists were arrested in connection with "Open Letter No. 12", an unofficially circulated report of violations of Adventists' right to freedom of conscience. In July Rostislav Galetsky, leader of the "dissenting" Seventh-Day Adventists, was arrested and charged with "anti-Soviet slander" and with violating regulations circumscribing believers' freedom of conscience. He was tried in Ryazan in March and sentenced to five years' imprisonment.

Since the 1960s a large movement for emigration from the USSR has developed among "dissenting" Soviet Pentecostalists because of official restrictions on their freedom of conscience. Two leaders of this movement were among the Pentecostalists imprisoned during the year. Pastor Nikolai Goretoi, who had been held in custody since his arrest in November 1979, was sentenced in August 1980 to 12 years' imprisonment and internal exile for "anti-Soviet agitation and propaganda". In August Boris Perchatkin was arrested in the far east of the USSR and sentenced to two years' imprisonment.

Two Russian Orthodox activists were among religious believers given long sentences for their dissenting activities. In August 1980 Father Gleb Yakunin, a leading campaigner for religious rights, received 10 years' imprisonment and internal exile for "anti-Soviet agitation and propaganda". Prisoner of conscience Alexander Ogorodnikov, a member of an unofficial seminar of Russian Orthodox Christians and already serving a one-year sentence, was faced with an additional charge of "anti-Soviet agitation and propaganda" and sentenced in September to a further 11 years' imprisonment and internal exile. A number of Lithuanian Roman Catholics were also imprisoned, including Genovaite Naviskaite and Ona Vitkauskaite, sentenced in November to two years' and eighteen months' imprisonment respectively for circulating the unofficial journal *A Chronicle of the Lithuanian Catholic Church.* Another Lithuanian woman, Gemma-Jadvyga Stanelyte, was arrested in June after organizing the annual religious procession to a shrine. She was charged with "organization of, or active participation in, group actions which violate public order", and in December imprisoned for three years.

Amnesty International continued to receive reports of conscientious objectors imprisoned for refusing military service. They included Baptists, Jews, ethnic Germans, Ukrainians and Russians.

People trying to emigrate were arrested, including several activists in the Jewish emigration movement — Viktor Brailovsky, Vladimir Kislik and Kim Fridman — Pentecostalists, ethnic Germans, Russians and others. In February two members of an unofficial "Committee for the Right to Emigrate" were arrested; Vasily Barats was briefly confined in a psychiatric hospital, and Georgy Shepelev sentenced to six months' imprisonment.

During the year more well-known human rights campaigners were imprisoned. These included Tatyana Velikanova, sentenced in August 1980 to a total of nine years' imprisonment and internal exile; Alexander Lavut, given three years' in December; and Genrikh Altunyan, given a 12-year sentence in March. In March the Soviet authorities arrested the former prisoner of conscience, Anatoly Marchenko. Amnesty International also worked on the case of Vazif Meylanov, a mathematician from Dagestan, who demonstrated peacefully against the internal exile of Dr Andrei Sakharov, and was sentenced in December to a total of nine years' imprisonment. Others adopted during the year as prisoners of conscience included campaigners for workers' rights (Vsevolod Kuvakin), feminists (Natalya Maltseva, Natalya Lazareva) and distributors of unofficial writings (Iosif Dyadkin, Sergei Gorbachev).

Some prisoners of conscience were convicted on false criminal charges. Would-be emigrants Alexander Maximov and Father Myron Sas-Zhurakovsky were sentenced for "violation of passport regulations". Another would-be emigrant, Valery Pilnikov, was given a five-year sentence after being falsely charged with "malicious hooliganism" and a Baptist, Vladimir Kishkun, a one-year sentence for "hooliganism". Some dissenters, like the Estonian Methodist Herbert Murd, lost their jobs as a result of official harassment and were charged with "parasitism": this may consist of not having paid employment for four months in any year.

The Soviet authorities continued to confine dissenters in psychiatric hospitals for political rather than medical reasons. Several prisoners of conscience were arrested and confined indefinitely to special psychiatric hospitals, the most severe form of psychiatric detention, intended for people who "represent a special danger to society". They included Algirdas Statkevicius, a Lithuanian Helsinki monitor, Viktor Davydov, a legal consultant, Anatoly Cherkasov, who attempted to leave the Soviet Union illegally, Aleksander Kuzkin, who circulated unofficial writings and leaflets, and Alexei Nikitin, a campaigner for workers' rights. However confinement to ordinary psychiatric hospitals has been more common. For example this was the fate of Hanna Mykhaylenko, a Ukrainian teacher, arrested for circulating unofficial reports of human rights violations; Lutheras Lukavicius, a Lithuanian former prisoner of conscience; Vladimir Khailo, a Baptist would-be emigrant; and two "dissenting" Adventists, Anatoly and Pavel Lysenko.

Many dissenters were confined in psychiatric hospitals for brief periods, particularly during the summer of 1980 when the Olympic Games took place in Moscow. Many prisoners of conscience in custody awaiting trial were sent to psychiatric hospitals to undergo psychiatric examination.

Amnesty International continued to receive reports of prisoners of conscience being ill-treated in psychiatric hospitals, particularly with powerful drugs. At the beginning of 1981 Alexei Nikitin was confined in the Dnepropetrovsk Special Psychiatric Hospital after discussing his workers' rights activities with foreign journalists, in spite of the fact that shortly before his arrest he had been independently examined by a Soviet psychiatrist, Dr Anatoly Koryagin, and found to be mentally sound. From mid-January to mid-March he was reported to have been held in isolation and given multiple injections of drugs "bringing him severe pain and disorientation". Other prisoners of conscience reported to have been ill-treated in this way included: Anna Chertkova, Vladimir Klebanov, Iosif Terelya, and Alexander Shatravka, who was again confined in a psychiatric hospital not long after being released. Amnesty International was concerned that prisoners of conscience were kept with criminally insane and violent inmates. For example Algirdas Statkevicius was reported to be held in Chernyakhovsk Special Psychiatric Hospital in a ward containing four psychotic murderers; in Alma-Ata Special Psychiatric Hospital Nikolai Baranov was reported to have twice been severely beaten.

During the year the authorities imprisoned the remaining active members of the unofficial Working Commission to Investigate the Use of Psychiatry for Political Purposes. Since its inception in early 1977 this group has played a major role in exposing political abuses of psychiatry and in September 1980 issued its 24th *Information*

Bulletin. Those imprisoned were: Vyacheslav Bakhmin, sentenced in September 1980 to three years' imprisonment; Dr Leonard Ternovsky, a physician and Helsinki monitor, sentenced in December to three years' imprisonment; Irina Grivnina, in custody; Felix Serebrov, in custody; and Dr Anatoly Koryagin, a psychiatrist, in custody. Alexander Podrabinek, the sixth member of the group, was rearrested while serving a sentence of internal exile and in January 1981 sentenced to three years' imprisonment. His brother, Kirill Podrabinek, was rearrested at the end of a previous sentence and in January was also sentenced to three years for "anti-Soviet slander".

Further charges were brought against several prisoners of conscience before the end of their sentences leading to their continued detention: Vasyl Lisovy and Razmik Markosyan were arrested and convicted on false charges while serving sentences of internal exile; Mark Morozov was charged with "anti-Soviet agitation and propaganda" in his place of internal exile and in December 1980 given a further 13 years' imprisonment and internal exile; Vasyl Barladyanu was given an additional three years for allegedly carrying out "anti-Soviet slander" among prisoners in his place of imprisonment; Alexander Bolonkin was charged with conducting "anti-Soviet propaganda" within a corrective labour colony and for the second time faces an extension of his prison sentence.

Conditions in Soviet corrective labour colonies and prisons continued to be characterized by chronic hunger, overwork in difficult conditions, inadequate medical treatment and arbitrary deprivation of the limited rights to correspondence and family visits. Amnesty International received detailed information on the harsh conditions in the new "special regime" zone (the most severe category) in Perm corrective labour colony No. 36. Prisoners of conscience imprisoned there protested in September 1980 that conditions were calculated to bring about their "gradual psychological and physical destruction". In September Amnesty International issued a paper: *Conditions of Imprisonment in Chistopol Prison.*

Amnesty International learned of numerous prisoners of conscience being punished while serving their sentences. Among those known to have been confined for long periods in prison conditions within corrective labour colonies were Yury Orlov, Mykola Matusevych (subsequently transferred to even harsher conditions in Chistopol prison), Sergei Kovalyov (also transferred to Chistopol prison), Anatoly Shcharansky and Myroslav Marynovych. At the beginning of 1980 the Baptist pastor, Mikhail Khorev, was reported to have been placed in a punishment cell in a corrective labour colony in Omsk after officials had found a Bible in his possession.

During the year Amnesty International interceded on behalf of a number of prisoners of conscience whose poor state of health was giving cause for concern. Among those for whom it issued special appeals were: Vyacheslav Chornovil, on hunger-strike, Alexander Bolonkin, Oksana Meshko, Dmitry Minyakov, on hunger-strike, Mart Niklus, on hunger-strike, Yuri Kukk, died on hunger-strike, Mykola Rudenko, on hunger-strike and Zinovy Antonyuk.

Amnesty International received persistent reports about hardships facing prisoners of conscience sentenced to internal exile in remote areas. It continued to campaign for the release of Dr Andrei Sakharov, who remained in enforced exile in the city of Gorky.

During the year Amnesty International learned of about 30 death sentences, most for murder or war crimes. However, several people are known to have been sentenced to death for non-violent crimes. For example Yuri Khorobidze, a Georgian official, was reported in the Soviet press to have been executed after being convicted of taking bribes. Four other Georgians were sentenced to be shot for economic crimes. Two of them were convicted of "illegally producing and selling adulterated fruit juice"; the other two were sentenced for their part in a swindle involving illegally-made knitted goods. Amnesty International, being unconditionally opposed to the use of the death penalty, appealed against the death sentence in all these cases.

During the year the Soviet news media made several attacks on Amnesty International. On 25 and 26 August 1980 the Soviet newspaper *Izvestia* accused Amnesty International of committing "anti-Soviet sabotage" and of being "maintained by imperialist secret services". Amnesty International issued an international news release on 12 November rejecting these charges. It pointed out that:

> "governments at the other end of the political spectrum have accused us of being run by the KGB . . . They have attacked us after we published detailed information about human rights violations in their countries. Instead of replying to the information or ending the abuses, they have tried to discredit us."

A further attack on Amnesty International at the end of November in the newspaper *Sovietskaya Rossiya* accused it of waging psychological warfare against the Soviet Union. In February V. Skosyrev, an *Izvestia* correspondent, interviewed Amnesty International's Secretary General. On 16 and 19 March *Izvestia* repeated its accusation.

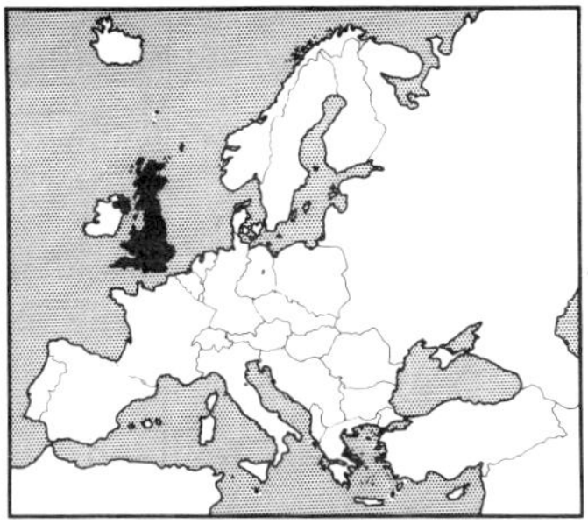

United Kingdom

The situation in the Maze prison in Northern Ireland was the main concern of Amnesty International.

Inmates of that prison convicted of politically motivated offences continued a protest begun in 1976 by refusing to wear prison clothes or do prison work. All the prisoners concerned had been convicted of offences involving the use or advocacy of violence and none have been adopted by Amnesty International as prisoners of conscience. Their demands have been expressed differently during the protest: originally, the prisoners demanded "special category status", the favourable status granted by the government to prisoners convicted of politically motivated offences carried out before March 1976. Later they demanded less specifically "political status", which finally crystallized into five demands. The two most important were that prisoners convicted of politically motivated offences be exempt from the requirement to do prison work and be allowed to wear their own clothing.

From the start the authorities responded by punishing the protesting prisoners for violating the prison rules. The regime of punishments consisted of substantial loss of remission, loss of all privileges (including association with other prisoners and access to educational and recreational facilities), and regular periods of confinement to cells. Certain facilities, such as exercise, could be taken only in prison uniform or naked; the prisoners refused to comply with these conditions. The government maintained its position when, from 1978 onwards, the prisoners refused to wash or clean their cells, which they smeared with excreta. Amnesty International takes no position on the issue of special status for any prisoners, and did not support the aims of the protest. However on several occasions it expressed its concern to the authorities that the cumulative effect of the punishments and conditions might deprive the prisoners of facilities which should be unconditional and afforded to all prisoners at all times.

In August 1978 some of the prisoners submitted a complaint to the European Commission of Human Rights, alleging that the government subjected them to "torture, inhuman or degrading treatment or punishment". They also claimed that the requirement to wear a prison uniform and to work, despite their deeply held beliefs, violated their right of freedom of belief and conscience. Although stating that they were not complaining about their trials as such, they argued that the state, in trying them under emergency legislation, had recognized, at least for the purpose of their trial, that their acts and their associations were political in character.

The commission's decision was published in June 1980. The commission had no doubt that the prisoners' conditions, especially those resulting from the "dirty protest", were inhuman and degrading, but found that they were self-imposed. The combination of disciplinary punishments and conditions of detention did not constitute a breach of the convention. The prisoners were not entitled to a status of political prisoner, under either national or international law.

On the other hand the commission considered that if prisoners undertake what is regarded as an unlawful challenge to the authority of the prison administration, this does not absolve the state from its obligation to safeguard the health and well-being of all prisoners.

The commission expressed its concern "at the inflexible approach of the state authorities which has been concerned more to punish offenders against prison discipline than to explore ways of resolving such a serious deadlock". Following the commission's report, the authorities expressed their willingness to seek a solution, but said that they would not treat prisoners convicted of politically motivated offences any differently than they treated all prisoners. During the spring and summer of 1980 there were a number of improvements in the facilities offered to protesting prisoners which considerably abated Amnesty International's concerns, but these did not meet the prisoners' central demands regarding exemption from prison work and clothing.

On the crucial issue of clothing the government offered the prisoners exercise in physical training clothes, rather than in prison uniform, and on 23 October 1980 decided to abolish the prison uniform altogether, substituting prison-issue "civilian-type" clothes. This did not satisfy the prisoners' demand that they be allowed to wear their own clothes, and the protesting prisoners rejected these prison-issued clothes.

On 27 October 1980 seven prisoners went on hunger-strike in support of the "five demands". In early December 1980 they were joined by another 33 prisoners, including three women in Armagh prison.

On 28 November 1980 an Amnesty International delegation met representatives of the government. Amnesty International suggested that, without granting special category or political status, there were still options left to the government within its stated policy of not granting any different treatment to politically motivated prisoners. The government outlined the relaxations on punishments it had introduced and the changes affecting conforming prisoners, such as the "civilian-type" clothing and the possibility for prisoners to follow educational courses instead of doing prison work. If the prisoners were to give up their protest, they, too, would benefit from these new aspects of the regime; they could also have lost remission restored with good behaviour.

When loss of life appeared imminent on 18 December 1980, Amnesty International sent an urgent telex to the Secretary of State for Northern Ireland, suggesting that the authorities allow all prisoners, including those involved in the protest, to wear their own clothes during visits, evening and weekend association, in the hope that this would end the hunger-strike and save life. As conforming prisoners already had this as a privilege, it would not amount to any different treatment. The prisoners decided to end the hunger-strike that same day, before this message was conveyed to them. The prisoners appear to have decided to end their fast after being informed in detail of the facilities available to all conforming prisoners. However, after the strike ended, confrontation soon resumed.

By the end of January 1981 more than 400 prisoners had returned to the "dirty protest".

On 1 March 1981 Bobby Sands, serving a 14-year sentence for firearms offences, went on hunger-strike in support of full "political status" for all republican prisoners in the Maze prison. On 19 March three more prisoners joined the hunger-strike. Meanwhile on 2 March all the other protesting prisoners ended their "dirty" protest, in order not to distract attention from the hunger-strike. On 10 April 1981 Amnesty International wrote again to the Secretary of State, reiterating its suggestion that the impasse might be broken if all prisoners, including those refusing prison work and prison-issue clothing, were allowed to wear their own clothes during visits, evening and weekend association. Amnesty International suggested that, since the prisoners had come off the "dirty protest" and were willing to clean their own cells, the level of punishments or withdrawal of privileges could be reduced accordingly. All the women prisoners in Armagh prison had been allowed to wear their own clothes since 1972; even those refusing prison work were allowed a degree of association and educational facilities.

However the government remained firm in its position and the prisoners continued their hunger-strike. By the end of April 1981 Bobby Sands, who had been elected as a Member of the United Kingdom Parliament in a by-election on 9 April 1981, was nearing death.

An Irish prisoner in Britain who refused to wear prison clothes from 1 January 1980 as a gesture of solidarity with the prisoners in the Maze was disciplined with the full range of punishments, including confinement in the segregation unit of Wakefield prison. Exercise outside his cell, visits and attendance at religious services were made conditional upon his wearing prison uniform. As a result of his refusal to wear this uniform, Joseph Patrick Hackett, who has an artificial leg, spent 11 months in continuous solitary confinement in his cell with no facilities for exercise. On 9 March 1981 Amnesty International wrote to the Home Office saying that it believed that the combined effect of the punishments, including the withdrawal of basic facilities unless the prisoner conformed fully to the prison rules, amounted to inhuman and degrading treatment.

There have been alterations to almost every stage of the criminal justice process in Northern Ireland, as applied in cases of offences with a political background. Although specific changes often purport to be mere technical adjustments to meet the exceptional situation, the overall effect has been a weakening of the legal system entailing a threat to fundamental rights.

The *Report of an Amnesty International Mission to Northern Ireland (28 November-6 December 1977)* published in 1978 had linked the ill-treatment of people detained in police custody to such changes in the law. Following certain recommendations by a government committee of inquiry allegations of ill-treatment have been considerably reduced. However Amnesty International was still concerned about alleged abuses of the extended powers of arrest and detention.

People arrested under the Prevention of Terrorism (Temporary Provisions) Act 1976 (which apllies throughout the United Kingdom) can be held for 48 hours on the authority of the police alone. The Secretary of State for Northern Ireland (or, in Great Britain, the Home Secretary) can extend this period for another five days. Although these powers may only be applied to people suspected of involvement in acts of terrorism, they have allegedly been used to detain people holding minority political opinions, or regarded as supporters of the aims (though not necessarily the means) of violent political groups.

A decision by Lord Chief Justice Lowry in June 1980 in the case of Martin Lynch virtually nullified the control of the courts in Northern Ireland over the arrest and detention of suspects by the police under the emergency legislation. Lord Chief Justice Lowry rejected any judicial responsibility to provide the remedy of *habeas corpus* even against "an unacceptable but ostensibly lawful exercise of the powers of arrest" such as repeated arrest and detention by the police of the same individual on the same suspicion, without bringing charges. The court had no power to inquire into the reasonableness of the arrest, he said; a remedy should be provided by the executive. There was therefore no effective remedy against arbitrary use of the emergency powers of arrest and detention by the police — contrary to international law.

The ruling in the Martin Lynch case also exposed the fact that, at least in Northern Ireland, the writ of *habeas corpus* does not provide a safeguard against irregular or even unlawful treatment of people detained under these powers. Reference to a case decided in 1654 made it clear that the ill-treatment of a prisoner would not itself be a ground for *habeas corpus.*

Amnesty International sent an observer to the appeal hearing on 12 September 1980 in the case of Stephen Paul McCaul. In December 1979 he was found guilty of hijacking buses, burning a bus, burglaries and certain associated firearms offences. The evidence against him consisted of oral and written statements alleged to have been made by him while he was questioned at Castlereagh police station in Belfast. Stephen Paul McCaul was 15 years old at the time. He was mentally retarded, attended a special school and could neither read nor write, although he could write his name. Although the police were aware of these facts he was held incommunicado and questioned without his parents or a lawyer or other third party present, in breach of regulations. According to uncontroverted psychiatric evidence the boy had a mental age of seven and was highly suggestible. The psychiatrist said that he could not accept that Stephen McCaul could have dictated the statement alleged to have been made by him. The judge rejected the defence's case and sentenced Stephen Paul McCaul to three years' detention in a Young Offenders Centre. The judgment was upheld on appeal.

During its meeting with the government about the Maze prison Amnesty International raised the case and expressed serious concern about what it regarded as a highly unsafe conviction. The authorities said they would look into the case. Amnesty International was subsequently informed that Stephen Paul McCaul had been released in early 1981.

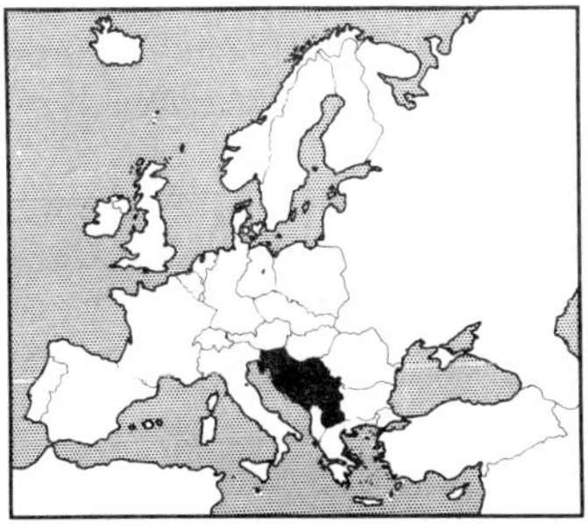

Yugoslavia

The past year has seen an increase in political trials. In June 1980 the Federal Public Prosecutor spoke in a newspaper interview of a rise in the number of political offences since the end of 1979, which he attributed to international tensions and to increased activity by political emigres and internal "enemies" following the illness and death (on 4 May 1980) of President Tito. In July 1980 Amnesty International wrote to the Federal Public Prosecutor expressing concern at the rising number of political trials and at the heavy sentences imposed on people convicted of "hostile propaganda" under Article 133 of the criminal code. It also reiterated its concern at the vague formulation of this article which enabled it to be used to imprison individuals for the non-violent expression of their beliefs, in contravention of international human rights instruments to which Yugoslavia is a party. *Tanjug,* the official Yugoslav news agency, reported that a meeting of public prosecutors on 21 April 1981 had noted that the number of political offences had risen over the previous year to 553, of which 93 per cent were characterized as "minor verbal misdemeanours", and had decided that no more "compromises" would be made in dealing with political offenders. This decision appears to have been partly prompted by a renewed outbreak of nationalist unrest in the predominantly Albanian-populated autonomous province of Kosovo in March and early April.

Prisoners of conscience adopted by Amnesty International in the past year have included 11 ethnic Albanians. Eight from Kosovo were sentenced on 9 June 1980 to between three and eight years' imprisonment by the district court of Pristina on charges of "hostile propaganda" and "association to carry out hostile activity". The eight accused — Shefqet Jashari, Ramadan Pllana, Avdi Kelmendi, Avdyl Lahu, Isa Demaj, Sulejman Quqalla, Skender Jashari and Hysen Gervalla — were reportedly among several hundred people detained in Kosovo in late 1979 after anti-government pamphlets had been circulated and anti-government slogans had been painted on walls in towns in the province. In July 1980 a further three ethnic Albanians, from Macedonia, were sentenced by the district court of Skopje to between three and six years' imprisonment. They were charged under Article 133 with having presented "a malicious picture of the position of the Albanian nationality in Yugoslavia with a view to destroying the Yugoslav nations' and nationalities' brotherhood, unity and equality". Amnesty International received unconfirmed reports that there was at least one other trial of Albanian nationalists in Prizren in early summer 1980.

Other cases taken up for adoption or investigation by Amnesty International in the past year included those of a Franciscan novice and a student at a Franciscan seminary, two Moslem religious officials, and an Orthodox priest, his brother and two acquaintances — all from the Republic of Bosnia-Hercegovina.

According to reports Franjo Vidovic (22), a Franciscan novice and Ivan Turudic (20), a student at the Franciscan seminary in Visoko were arrested early in April, following a police raid on the seminary at the end of March 1980. It was reported that during searches police found cuttings from the newspaper *Frankfurter Allgemeine Zeitung* (published in the Federal Republic of Germany (FRG)), articles from a Croatian emigre journal and nationalist poems. On 26 May 1980 Franjo Vidovic and Ivan Turudic were sentenced by the district court of Sarajevo on charges of "hostile propaganda" to six and five and a half years' imprisonment respectively.

Amnesty International was investigating the cases of Muharem Hasenbegovic (aged 35), chief Imam of the mosque in Gorazde and Ago Curovac (aged 52), a watch-maker and the mosque's treasurer. In September 1980 they were sentenced to four years' imprisonment on charges of having "provoked national and religious hatred or intolerance". The charges were allegedly based on conversations in which Ago Curovac criticized the authorities, and on a sermon preached by Muharem Hasanbegovic in which he urged parents to bring up their children in Moslem traditions.

On 30 December 1980 the district court of Sarajevo sentenced the Orthodox priest, Father Nedjo Janjic, his brother Momcilo Janjic, and two friends to prison terms of between four and six years on charges of "provoking religious and racial hatred". According to an official press report, Father Janjic (aged 24):

> "took advantage of the religious ceremony of the christening of his son to sing at his house, together with a number of guests, including members of the parish church council, nationalist songs, and to incite those present to chauvinist euphoria".

Although the prohibition of incitement to national, racial or religious hatred is an internationally accepted restriction of the right to freedom of expression Amnesty International considers that the singing of nationalist songs at a private christening party could not reasonably be held to constitute such incitement. Amnesty International has therefore adopted all four men as prisoners of conscience.

In October 1980 Amnesty International sent two observers to the trial of Dragutin Trumbetas by the district court of Zagreb. In May 1980 Dragutin Trumbetas, a 42-year-old typesetter and artist, was arrested on his return to Yugoslavia after 14 years as a migrant worker in the FRG. Customs officials had found a number of Yugoslav emigre journals in his luggage and letters he had received from the editors of one of them. He was charged with "participation in hostile activity" and "hostile propaganda". He was released from preventive detention after a month. The court found him guilty on both charges, but taking into account mitigating circumstances imposed a sentence below the prescribed minimum. He received a sentence of 18 months' imprisonment, and at the end of April 1981 was still at liberty pending appeal. In a letter to the Federal Secretary of Justice Amnesty

International stated that it considered that the evidence against him was not sufficient for conviction. Amnesty International considered that Dragutin Trumbetas' conviction contravened international human rights standards and was incompatible with Yugoslavia's international commitments. Amnesty International urged that his appeal be upheld.

In February 1981 Amnesty International sent an observer to the trial of Dr Franjo Tudjman (aged 59), a former prisoner of conscience, by the district court of Zagreb. Dr Tudjman, a historian, veteran partisan and former army general was indicted for "hostile propaganda" with aid from abroad. He was accused of having "falsely presented the position of the Croat people as well as the implementation of the democratic freedoms of Yugoslav citizens". The charges were based on statements in interviews with three foreign journalists between 1977 and 1980, and in a discussion with a Serbian student, Vladimir Markovic, an adopted prisoner of conscience (see *Amnesty International Report 1980*). Dr Tudjman was sentenced to three years' imprisonment; he remained at liberty pending appeal. To Amnesty International's knowledge Vladimir Markovic, who in February 1979 was confined by court order to psychiatric hospital following the publication in an emigre journal of a letter in which he had cited Dr Tudjman, was still detained in the psychiatric wing of Belgrade prison hospital at the end of the year.

On 16 February 1981, the eve of Dr Tudjman's trial, *Tanjug* announced that three petitions to the Yugoslav State Presidency had been rejected. The first petition, of June 1980, signed by 36 Belgrade intellectuals, called for an amnesty for people who had "committed the offence of expressing prohibited political views". The second, of October 1980, signed by over 100 academics, lawyers, writers and artists, called for the deletion of a passage making it a criminal offence to depict socio-political conditions in Yugoslavia "falsely and maliciously" from Article 133 of the criminal code, dealing with "hostile propaganda". The third, of November 1980, signed by 43 Zagreb intellectuals, called for an amnesty for political prisoners. Although the constitution guarantees the right of petition, the *Tanjug* statement said that the petitions had been rejected as "legally and politically unacceptable", and charged their authors with "evil and immoral intentions" and with having deliberately organized a "campaign to discredit Yugoslavia's high reputation in the world".

On 21 November 1980 Dobroslav Paraga, a 19-year-old law student from Zagreb who had collected signatures for the Zagreb petition was arrested. On 25 November he was brought before an examining magistrate, when he made a confession on which his subsequent indictment was based. He later retracted this confession, stating that he had made it under pressure from the police who had denied him food from his arrest until 26 November and had subjected him to repeated prolonged interrogations and to intimidation including death threats. This retraction was reportedly not recorded in the court dossier until 6 January 1981, nor was it mentioned in the indictment. On 16 March 1981 he was formally charged with "hostile propaganda" and "hostile activity". According to the indictment in July 1980 he had visited in the FRG Stjepan Bilandzic, a Croatian political emigre from whom he "received the task" of starting a dissident bulletin in Zagreb and money for this purpose as well as numerous emigre publications, found in the Zagreb flat of a friend of Dobroslav Paraga, Ernest Brajder. He was also accused of having obtained signatures for the petition under false pretences, and of having sent a copy of the petition and a list of signatories to *Der Spiegel,* a magazine published in the FRG. Ernest Brajder was arrested on 24 November 1980 and committed suicide on 27 November, according to official reports. No further details concerning his death were available at the end of April 1981. By the end of April 1981 Dobroslav Paraga was still detained awaiting trial. Amnesty International appealed to the authorities to release him and to drop all charges.

On 2 April 1981 Vlado Gotovac, a writer and former prisoner of conscience, was charged with "hostile propaganda" with aid from abroad and with "provoking national hatred and discord" in interviews he had given to three foreign journalists between 1977 and 1980 in which, according to the indictment, "he falsely represented the position of the Croatian people and also the realization of the democratic freedoms of the citizens of the Socialist Federal Republic of Yugoslavia". He remained at liberty pending trial, Amnesty International appealed for the charges to be withdrawn.

Dr Marko Veselica, an economist and former prisoner of conscience, was arrested on 24 April 1981 on similar charges, based on an interview he gave in August 1980 to a news magazine published in the FRG, in which he claimed that the Republic of Croatia was economically and politically disadvantaged within the Yugoslav federation. He was also accused of "participation in hostile activity", for allegedly sending articles about human rights violations to political emigres for publication and for presentation to the Conference on Security and Cooperation in Europe held in Madrid. Amnesty International appealed for his release from detention, and for the charges to be dropped.

In April 1981 after reports of numerous arrests in Kosovo, following nationalist demonstrations and riots by ethnic Albanians, Amnesty International asked the authorities for details of the charges against the detainees and called for an urgent review of all cases and the release of all those in detention for having exercised, non-violently, their right to freedom of expression. According to official statements in the press the demonstrations began on 11 March when some students at Pristina university protested about living conditions. On 25 and 26 March there were further demonstrations in Prizren and Pristina. According to official figures 23 demonstrators and 12 police were injured and 21 people arrested. These disturbances grew into widespread demonstrations and riots on 1, 2 and 3 April in Pristina and other towns in Kosovo. Demonstrators, including students, high school pupils, workers and peasants, reportedly demanded that Kosovo — a constituent part of the Republic of Serbia — be given the status of a republic within the Yugoslav federation. A number of demonstrators reportedly called for Kosovo's union with neighbouring Albania. The demonstrations culminated in clashes with security forces in which, according to official statements, up to 11 people were killed and 261 injured. Unofficial sources have alleged that the numbers were far higher. On 24 April Kosovo's Vice-Premier announced that 194 people had been sentenced in summary trials for their part in the demonstrations and that 28 others were detained for investigation as suspected organizers.

Violations of criminal procedure have undermined legal safeguards for the accused, contravening both the national law and international standards. A number of prisoners of conscience have been arrested without warrant. Yugoslav law stipulates that in exceptional cases the militia and state security police may detain a person without formal charges for up to three days. Several reports have indicated that during this period detainees have been subjected to severe psychological and sometimes physical pressure to obtain confessions, and that this period has sometimes been illegally extended beyond three days. Pressure has also been applied to witnesses to obtain testimonies, including holding them in police custody for up to three days. In several cases the power of the police to deny a passport, without giving reasons, has been used to pressurize witnesses, who were migrant workers on holiday or would-be migrant workers, into testifying against the accused. The investigation of political cases has sometimes been conducted almost exclusively by the state security police in contravention of legal provisions.

Amnesty International has also been concerned that the accused's right to a lawyer of his or her choice and access to this lawyer has in a number of cases been denied or seriously restricted. Contrary to Yugoslav law the accused has not always been informed of the right to defence counsel. Some have been obliged to accept a state-appointed lawyer. In one case the accused was not informed by the investigating magistrate that a lawyer had been engaged by his family for him, and this lawyer was denied access to his client. It was reportedly not until over four months after his arrest — two days before his trial — that the accused was granted access to defence counsel. There have also been complaints that lawyers have been denied the right to examine the dossier or have only been allowed to take handwritten notes of the contents of the dossier on court premises. The principle of public trial has also been violated by restricting access to the courtroom to a few people issued with official passes. The court has often refused to allow evidence and the calling of witnesses for the defence. Amnesty International believes that such trials have been weighted in favour of the prosecution and that internationally recognized standards of fair trial have not been met.

Amnesty International continued to be concerned about prison conditions for prisoners of conscience, in particular poor diet, ill-treatment by guards and punishment for disciplinary offences by isolation or solitary confinement, sometimes for long periods.

Despite numerous appeals by Amnesty International to the head of state to mark the state anniversary on 29 November by granting pardon to all prisoners of conscience, only five cases taken up by Amnesty International benefited from pardons granted to 82 criminal and political prisoners. Fatmir Salihu was released and Professor Davor Aras, whose sentence had been suspended on health grounds since March 1979, was exempted from serving the remainder. Three others received a reduction of sentence of between six months and one year.

The Yugoslav criminal code prescribes a discretionary death sentence for particularly grave murder cases, certain "crimes against the state" and acts of political terrorism. During the year Amnesty International learned of three death sentences passed and two executions.

The Middle East and North Africa

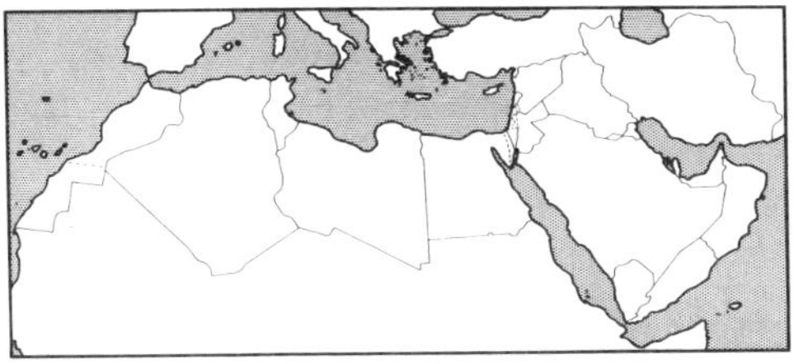

The year May 1980 to April 1981 saw political unrest in many countries of the region, which stretches from Morocco in the west to Iran in the east. However all the changes of government took place within the existing institutions. Open war broke out between Iran and Iraq in September 1980 influencing political developments throughout the region; the Palestinian question was affected by the continuing moves by Egypt and Israel towards normalized relations, by the growing tension between Syria and Israel, and by the complex state of affairs in Lebanon which threatened war as the year under review ended.

During the year Amnesty International called attention to human rights abuses taking place in many countries of the region. For a number — Saudi Arabia, Yemen Arab Republic, United Arab Emirates, Qatar, Kuwait, Oman and Lebanon — the information available on violations of concern to Amnesty International was not sufficient to allow an individual country entry in this report. Amnesty International addressed appeals and inquiries concerning human rights violations to most governments of the region. Many, including Libya, Tunisia, Egypt, Syria, People's Democratic Republic of Yemen (PDRY), Bahrain and Iran, occasionally acknowledged receipt but did not reply in detail. Some, such as Morocco and Iraq, responded infrequently but on rare occasions they did reply in substance; others, such as Jordan and Israel replied regularly and often in substance. When governments did respond, they invariably defended their actions.

During the year Amnesty International worked on behalf of more than 600 individual prisoners in the region known or suspected to be prisoners of conscience: in Morocco, Algeria, Tunisia, Libya, Egypt, Israel and the Occupied Territories, Jordan, Syria, Iraq, People's Democratic Republic of Yemen, Oman and Bahrain. Amnesty

International was concerned about deficient trial procedures and detention without trial of political prisoners in Morocco, Algeria, Libya, Israel and the Occupied Territories, Jordan, Syria, Iraq, Saudi Arabia, People's Democratic Republic of Yemen, Bahrain and Iran.

Serious allegations of torture or ill-treatment were received from many countries in the region including Morocco, Algeria, Tunisia, Libya, Egypt, Israel and the Occupied Territories, Jordan, Syria, Iraq, Bahrain and Iran. The *Report and Recommendations of an Amnesty International Mission to the Government of the State of Israel, 3-7 June 1979,* which was published in September 1980, found that administrative and legal procedures followed after arrest enhanced the possibility of ill-treatment of security suspects and did not enable the Israeli authorities to bring forward conclusive evidence to refute allegations of ill-treatment. In April 1981 Amnesty International published a report, *Iraq: Evidence of Torture,* which detailed medical findings that strongly supported allegations of torture in Iraq.

In a number of countries these human rights violations occur under emergency laws which provide the authorities with extraordinary powers restricting the rights of the individual. This is the case in Israel and the Occupied Territories, Jordan, Syria, and People's Democratic Republic of Yemen. Emergency law was lifted in Egypt during the year, but it is too early to assess the implications. In addition, most other states, although not having emergency law as such, have special procedures for offences against the security of the state which substantially restrict the rights of the defendant: such procedures were applied during the year in countries including Morocco, Algeria, Libya and Iraq.

All states in the region retain the death penalty in their legislation: from Israel and the Occupied Territories, where it applies to few offences and has not been inflicted since 1961, to Iraq and Iran, where a broad range of offences carry the death penalty and where, in the past year, hundreds of people have been executed. Official executions were carried out during the year in Tunisia, Libya, Egypt, Jordan, Syria, Iraq, Saudi Arabia, the People's Democratic Republic of Yemen and Iran. In addition a number of extrajudicial executions were reported in Syria and Iraq, and the Libyan authorities appear to have encouraged the shooting and killing of a number of Libyan citizens abroad. In Morocco, Kuwait and the United Arab Emirates death sentences were passed but, as far as Amnesty International is aware, none were carried out.

A growing regard for human rights was demonstrated in regional meetings both of governmental and of non-governmental organizations. Amnesty International noted with interest the formation in May 1980 of the *Union interafricaine des avocats,* Inter-African Lawyers Union, which has members from Morocco, Algeria, Tunisia and Egypt, and its creation of a *Commission permanente des droits de l'homme et des peuples,* Permanent Commission of Human and People's Rights. In December 1980 the Arab Lawyers Union (ALU) organized a conference on Islam and Human Rights jointly with the International Commission of Jurists, which was held in Kuwait. The June 1980 annual meeting of the ALU, which Amnesty International attended, passed a resolution in support of the Amnesty International Stockholm Declaration against the death penalty; and asked the Permanent Bureau of the ALU to seek joint action with other concerned groups, such as Amnesty International and the International Commission of Jurists, towards the abolition of torture and the death penalty. At this meeting the ALU also denounced the arrests of Syrian lawyers, called for the Syrian Government to reverse its decision to dissolve the elected councils of the Syrian Bar Association, and deplored the Libyan Government's moves to reduce the independence of lawyers. A meeting of the Permanent Bureau of the Arab Lawyers Union, held in Algiers in April 1981, decided to recommend strikes by Arab lawyers to protest against the Libyan measures.

Two promising developments took place on the intergovernmental level. The third Islamic Summit Conference was held in Taif, Saudi Arabia, from 25 to 28 January 1981, and was attended by all governments of the region with the exception of Libya and Iran, as well as several from Africa and Asia. It agreed to establish an Islamic Court of Justice and called upon experts from its member states to meet and draw up the statute of this court. The conference also decided to submit a modified draft document on human rights in Islam for consideration at the Twelfth Islamic Foreign Ministers Conference, to be held in Baghdad, Iraq, in June 1981.

In January 1981 a draft African Charter of Human Rights was adopted during an Organization of African Unity (OAU) meeting of Ministers of Justice of member states, which include Morocco, Algeria, Tunisia, Libya and Egypt. This charter, which envisages the formation of a commission to monitor compliance by States Parties to the charter with human rights principles would, if adopted by the 1981 conference of Heads of State and Government, then be submitted to member states of the OAU for ratification.

During the year Amnesty International published three reports on countries in the region: *Law and Human Rights in the Islamic Republic of Iran,* focusing on the summary proceedings of the Islamic Revolutionary Tribunals which fall far short of internationally recognized standards for a fair trial, and on the frequent use of the death penalty; *Report and Recommendations of an Amnesty International Mission to the Government of the State of Israel,* which found that the administrative and legal safeguards for security suspects in custody were insufficient to protect them from ill-treatment; and *Iraq: Evidence of Torture,* based on detailed medical findings of the examinations of 15 alleged victims of torture in Iraq. In February 1981 Amnesty International sent a mission to Morocco to discuss the organization's concerns with relevant Moroccan officials. A memorandum of that mission was to be submitted to the Moroccan Government during 1981.

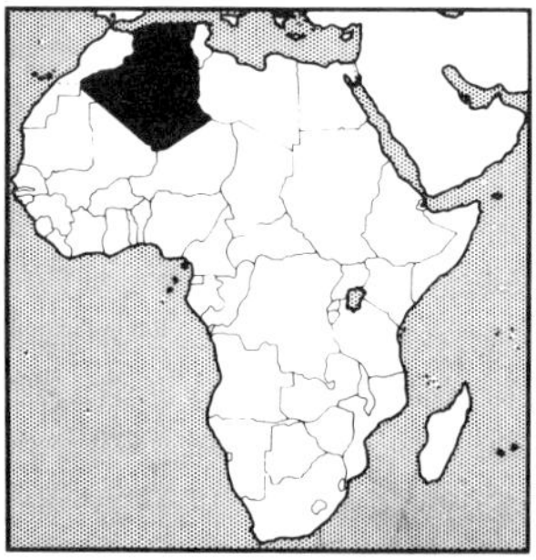

Algeria

During the year Amnesty International welcomed the lifting of all restrictions on its adopted prisoner of conscience, Ahmed Ben Bella; it also took up for further investigation the cases of four prisoners sentenced on charges of plotting against state security. It continued to follow the cases of those arrested in the aftermath of clashes that had taken place in March and April 1980 between security forces and demonstrators in the Berber Kabyle region. To Amnesty International's knowledge there were no executions in Algeria during the year.

On 30 October 1980 the government announced that all remaining restrictions on former President Ahmed Ben Bella would be lifted to mark the anniversary of the 1954 uprising against French occupation on 1 November. Ahmed Ben Bella, the first President of independent Algeria, had been arrested in June 1965, following a coup led by then Minister of Defence Houari Boumedienne. He was held in detention until July 1979, when he was transferred to house arrest in M'sila, southeast of Algiers, where he remained until all restrictions were lifted. In a recorded message which he sent to his Amnesty International adoption group in Madrid Ahmed Ben Bella said he wanted: "... the Amnesty International group in Madrid to know that my wife and I have and will keep a very, very great regard for what they did for us during those 15 years of silence .... We know that this action ... was not on behalf of one man or one idea, but on behalf of a concept of man, a concept of democracy, of human dignity ... I think that such acts are the best contribution to drawing together the peoples of the West and the Third World, to get them to know each other better and to put them all on the same level."

Following the conviction of five defendants (one of whom had escaped arrest and was tried in his absence) by the Military Tribunal at Blida on 27 December 1980, Amnesty International took up for further investigation the cases of the four who were serving sentences, two of three years and two of six years. The four — two trainee-officers from the Cherchell Military Academy and two civilians — were originally arrested on 2 November 1978, accused of having formed a local cell of the "International Communist Party" with links in Western Europe, and were charged with plotting against state security. Reports received by Amnesty International suggested that the political activities of these individuals were limited to the discussion of leftist literature and the dissemination of their own political views; they were said not to have used nor advocated violence. Amnesty International has not yet been able to confirm these reports.

Amnesty International continued to follow the cases of those arrested in Tizi-Ouzou (the administrative centre of the Berber Kabyle region) in March and April 1980, 24 of whom were charged and scheduled to appear before the State Security Court at Medea. On 21 May 1980 Amnesty International sent a telegram to President Chadli Benjedid urging that "the rights of the defence and the right to a public hearing be respected, in accordance with the International Covenant on Civil and Political Rights which Algeria has signed but has not yet ratified". In June 1980 the 24 accused were provisionally released. At the end of April 1981 they were still provisionally at liberty and Amnesty International continued to follow the cases as the charges had not yet been officially dropped. In March and April 1981 there were renewed demonstrations in the Berber Kabyle region calling for further official measures to promote Berber culture and for the demands of the previous year's actions to be fulfilled, including a chair of Berber studies at the University of Tizi-Ouzou. These demonstrations included the occupation of the University of Tizi-Ouzou for several weeks in March and April 1981 by students supporting increased freedom for Berber cultural expression, a general strike by merchants, students and civil servants, and the holding of public assemblies to secure more attention for Berber culture.

Amnesty International received serious allegations from a number of different sources of very bad prison conditions, and reports that those detained in the Kabyle region in March and April 1980 and the four prisoners sentenced in Blida had been ill-treated. So far Amnesty International has not been able to verify these reports.

Bahrain

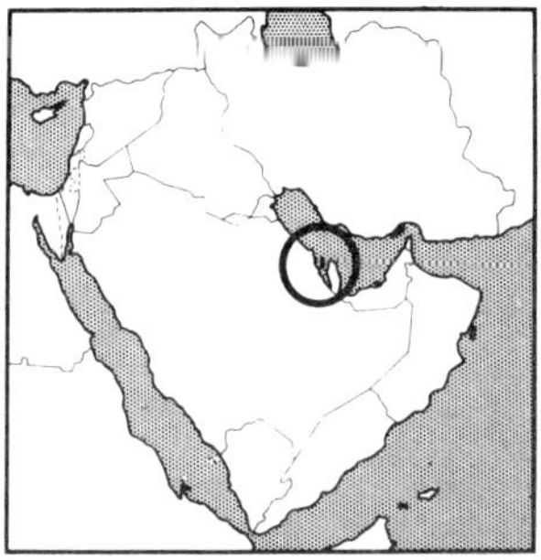

Amnesty International's principal concerns continued to be the arrest and imprisonment of prisoners of conscience, detention without trial, and reports of torture and ill-treatment.

At the end of April 1981 there were eight adopted prisoners of conscience, including: Ibrahim Sanad, an army officer arrested in 1972 and accused of organizing a political cell within the army; Abbas Abdullah'Awaji and Ahmed Al Thawadi, trade unionists who were arrested in 1974 following strikes at the Bahrain smelting works and accused of organizing workers; and Abdulwahid Ahmed Abdulrahman and Abbas Hillal, opposition members arrested in May and November 1976 following the dissolution of the National Assembly in August 1975. Several former adopted prisoners were released in August 1980 and in December on Bahrain's National Day.

Many arrests were reported after street clashes between the police and members of the Shi'i community demonstrating their support for the Iranian regime during several religious ceremonies and festivals. Reliable reports indicated that a considerable number of them, including all the women, were later released. Amnesty International continued to investigate the cases of those still in detention to ascertain whether they were prisoners of conscience.

Amnesty International was concerned about laws, including the State Security Law of 1974 which allows people to be held without charge or trial for up to three years. In practice the detention order is renewable (see *Amnesty International Report 1980*). In a letter of 7 October 1980 to the ruler of Bahrain, Sheikh Issa Bin Salman Al Khalifah, Amnesty International reiterated its concern that this and other laws curtail the freedom of expression and participation in public life, and facilitate imprisonment for the non-violent exercise of human rights. It added that these laws contravene the letter and spirit of the constitution of the State of Bahrain and the Universal Declaration of Human Rights.

A number of allegations reached Amnesty International of torture and ill-treatment. Of particular concern were reports that three people, Jamil Ali Muhsin Al Ali, Karim Al Hibshi, and Muhammad Hassan Madan, who died in May 1980, July 1980 and February 1981 respectively, had died as a result of torture. Each had reportedly been arrested on political charges. Amnesty International called upon the authorities to initiate an independent inquiry into the circumstances of these deaths, and urged that the findings be made public.

Bahrain retains the death penalty for a significant number of offences. However Amnesty International learned of no death sentences or executions during the year.

Egypt

Amnesty International's principal concerns in Egypt were arrest, detention and imprisonment for the non-violent expression of political beliefs, new legislation restricting the freedom of political expression and the death penalty.

During the year a number of significant developments took place which influenced human rights. In May 1980 President Muhammad Anwar Sadat assumed the premiership in addition to the presidency, and the state of emergency, which had been in force for many years, was lifted. The state of emergency was of considerable concern because it had invested the President with extraordinary powers over the judiciary, and had facilitated the arrest and detention of people subsequently considered by Amnesty International to be prisoners of conscience.

In May 1980, before the lifting of the state of emergency and restructuring of the cabinet, a group of prominent Egyptians, including former ministers, academics and lawyers had signed a statement criticizing the government's policies and in particular the political role of the President. They called for the independence of the judiciary, the abolition of all special courts such as state security or military courts, the lifting of all restrictions on freedom of opinion, publication, printing and the press, and the freedom to form associations, trade unions and political parties.

Several new laws were promulgated when the state of emergency was lifted. These included Law 105 on the establishment of state security courts, published in the Official Gazette on 31 May 1980, which established that the state security court comprises three judges from the court of appeal, and provided for two officers of the armed forces to be added by presidential decree. The state security court can try people accused of political offences with which prisoners of conscience have in the past been charged. There is no appeal against judgments made by the state security court. Perhaps the most significant change was that the President's power under the state of emergency to approve or veto court judgments was removed by Law 103 of 1980, which treats the court's decision as final.

On 15 May 1980 Law 95 on "the protection of values from shameful conduct" was promulgated. Offences punishable include opposing religious doctrines, inciting young people to renege on religious and moral values, disseminating false information, and certain offences punishable by imprisonment under existing laws relating to illegal political organizations. Many terms of this law are vague and ill-defined. Sanctions are non-custodial and include being barred from election to the People's Assembly, trade union organizations or press associations, not being allowed to set up or participate in political parties, and being barred from working in certain professions which may influence public opinion, such as journalism.

Amnesty International received reports of numerous arrests on political grounds during the year. These included the arrest in September 1980 of about 50 people accused of illegal political activities in connection with the Communist Party, and more than 20 alleged members of a splinter group of the Islamic Liberation Party. At the end of April 1981 it was not known whether any charges had been preferred.

Further arrests were reported in February 1981 during Cairo's International Book Fair, at which Israel was represented for the first time. Some of those arrested were accused of participating in protests against the Israeli bookstall; others, including Kamel Zouheiri, then head of the Egyptian Journalists' Union, were accused of disseminating anti-Israeli propaganda when they signed a petition calling for a boycott of the Israeli bookstall. All have since been released from detention.

Shortly afterwards President Sadat called on Egyptian journalists working abroad who had written material critical of the Egyptian Government or its policies to return to Egypt before 15 May 1981, when they would benefit from an amnesty.

More than 70 arrests took place in March 1981 when the intelligence services claimed to have uncovered an illegal communist organization. Those arrested were held initially at the Citadel Prison for interrogation but were subsequently transferred to Tora Agricultural Prison, in a suburb of Cairo. A considerable number of those detained were already facing trial before the state security court in Cairo on charges of illegal Communist Party activities between the end of 1977 and August 1979, and had been provisionally released pending the outcome of the trial. Their rearrest caused the trial which began in October 1980 to be postponed again. Amnesty International viewed this trial of 30 people with particular concern because the defendants appeared to be on trial for the non-violent expression of their political beliefs, and they faced a maximum punishment of life imprisonment with hard labour under Law 40 of 1977.

On 29 April 1981 the popular poet Ahmed Fu'ad Negm was arrested in Cairo. He had been in hiding since March 1978, just before being sentenced by a military court on 25 March 1978 to one year's imprisonment with hard labour. His trial followed a meeting with students at Ain Shams University in November 1977 when his poetry was recited and sung. Charges against him included insulting the head of state. Ahmed Fu'ad Negm has been imprisoned many times because of his work, and has been adopted as a prisoner of conscience. He was held in the Citadel Prison in Cairo.

In September 1980 Amnesty International learned of the execution by hanging at Beni Suef Prison of a man convicted of murder. In January and February 1981 it learned of five death sentences passed by criminal courts in Cairo, Mansoura, Minia and Zagazig. All five people, including two women, had been convicted of murder. Amnesty International appealed to President Sadat to commute all the death sentences on humanitarian grounds. In September 1980 press reports indicated a change in legislation which would increase the number of offences punishable by death under Egyptian law. The maximum punishment of life imprisonment with hard labour for rape would be replaced by the death penalty.

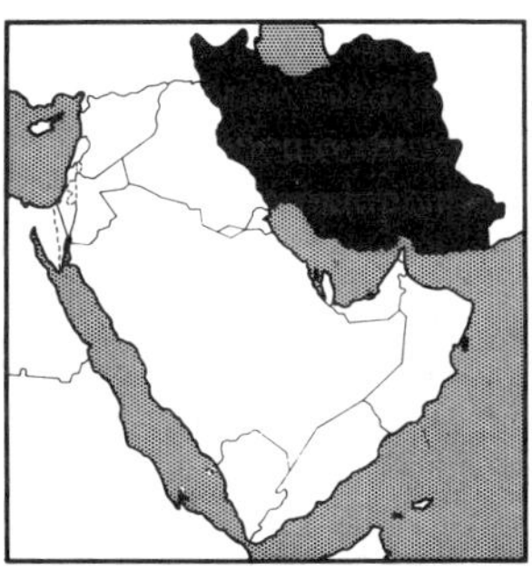

Iran

The main concerns of Amnesty International were executions, the ill-treatment of prisoners, the imprisonment of prisoners of conscience, and the lack of fair trials for political prisoners.

More than 700 executions have taken place in Iran during the past year. This figure, which is based on reports which have appeared in the press outside Iran, must be regarded as the minimum because not all executions have been reported. Offences for which people have been executed included alleged plots against the government, drug-smuggling and selling, espionage, collaboration with Iraqi forces, sexual offences, support of the Kurdish Democratic Party, murder and robbery. Baha'is and Jews have been among those executed, usually on charges of espionage apparently based on the connections members of these religions have with Israel (Baha'i world headquarters are in Israel).

Throughout the year Amnesty International appealed to the authorities to halt executions and on 19 August 1980 wrote to Prime Minister Mohammed Ali Rajai "... we appealed time and time again to the late Shah for a stop to executions ... Since the Revolution we have been sad to observe the continuation of human rights violations and especially the large number of executions which have taken place".

In December 1980 Ayatollah Khomeini ordered an inquiry into reports of torture in Iranian prisons. President Abolhassan Bani-Sadr and subsequently a group of 133 Iranian intellectuals had stated publicly that torture was once again taking place in Iran, but had not mentioned specific instances. The report of the investigating commission had not been made public by the end of April 1981, but two members of the commission, Ali Mohammad Besharati Jahromi and Hojatoleslam Mohammad Montazeri, stated on 12 April and 19 April that allegations of torture were totally unfounded. Amnesty International did not receive any specific allegations of torture during the year, but on several occasions was told that torture was taking place. It has been unable to verify these reports.

In May 1980 Amnesty International published a report *Law and Human Rights in the Islamic Republic of Iran* which found that defendants before Islamic Revolutionary Tribunals were consistently denied fair trials (see *Amnesty International Report 1980*). Many people were executed almost immediately after the imposition of the death sentence, leaving little or no time for the defendant to appeal or petition for clemency. On 20 July 1980 five officers convicted of participation in a conspiracy to overthrow the government were executed approximately 16 hours after their trial was reported to have begun.

Amnesty International expressed its concern about the imprisonment and execution of members of religious minorities to President Abolhassan Bani-Sadr on 24 March 1981 following the execution of two Baha'is.

> "These executions and the imprisonment and execution of other members of the Baha'i religion appear to Amnesty International to indicate a deliberate government policy of religious persecution, in violation of Article 18 of the International Covenant on Civil and Political Rights to which Iran is a State Party. This article states: 'Everyone shall have the right to freedom of thought, conscience and religion. This right shall include freedom to have or to adopt a religion or belief of his choice, and

freedom, either individually or in community with others and in public or private, to manifest his religion or belief in worship, observance, practice and teaching.' "

Amnesty International asked the President about the whereabouts of nine members of the National Spiritual Assembly of the Baha'is of Iran and two other Baha'is, who were arrested in Teheran on 21 August 1980 and whose relatives had received no information about them since.

The number of prisoners of conscience in Iran was not known to Amnesty International. It has often been difficult to establish whether a person was a prisoner of conscience because the charges faced were not known or were couched in vague and general terms, without mention of a specific offence. Even when people were charged with offences which would suggest that they were not prisoners of conscience, the lack of fair trials usually made it impossible to know to what extent the charges were justified.

Many people have been held for long periods without charge or trial. Abolfazle Ghassemi, one of the leaders of the Iranian National Front and Secretary General of the Iran Party, who was elected to the Iranian parliament in the first elections after the February 1979 revolution, was arrested on 14 July 1980, after his parliamentary mandate had been contested by the Minister of the Interior. In January 1981 Amnesty International appealed to President Bani-Sadr and Ayatollah Beheshti, Head of the Supreme Court, for his release, expressing particular concern because he was 60 years old and suffered from heart disease. In April 1981 he was still being held without charge or trial.

Other prisoners of conscience included members of ethnic and religious minorities; members of political parties and groups opposed to the existing authorities; and people connected in some way with the previous government, who appeared to be regarded as guilty by association.

Mohammad Reza Sa'adati, former leader of the *Mojaheddin-e-Khalq,* a left-wing organization active in the opposition to the Shah, was sentenced to 10 years' imprisonment on 15 November 1980 on charges of spying for the Soviet Union (see *Amnesty International Report 1980*). He denied the charges and conducted his own defence after his lawyer was barred from the court. On 26 January 1981 Teheran State Radio announced that he was to be retried, but by the end of April 1981 no further information had reached Amnesty International.

On 8 April 1981 Amnesty International wrote to the Iranian Embassy in London, asking to be informed of the charges against Ali-Asghar Amirani, proprietor and editor-in-chief of the former weekly journal *Khandaniha*, who had been imprisoned. No further information about Ali-Asghar Amirani had reached Amnesty International by the end of April 1981.

In January 1981 the hostages held in the United States Embassy in Teheran since November 1979, for whose release Amnesty International had appealed, were released.

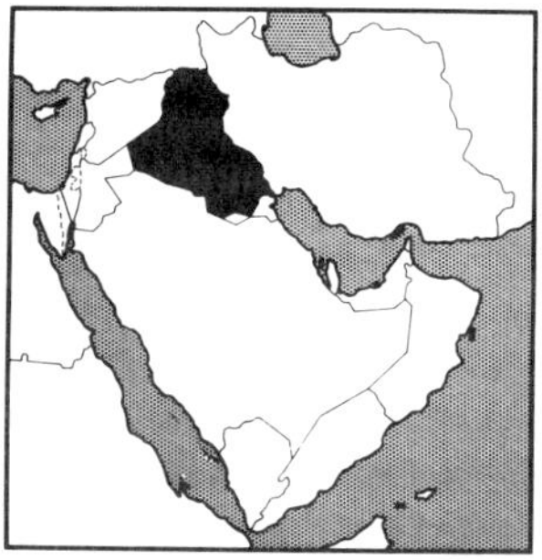

Iraq

Amnesty International continued to be concerned about widespread arrests and imprisonment on political grounds, and the lack of legal safeguards in trials of political prisoners by revolutionary and special courts. It was also concerned about the use of torture to extract confessions during interrogation, and about the many executions during the year. On 12 June 1980 Amnesty International launched an international campaign to persuade the Iraqi authorities to halt their frequent use of the death penalty, and to reduce the large number of offences, many political and some non-violent, which carry the death penalty. On 29 April 1981 Amnesty International published *Iraq: Evidence of Torture*.

During the year Amnesty International worked on behalf of 37 prisoners whose cases were being investigated. These included 31 former government officials of the ruling Ba'ath Party, arrested in July 1979, and serving sentences of up to 15 years' imprisonment in Abu Ghraib prison in Baghdad. They were convicted of being party to, or withholding information about, a conspiracy against the government allegedly uncovered in mid-July 1979. Reports reached Amnesty International that one prisoner from this group, Murthadha Abdul Baqi al Hadithi, sentenced to 15 years' imprisonment, died in prison in mid-June 1980. Unofficial sources claimed that he died from "unnatural causes" but Amnesty International has been unable to verify this.

Amnesty International was also concerned about two members of the Iraqi Communist Party (ICP), Dr Safa al-Hafidh and Dr Sabbah al-Durrah. Both were arrested on 8 February 1980 because of their alleged activities within the ICP and have since been held in incommunicado detention without being charged or tried.

Amnesty International was investigating the cases of three scientists —

Dr Hussain al-Shahristani, Dr Hassan al-Rajai and Dr Ja'afar Dhia Ja'afar — arrested at the end of 1979. The first two were arrested because of alleged connections with *al-Da'awa al-Islamiya,* a predominantly Shi'i party which has existed illegally since the mid-1950s, and were sentenced to 10 and seven years' imprisonment respectively. As far as Amnesty International knows Dr Ja'afar has not been charged or tried. On 30 January 1980 Amnesty International sent an urgent appeal to the authorities on behalf of Dr al-Shahristani after reports that he had been severely tortured but has received no reply. According to the *New Scientist,* 2 April 1981, "Dr Shahristani has been killed while in custody; he was tortured and spent his last days in the al-Rashid Military Hospital in Baghdad".

During the year Amnesty International learned of the arrest of seven religious men, assistants to Ayatollah Al Kho'i, a prominent leader of the Shi'i community in Iraq. The seven men were reportedly arrested around the start of the war with Iran in September 1980. In December 1980 Amnesty International received the names of 49 people said to be teachers, students, engineers and other workers, who had reportedly been arrested on suspicion of opposition to the government. In January 1981 Amnesty International wrote to the authorities seeking confirmation of these arrests, details of the prisoners' whereabouts and of the charges against them, but received no reply.

Amnesty International viewed with concern reports in February 1981 of the arrest of several members and supporters of the ICP, after a house-to-house search by security forces in the Sulaymaniah area. The whereabouts of those arrested and the charges against them were still unknown at the end of April 1981.

On 29 April 1981 Amnesty International published a report, *Iraq: Evidence of Torture.* This contains detailed medical findings and other evidence that political prisoners were tortured in Iraq. In October 1979 and March 1980 a panel of Amnesty International doctors interviewed and examined 15 Iraqi exiles who alleged that they had been tortured while in the custody of Iraqi security forces between September 1976 and August 1979. All 15 said that they were questioned under torture about their views and those of other people, and in some cases were pressed to join the ruling Ba'ath Party. Torture techniques allegedly ranged from crude physical assaults with fists, boots, truncheons and whips to sustained beatings of the soles of the feet *(falaqa),* rape and threats of rape, systematic electric shock torture and mock executions. In all cases the doctors found that the results of the physical examination were consistent with the tortures described. In addition the accounts were markedly consistent — even though the former detainees were arrested independently and at different times and places.

None of the prisoners had been allowed access to a lawyer during detention. Their families were often unable to obtain confirmation of their arrest or whereabouts. In all cases interrogation by members of the security forces started on the first or second day of detention. Only two of the 15 were brought to trial and neither was found guilty of any offence.

On 29 April 1981 Amnesty International issued a news release stating that all the information available, including details in the new report, provided convincing evidence that torture was continuing and widespread in Iraq. In the report Amnesty International recommended concrete measures to protect prisoners, including: an end to incommunicado detention; allowing lawyers, family and doctors prompt access to prisoners; and bringing people to court without delay after arrest. It called on the Iraqi Government to honour its commitments under the International Covenant on Civil and Political Rights, which Iraq ratified in 1971 and which prohibits torture.

On 27 April 1981 the government described the report as "without foundation". The 1,500-word government response, passed to Amnesty International by the Iraqi Embassy in London, emphasized that torture was banned by the nation's constitution and laws. However it did not reply in detail to the specific allegations of torture in the report and did not allay Amnesty International's concern.

During the year Amnesty International continued to receive allegations of torture and deaths under torture; bodies of political detainees are said to have been returned to their families bearing marks of torture and in some cases badly mutilated. Amnesty International has the names of 13 people reported to have died under torture since June 1979.

Since May 1980 Amnesty International has received disturbing information about the alleged poisoning of political suspects. A number of people arrested on suspicion of political opposition were said to have been given drinks shortly before being released, and then to have become ill some time after their release from custody. Detailed evidence on three people alleged to have been given slow-acting poison while in custody in Iraq has reached Amnesty International. Two were examined by doctors in the United Kingdom after they left Iraq and both were found to be suffering from thallium poisoning (thallium is a heavy metal used commercially in rat poison). One person died and the other recovered. The third case was of a women reported to have died in Iraq. On 2 September 1980 Amnesty International wrote to President Saddam Hussain urging him to open an inquiry into the reported poisonings and to make public its findings. No reply has been received.

After receiving an average of 100 names each year since 1974 of political prisoners reported to have been executed in Iraq, and reports of up to 100 executions in a six-week period from the beginning of March 1980, Amnesty International launched an international campaign in June 1980 to call attention to these facts and to persuade the authorities to cease the executions.

On 11 July 1980 Amnesty International appealed on behalf of 20 Kurds from the Autonomous Region of Kurdistan after they had been sentenced to death by the Special Court of Kirkuk. It learned later that six of the 20 were executed on 25 November 1980 in Mosul prison.

The majority of death sentences were passed either by the Revolutionary Court in Baghdad, or by special courts such as the Special Court of Kirkuk. Amnesty International continued to be concerned about the procedures of these courts, which did not conform to the legal safeguards guaranteed by Iraqi law and stipulated by the International Covenant on Civil and Political Rights: all trials were summary and held *in camera*; tribunals consisted of representatives of the executive and not of the judiciary; defendants were held incommunicado during pre-trial detention; there were very severe restrictions on the rights of the defence in the Revolutionary Court and no right of defence at all in special courts; convictions in both courts were often based on confessions extracted under torture; there was no right of appeal to a higher court, although the death sentence had to be ratified by the President and the prisoner could petition the President for clemency.

In January 1981 Kurdish sources claimed that 19 Kurds, allegedly members and supporters of the Kurdistan Democratic Party (KDP) of Iraq were executed in November 1980. A further 61 were under sentence of death. On 16 March 1981 the Syrian daily newspaper *Al Ba'ath* reported that 176 members of the Iraqi armed forces had been executed and many others had been arrested, including members of the armed forces, a former government minister, and a writer. Amnesty International sought confirmation of these reports.

Israel and the Occupied Territories

Amnesty International's concerns in Israel and the Occupied Territories were the arrest and conviction of prisoners of conscience, including conscientious objectors to military service; the use of administrative measures to physically restrict individuals and to detain them without trial; the secrecy of certain military trials; the lack of effective safeguards to protect those in custody from ill-treatment; and the use of excessive force by security forces to quell public disturbances. Israel retains the death penalty; however it is not mandatory and no death sentences were passed during the year.

In September 1980 Amnesty International published *Report and Recommendations of an Amnesty International Mission to the Government of the State of Israel.* This concentrated on the lack of administrative and legal safeguards for security suspects — individuals detained on suspicion of threatening the security of the state. This publication included the government's response to the mission report and Amnesty International's comments.

During the year Amnesty International worked on behalf of 25 prisoners who had been tried and convicted of security offences: seven of these were adopted as prisoners of conscience and 18 cases were being investigated.

Security offences are specified in the Defence (Emergency) Regulations (DER) promulgated by the British in 1945 for the whole of Palestine and still valid for both Israel and the Occupied Territories, except where superseded by more recent legislation, and in the more than 800 orders issued by the Regional Commander of the West Bank since 1967. They include a wide range of acts, some of which may involve the use or advocacy of violence. However Amnesty International believes that the regulations and orders, as interpreted and applied by military courts, have led to some individuals being sentenced to prison terms for acts which were expressions of political belief and did not involve the use or advocacy of violence. In one such case Amnesty International adopted as a prisoner of conscience Ahmed Abu Ayish, a 19-year-old resident of Halhoul (West Bank), who was arrested with two other teenagers on 18 December 1979 after a mock funeral procession to commemorate the death of an official of the Palestine Liberation Organization who had been a native of the town. Ahmed Abu Ayish was charged before the

Military Court at Hebron with activity against public order and participating in a procession without a licence, but was not specifically charged with advocating or using violence. He was sentenced to two years' imprisonment and an additional two years' suspended sentence, and was held in Hebron prison.

Amnesty International noted with concern the amendment of the Prevention of Terrorism Ordinance in July 1980 making public expression of sympathy for illegal organizations by means of placards, slogans, flags or anthems an offence punishable by up to three years' imprisonment. Amnesty International believes that applying such a law might create prisoners of conscience and noted that opponents of the bill asserted during debate that "it was designed to stifle legitimate expression of opinion" (*Jerusalem Post,* 29 July 1980).

Amnesty International adopted as a prisoner of conscience Gadi Elgazi, a member of a group of 27 Israeli high school students who had sent an open letter to the Minister of Defence in July 1979 stating that they would refuse military service in the Occupied Territories.

Gadi Elgazi was arrested in June 1980 after refusing to serve at an army base in the West Bank. He applied to the Israeli High Court of Justice to force the army to allow him, for reasons of conscience, to serve only within Israel's pre-1967 borders. In September 1980 this was rejected and on 6 January 1981 Gadi Elgazi was sentenced by the Southern District Military Court to one year's imprisonment. Two months later, in March 1981, after having spent more than six months in prison, Gadi Elgazi was released following the commutation of his sentence. He was later discharged without penalty from the Israeli Defence Forces.

Amnesty International continued to work on behalf of individuals who were imprisoned or physically restricted in their movements under administrative orders. In January 1980 the law governing administrative detention in the Occupied Territories was amended by Military Order No. 815. This provides for some judicial review, allows the detainee the right of appeal to the President of the Military Courts and limits the duration of each order to six months, after which a new order must be issued. However, the principle of detention without charge or trial is maintained and at no stage need the detainee or lawyer be informed of the reason for detention nor of the evidence against the detainee. During the year Amnesty International worked on behalf of 10 administrative detainees, of whom the longest held was Ali Awad Jamal, detained since May 1975.

Amnesty International began work on a number of cases of people whose movement was restricted by administrative order, although they were not imprisoned. Such orders do not give the restricted person details of the charges nor the right to refute evidence. They are issued by the military authorities under Article 110 of the DER in Israel and under Article 86 of Security Provisions Order 378 for the Occupied Territories. The restrictions include house arrest, "banning", limits to travel, restricted residence and the requirement to fulfil official formalities such as periodic registering.

Amnesty International learned of more than 30 Arabs from both Israel and the Occupied Territories who were subjected to restriction orders. Three were editors of important East Jerusalem publications: Bashir Barghouti of *Al-Tali'a,* Ma'mun Al-Sayyid of *Al-Fajr* and Akram Haniyyeh of *Al-Sha'ab.* They were placed under town arrest on 7 August 1980 and were still under this restriction at the end of April 1981. The restriction orders made it impossible for them to carry out their journalistic work. Two others, Ibrahim Nassar and Walid Fahoum, were lawyers who often represented Palestinian prisoners in the Occupied Territories. They were issued with administrative orders prohibiting them from entering the West Bank and making it difficult, if not impossible, to represent many of their West Bank clients. Ibrahim Nassar was also placed under house arrest by administrative order on 5 July 1980, and was still under house arrest at the end of the year.

Amnesty International continued to be concerned about the secrecy imposed on certain military trials in both the West Bank and, under the DER, in Israel proper. In particular it noted with concern the arrest of approximately 60 Israeli Arabs in early 1981, and the strict military censorship surrounding the case: the Jerusalem newspaper *Al-Quds* was suspended for five days after revealing certain details. At least four people were sentenced in a secret trial before a military tribunal to up to 20 months in prison. Amnesty International sought further information on these and related cases. Amnesty International also noted the release, in December 1980, of two Germans whose cases it had been investigating. Thomas Reuter and Brigitte Schultz had both been formally charged and tried before a secret military tribunal, beginning in December 1976, and few details have been made public by the Israeli authorities. Three Arabs who were arrested with them in January 1976 and were sentenced to 18-year prison terms remained in prison.

Amnesty International was concerned by reports that Israeli security forces were using unnecessarily harsh methods to quell public disturbances and were ill-treating people in custody. Reports reached Amnesty International that in November 1980 at least nine students were shot and injured by the Israeli Defence Forces in the West Bank towns of Bethlehem and Ramallah, as the army attempted to disperse demonstrators supporting Palestine Week and protesting against the closure of Bir Zeit university. There were also numerous allegations of police and army brutality and, in one instance at least, an offending official was punished: on 9 September 1980 the High Court of Justice upheld a two-year prison sentence on an Israeli police sergeant convicted of brutally beating a man from Hebron (West Bank) to extract a confession.

Amnesty International was concerned at the death in July 1980 of two hunger-strikers in Nafha prison after reports that they had been forcibly fed. In a message to Prime Minister Begin it urged that "all necessary steps to be taken to prevent such occurences and that a full public explanation be given of the methods utilized and the circumstances leading to the deaths". A special committee appointed by the Minister of the Interior to investigate the deaths of Ali Jafri and Muhamed Halwa reached the following conclusions:

> "As to the circumstances of the death of the two prisoners, the committee stated [for Ali Jafri:] . . . the findings indicate that the cause of death was 'aspiration pneumonia' but since it was proven that the prisoner was not force-fed, the committee stated that the pneumonia was caused by aspiration of stomach liquids into the lungs.
> As to Muhamed Halwa, the committee stated that the prisoner was force-fed through a tube and his death was caused by 'aspiration pneumonia', due to aspiration of gastric acid and food from the stomach to the lungs. There exists a reasonable possibility that as a result of his general condition a certain amount of food entered his lungs due to a misinsertion of the tube . . . . The committee stated that all actions taken were carried out according to the prevailing orders and procedures."

However this failed to satisfy nine inmates of Nafha prison or Fatma Jafri, sister of one of the dead hunger-strikers. In March 1981 they applied to the Israeli Supreme Court for the suspension and trial of several prison and medical staff they accused of responsibility for the deaths of the hunger-strikers. In March 1981 the Israeli police were reported to be opening files on these individuals to investigate their role in the deaths.

In September 1980 Amnesty International published *Report and Recommendations of an Amnesty International Mission to the Government of the State of Israel* which included a reply from Israel's Attorney General and Amnesty International's comments. The report concentrated on administrative and legal safeguards, applying to security suspects in custody in the Occupied Territories, and found these safeguards to be inadequate, "[enhancing] the possibility that the basic rights of prisoners may be routinely violated". (See *Amnesty International Report 1980.*)

Amnesty International therefore recommend that: "a public and impartial committee of inquiry should be established to investigate the allegations of ill-treatment in their totality and the administrative and legal procedures and practices relevant to the arrest, confinement, interrogation and trial of security suspects. The committee's findings, conclusions and recommendations should be made public."

The publication included a reply from the Attorney General on behalf of the authorities which rejected the conclusions and recommendations.

As the report was being published Amnesty International received a document from Acting Attorney General Gabay which reiterated many of the points in the earlier reply. Amnesty International wishes to draw attention to an error in its report that was addressed by the Acting Attorney General. It is not true that: "one important limitation to the free choice of defence counsel [in the Occupied Territories is that]: in situations where the court has determined that the security interests of the state require the military trial to be held in secret, the defendant must select legal counsel from among those on a specially approved list" (page 31). This limitation does not obtain in the Occupied Territories and is only relevant to military trials held in Israel proper.

In this document the Acting Attorney General emphasized that: "Israel makes every effort, under the most difficult circumstances to safeguard the human rights of the security detainees in the areas under her administration . . . the Israeli authorities responsible for the administration of justice, conduct an ongoing review of the treatment of security detainees and will continue to ensure that their civil rights are duly respected . . . we are of the opinion that nothing is to be gained by having the sort of committee of inquiry proposed."

In January 1981 the *Knesset* (parliament) State Control Committee announced that it would begin an examination of police detention and interrogation procedures, and that the Knesset Interior Committee and the Law Committee had decided to form a joint panel to examine these matters. These developments followed a report by the State Comptroller that police officers had been lax in their required supervision of detentions and interrogations.

On 1 April the *Knesset* passed a government-sponsored amendment to the Criminal Procedure Law, relating to the rights of suspects in police custody. A suspect "has the right to remain silent during interrogations, but police do not have to tell him of that right after he is brought to the station" (*Jerusalem Post,* 3 April 1981). The amendment, which applies to Israel but not to the Occupied Territories, also enables the detainee to notify a lawyer and relatives of the place of detention, immediately after arrest. This may be delayed by up to

48 hours on the authority of a senior officer, and by up to 21 days in cases of terrorism and espionage. Under the amendment an arrested person may apply for financial compensation and defence costs in cases of unjustified arrest.

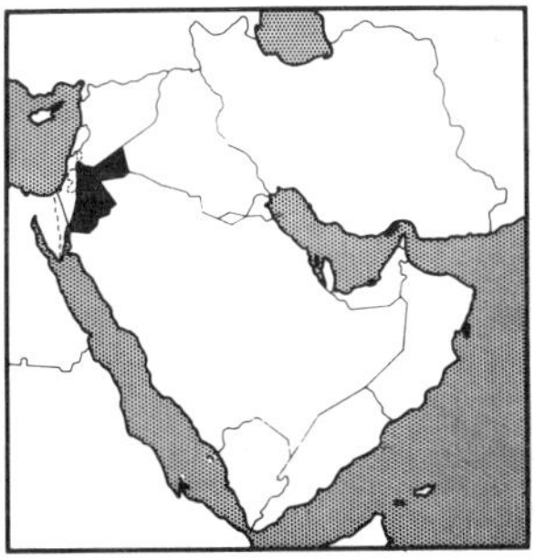

Jordan

Amnesty International's concerns during the year included the imprisonment of prisoners of conscience, the prolonged detention without trial of political prisoners, the lack of legal safeguards in military court trials and the death penalty.

Martial law has been in force in Jordan for the last 14 years. Its provisions suspend a broad range of constitutional guarantees and invest the Prime Minister, in his capacity as martial law governor, with wide powers of arrest and detention. Under martial law political prisoners were either held for long periods without trial or were tried before military courts.

During the year Amnesty International worked on behalf of 16 political prisoners and learned of the release of 10. Four of the 16, who had each been sentenced to 10 years' imprisonment for alleged membership of the Communist Party, prohibited under the Anti-Communist Law of 1953, were adopted as prisoners of conscience by Amnesty International. One of these, Hashim Gharaibeh, a 31-year-old student from Yarmuk, was granted an amnesty in August 1980. The others, Nabil Ja'anini, Muhammad Abu-Shama'a and Imad Mulhim, were still serving their sentences. The Prime Minister's Office responded to appeals for the release of Nabil Ja'anini, who had featured as Prisoner of the Month in the *Amnesty International Newsletter* in February 1981, by stating that "Ja'anini is currently serving a 10-year sentence for his involvement in subversive activities and organizing illegal cells to undermine the security of the state . . . Ja'anini was only arrested when he began organizing a Communist cell." Nabil Ja'anini was officially charged and sentenced for membership of the Communist Party and for possession of prohibited communist leaflets.

Amnesty International was concerned about the prolonged detention without trial of political prisoners. Between June and August 1980 it took up for investigation the cases of nine untried detainees. They included two members of the Palestine National Council:

Oussama Shannar, who was detained in October 1977; and Taysir al Zabri, detained in May 1979, who was also a member of the Secretariat of the *Rassemblement des forces populaires en Jordanie* (RFPJ), Assembly of Popular Forces in Jordan. Hamadeh Fara'neh, another member of this group, was in his fifth year of detention without trial at al-Ma'an Prison in southern Jordan. All nine prisoners were among 83 prisoners, mostly untried detainees, who were released on 10 August 1980 after an amnesty was proclaimed to commemorate the *'Id al-Fitr* (end of Ramadan) in Jordan.

In a letter to Minister of Interior Ali al-Bashir on 13 April 1981 Amnesty International repeated its concern about detention without trial and referred to assurances given to an Amnesty International delegation to Jordan in March 1978 that all prisoners were brought to trial within a reasonable time. Amnesty International submitted 131 names of untried detainees at al-Mahatta Central Intelligence Prison in Amman and asked the Minister of Interior to investigate the status of their cases and to give details of any planned trial procedures. The Jordanian Ambassador in London, Ibrahim Izziddin, has since informed Amnesty International that he has asked the authorities in Jordan to provide him with the information.

Over the past year there have been a number of reports of death sentences and executions. On 22 September 1980 a military court sentenced to death five Palestinian members of *al-Fatah,* the largest group within the Palestine Liberation Organization. They had reportedly been arrested after returning to Jordan from Israeli occupied territory. They were Musa Mahmud Fadillat, Mahmud Abbas Abu-'Ubaid, Salameh Mahmud Shatrat, Lutfi Muhammad Alloush and Salih Muhammad Alloush. In the same month two Arabs, Halwa Khalil Hammudeh and Ahmad Hassan, were sentenced to death in their absence for selling their property in Jerusalem to Israelis. Although they have not been executed, their sentences have not been commuted and fears remained that they might be executed at any time.

In a letter of 4 November 1980 to King Hussein Amnesty International said it was disturbed at the growing number of reports of death sentences and expressed its grave concern at the executions on 28 October 1980 of two Syrians, Muhammad Walid Muti'al-Ijaz and Muhammad Yusuf Hasan Sha'ibi, at al-Mahatta Prison in Amman. The two had been found guilty of the murder of Abdul Wahhab al-Bakri, a Syrian political refugee in Jordan and a senior member of the Muslim Brotherhood. It has appealed to King Hussein to commute all remaining death sentences.

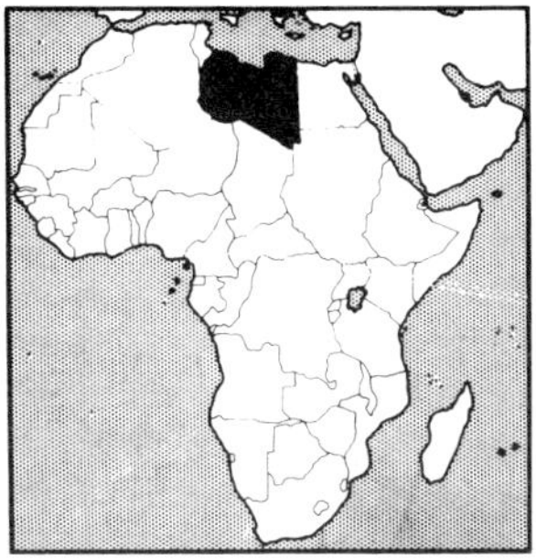

Libyan Arab Jamahiriya

The major concerns of Amnesty International were the imprisonment of prisoners of conscience, frequent allegations of torture and ill-treatment, executions and extrajudicial killings. It was particularly alarmed by official calls for the "physical liquidation of enemies of the revolution" and the subsequent killing or wounding of a number of Libyan citizens living abroad.

During the year Amnesty International worked on behalf of 74 prisoners of conscience and learned of the release of 12. Most prisoners of conscience were believed to be held in Tripoli Central prison and in Kuweifiya prison, Benghazi.

Amnesty International continued to follow two trials involving prisoners of conscience (see *Amnesty International Report 1980*). The first trial involved a group of 18 journalists and writers arrested in December 1978 and accused of forming a Marxist organization. The second was a retrial of 10 defendants originally arrested in 1975 on charges of forming a secret political organization. According to unofficial sources five of the 18 journalists and writers were released and the other 13 sentenced to life imprisonment; and two of the 10 defendants in the retrial were sentenced to life imprisonment, and the rest acquitted but not necessarily released. Amnesty International has so far been unable to verify these reports.

Amnesty International received reports of widespread arrests among Muslim activists. A number of senior military and civilian officials were also allegedly arrested early in 1980 and tried in February 1981 by Revolutionary Courts set up at the Revolutionary Committees' meeting in February 1980. Amnesty International was concerned that the legal safeguards at these trials were inadequate: the tribunals were composed of members of the Revolutionary Committees rather than the judiciary, and the rights of the defence were severely restricted.

At the beginning of March several alleged former members of the pro-Iraqi wing of the Ba'ath Party, which is banned in Libya, were arrested, and later tried. Amnesty International has not yet been able to ascertain the precise charges against them, the type of court in which they were tried, nor the outcome of the trial.

Amnesty International noted the passage on 27 January 1981 of Law No. 4 of 1981 which prohibits lawyers from practising privately. Under this law all lawyers become employees of the Secretariat of

Justice. Fears were expressed by the Arab Lawyers Union and individual Libyan lawyers about the effects of this measure on the independence of lawyers and on their freedom to provide proper legal defence for political prisoners.

Towards the end of the year first-hand reports of torture reached Amnesty International. Detainees were allegedly tortured in various centres belonging to the intelligence services in Tripoli and Benghazi. Detainees were apparently held incommunicado for unlimited periods and their families were not informed of their whereabouts. According to these reports, the most common torture techniques were electric shocks, in particular to the head and genitals, and beatings on the soles of the feet *(falaqa)*. Several deaths in custody have been reported, including three lawyers who were former members of the Ba'ath Party. Reliable unofficial reports suggested that these deaths resulted from torture.

Amnesty International has also learned of a serious deterioration in prison conditions for prisoners of conscience. Many have allegedly been transferred to overcrowded cells, compelled to wear prison clothes and their books and writing materials have been confiscated. Amnesty International was particularly disturbed by the report of a riot at Tripoli Central prison on 4 September 1980 during which five prisoners were shot and wounded by prison officers.

Libya retains the use of the death penalty for a wide number of offences, many of a political nature and not involving use or advocacy of violence. In addition official calls for the "physical liquidation of enemies of the revolution" have been followed by a number of extra-judicial killings. On 5 February 1980 the third meeting of the Revolutionary Committees held at Gar Younis university, Benghazi, issued a declaration calling for, among other things, the "physical liquidation" of enemies of the revolution living abroad as well as of other "elements obstructing revolutionary change" in Libya. Since then more than a dozen Libyan citizens have been killed or wounded in assasination attempts in Great Britain, Federal Republic of Germany, the United States of America, Italy, Greece and the Lebanon. On 30 April 1980 Amnesty International submitted a memorandum to the authorities in which it called upon them to renounce immediately the declaration concerning the "physical liquidation" of its opponents and to implement fully the provisions of the International Covenant on Civil and Political Rights, which Libya ratified in 1970. No reply has been received.

At the beginning of March 1980 press reports quoted Colonel Mu'ammar Gaddafi declaring "the masses have the right to liquidate their enemies at home and abroad", in a speech marking the fourth anniversary of the establishment of People's Congresses in Libya. He added later "It is a matter of honour to jail or liquidate the enemies of the authorities". On 3 March 1981 at the final session of the fourth meeting, Libyan Revolutionary Committees were reported to have "reaffirmed their determination to continue the physical liquidation of the enemies of people's authority at home and abroad".

On 25 February 1981 a revolutionary tribunal in Tripoli passed the death sentence in their absence on four Libyans in exile. Mohammad Youssif Lamgarief, former Libyan Ambassador to India, was reported to be among those sentenced to death. Mohammad Lamgarief was one of three high-ranking Libyan officials who reportedly resigned during the year, and joined the Libyan opposition in exile. The others were Ahmed Ibrahim Ehwas, former Libyan chargé d'affaires in Guyana, and Abdul Salam Ali Aila, former chargé d'affaires in India.

In December 1980 Amnesty International received information about the arrest of 15 people in a mosque in Tripoli, five of whom were allegedly executed, including Sheikh El Bishti, a mosque official. In a cable to the Libyan Secretary of Justice on 24 December 1980 Amnesty International asked for clarification of these reports and information on the whereabouts of those detained and the charges against them. It has received no reply.

Morocco and Western Sahara

During the year to 30 April 1981 Amnesty International's concerns were the imprisonment of prisoners of conscience, long-term incommunicado detention, "disappearances", and allegations of ill-treatment and inadequate medical care for prisoners. In addition Amnesty International was concerned about reports of human rights violations committed by the Polisario Front.

After a period of relative quiet, in early 1981 there was renewed unrest which led to a number of arrests among students and members of the major left-wing opposition party, the *Union socialiste des forces populaires* (USFP), Socialist Union of Popular Forces. Two referendums were held in May 1980: one modifying the rules of succession to the throne and the composition of the Regency Council, the other extending the term of parliament from four to six years. They both received an overwhelmingly positive vote, but the second was opposed by the USFP which promised to withdraw its elected deputies from parliament when their four-year term expired in 1981. In the background was Morocco's continuing war with the Algerian and Libyan-backed Polisario Front over the Western Sahara. Morocco claims the Western Sahara as part of its national territory while the Polisario Front claims the area should constitute an independent Saharan Arab Democratic Republic.

Despite amnesties in July 1980 affecting 91 political prisoners, Amnesty International was concerned about new arrests and about the continued imprisonment of substantial numbers of prisoners of conscience. It was also concerned about prolonged incommunicado detention and allegations of ill-treatment in police detention centres. Medical care for prisoners was also reported to be inadequate. Morocco retains the death penalty but no executions were reported during the year. In February 1981 Amnesty International sent a mission to Morocco to discuss its concerns with officials; a memorandum was to be submitted to the authorities presenting these concerns in detail.

During the year Amnesty International worked on behalf of more than 250 individual prisoners. Among cases from previous years were more than 130 members of various Marxist-Leninist movements and of the *Union nationale des forces populaires* (UNFP), National Union of Popular Forces, tried and sentenced in 1977 or earlier; two trade unionists arrested in April 1979 and both now released; 15 peasants from Beni Mellal arrested in December 1979 and sentenced to up to three years in prison; and approximately 30 people from southern Moroccan towns who were taken into custody as long ago as 1975 and most of whom have not reappeared. During the year Amnesty International took up for investigation the cases of more than 60 other inhabitants of southern Moroccan towns such as Tan-Tan and Goulimine, who were also reportedly taken into custody by the security forces as long ago as 1975 and whose whereabouts were still not known. Repeated inquiries to the authorities concerning the whereabouts of these latter two groups have so far had no result. Unofficial reports, which Amnesty International has not been able to verify, have indicated that several hundred such people were in custody and that they were held in secret detention centres in southern Morocco, as well as in local police detention centres.

Several other groups of cases were closely followed. During 1980 26 people, most of whom called themselves Saharans and who had all been arrested in 1977, were convicted and sentenced in four separate trials to terms of up to five years' imprisonment on charges of forming an illegal association and plotting against the security of the state. Amnesty International was seeking further information to determine whether or not they were prisoners of conscience. Over 20 members and officials of the USFP, arrested principally in Tiznit and Fqih ben Saleh in January and March 1981, received prison sentences of up to 13 months in trials on charges including disturbing public order, incitement to unrest, unlicensed association and disrespect towards authority. The results of several appeals in the USFP cases were due in May 1981.

In July 1980, under royal amnesties which freed 91 political prisoners, 20 prisoners adopted by Amnesty International as prisoners of conscience were released, all of whom had been tried in 1977 or earlier. They included the poet Abdellatif Laabi. Amnesty International had appealed urgently on his behalf on 8 May 1980 after reports that he was being denied urgently needed medical care while in custody. Like many other amnestied prisoners Abdellatif Laabi was subjected to restrictions after release: in particular, he has not been issued a passport which would allow him to accept offers of specialist medical care from abroad and has not been permitted to take up his former occupation as a teacher in the public education system. Despite press speculation at the time of the July amnesties that all political prisoners would be released — such a measure had already been called for by all parties represented in the Moroccan parliament — no further amnesties affecting political prisoners were announced, other than informal assurances that a number of exiles would be permitted to return. Among them was Abderrahman Youssoufi, Deputy Secretary General of the Arab Lawyers Union and member of the political bureau of the USFP, who had been in exile since 1965.

On 23 July 1980 Amnesty International sent a cable welcoming the amnesties, but on 3 September it expressed its disappointment at their limited application. No further royal amnesties took place during the year. There was particular disappointment on 3 March 1981, the 20th anniversary of King Hassan II's accession to the throne, since Amnesty International's delegation to Morocco had been informally assured by responsible government officials that this occasion was likely to be marked by a substantial amnesty for political prisoners. On 23 March 1981 Amnesty International sent a telegram to Prime Minister and Minister of Justice Maati Bouabid expressing its "profound disappointment that . . . the pardons granted on the occasion of the Feast of the Throne did not affect either prisoners taken up by Amnesty International nor other political prisoners still held in Moroccan prisons".

Among the prisoners released during the year whose cases Amnesty International had followed were more than 80 people detained without trial since 1977 in Meknes civil prison. They had spent almost three years in detention without trial, and many had been held incommunicado for more than one year, when in March 1980 they went on hunger-strike calling for their release or trial. Shortly afterwards, charges against more than 40 were dropped and they were set free. The rest were provisionally released pending trial and were tried in the months that followed. All were freed by the end of April 1981, most having been convicted but sentenced to terms shorter than the time they had already served; a small number were either acquitted or required to spend some additional months in prison to complete their sentences.

Amnesty International continued to be concerned at the use of prolonged incommunicado detention, which is provided for under *garde-à-vue* procedures, which allow the detainee to be held without access to lawyers, family or independent medical staff for 96 hours, with a possible extension of 48 hours. These periods are doubled for acts threatening the security of the state according to the code of criminal procedure. However these extensions have often been renewed repeatedly, leading to incommunicado detention lasting months and sometimes years. It is to this period that allegations of ill-treatment usually refer. Although a new code of criminal procedure which might limit such incommunicado detention is said to be under consideration by the government, all the practices, laws and legal precedents which facilitate incommunicado detention remain and may be invoked at any time.

Serious allegations have reached Amnesty International that many individuals in southern Moroccan cities such as Goulimine and Tan-Tan and in areas farther south have been held in incommunicado detention for long periods; the whereabouts of many were unknown.

A number of military officers convicted of involvement in coup attempts of 1971 and 1972 have served their sentences but have not yet been released. Despite repeated inquiries from Amnesty International, the Morrocan authorities have refused to say where they were being held. Recent reports indicated that a number were held in appalling conditions in secret prisons, and that up to 10 may have died as a result.

Amnesty International continued to be concerned about inadequate medical care for prisoners. Vital specialist care was frequently unavailable and routinely prisoners had to wait more than a month for a medical examination by a qualified doctor. In addition the supply of prescribed medicine was often unacceptably delayed, frequently for more than a month. Amnesty International continued to receive worrying reports about the health of individual prisoners. On 16 June 1980 Amnesty International cabled Prime Minister and Minister of Justice M. Bouabid, Minister of Interior Idris Basri, and Minister of Health Rahal Rahali, to express concern over reports that prisoners held at Kenitra civil prison, who had gone on hunger-strike on 15 May 1980, had been refused medical care. In July 1980 Amnesty International medical groups urged the authorities to provide independent psychiatric examinations for three prisoners: Hassan el-Bou, Miloud Achdini and Zaoui el-Meliani, all reportedly severely mentally disturbed and being treated only with tranquillizers. Hassan el-Bou and Miloud Achdini had been adopted as prisoners of conscience and Amnesty International urged their immediate release. Zaoui el-Meliani was released under the amnesties of July 1980 but Hassan el-Bou and Miloud Achdini remained in prison and, despite another urgent appeal from Amnesty International on 26 September 1980, their condition was reported to be serious. The treatment prisoners received in hospital wards reserved for them was apparently inadequate, and frequent complaints have reached Amnesty International that prisoners have been harassed by police officers on duty in the wards.

Allegations of ill-treatment in police custody included the case of several USFP activists arrested in Tiznit in January 1981 who showed the court marks on their bodies which they claimed were evidence of ill-treatment at the hands of the police. The court rejected their request for medical examinations to verify these claims.

Morocco retains the death penalty for several crimes. Although a number of prisoners remained under sentence of death no one was executed during the year. There have been no executions since 1973, when at least 26 people were executed, although more than 50 death sentences have been passed since then. On 21 September 1980 Amnesty International appealed urgently for the commutation of death sentences passed on two men convicted of murdering Omar Benjelloun, director of the newspaper *Al-Muharrir* and member of the political bureau of the USFP, in December 1975. The prisoners have not been executed, but it is not yet known whether the sentences have been officially commuted.

Amnesty International was also concerned about serious allegations of human rights violations committed by the Polisario Front. In particular it received information that a number of Polisario Front members had been arrested by the Polisario Front between 1975 and 1979. None of the people arrested have been heard of since. Amnesty International raised this matter with representatives of the Polisario Front on several occasions and provided a number of names. After the Polisario Front had persistently denied the allegations, but had failed to refute them in detail or provide further information on the fate of the named individuals, Amnesty International issued a public statement on 10 February 1981:

"According to the allegations reaching Amnesty International, hundreds of Polisario members have been arrested since 1975 for criticizing the movement's internal policies . . . The present whereabouts of most of the alleged prisoners are not known . . . These reports say political prisoners were made to do hard labour and were ill-treated . . .

. . . Polisario has consistently denied such reports. Amnesty International said . . . Polisario had not refuted the allegations in detail or provided information which might allay its concerns. Amnesty International added that as far as it knew, no impartial international organization had been able to investigate fully the situation in the Western Sahara as it affects prisoners."

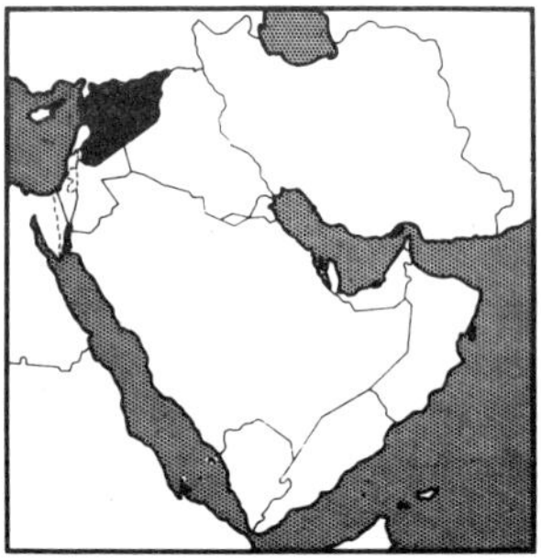

Syria

Amnesty International continued to be concerned about prolonged detention without trial, the lack of legal safeguards in the trials of political prisoners, the use of torture and the death penalty. It was also concerned about increasing reports of arbitrary imprisonment, "disappearances" of detainees, extrajudicial killings and torture by the Syrian security forces during the year.

The state of emergency, now in its 19th year, suspends all constitutional guarantees and gives the Minister of Interior, in his capacity as emergency law governor, extraordinary powers of arrest and detention. During the year various sectors of society expressed opposition to the emergency regulations, including some professional associations, trade unions, political parties outside the ruling National Progressive Front and the *Ikhwan al-Muslimin* (Muslim Brotherhood). In some instances the government retaliated by punishing opponents.

During the year Amnesty International worked on behalf of 107 political detainees, 70 of them adopted prisoners of conscience. It has continued to seek the fair trial or release of 18 members or supporters of the previous government, detained since 1970; of seven members of the Kurdish Democratic Party detained without trial since 1973; and of 20 alleged political opponents of the government who had been abducted at various times from the Lebanon. In November 1980 a number of reports indicated that former President Nur al-Din Atassi had been moved from al-Mezze prison to house detention where he was allowed to live with his family. However later reports suggested that he was returned to prison in March 1981.

In December 1980 Amnesty International adopted as prisoners of conscience 23 Syrian lawyers detained following the dissolution on 9 April 1980 of the General Congress and the regional assemblies of the Syrian Bar Association. The arrests came after the lawyers staged a one-day national strike on 31 March 1980 in support of their call for an end to the state of emergency and for reforms in the emergency legislation; for the abolition of the state security courts; for a boycott of such courts by all lawyers; and for the release of all untried detainees. Amnesty International appealed on behalf of the detained lawyers in June and July 1980 and their release was urged by the international legal community. The strike was supported by the doctors', engineers' and architects' associations as well as by several trades unions which went on strike for several weeks in a number of northern towns. In response the government closed down the national and regional assemblies of the Bar, medical and engineers' associations and arrested many of their members. Their places of detention have not been made public and those detained have not been allowed visits from relatives or lawyers.

In February 1981 Amnesty International adopted as prisoners of conscience 10 members of the banned Syrian Communist Party Political Bureau including its Secretary General, Riad al-Turk, and his wife Asmah al-Feisal. Amnesty International had appealed urgently on behalf of Riad al-Turk after receiving reports that he had been severely tortured and had been rushed to an intensive care unit at a Damascus hospital for emergency treatment. At the end of April 1981 his place of detention was not known. Another member of this organization, Omar Kashash, arrested in February 1981, is a former adopted prisoner of conscience detained without trial from June 1978 until February 1980.

Amnesty International received several first-hand accounts of ill-treatment and torture of suspects during interrogation. A doctor who was briefly detained in September 1979 before being released and fleeing the country said that he had been tortured by systematic beatings on the soles of his feet and by electricity applied to his shoulder blades and his genitals. He was medically examined by a British doctor in September 1980, a year after the alleged torture; the examination revealed 50 to 100 healed scars on his back and two similar scars on his genitals which according to the doctor's report "are not compatible with natural causes and are the result of external trauma, which could have been electrical."

Amnesty International continued to receive disturbing information on human rights violations by the security forces and specifically by the *Saray al-Difa'* (Special Defence Units) under the command of President Assad's brother, Rifa'at Assad. Eye-witnesses have reported seeing security forces ill-treating and torturing people under interrogation in makeshift detention centres. Relatives have said they were unable to trace people arrested because they did not know where the security forces had taken them or because prisoners were moved from prison to unknown destinations. Executions were reported after trials by military court with summary rules of procedure which denied the defendants the right to defence by lawyers and the right of appeal.

Over the past year there have been a number of reported executions. In June 1980 the international press reported that 17 army officers had been executed for "treason and disaffection" after criticizing President Assad's brother. Amnesty International cabled President Assad requesting confirmation and urging commutation of any remaining death sentences on humanitarian grounds. In July 1980 the Syrian People's Assembly ratified a law making membership of the Muslim Brotherhood a capital offence. An amnesty was declared for all members who gave themselves up within one month and this was later extended to two months. In September 1980 the Jordanian News Agency *Petra* carried a report that 200 Muslim Brothers had been executed at a camp in al-Raqqa after having given themselves up under the terms of the amnesty. The same news agency carried reports in January 1981 that 200 members and supporters of the Muslim Brotherhood were executed at al-Mashraqiyya square in Aleppo, and a few days later it reported the execution of nine pilots. These reports were publicly dismissed by the Syrian authorities as hostile propaganda and as exaggerated accounts of raids by the security forces on Muslim Brotherhood hiding-places. Amnesty International has not been able to confirm these accounts.

In a letter to President Assad in August 1980 Amnesty International expressed concern over the growing number of reported executions and said it was greatly disturbed by recent moves to increase the number of capital offences. Amnesty International also expressed its grave concern over the reported killing by security forces of hundreds of prisoners, mainly Muslim Brothers, at Tadmur (Palmyra) Prison on 27 June 1980 and urged President Assad to set up a committee of inquiry and make public its findings. In 1981 two Syrian members of the *Saray al-Difa'* (Special Defence Units) arrested in Jordan gave details of the massacre on Jordanian Television and admitted having taken part in it. Amnesty International has received no response from the authorities.

Also of concern were allegations that the security services were responsible for the assassination abroad of several prominent figures opposed to the government, including Salah al-Din al-Bitar, a founder of the Ba'ath Party, who was shot in Paris in July 1980, and Banan Ali-Tantawi, wife of Issam al-Attar, the Director of the Islamic Centre in Aachen and a leader of the Muslim Brotherhood, who was shot in March 1981.

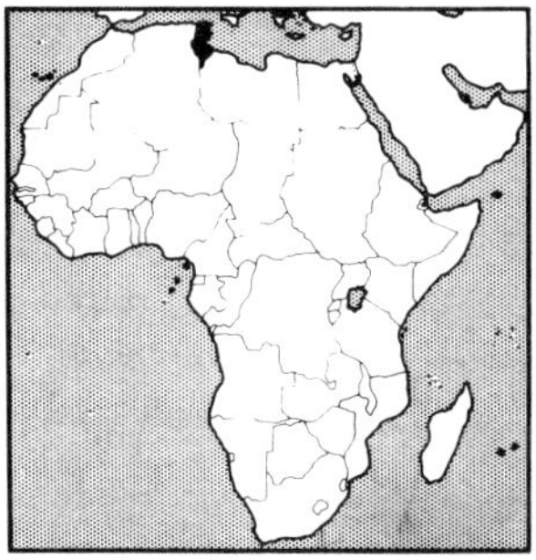

Tunisia

During the year all Amnesty International adopted prisoners of conscience were released from prison. Amnesty International welcomed this but was still concerned that some former prisoners were subjected to restrictions, including house arrest. It was also concerned about continuing allegations of torture, and the death penalty.

Although the *Parti socialiste destourien* (PSD), Socialist Destour Party, was the only legal party, President Habib Bourguiba indicated at the opening of the PSD conference on 10 April 1981 that other political movements would be authorized during the year, provided that they were representative and complied with the constitution. The year was marked by a government policy of "liberalization" which included elections at the end of April 1981 for the leadership of the *Union générale des travailleurs tunisiens* (UGTT), General Union of Tunisian Workers, in which former prisoner of conscience Taieb Baccouche was elected Secretary General. More newspapers were authorized. However there were also periods of renewed unrest as strikes and student troubles continued in early 1981, resulting in some arrests.

On 18 November 1980 charges were dropped for lack of evidence against 12 trade unionists from Sousse by the State Security Court in Tunis. They were the last of a group of 101 defendants who appeared before the Sousse Criminal Court in July 1978, on various charges relating to the general strike of 26 January 1978. Charges against 89 of the defendants were dropped in November 1978.

President Bourguiba granted several amnesties benefiting Amnesty International adopted prisoners of conscience and a considerable number of other political and non-political prisoners. While some of the amnesties were unconditional and without restrictions, others were conditional or partial, granting release from prison but not the restoration of all constitutionally guaranteed rights.

On 1 May 1980 four former members of the leadership of the

UGTT serving prison sentences of up to eight years were released. On 1 June eight members of the group *El Amel El Tounsi,* The Tunisian Worker, and some associated with *Ech-Chaab,* The People, an underground version of the UGTT newspaper circulated in 1978, were freed. In July and August 1980 the remaining six members of *El Amel El Tounsi* were released to mark the President's birthday. They were serving up to nine years' imprisonment. The only two members of the UGTT leadership remaining in prison were granted amnesty: Abderrazak Ghorbal, who had been sentenced to 10 years' imprisonment; and Salah B'rour, personal secretary to Habib Achour (former Secretary General of the UGTT), who was sentenced to six years' imprisonment at the same trial before the State Security Court in October 1978.

In February 1981 President Bourguiba granted an amnesty for members of the *Mouvement d'unité populaire* (MUP), Movement for Popular Unity, although none was in prison at the time. This amnesty reportedly extended to members of MUP tried in their absence and living abroad, with the sole exception of the leader of MUP, former cabinet minister Ahmed Ben Salah.

Many former prisoners of conscience have initially faced considerable restrictions after their release. These included restricted residence and being required to register every day at a local police station. In the majority of cases these restrictions have been gradually lifted.

In August 1980 former Minister of Foreign Affairs Mohamed Masmoudi, who had been the principal exponent of the union between Tunisia and Libya in 1974, was released from house arrest after more than two years. The release followed his hunger-strike in protest against the restrictions placed upon him and in support of his demand to be allowed to travel abroad.

Although no prisoners of conscience were known to be in prison at the end of the year, Habib Achour, former Secretary General of the UGTT, remained under strict house arrest and one of his sons was reportedly also placed under house arrest in March 1981. In a letter to President Bourguiba in November 1980 Amnesty International welcomed the release of prisoners of conscience and urged an unconditional amnesty for them to enable them to exercise fully their human rights, as guaranteed by the constitution and the International Covenant on Civil and Political Rights, ratified by Tunisia in 1969. It urged that all conditions and restrictions be lifted at the earliest opportunity.

There have been occasional reports of torture and ill-treatment despite indications that the authorities intended to investigate the use of torture. In November 1980 Amnesty International welcomed the news that at least one former adopted prisoner of conscience who had been tortured during pre-trial detention had been sent abroad for medical treatment at the expense of the government. Amnesty International urged the authorities to ensure medical treatment free of charge either within the country or abroad for all former prisoners of conscience whose health was impaired as a result of ill-treatment or prolonged imprisonment.

At the end of January 1981 two Tunisian newspapers reported the death of 24-year-old Jamel Zkir, allegedly as a result of torture and poor prison conditions. In appeals to President Bourguiba and to the Prime Minister, Mohamed M'zali, Amnesty International expressed concern at these reports, and urged an inquiry into the circumstances.

Tunisia retains the death penalty for a considerable number of political and non-political offences. During the year Amnesty International learned of seven executions in June and November 1980 at Tunis Civil Prison. All those executed had been found guilty of murder. In February 1981 Amnesty International learned that a 23-year-old Tunisian had been sentenced to death by the Tunis Criminal Court for murder. It appealed to President Bourguiba to commute this and any other death sentences on humanitarian grounds. He was executed on 22 April 1981.

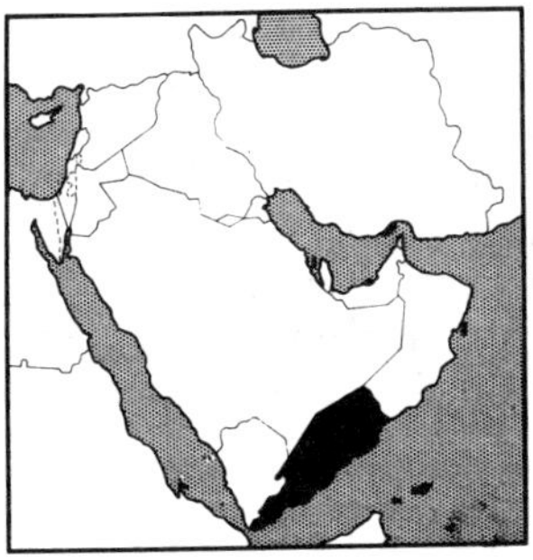

Yemen (People's Democratic Republic of)

Amnesty International's concerns included prolonged detention without trial, inadequate procedures in the trials of political prisoners, "disappearances" and the death penalty.

During the year it worked on behalf of 40 prisoners, of whom 30 were adopted prisoners of conscience; they probably represented only a small portion of the total. Official news of the prisoners was rarely available and in the recent past no responses of substance have been received from the authorities to the numerous inquiries made by Amnesty International.

The 30 prisoners of conscience included 12 members of the former Federal Government which operated under British colonial rule before independence in November 1967. Five were sentenced in February 1968 to between 10 and 15 years' imprisonment on charges of high treason and feudalism. The remaining seven have been held since 1967 without charge or trial at al-Mansurah Prison. During 1980 Amnesty International learned of the release of two of this group, Ali Atif Kalidi and Nasir bin Abdullah al-Wahidi, both of whom had been sentenced to 10 years' imprisonment in 1968 but had remained in prison after completing their sentences.

Amnesty International also adopted as prisoners of conscience 10 farmers arrested on 16 November 1976 for protesting against a government decision to ban the consumption, sale and purchase of the narcotic shrub *qat*. Eight were originally sentenced to death and two were sentenced to 10 years' imprisonment. The death sentences were later commuted to between 10 and 15 years' imprisonment, and the two 10-year sentences were commuted to eight years. The prisoners' place of detention was unknown.

Amnesty International has continued to work on behalf of 18 political prisoners detained between 1970 and 1975 who have not been charged or brought to trial. The whereabouts of 10 of these prisoners was not known and there were fears that they might no longer be alive. One was Abdul Malik Ismail Muhammad, former Ambassador to Cairo, who was arrested at Aden airport in May 1975. Neither his family nor friends have seen or heard of him since.

According to reports hundreds of people have "disappeared" since independence in 1967 and some have "disappeared" from prisons where they had been receiving regular visits from their families. Despite persistent inquiries their families have not been able to trace their whereabouts or confirm whether they were still alive.

On 9 March 1981 Amnesty International cabled President Ali Nasir Mohammad expressing concern and seeking official confirmation of a report in the Lebanese newspaper *As-Safir* of the execution of Mohammad Saleh Muti', former Minister of Internal and Foreign Affairs. In a later unconfirmed report the Kuwaiti newspaper *Al-Watan* said that the Minister had been killed trying to escape from prison.

Missions: May 1980-April 1981

Country	*Date*	*Delegate(s)*	*Purpose*
	1980		
Zimbabwe/Namibia	May	Malcolm Smart (International Secretariat)	To hold talks with government officials in Zimbabwe and to carry out research in Namibia
Republic of Ireland	May	Mathole Motshekga (South Africa)	To attend appeal hearing of member of Irish Republican Socialist Party convicted of armed robbery of mail train
Turkey	May	Anne Burley (International Secretariat)	To carry out research
Poland	June	Gunther Hagen (Austria)	To observe trials of Miroslaw Chojecki and Bogdan Grzesiak
USA	June	Anthony Dunbar (USA) José Zalaquett (International Executive Committee)	To appeal to Governor Busbee of Georgia to suspend/commute death sentence passed on Jack Potts and to present arguments in favour of abolition
Nicaragua	August	Hipólito Solari Yrigoyen (Argentina)	To observe trials of suspected members of and collaborators with the National Guard of the Somoza regime

Country	Date	Delegate(s)	Purpose
USA	September	Professor Robert Daly (Eire) Douwe Korff (International Secretariat)	To investigate allegations of ill-treatment at Marion Prison, Illinois
Northern Ireland	September	Richard Elsner (International Secretariat)	To attend appeal hearing of Stephen Paul McCaul
Federal Republic of Germany (FRG)	September	Frits Rüter (Netherlands) Sarah Oliver (International Secretariat)	To discuss with relevant FRG authorities the "buying out" scheme and other arrangements between the FRG and the German Democratic Republic
Yugoslavia	October	Hipólito Solari Yrigoyen (Argentina) Melanie Anderson (International Secretariat)	To observe trial of Dragutin Trumbetas
Italy	October	Wilson Finney (UK)	To observe trial of conscientious objector
Spain	October	Hans Rau (FRG)	To observe trial of José Orive
Northern Ireland	October	Douwe Korff (International Secretariat)	To collect research material on trials
Bolivia	November	Admiral Antoine Sanguinetti (France) Michael Klein (International Executive Committee) Tricia Feeney (International Secretariat)	To hold talks with government officials and to monitor release of prisoners promised for early November by the government

Country	*Date*	*Delegate(s)*	*Purpose*
Vatican	December	José Zalaquett (International Executive Committee) Thomas Hammarberg (Secretary General) Julia Collier (International Secretariat)	To meet the Pope and the Pontifical Commission of Justice and Peace
Gambia	December	Kevin Boyle (UK)	To observe trial of six people accused of belonging to an "unlawful society" and of "possession of firearms and ammunition"
Grenada/Suriname	January	Stelios Nestor (International Executive Committee) Anne Burley (International Secretariat)	To hold high-level talks with government officials and carry out research
France	January/ February	Amand d'Hondt (Belgium)	To observe trial of Corsican nationalists
Yugoslavia	February	Sotiris Dedes (Greece)	To observe trial of Franjo Tudjman
Suriname	February	Hector Faundez-Ledesma (Chile)	To observe trial of former government officials by special court

Country	*Date*	*Delegate(s)*	*Purpose*
Morocco	February	Martin Ennals (former Secretary General) Michael Klein (International Executive Committee) Kevin Dwyer (International Secretariat)	To hold talks with government officials on current Amnesty International concerns
Turkey	April	Admiral Jan Dam Backer (Netherlands) Anne Burley (International Secretariat)	To hold high-level talks with government officials on Amnesty International concerns, especially torture
Bangladesh	April	Desmond Fernando (Sri Lanka)	To observe trial of five men charged with plotting to overthrow the government and to discuss legal concerns with the government

Amnesty International Accounts, Treasurer's and Auditors' Reports

TREASURER'S REPORT FOR THE YEAR ENDED 30 APRIL 1981

During the financial year ended 30 April 1981 Amnesty International received a total of £2,236,807 for the operation of its International Secretariat in London and for the implementation of its program by the International Executive Committee. Of this total £2,089,260 was directly contributed by its membership through national sections, and £147,547 was received from other sources, including sales of publications and audio-visual materials, interest income and so forth. In addition £185,791 was received for direct distribution as relief to individuals covered by Amnesty International's relief policies.

Before accepting any income, whether directly or through national sections, Amnesty International carefully ascertains that such contributions are in accordance with the general principles of its guidelines to ensure that:

— it is, and remains, and is seen to remain, an independent and impartial organization;

— it is, and remains, a broadly based and self-supporting organization;

— funds are given in accordance with the objects of its Statute.

In spite of the overall growth of the organization and the continuing high rate of inflation in the United Kingdom, stringent measures to control and reduce costs succeeded in keeping expenditure below the budgeted provision. For the first time in years it was possible to recover the considerable direct costs of the publications program from sales revenue. In addition the membership responded with admirable solidarity in providing its assessed contribution despite the heavy burden this undoubtedly created for many national sections.

It must be recognized, however, that for three years the International Secretariat budget has been held unchanged in real terms. In fact this has meant a reduction in resources considering the continuing growth of the movement. This cannot continue in the future without seriously affecting the implementation of the movement's program. To avoid this, major fund-raising efforts will be needed at all levels.

During the year, total expenditure for program activities amounted to £2,027,756 and £144,306 was distributed in relief payments.

Dirk Börner
Treasurer

AUDITORS' REPORT

To the International Council, Amnesty International:

We have examined the balance sheets of AMNESTY INTERNATIONAL as of 30 April 1981 and 1980 and the related statements of income and expenditure, changes in financial position and movement on Relief and Special Projects funds for the years then ended. Our examination was made in accordance with generally accepted auditing standards, and accordingly included such tests of the accounting records and such other auditing procedures as we considered necessary in the circumstances.

In our opinion, the accompanying financial statements set out on pages 390 to 401 present fairly the financial position of Amnesty International as of 30 April 1981 and 1980, the results of its activities, changes in financial position and movement on Relief and Special Projects funds for the years then ended, in conformity with generally accepted accounting principles, applied on a consistent basis.

Arthur Andersen & Co.

London
18 June 1981

AMNESTY INTERNATIONAL
BALANCE SHEETS — 30 APRIL 1981 AND 1980

ASSETS

	1981	1980
CURRENT ASSETS:		
Cash (Note 2)	£864,571	£473,024
Due from National Sections	40,172	186,033
Sundry debtors and prepaid expenses	76,482	72,701
Publications stocks (Note 3c)	16,598	12,472
Total current assets	997,823	744,230
PROPERTY AND EQUIPMENT (Notes 3b and 4):		
Cost	155,260	147,362
Accumulated depreciation	131,468	106,697
Net book value	23,792	40,665
Total assets	£1,021,615	£784,895

The accompanying notes are an integral part of these balance sheets.

Balance Sheets — 30 April 1981 and 1980 continued

LIABILITIES AND ACCUMULATED RESERVES

	1981	1980
CURRENT LIABILITIES:		
Creditors and accrued liabilities	£102,642	£116,906
Due to National Sections	66,932	58,309
Relief funds, per attached statement (Note 2)	192,108	158,218
Special Projects fund, per attached statement (Note 6)	201,336	177,828
Total current liabilities	563,018	511,261
PAST SERVICE SUPERANNUATION LIABILITY (Note 9)	7,540	8,120
Total liabilities	570,558	519,381
ACCUMULATED RESERVES (Note 7)	451,057	265,514
Total liabilities and accumulated reserves	£1,021,615	£784,895

The accompanying notes are an integral part of these balance sheets.

AMNESTY INTERNATIONAL
STATEMENTS OF INCOME AND EXPENDITURE
FOR THE YEARS ENDED 30 APRIL 1981 AND 1980

	1981	1980
INCOME:		
Contributions from National Sections (Note 3a)—		
Regular	£1,937,812	£1,586,762
Special contributions for contingencies	–	80,000
Additional contribution to increase the accumulated reserves	27,190	23,489
	1,965,002	1,690,251
Donations (Note 3a)	20,495	60,746
Other—		
Publications revenue (Note 3a)	53,345	31,453
Interest income	51,587	39,869
Write-back of over-provisions in prior years	8,756	11,420
Other receipts	13,364	8,562
	2,112,549	1,842,301
EXPENDITURE (Notes 3 and 5):		
Salaries and related costs	1,222,000	977,973
Administrative and program support expenses	195,931	201,866
Publications and printing	116,481	149,611
Travel and subsistence	74,377	80,219
Office expenses	255,670	240,097
Other expenses	32,462	22,060
Bad debts expense (Note 3a)	11,630	33,286
Exchange losses (Note 3d)	2,512	7,023
Expenditure relating to Nobel Peace and Erasmus Prizes (Note 7)	10,138	21,240
	1,921,201	1,733,375
Net surplus for the year	191,348	108,926

The accompanying notes are an integral part of these statements.

Analysis of net surplus for year—		
Operating surplus of the International Secretariat for the year	159,735	60,467
Contribution for accumulated reserves	27,190	23,489
Write-back of over-provisions in prior years	8,756	11,420
Donations allocated by the International Executive Committee to Special Projects fund	5,805	34,790
Expenditure relating to Nobel Peace and Erasmus Prizes	(10,138)	(21,240)
	£ 191,348	£ 108,926

DONATIONS ALLOCATED BY INTERNATIONAL EXECUTIVE COMMITTEE TO SPECIAL PROJECTS FUND	5,805	34,790
Net surplus for the year allocated to Accumulated Reserves	185,543	74,136
ACCUMULATED RESERVES, beginning of year	265,514	191,378
ACCUMULATED RESERVES, end of year	£ 451,057	£ 265,514

The accompanying notes are an integral part of these statements.

AMNESTY INTERNATIONAL
STATEMENTS OF CHANGES IN FINANCIAL POSITION FOR THE YEARS ENDED 30 APRIL 1981 AND 1980

	1981	1980
SOURCES OF FUNDS:		
Accumulated reserves—		
Net surplus for year	£191,348	£ 108,926
Depreciation, which does not involve cash flow during the year	24,771	29,212
	216,119	138,138
Relief funds receipts	185,791	175,132
Special Projects fund receipts	124,258	88,462
	526,168	401,732
Other sources—		
Decrease in debtor balances	142,080	–
Decrease in publications stocks	–	1,457
	668,248	403,189
USES OF FUNDS:		
Purchase of property and equipment	7,898	7,663
Increase in debtor balances	–	101,071
Decrease in creditor balances	6,221	34,880
Relief fund payments	151,901	202,172
Special Projects fund expenditure	106,555	164,332
Increase in publications stocks	4,126	–
	276,701	510,118
Increase (decrease) in cash during the year	£391,547	£(106,929)

The accompanying notes are an integral part of these statements.

AMNESTY INTERNATIONAL
STATEMENTS OF MOVEMENT ON RELIEF FUNDS
FOR THE YEARS ENDED 30 APRIL 1981 AND 1980
(Note 2)

	1981	1980
INCREASES:		
Specific relief funds received	£162,438	£154,779
Interest income	23,353	20,353
	185,791	175,132
DECREASES:		
Payments by geographical region—		
Africa	29,089	64,383
Asia	60,327	78,254
Europe	4,799	5,588
Americas	48,885	45,931
Middle East	309	8,016
Other (including administration charge)	8,492	–
	151,901	202,172
Net increase (decrease) for the year	33,890	(27,040)
BALANCE OF RELIEF FUNDS, beginning of year	158,218	185,258
BALANCE OF RELIEF FUNDS, end of year	£192,108	£158,218

The accompanying notes are an integral part of these statements.

AMNESTY INTERNATIONAL
STATEMENTS OF MOVEMENT ON SPECIAL PROJECTS FUND FOR THE YEARS ENDED 30 APRIL 1981 AND 1980
(Note 6)

	1981	1980
INCREASES:		
Donations for the Special Projects fund	£124,258	£ 88,462
Donations allocated to the Special Projects fund by the International Executive Committee	5,805	34,790
	130,063	123,252
DECREASES:		
Expenditure by Special Projects category comprised—		
Missions	24,079	57,861
National Section development	41,704	62,814
The Campaign Against Torture	1,661	21,925
Medical projects	14,682	2,463
Human rights awareness and education	651	–
Office premises and equipment	–	485
Research	4,201	9,317
International meetings	14,119	3,121
Other	5,458	6,346
	106,555	164,332
Net increase (decrease) for the year	23,508	(41,080)
FUND BALANCE, beginning of year	177,828	218,908
FUND BALANCE, end of year	£201,336	£177,828
Comprising—		
Amounts allocated to identified projects	£ 38,144	£ 52,156
Unallocated portion	163,192	125,672
	£201,336	£177,828

The accompanying notes are an integral part of these statements.

AMNESTY INTERNATIONAL
NOTES TO ACCOUNTS — 30 APRIL 1981 AND 1980

1. *AIMS AND ORGANIZATION:*

Amnesty International is an unincorporated, non-profit organization which has as its object the securing, throughout the world, of the observance of the provisions of the Universal Declaration of Human Rights. The specific objects, the methods to be applied in achieving these objects, and details of its organization are covered by the Statute of Amnesty International, as amended by the Twelfth International Council Meeting in Leuven, Belgium, in September, 1979.

The objects of Amnesty International include providing assistance to and working towards the release of persons who, in violation of the provisions of the Universal Declaration of Human Rights, are imprisoned, detained, restricted or otherwise subjected to physical coercion or restriction by reason of their political, religious, or other conscientiously held beliefs or by reason of their ethnic origin, colour or language (provided that they have not used or advocated violence). These persons are referred to as "prisoners of conscience". Amnesty International is organized on the basis of National Sections, whose activities are assisted by the International Secretariat in London, under the control of the International Executive Committee. One of the main functions of the International Secretariat is to carry out research to identify prisoners of conscience and to report on its findings.

The International Secretariat is financed principally by contributions from National Sections. The accompanying accounts include only those finances for which the International Executive Committee is responsible, namely those of the International Secretariat. Accordingly these accounts exclude amounts related to the resources of individual National Sections.

2. *RELIEF FUNDS:*

The International Secretariat is responsible for the administration and disbursement of relief funds. Not all such funds received have been applied, as yet, towards relief, and such unpaid funds are held in separate bank accounts. Relief funds are reflected as a current liability of the International Secretariat.

Payments of relief are usually made to prisoners or their families via intermediaries. This involves entrusting persons whom the International Secretariat considers to be responsible with relief monies and relying extensively on their integrity and dedication to ensure that the proper persons benefit from relief. It is not always possible or practicable to obtain receipts from beneficiaries of relief monies, but the International Secretariat does have additional sources of information which, it believes, would report any significant instances where relief monies, for one reason or another, did not reach prisoners or their families. No such significant instances have been reported.

The movement on relief funds is summarized in the attached statement; receipts and payments of relief funds do not comprise income and expenditure of the International Secretariat.

3. *ACCOUNTING POLICIES:*

a) Income—

National Section contributions to the International Secretariat represent the agreed share of each Section towards the budget of the International Secretariat. Reserves have been provided against unpaid contributions which National Sections have stated they will not or cannot meet.

Donations are accounted for on a cash basis, and include amounts received from National Sections over and above their agreed contributions.

Publications revenue represents the sale of publications to National Sections and third-parties.

b) Property and equipment—

Property and equipment are stated at cost less accumulated depreciation. Depreciation is provided at the following rates—

Leasehold improvements — over the period of the lease
Office equipment — over a period of four years

Depreciation provided in respect of assets purchased out of the Special Projects fund has been charged to the fund.

c) Publications stocks—

Publications stocks are stated at the lower of cost and net realisable value.

d) Foreign currencies—

Foreign currency assets and liabilities have been translated into pounds sterling at the exchange rates ruling at the balance sheet dates.

Foreign currency income and expenditure are translated into pounds sterling at average exchange rates for the year.

4. *PROPERTY AND EQUIPMENT:*

Movement on the account for the year was—

	Balance, 30 April 1980	Additions/ Provisions	Balance, 30 April 1981
Cost—			
Leasehold improvements	£ 48,146	£ –	£ 48,146
Office equipment	99,216	7,898	107,114
	147,362	£ 7,898	155,260
Accumulated depreciation—			
Leasehold improvements	34,727	5,369	40,096
Office equipment	71,970	19,402	91,372
	106,697	£24,771	131,468
Net book value	£ 40,665		£ 23,792

5. *PUBLICATIONS DEPARTMENT:*

The income and expenditure of the Publications Department of the International Secretariat (included in the statement of income and expenditure) was as follows—

	1981	1980
Publications revenue	£ 53,345	£ 31,453
Publications cost of sales	(44,163)	(65,753)
Gross profit (loss)	9,182	(34,300)
Salaries and related costs	(70,980)	(52,934)
Other costs	(35,317)	(25,855)
Deficit for year	£(97,115)	£(113,089)

6. *SPECIAL PROJECTS FUND:*

The Special Projects fund, replenished from time to time by National Sections and other sources, is maintained to enable the organization to carry out specific projects for which resources would not otherwise be available. Examples of these projects include missions to attend trials of prisoners of conscience, investigations into prison conditions and the provision of information services for certain regions.

The movement on the Special Projects fund is summarized in the attached statement; receipts and payments of the Special Projects fund do not comprise income and expenditure of Amnesty International.

7. *ACCUMULATED RESERVES:*

The accumulated reserves represent—

	1981	1980
General accumulated reserve	£411,419	£215,738
Nobel Peace Prize	22,654	32,184
Erasmus Prize	16,984	17,592
	£451,057	£265,514

At its meeting in May 1980, the International Executive Committee agreed that the level of the general accumulated reserve should represent approximately 25 per cent of the annual expenditure of the International Secretariat. At 30 April 1981 and 1980, the general accumulated reserve represented 21 per cent and 13 per cent respectively of the expenditure incurred during the years then ended (excluding expenditure relating to the Nobel Peace Prize and the Erasmus Prize).

During the year ended 30 April 1978, Amnesty International was awarded the Nobel Peace Prize. On the recommendation of the International Executive Committee, the prize has been placed in a special fund, for the purpose of strengthening the worldwide organization of Amnesty International and for special programs identified with peace. During the year ended 30 April 1981, £9,530 was expended from this fund.

The Erasmus Prize was awarded to Amnesty International during the year ended 30 April 1977. The prize, which can only be used for specified purposes, is being used to establish a document centre. During the year ended 30 April 1981, £608 was expended from the fund.

8. *LEASE COMMITMENTS:*

In 1979, the organization renegotiated the terms of the lease of its premises at Southampton Street, London WC2. The lease extends to 25 December 1983 at an annual rental of £110,000 but can be terminated in December 1982 at the option of the landlord.

Under the terms of the lease, the organization has paid a deposit of £12,250 as surety, which is held jointly by the solicitors of Amnesty International and the lessor until the expiry of the lease.

9. *PAST SERVICE SUPERANNUATION LIABILITY:*

The International Secretariat's Retirement Benefits Scheme became effective in January 1974. The scheme is fully-insured and covers most employees. The past service liability at inception of the scheme amounted to £11,600. A provision of this amount was made in 1974, and is being amortized over 20 years on a straight-line basis; the unamortized balance at 30 April 1981 was £7,540.

10. *TAXATION:*

Amnesty International is regarded for tax purposes as a body corporate and is chargeable to Corporation Tax on profits arising from any trading activity and on interest income. No provision for Corporation Tax has been made in these accounts as trading losses (from publications) exceed interest income.

11. *INCORPORATION OF AMNESTY INTERNATIONAL:*

Subsequent to 30 April 1981 proceedings have been initiated to incorporate Amnesty International, International Secretariat, as a company limited by guarantee. Incorporation with liability limited by guarantee is a form of incorporation commonly used by non-profit making organizations in the United Kingdom.

Appendices

APPENDIX I

Statute of Amnesty International

As amended by the 12th International Council, meeting in Leuven, Belgium, 6-9 September 1979

OBJECT

1. CONSIDERING that every person has the right freely to hold and to express his or her convictions and the obligation to extend a like freedom to others, the object of AMNESTY INTERNATIONAL shall be to secure throughout the world the observance of the provisions of the Universal Declaration of Human Rights, by:
   a) irrespective of political considerations working towards the release of and providing assistance to persons who in violation of the aforesaid provisions are imprisoned, detained or otherwise physically restricted by reason of their political, religious or other conscientiously held beliefs or by reason of their ethnic origin, sex, colour or language, provided that they have not used or advocated violence (hereinafter referred to as "Prisoners of Conscience");
   b) opposing by all appropriate means the detention of any Prisoners of Conscience or any political prisoners without trial within a reasonable time or any trial procedures relating to such prisoners that do not conform to internationally recognized norms;
   c) opposing by all appropriate means the imposition and infliction of death penalties and torture or other cruel, inhuman or degrading treatment or punishment of prisoners or other detained or restricted persons whether or not they have used or advocated violence.

METHODS

2. In order to achieve the aforesaid object, AMNESTY INTERNATIONAL shall:
   a) at all times maintain an overall balance between its activities in relation to countries adhering to the different world political ideologies and groupings;
   b) promote as appears appropriate the adoption of constitutions,

conventions, treaties and other measures which guarantee the rights contained in the provisions referred to in article 1 hereof;

c) support and publicize the activities of and cooperate with international organizations and agencies which work for the implementation of the aforesaid provisions;

d) take all necessary steps to establish an effective organization of national sections, affiliated groups and individual members;

e) secure the adoption by groups of members or supporters of individual Prisoners of Conscience or entrust to such groups other tasks in support of the object set out in article 1;

f) provide financial and other relief to Prisoners of Conscience and their dependants who have lately been Prisoners of Conscience or who might reasonably be expected to be Prisoners of Conscience or to become Prisoners of Conscience if convicted or if they were to return to their own countries, and to the dependants of such persons;

g) work for the improvement of conditions for Prisoners of Conscience and political prisoners;

h) provide legal aid, where necessary and possible, to Prisoners of Conscience and to persons who might reasonably be expected to be Prisoners of Conscience or to become Prisoners of Conscience if convicted or if they were to return to their own countries, and where desirable, send observers to attend the trials of such persons;

i) publicize the cases of Prisoners of Conscience or persons who have otherwise been subjected to disabilities in violation of the aforesaid provisions;

j) send investigators, where appropriate, to investigate allegations that the rights of individuals under the aforesaid provisions have been violated or threatened;

k) make representations to international organizations and to governments whenever it appears that an individual is a Prisoner of Conscience or has otherwise been subjected to disabilities in violation of the aforesaid provisions,

l) promote and support the granting of general amnesties of which the beneficiaries will include Prisoners of Conscience;

m) adopt any other appropriate methods for the securing of its object.

ORGANIZATION

3. AMNESTY INTERNATIONAL shall consist of national sections, affiliated groups and individual members.
4. The directive authority for the conduct of the affairs of AMNESTY INTERNATIONAL is vested in the International Council.
5. Between meetings of the International Council, the International Executive Committee shall be responsible for the conduct of the affairs of AMNESTY INTERNATIONAL and for the implementation of the decisions of the International Council.
6. The day to day affairs of AMNESTY INTERNATIONAL shall be conducted by the International Secretariat headed by a Secretary General under the direction of the International Executive Committee.
7. The office of the International Secretariat shall be in London or such other place as the International Executive Committee shall decide and which is ratified by at least one-half of national sections.

NATIONAL SECTIONS

8. A national section of AMNESTY INTERNATIONAL may be established in any country, state or territory with the consent of the International Executive Committee. In order to be recognized as such, a national section shall (a) consist of not less than two groups or 10 members (b) submit its statute to the International Executive Committee for approval (c) pay such annual fee as may be determined by the International Council (d) be registered as such with the International Secretariat on the decision of the International Executive Committee. National sections shall take no action on matters that do not fall within the stated object of AMNESTY INTERNATIONAL. The International Secretariat shall maintain a register of national sections. National sections shall act in accordance with the working rules and guidelines that are adopted from time to time by the International Council.
9. Groups of not less than three members or supporters may, on payment of an annual fee determined by the International Council, become affiliated to AMNESTY INTERNATIONAL or a national section thereof. Any dispute as to whether a group should be or remain affiliated shall be decided by the International Executive Committee. An affiliated adoption group shall accept for adoption such prisoners as may from time to time be allotted to it by the International Secretariat, and shall

adopt no others as long as it remains affiliated to AMNESTY INTERNATIONAL. No group shall be alloted a Prisoner of Conscience detained in its own country. The International Secretariat shall maintain a register of affiliated adoption groups. Groups shall take no action on matters that do not fall within the stated object of AMNESTY INTERNATIONAL. Groups shall act in accordance with the working rules and guidelines that are adopted from time to time by the International Council.

INDIVIDUAL MEMBERSHIP

10. Individuals residing in countries where there is no national section may, on payment to the International Secretariat of an annual subscription fee determined by the International Executive Committee, become members of AMNESTY INTERNATIONAL with the consent of the International Executive Committee. In countries where a national section exists, individuals may become international members of AMNESTY INTERNATIONAL with the consent of the national section and of the International Executive Committee. The International Secretariat shall maintain a register of such members.

11. Deleted.

INTERNATIONAL COUNCIL

12. The International Council shall consist of the members of the International Executive Committee and of representatives of national sections and shall meet at intervals of approximately one year but in any event of not more than two years on a date fixed by the International Executive Committee. Only representatives of national sections and elected members of the International Executive Committee shall have the right to vote on the International Council.

13. All national sections shall have the right to appoint one representative to the International Council and in addition may appoint representatives as follows:

10- 49 groups	:	1 representative
50- 99 groups	:	2 representatives
100-199 groups	:	3 representatives
200-399 groups	:	4 representatives
400 groups or over	:	5 representatives

National sections consisting primarily of individual members rather than groups may in alternative appoint additional representatives as follows:

500-2,499	:	1 representative
2,500 and over	:	2 representatives

Only sections having paid in full their annual fee as assessed by the International Council for the previous financial year shall vote at the International Council. This requirement may be waived in whole or in part by the International Executive Committee.

14. Representatives of groups not forming part of a national section may with the permission of the Secretary General attend a meeting of the International Council as observers and may speak thereat but shall not be entitled to vote.

15. A national section unable to participate in an International Council may appoint a proxy or proxies to vote on its behalf and a national section represented by a lesser number of persons than its entitlement under article 13 hereof may authorize its representative or representatives to cast votes up to its maximum entitlement under article 13 hereof.

16. Notice of the number of representatives proposing to attend an International Council, and of the appointment of proxies, shall be given to the International Secretariat not later than one month before the meeting of the International Council. This requirement may be waived by the International Executive Committee.

17. A quorum shall consist of the representatives or proxies of not less than one quarter of the national sections entitled to be represented.

18. The Chairperson of the International Executive Committee, or such other person as the International Executive Committee may appoint, shall open the proceedings of the International Council, which shall elect a chairperson. Thereafter the elected Chairperson, or such other person as the Chairperson may appoint, shall preside at the International Council.

19. Except as otherwise provided in the statute, the International Council shall make its decisions by a simple majority of the votes cast. In case of an equality of votes the Chairperson of the International Council shall have a casting vote.

20. The International Council shall be convened by the International Secretariat by notice to all national sections and affiliated groups not later than 90 days before the date thereof.

21. The Chairperson of the International Executive Committee shall at the request of the Committee or of not less than one-third of the national sections call an extraordinary meeting of the

International Council by giving not less than 21 days notice in writing to all national sections.

22. The International Council shall elect a Treasurer, who shall be a member of the International Executive Committee.

23. The International Council may appoint one or more Honorary Presidents of AMNESTY INTERNATIONAL to hold office for a period not exceeding three years.

24. The agenda for the meetings of the International Council shall be prepared by the International Secretariat under the direction of the Chairperson of the International Executive Committee.

INTERNATIONAL EXECUTIVE COMMITTEE

25. a) The International Executive Committee shall consist of the Treasurer, one representative of the staff of the International Secretariat and seven regular members, who shall be members of AMNESTY INTERNATIONAL, or of a national section, or of an affiliated group, elected by the International Council by proportional representation by the method of the single transferable vote in accordance with the regulations published by the Electoral Reform Society. Not more than one member of any national section or affiliated group may be elected as a regular member to the Committee, and once one member of any national section or affiliated group has received sufficient votes to be elected, any votes cast for other members of that national section or affiliated group shall be disregarded.

b) Members of the permanent staff, paid and unpaid, shall have the right to elect one representative among the staff who has completed not less than two years' service to be a voting member of the International Executive Committee. Such member shall hold office for one year and shall be eligible for re-election. The method of voting shall be subject to approval by the International Executive Committee on the proposal of the staff members.

26. The International Executive Committee shall meet not less than twice a year at a place to be decided by itself.

27. Members of the International Executive Committee, other than the representative of the staff, shall hold office for a period of two years and shall be eligible for re-election. Except in the case of elections to fill vacancies resulting from unexpired terms of office, the members of the Committee, other than the representative of the staff, shall be subjected to election in equal

proportions on alternate years.

28. The Committee may co-opt not more than four additional members who shall hold office until the close of the next meeting of the International Council; they shall be eligible to be reco-opted. Co-opted members shall not have the right to vote.

29. In the event of a vacancy occurring on the Committee, other than in respect of the representative of the staff, it may co-opt a further member to fill the vacancy until the next meeting of the International Council, which shall elect such members as are necessary to replace retiring members and to fill the vacancy. In the event of a vacancy occurring on the Committee in respect of the representative of the staff, the staff shall have the right to elect a successor representative to fill the unexpired term of office.

30. If a member of the Committee is unable to attend a meeting, such member may appoint an alternate.

31. The Committee shall each year appoint one of its members to act as Chairperson.

32. The Chairperson may, and at the request of the majority of the Committee shall, summon meetings of the Committee.

33. A quorum shall consist of not less than five members of the Committee or their alternates.

34. The agenda for meetings of the Committee shall be prepared by the International Secretariat under the direction of the Chairperson.

35. The Committee may make regulations for the conduct of the affairs of AMNESTY INTERNATIONAL, and for the procedure to be followed at the International Council.

INTERNATIONAL SECRETARIAT

36. The International Executive Committee may appoint a Secretary General who shall be responsible under its direction for the conduct of the affairs of AMNESTY INTERNATIONAL and for the implementation of the decisions of the International Council.

37. The Secretary General may, after consultation with the Chairperson of the International Executive Committee, and subject to confirmation by that Committee, appoint such executive and professional staff as are necessary for the proper conduct of the affairs of AMNESTY INTERNATIONAL, and may appoint such other staff as are necessary.

38 In the case of the absence or illness of the Secretary General, or of a vacancy in the post of Secretary General, the Chairperson of the International Executive Committee shall, after consultation with the members of that Committee, appoint an acting Secretary General to act until the next meeting of the Committee.

39. The Secretary General or Acting Secretary General, and such members of the International Secretariat as may appear to the Chairperson of the International Executive Committee to be necessary shall attend meetings of the International Council and of the International Executive Committee and may speak thereat but shall not be entitled to vote.

TERMINATION OF MEMBERSHIP

40. Membership of or affiliation to AMNESTY INTERNATIONAL may be terminated at any time by resignation in writing.

41. The International Council may, upon the proposal of the International Executive Committee or of a national section, by a three-fourths majority of the votes cast deprive a national section, an affiliated group or a member of membership of AMNESTY INTERNATIONAL if in its opinion that national section, affiliated group or member does not act within the spirit of the object and methods set out in articles 1 and 2 or does not observe any of the provisions of this statute. Before taking such action, all national sections shall be informed and the Secretary General shall also inform the national section, affiliated group or member of the grounds on which it is proposed to deprive it or such person of membership, and such national section, affiliated group or member shall be provided with an opportunity of presenting its or such member's case to the International Council.

42. A national section, affiliated group or member who fails to pay the annual fee fixed in accordance with this statute within six months after the close of the financial year shall cease to be affiliated to AMNESTY INTERNATIONAL unless the International Executive Committee decides otherwise.

FINANCE

43. An auditor appointed by the International Council shall annually audit the accounts of AMNESTY INTERNATIONAL, which shall be prepared by the International Secretariat and presented to the International Executive Committee and the International Council.

44. No part of the income or property of AMNESTY INTERNATIONAL shall directly or indirectly be paid or transferred otherwise than for valuable and sufficient consideration to any of its members by way of dividend, gift, division, bonus or otherwise howsoever by way of profit.

AMENDMENTS OF STATUTE

45. The statute may be amended by the International Council by a majority of not less than two-thirds of the votes cast. Amendments may be submitted by the International Executive Committee or by a national section. Proposed amendments shall be submitted to the International Secretariat not less than three months before the International Council meets, and presentation to the International Council shall be supported in writing by at least five national sections. Proposed amendments shall be communicated by the International Secretariat to all national sections and to members of the International Executive Committee.

APPENDIX II

Amnesty International News Releases May 1980-April 1981

1980

4 May — AI expressed fears that former members of an East Timor independence movement have been executed after surrendering under an amnesty offered by *Indonesian* authorities. A number "disappeared" after being rearrested by Indonesian troops, and others have been missing since they surrendered.

9 May — AI urged the authorities in *Iran* to conform to internationally agreed standards for trials and treatment of prisoners, to which Iran is committed by international treaty. A report sent to the new government found that many people had been sentenced to death and executed without fair trials.

20 May — AI launched a campaign against human rights violations in *Zaïre*. Hundreds of people have been arbitrarily arrested and then confined indefinitely in remote camps in the jungle and bush where deaths

by summary execution, torture or starvation are common.

20 May — AI received a written response from the Government of *Zaïre* in reply to the report and memorandum on arrests and ill-treatment of prisoners.

22 May — AI received an assurance from the chairperson of *Uganda's* ruling Military Commission about former President Godfrey Binaisa.

26 May — AI urged President Carter to establish a presidential commission to study the death penalty in the *United States of America,* and examine whether executions violate the country's international commitments to human rights.

28 May — AI said that prisoners held in connection with politically motivated crimes in the *Federal Republic of Germany* were kept in conditions that could — and sometimes did — cause serious physical and psychological damage.

3 June — AI appealed to President Carter of the *United States of America* to intervene personally with Governor George Busbee of Georgia to stay the execution of Jack Howard Potts, scheduled to take place on 5 June 1980.

9 June — AI reported that torture in *Turkey* had become widespread and systematic; that most people being arrested by police and martial-law authorities were tortured; and that in some cases it was alleged to have ended in death.

12 June — AI launched an international campaign to persuade the *Iraqi* authorities to halt their increasing use of the death penalty, often imposed by special courts for non-violent political activity.

16 June — AI called on the *Jamaican* Committee on Capital Punishment and Penal Reform to pave the way for the abolition of the death penalty.

30 June — AI said that the authorities in *Romania* used a wide range of legal and extra-legal penalties against those breaching official limits on the expression of political, religious and social views.

30 June — AI publicized reports that two Argentinians had been tortured to death after being seized in *Peru* and

that three others had been secretly taken back to Argentina.

16 July — AI warned that proposed United States security assistance to *El Salvador* would worsen the widespread murder and torture of peasants and suspected opponents of the government. In a letter to US Secretary of State Edmund Muskie, AI said that since early January "at least 2,000 Salvadorians have been killed or 'disappeared' while in the hands of conventional and auxiliary security forces".

28 July — AI reported that 10 political prisoners being held without trial in *Angola* were seriously ill after more than three weeks on hunger-strike.

5 August — AI announced that a fact-finding mission to the *Republic of Korea* had been refused entry. The mission was to investigate reports of large-scale arrests and torture of political prisoners.

8 August — AI appealed to the new military leader of *Bolivia* to release all political prisoners and to publish a list of people imprisoned or killed since he took power on 17 July 1980. AI estimated that 1,000 people had been arrested since the coup, and cited reports of summary executions, arbitrary arrests and torture.

21 August — AI publicized an eye-witness account of *Bolivian* troops rampaging through a mining town, killing, abducting and raping. As many as 900 people had "disappeared" from Caracoles after the attack. The town is in a mining region whose inhabitants are suspected of political opposition to the new military leaders.

29 August — AI appealed to the newly appointed prime minister of *Iran* to halt executions and the imprisonment of people for their beliefs or origins. AI was saddened to see continued human rights violations since the Iranian Revolution "and especially the large number of executions".

2 September — AI called on the Government of *Israel* to set up a public and impartial inquiry into persistent complaints of brutality towards people arrested on suspicion of security offences in the Occupied Territories.

9 September — AI reported that political arrests and systematic

torture of suspects increased sharply as *Chile* approached the seventh anniversary of the military coup that brought its present government to power.

15 September	AI called on the United Nations General Assembly to declare the death penalty a violation of fundamental human rights. The supreme governing body of AI, meeting in Vienna, urged its national sections and members to seek support for such a declaration.
17 September	AI was appalled by the death sentence passed by a *Republic of Korea* military court on opposition leader Kim Dae-jung. The trial of Kim and 23 co-defendants, who received prison sentences, failed to meet international standards of fairness.
22 September	AI sent the Government of *Colombia* detailed and conclusive evidence of widespread arbitrary arrests and systematic torture of political prisoners by government forces.
29 September	AI urged President Saddam Hussein of *Iraq* to inquire into reports that political suspects had been given slow-acting poison while in custody. The organization had received detailed evidence about three people, two of whom had been examined by doctors in the UK after leaving Iraq.
12 October	AI launched a worldwide week of action on behalf of victims of political repression. Prisoner of Conscience Week 1980 was organized around the theme "the different faces of imprisonment", spotlighting the different methods of repression — including abduction, house arrest, prosecution on false criminal charges and short-term arrest.
15 October	AI announced that it had submitted a series of detailed recommendations to the Government of *Spain,* designed to protect political detainees from torture.
22 October	Willy Brandt, Pierre Trudeau and Morarji Desai were among thousands of prominent people from around the world who joined in an AI appeal to the United Nations for international action to abolish the death penalty.
3 November	AI called on President Zia ul-Haq to release all prisoners of conscience held in *Pakistan* and to take immediate steps to halt torture, floggings and executions.

6 November AI asked the Government of the *United States of America* to clarify what treatment and status Haitians seeking asylum in the US would receive. AI had reports that they were to be sent to a military camp in Puerto Rico.

12 November AI rejected accusations by the *Soviet* newspaper *Izvestia* that it was "maintained by imperialist secret services".

28 November AI said that a new constitution proposed by the military rulers of *Uruguay* would institutionalize a system marked by repression and torture, and give a semblance of legality to violations of basic human rights which have been occurring since the military took full power in 1973.

3 December AI published medical evidence of maltreatment amounting to torture inflicted on political detainees held incommunicado in *Spanish* police stations.

9 December AI appealed to the heads of government of each of the 43 nations represented on the United Nations Commission of Human Rights in an effort to prevent the execution of *Republic of Korea* opposition leader Kim Dae-jung.

10 December The *Amnesty International Report 1980* highlights the political death toll: people were murdered by government forces or executed for political reasons in more than 30 countries during the 12 months reviewed.

1981

21 January AI said that courts in the *Soviet Union* were passing severe sentences in a sustained crackdown on dissenters, more than 200 of whom had been imprisoned during the previous 15 months.

23 January AI appealed to President Chun Doo-hwan of the *Republic of Korea* for the immediate and unconditional release of opposition leader Kim Dae-jung.

25 January AI urged the authorities in *China* to commute the death sentences passed by a special court on Jiang Ching and Zhang Chunqiao in the "gang of four" trial.

4 February AI appealed to the Government of the *German Democratic Republic* to review the country's cri-

minal laws to bring them in line with its international commitments on human rights.

13 February	AI cabled the Government of *Nicaragua* to express concern about reports that the Ministry of Justice had ordered the closure of the independent Nicaraguan Commission on Human Rights.
18 February	AI said that a long-established government program of murder and torture in *Guatemala* was run from an annex to the National Palace, under the control of President Romeo Lucas García.
25 February	AI reported that *Bolivian* troops and government agents had killed, tortured and abducted people in total disregard of law and constitutional principles since a military junta took power in a coup in July 1980.
2 March	AI launched a worldwide campaign to persuade the authorities of the *Republic of Korea* to stop political imprisonment, torture and unfair trials.
20 March	AI appealed to President Giscard d'Estaing of *France* to commute the death sentence on Philippe Maurice and prevent France's first execution since 1977.
9 April	AI called on the Government of *El Salvador* to guarantee the safety of people named on an apparent death list of 138 names published by the Salvadorian army.
29 April	AI published detailed medical findings supporting other convincing evidence that political prisoners are tortured in *Iraq*.

APPENDIX III

Amnesty International Publications May 1980-April 1981

Amnesty International Publications are available in English, French and Spanish. Editions in many other languages are also produced. Copies of publications and details of the Amnesty International multilingual publishing program may be obtained from the offices of national sections. For addresses see page 421.

Reports

Zaïre: *Human Rights Violations in Zaïre* (1980)

United States of America: *Proposal for a Presidential Commission on the Death Penalty* (1980)

Romania: *Amnesty International Briefing on Romania,* No. 17 (1980)

Israel: *Report and Recommendations of an Amnesty International Mission to the Government of the State of Israel, 3-7 June 1979* (1980)

Annual Report: *Amnesty International Report 1980* (1980)

Spain: *Report of an Amnesty International Mission to Spain 3-28 October 1979* (1980)

German Democratic Republic: *Amnesty International Briefing on the German Democratic Republic,* No. 18 (second edition) (1981)

Guatemala: *Guatemala — A government program of political murder* (1981)

Republic of Korea: *Republic of Korea: violations of human rights* (1981)

Iraq: *Iraq: evidence of torture* (1981)

Colombia: *Informe de una misión de Amnistia Internacional a la República de Colombia, 15 de enero-31 de enero de 1980* (1980)

A Chronicle of Current Events

A Chronicle of Current Events (the *samizdat* journal of the human rights movement in the USSR) is translated and published by Amnesty International. Orders for subscriptions, back issues or single copies should be sent to the distributor: Routledge Journals, Broadway House, Newtown Road, Henley on Thames, Oxon RG9 1EN, UK, or to: Routledge Journals, 9 Park Street, Boston, Mass 02108, USA.

A Chronicle of Current Events, No. 54 (1980), Nos. 55-56 (1981), and No. 57 (1981).

Amnesty International Newsletter

The *Amnesty International Newsletter* provides a monthly account of Amnesty International's work for human rights in countries throughout the world. It includes the latest reports of fact-finding missions, details of the arrest and release of prisoners of conscience, and reliable reports of torture and execution. It also gives practical information for Amnesty International supporters: each issue includes appeals on behalf of prisoners of conscience and victims of torture.

Documents

In addition to major reports, Amnesty International publishes documents on its missions and related research work.

Iran: *Law and Human Rights in the Islamic Republic of Iran. (A report covering events within the seven-month period following the Revolution of February 1979.)* (1980)

Federal Republic of Germany: *Amnesty International's work on prison conditions of persons suspected or convicted of politically-motivated crimes in the Federal Republic of Germany: Isolation and Solitary Confinement* (1980)

Bolivia: *Memorandum from Amnesty International to His Excellency General Luis Garcia Meza, President of the Republic of Bolivia* (1981)

APPENDIX IV

Resolution 5 adopted by the Sixth United Nations Congress on the Prevention of Crime and the Treatment of Offenders (on 1 September 1980)

Extra-legal executions

The Sixth United Nations Congress on the Prevention of Crime and the Treatment of Offenders,

Alarmed by reports of widespread killings of political opponents or suspected offenders carried out by armed forces, law enforcement or other governmental agencies or by political groups often acting with the tacit or other support of such forces or agencies,

Recalling that article 3 of the Universal Declaration of Human Rights guarantees to everyone the right to life, liberty and security of person,

Recalling article 6, paragraph 1, of the International Covenant on Civil and Political Rights, according to which no one shall be arbitrarily deprived of his life,

Recalling that the four Geneva Conventions,[1] of 12 August 1949, provide that wilful killings are grave breaches of the conventions and that article 3, common to the four conventions, in respect of non-international armed conflict, further prohibits at any time and in any place whatsoever violence to life and person, in particular murder of all kinds,

Considering that murder committed or tolerated by Governments is condemned by all national legal systems and, thus, by general principles of law,

Recalling General Assembly resolution 33/173 of 20 December 1978 on Disappeared Persons, and the fact that the enforced or involuntary disappearances referred to in that resolution are frequently related to murder committed or tolerated by Governments,

Considering that the above-mentioned acts also violate the Declaration on the Protection of All Persons from Being Subjected to Torture or Other Cruel, Inhuman or Degrading Treatment or Punishment,

1. *Deplores and condemns* the practice of killing of political opponents or of suspected offenders carried out by armed forces, law enforcement or other governmental agencies or by political groups acting with the tacit or other support of such forces or agencies;

2. *Affirms* that such killings constitute a particularly abhorrent crime the eradication of which is a high international priority;

3. *Calls upon* all Governments to take effective measures to prevent such killings;

4. *Urges* all organs of the United Nations dealing with questions of crime prevention and of human rights to take all possible action to bring such killings to an end.

1 United Nations, *Treaty Series,* vol. 75.

APPENDIX V

Amnesty International

APPEAL TO THE UNITED NATIONS FOR THE ABOLITION OF THE DEATH PENALTY

We, the undersigned,

ALARMED BY

executions of political opponents and criminal offenders in many countries;

AFFIRMING THAT

the death penalty is incompatible with the right to life and the prohibition of cruel, inhuman or degrading treatment;

CONVINCED THAT

the abolition of the death penalty in all countries would represent a great advance in the respect of governments for the human person;

APPEALS TO

the United Nations and its member states to take all necessary steps for the immediate and total abolition of the death penalty throughout the world.

APPENDIX VI

Amnesty International

DECLARATION ON THE PARTICIPATION OF DOCTORS IN THE DEATH PENALTY

Amnesty International,

RECALLING

that the spirit of the Hippocratic Oath enjoins doctors to practise for the good of their patients and never to do harm,

CONSIDERING

that the Declaration of Tokyo of the World Medical Association provides that "the utmost respect for human life is to be maintained even under threat, and no use made of any medical knowledge contrary to the laws of humanity",

FURTHER CONSIDERING THAT

the same Declaration forbids the participation of doctors in torture or other cruel, inhuman or degrading procedures,

NOTING

that the United Nations Secretariat has stated that the death penalty violates the right to life and that it constitutes cruel, inhuman or degrading punishment,

MINDFUL

that doctors can be called on to participate in executions by, *inter alia,*

—determining mental and physical fitness for execution,
—giving technical advice,
—prescribing, preparing, administering and supervising doses of poison in jurisdictions where this method is used,
—making medical examinations during executions, so that an execution can continue if the prisoner is not yet dead,

DECLARES

that the participation of doctors in executions is a violation of medical ethics;

CALLS UPON

medical doctors not to participate in executions;

FURTHER CALLS UPON

medical organizations to protect doctors who refuse to participate in executions, and to adopt resolutions to these ends.

This declaration was formulated by the Medical Advisory Board of Amnesty International and was adopted by Amnesty International's International Executive Committee on 12 March 1981.

APPENDIX VII

National Section Addresses

Australia: Amnesty International, Australian Section, PO Box No. A159, Sydney South, New South Wales 2000

Austria: Amnesty International, Austrian Section, Esslinggasse 15/4, A-1010 Wien

Bangladesh: Amnesty Bangladesh, GPO Box 2095, Dacca

Barbados: Amnesty International, Barbados Section, PO Box 65B, Brittons Hill, Bridgetown

Belgium: *(Flemish branch)* Amnesty International, Blijde Inkomststraat 98, 3000 Leuven

(Francophone) Amnesty International, 145 Boulevard Leopold II, 1080 Brussels

Canada: *(English-speaking)* Amnesty International, Canadian Section (English-speaking), PO Box 6033, 2101 Algonquin Avenue, Ottawa, Ontario K2A 1T1

(Francophone) Amnistie Internationale, Section canadienne (francophone), 1800 Ouest Boulevard Dorchester, Local 400, Montreal, Quebec H3H 2H2

Denmark: Amnesty International, Frederiksborggade 1, 1360 Copenhagen

Ecuador: Casilla de Correo 8994, Guayaquil

Faroe Islands: Amnesty International, c/o Anette Wang, PO Box 1075, Tróndargøta 47, 3800 Tórshavn

Finland: Amnesty International, Finnish Section, Munkkisaarenkatu 12A51, 00150 Helsinki 15

France: Amnesty International, Section français, 18 rue Theodore Deck, 75015 Paris

Germany, Federal Republic of: Amnesty International, Section of the FRG, Heerstrasse 178, 5300 Bonn 1

Ghana: Amnesty International, Ghanaian Section, PO Box 9852, Kotoka Airport, Accra

Greece: Amnesty International, Greek Section, 22 Kleitomachou Street, Athens 502

Iceland: Amnesty International, Icelandic Section, Hafnarstraeti 15, PO Box 7124, 127 Reykjavik

India: Amnesty International, Indian Section, Vivekananda Vihar, C4/3 Safdarjung Development Area, New Delhi-110016

Ireland: Amnesty International, Irish Section, Liberty Hall, 8th Floor, Dublin 1

Israel: Amnesty International, Israel National Section, PO Box 37638, 61 375 Tel Aviv

Italy: Amnesty International, Italian Section, viale Mazzini 146, 00195 Rome

Ivory Coast: Amnesty International, Section ivoirienne, 04 BP 895, 04 Abidjan

Japan: Amnesty International, Japanese Section, Daisan-Sanbu Building, 3F, 2-3-22, Nishi-Waseda, Shinjuku-ku, Tokyo 160

Korea, Republic of: c/o International Secretariat, 10 Southampton Street, London WC2E 7HF, United Kingdom

Luxembourg: Amnesty International Luxembourg, Boîte Postale 1914, Luxembourg-Gare

Mexico: Apartado Postal No. 20-217, Mexico 20 DF

Nepal: Amnesty International, Nepal Section, Post Box 918, 21/94 Bagbazar, Kathmandu

Netherlands: Amnesty International, Dutch Section, Postbus 61501, 1005 HM Amsterdam

New Zealand: Amnesty International, New Zealand Section, PO Box 11648, Manners Street, Wellington 1

Nigeria: Amnesty International, Nigerian Section, 7 Onayade Street, Fadeyi-Yaba, Lagos

Norway: Amnesty International, Norwegian Section, Rosenkrantz-gatan 18, Oslo 1

Pakistan: Amnesty International, Pakistan Section, 615 Muhammadi House, I.I. Chundrigar Road, Karachi

Peru: Casilla 2319, Lima 1

Senegal: Amnesty International, Section sénégalaise, Boîte Postale 3813, Dakar

Spain: Amnesty International, Paseo de Recoletos 18, Escalera Interior, 6ª Planta, Madrid 1

Sri Lanka: Amnesty International, Sri Lankan Section, c/o E.A.G. de Silva, 79/15 Dr C.W.W. Kannangara Mawatha, Colombo 7

Sweden: Amnesty International, Swedish Section, Surbrunnsgatan 44, S-113 48 Stockholm

Switzerland: Amnesty International, Swiss Section, PO Box 1051, CH-3001 Bern

Turkey: c/o International Secretariat, 10 Southampton Street, London WC2E 7HF, United Kingdom

United Kingdom: Amnesty International, British Section, 8-14 Southampton Street, London WC2E 7HF

USA: Amnesty International of the USA, 304 West 58th Street, New York, NY 10019
Western Regional Office: Amnesty International, Western Regional Office, 3618 Sacramento Street, San Francisco, CA 94118

Venezuela: Av. Las Mercedes/Guaicapuro, Quinta Otawa, Caracas 1060

Appendix VIII

Places where there are individual subscribers or supporters

Algeria
Andorra
Antigua
Argentina
Bahamas
Bahrain
Belize
Benin
Bermuda
Bhutan
Bolivia
Botswana
Brazil (groups)
Brunei
Bulgaria
Burma
Burundi
Cameroon
Central African Republic
Chad
Chile (group)
China
Colombia (group)
Congo
Costa Rica (groups)
Cuba
Cyprus
Czechoslovakia
Dominican Republic
Egypt
El Salvador
Ethiopia
Falkland Islands
Fiji
French Guiana
Gabon (groups)
Gambia
Gibraltar
Grenada
Guadeloupe
Guatemala
Guyana (group)
Haiti
Honduras
Hong Kong (group)
Indonesia
Iran
Iraq
Jamaica
Jordan
Kenya
Kuwait
Lebanon
Lesotho
Liberia
Libya
Madagascar
Malawi
Malaysia
Maldives
Mali
Malta
Martinique
Mauritania
Mauritius (groups)
Morocco
Mozambique
Namibia
Netherlands Antilles
Nicaragua
Niger
Oman
Pakistan
Panama
Papua New Guinea (group)
Paraguay

Poland
Portugal (group)
Puerto Rico (group)
Réunion (group)
Romania
Rwanda
Saint Lucia
Saudi Arabia
Senegal
Seychelles
Sierra Leone
Singapore
Solomon Islands
South Africa
Sudan
Suriname
Swaziland
Syria
Taiwan
Tanzania
Thailand
Togo
Trinidad and Tobago (groups)
Tunisia
Uganda
United Arab Emirates
Upper Volta
USSR
Vanuatu
Viet Nam
Yemen (PDR)
Yugoslavia
Zaïre
Zambia
Zimbabwe

APPENDIX IX

International Executive Committee

Andrew Blane (Vice-Chairperson)	United States of America
Stelios Nestor	Greece
Dirk Börner (Treasurer)	Federal Republic of Germany
Jan Egeland	Norway
Stephanie Grant (co-opted September 1980)	United Kingdom
Edy Kaufman	Israel
Michael Klein	Federal Republic of Germany
Tricia Feeney	International Secretariat
Suriya Wickremasinghe (Vice-Chairperson)	Sri Lanka
José Zalaquett (Chairperson)	Chile

Secretary General

On 1 July 1980 Thomas Hammarberg became Secretary General of Amnesty International.

APPENDIX X

Selected Statistics 1981

On 1 May 1981 there were 2,560 Amnesty International adoption groups in 54 countries — an increase of 133 groups over the year before. There were over 250,000 members, subscribers and supporters in 151 countries or territories, with national sections in 40.

On 1 May 1981, 4,517 prisoners were adopted as prisoners of conscience or being investigated as possible prisoners of conscience. They were imprisoned in 64 countries. During the year 1,475 new cases were taken up, and 894 prisoners were freed. Over 310 urgent appeals were issued on behalf of prisoners in 63 countries.